A Nearly Infallible
History of Christianity

A Nearly Infallible
History of Christianity

Nick Page

HODDER &
STOUGHTON

First published in Great Britain in 2013 by Hodder & Stoughton
An Hachette UK company

7

Copyright © Nick Page, 2013

A CIP catalogue record for this title is available from the British Library

ISBN 978 1 444 75013 3
eBook ISBN 978 1 444 75014 0

Typeset in Sabon MT by Palimpsest Book Production Limited, Falkirk, Stirlingshire

Printed and bound in the UK by Clays Ltd, Elcograf S.p.A.

Hodder & Stoughton policy is to use papers that are natural, renewable and recyclable products
and made from wood grown in sustainable forests. The logging and manufacturing processes
are expected to conform to the environmental regulations of the country of origin.

Hodder & Stoughton Ltd
338 Euston Road
London NW1 3BH

www.hodderfaith.com

'We have seen truth crucified and goodness buried, but we have kept going with the conviction that truth crushed to earth will rise again.'
                                                    Martin Luther King

'Jesus came preaching the kingdom and what arrived was the church.'
                                                    Alfred Loisy

'With great power, comes great responsibility.'

                                    Stan Lee, Amazing Fantasy #15

Contents

Introduction

In AD 542 plague struck the eastern Mediterranean.

A well-known Egyptian Christian called Barsanuphius wrote a letter to comfort and encourage anxious Christians. I would call him a 'public figure', except that he had retired to a cave as a young monk, and nobody had set eyes on him since.* But he was a great letter writer. He told his correspondents that although God loved humanity and wanted to show mercy, 'the mass of sins committed in the world stands in his way'. But, he continued, there were three men he could think of who were perfect before God, and who had the power 'to bind and loose, to remit our faults or to retain them'.

Those men were John, at Rome, Elias at Corinth and another – whose name he didn't seem to recall – in the province of Jerusalem.

Eh? Surely some mistake? Not the pope? Not the Patriarch of Constantinople or Antioch or Alexandria? Not the emperor?

Nope. According to Barsanuphius, the three most holy men in the world in 542 were John, Elias and some bloke in Jerusalem, whose name he couldn't quite remember.†

That is why I wrote this book. Because of people like John, Elias, and whatsisface from Jerusalem. Because of all the truly holy men who have been forgotten along the way.

—⁓—

* He remained a total recluse for fifty years before, eventually, making a brief trip to Jerusalem to tell the emperor off.
† Barsanuphius himself was noted for his piety, which took the shape of a retiring disposition, a refusal to get involved with local politics and the fact that he covered himself up when he went to the public baths. It didn't take much to be a holy man in those days.

This book is the story of how a Mediterranean peasant inspired a movement of followers that eventually became the biggest religion in the world.

And of how those followers – who called themselves Christians – did extraordinary, inspirational, world-changing things because they believed that's what that Mediterranean carpenter wanted them to do and because somehow he gave them the power to do it. And how, even today, we're living with the consequences of their actions.

And of how a lot of other people – who also called themselves Christians – did awful, appalling things in the name of Christ. And how, even today, we're living with the consequences of *their* actions as well.

This is the story of some people who tried to live like Jesus, and many people who didn't try very hard to live like Jesus, and a few people who couldn't even be arsed to try it at all. The strange thing is that they *all* called themselves Christians, even though, with hindsight, it is clear that some of them had little idea of who Jesus was and what he represented.

The whistle-blower

There are three main tasks to this thing we call history: explanation, whistle-blowing and celebration.

The first task is to explain why things are the way they are.

The second task is to reveal who is to blame for why things are the way they are.

And the third task is to celebrate wonderful heroic people and events that show things don't always have to be the way they are.

Those three things are the reason I wanted to write this book.

First, I wanted to find out for myself how we, as Christians, got here. Why do we believe the things that we do? Who first came up with the phrases that are so familiar and the practices that so baffle us? Who, seriously, thought that the Crusades were a good idea? So this is a book for all those who look at the church and go, 'Huh?' For anyone who thinks that Pope John Paul II was named after half of the Beatles. For those, who, frankly, don't know their apse from their elders.

Second, I wanted to tell the truth about some of those we think are heroes but who prove to be not very heroic at all. I realise that this will upset some people. They may think that I have been rude to the

Catholics. Or to the Lutherans. Or to the Puritans. Or to the Anglicans. Or to the Orthodox. Actually, I've tried to be equally outspoken about everybody. I am ecumenically rude.*

Third, I wanted to celebrate the *real* heroes of Christianity. Most of the time, these are people who often lived their whole lives under the radar: the losers, the members of underground movements who faithfully carry out Jesus' instructions only to find themselves mocked, ostracised, imprisoned or even killed. Sometimes all four. Simultaneously. Most of them didn't have wealth or power or status. They had better things to do. And many of them got completely mullered by the people mentioned under the aforementioned category of whistle-blowing. Of course, had they had the power they might have been just as monstrous as their oppressors. But they didn't. So they weren't.

I know at times it might appear as though this book has lost all objectivity. But that's wrong. Because it never had any objectivity in the first place, and you can't lose what you never had. The fact is, I *care* about this. It matters to me how my faith is represented. Grown-up historians are supposed to have 'detachment': the best I can manage is semi-detachment.

A lot of historians excuse the very unchristian behaviour of Christians in history on the grounds of historical relativism – that it was a different era, with a different set of cultural values. But I don't get this. I mean, for Christians, which part of 'Love your enemies' is so hard to understand? Where exactly does Jesus say that burning people is perfectly OK? It's not like 'Love your enemies' suddenly popped up in some previously undiscovered record of the words of Jesus. It's always been there. And 'they had different standards back then' may be OK when it comes to personal hygiene. But it doesn't cut it when we're talking about one Christian burning another Christian to death just because the second one believed something different about a piece of bread.

I have to admit this book focuses largely on the Mediterranean and the west. Christianity is now huge in Africa and in Asia and has a long

---

* And another thing: this is a serious *book* of history – well, semi-serious, at any rate – but it has a lot of jokes in it. You might not find them funny. That's OK. I can handle rejection. My therapist says I'm doing very well and if I carry on improving, there's every chance I'll be allowed to use sharp objects again in the future. And anyway, you try finding something funny to say about the Nestorians. But don't write to me and complain that there are jokes in the book. I know. I put them there.

history in those continents, but I ran out of space to tell the story of all the heroes in those parts. Sorry.

But the fact is that there *are* heroes. There are good guys – and girls – in this story. Quite a lot of them are wonderful. Weird, eccentric, other-worldly, outrageous. But wonderful.

First, though, we have to go to a dark place . . .

Prologue: The Nightmare Begins

Greece. 300 BC.

Ctesibius of Alexandria unveiled his latest invention. It looks like a large set of pan pipes. In front of the pipes was a box with channels cut into it, along which close-fitting sliders could be moved. Was it a weapon? An instrument of torture?

No. It was worse than that. As slaves pumped the bellows, he moved some sliders and suddenly a terrible noise started to emerge.

Greece. 300 BC. Ctesibius had invented the organ.*

---

* He called it the *hydraulis*, but in the end there was no word that could sum up the terror, so they called it after the Greek word for 'instrument' or 'tool'. They called it an *organon*.

THINGS YOU LEARN FROM CHRISTIAN HISTORY

NO. 1
It's the resurrection, stupid

The history of the church begins on a Sunday morning in AD 33, when a man whom everyone thought was dead was found walking about in a graveyard. Christianity's core business is resurrection. There is always life after death. There is always hope.

Given some of the places we are going to go on this journey, it might be worth holding on to that fact.

1 Resurrection, Rome and Revelation

Er... no

It was AD 33 and the people in charge of Jerusalem were *extremely* annoyed.

This was not new. There was a lot in life to annoy them – the workload, the pressures of responsibility, the sheer cost of buying the position of high priest from the ruling Romans, remembering to wear the right robes for the festivals, not to mention the fact that everyone hated them and viewed them as collaborators.

And now there was this: two Galilean fishermen who had been teaching and causing a disturbance in the temple. That was not the problem, the temple was always full of religious agitators of one sort or another: Pharisees, Essenes, would-be-Messiahs, Young Conservatives. Nor was it the fact that these men were rumoured to have performed miracles. That was *supposed* to happen in Jerusalem and was officially Very Good for Tourism. No, what really annoyed them was that these men were claiming that their leader had come back from the dead. And since the temple elite had gone out of their way to organise the man's death in the first place, this was a flagrant threat to their authority.

His name was Jesus of Nazareth. Yeshua – to give him his real name – was a miracle-worker, teacher, radical preacher from Galilee. He had led his followers to Jerusalem, caused a riot in the temple, and said a lot of things the authorities found very hurtful, actually. So they had arrested him, taken him to the Roman prefect Pontius Pilate, and persuaded Pilate to have him killed. (They weren't allowed to execute him themselves. Which was *another* annoying thing.)

Now the followers of this Jesus were claiming that he had risen from the dead, which was not only impossible, but was directly in contravention of their theology.* More, they claimed that he was the long-awaited Jewish Messiah. (Later on, his followers used the Greek word for Messiah – *Christos* – which means 'anointed one'. Hence 'Jesus Christ'. It's not his surname; just his job description.)

The two men – Peter and John – were instructed by the high priest and the other people in charge of the temple 'not to speak or teach at all in the name of Jesus'. And here is their reply: 'Whether it is right in God's sight to listen to you rather than to God, you must judge; for we cannot keep from speaking about what we have seen and heard' (Acts 4.18–20).

Or, in other words, 'No.'

And there you have it. Right at the start of Christianity we have one of its most characteristic acts: a lack of respect for authority. A refusal to be silenced. The truth is that, right from the start, authentic Christianity has been deeply, *deeply* annoying.

Dead man walking

The account of the hearing comes from the book of Acts. But the earliest account we have of these resurrection appearances comes from a letter written around AD 54 to a group of Christians misbehaving in Asia Minor:

> Christ died for our sins in accordance with the scriptures, and that he was buried, and that he was raised on the third day in accordance with the scriptures, and that he appeared to Cephas, then to the twelve. Then he appeared to more than five hundred brothers and sisters at one time, most of whom are still alive, though some have died. Then he appeared to James, then to all the apostles. Last of all, as to one untimely born, he appeared also to me. (1 Cor. 15.3–8)

The 'me' in question here is a man called Paul of Tarsus, aka Saul, of whom more, later. He's reminding the badly behaved Christian

---

* The ruling parties in Jerusalem were Sadducees, who didn't believe in the resurrection of the dead. They also didn't believe in fate, angels or the immortality of the soul. Or Father Christmas.

community in Corinth that witnesses to this resurrection were still around. A number of these were key leaders of the church – Cephas, aka Peter, and James; but he also mentions the 'apostles', an amorphous group that generally refers to anyone who saw the risen Jesus. Twenty years later, according to Paul, many of these were still alive. By then they were telling the story to anyone who would listen (and many who wouldn't).

The first time the wider world heard about the resurrection was forty days after the event. The followers of Jesus had gathered together in one place to pray, during the Jewish festival of Pentecost, when the Holy Spirit descended on them. The city was full of Jews from other parts of the world: Parthians, Asians, Egyptians, Romans, Welsh – they were all there.* And with the outpouring of power Jesus' followers started to speak about Jesus in the visitors' languages. From the start, the Jesus movement was international.

Many people joined the new movement that day. But what, exactly, were they joining? The church itself, let alone many of its core doctrines, hadn't been invented. These converts didn't go home with an informative tract, a copy of the Gideons' Bible and a newsletter giving times of the church services. All they had was the story of what happened: what people had seen Jesus do and heard him say. Things that had been passed on.

Pass it on

Paul says of Jesus' resurrection appearances that he didn't invent them: they have been 'handed on' to him. He is quoting a Christian statement of faith – a kind of creed. He learned other things as well:

> For I received from the Lord what I also handed on to you, that the Lord Jesus on the night when he was betrayed took a loaf of bread, and when he had given thanks, he broke it and said, 'This is my body that is for you. Do this in remembrance of me.' In the same way he took the cup also, after supper, saying, 'This cup is the new covenant in my blood. Do this, as often as you drink it, in remembrance of me.' For as often as you eat this bread and drink the cup, you proclaim the Lord's death until he comes. (1 Cor. 11.23–26)

---

* Not the Welsh, obviously. Pay attention.

From the start Christians *learned* the story of Jesus. This was an age when, for the most part, you couldn't look anything up. Most people couldn't read. That, and the fact that the internet wouldn't be invented for another two thousand years or so made Googling something pretty tricky. There were libraries but these were for posh people with togas. So ordinary Christians learned by memorising and repeating. And, in one of Christianity's best innovations, they also learned through eating, which is absolutely my favourite kind of learning. The story was embedded in a meal, which Paul calls 'the Lord's supper'. It became known as 'the Eucharist' – from the Greek word for thanksgiving. It was a thank-you meal.

The meal was both symbolic and practical. Christians from all social classes shared the food, to demonstrate that 'we who are many are one body' (1 Cor. 10.17). And it was a proper meal. Today, when communion consists of something that claims to be wine but that manifestly isn't, and something that claims to be bread but is either (a) a day-old Hovis, or (b) a bit of cardboard called a *wafer*. We forget this. Their meal was actually, you know, a *meal*.

In their meetings they did other things as well. They prayed, read and discussed the Scriptures, and sang stuff as well. Indeed, from another of Paul's letters we get what is probably an ancient Christian hymn. The lyrics tell about Jesus being 'in the form of God' but choosing to become a slave, taking human form and dying on the cross. And therefore God 'highly exalted him' and every knee will bow, 'every tongue confess that Jesus Christ is Lord, to the glory of God the Father'.[*]

These are radical views. And though Paul is writing a couple of decades after the events, very early on the central contradictions of all this must have been clear. These people were following a man who had died on the cross – a death reserved for slaves and foreign rebels. They claimed that he was not just *their* Lord, but the Lord of everything and everybody, which would come as a bit of a shock to a few Romans, to say the least. Most of all, Jesus was, in some way, 'in the form of God'.

These were not the kinds of views that were going to go down well. As Paul admitted, Jesus was 'a stumbling-block to Jews and foolishness to Gentiles' (1 Cor. 1.23). Which has everyone more or less covered.

---

[*] It's in Philippians 2.5–11.

As the conflict with the Jerusalem temple authorities shows, some Jews reacted badly to all this. But not all Jews, of course. Because these first followers of Jesus were Jewish. And they carried on with many Jewish practices – going to synagogue, praying at the set times, eating ritually clean food, feeling guilty, phoning their mothers regularly, etc. This was to cause conflict once non-Jews started to adopt the faith. But Jesus' first followers did not know that they were starting a new religion: they thought they were fulfilling the old one.

Indeed, the relationship of Christianity to Judaism lies behind much of the writing of their most influential early thinker: Paul of Tarsus.

PAUL

Paul, from a third-century medallion. Presumably this must have been after one of his shipwrecks, as he appears to have some kind of squid attached to his jaw

Name: Paul of Tarsus.
Aka: Saul.
Nationality: Greek-speaking Jew from Cilicia.
Dates: c.1–c.68.
Appearance: Bald, bandy-legged, monobrowed, hook nosed. But apart from that, curiously attractive.
Before he was famous: Tent-maker. Rabbinic student.
Famous for: Letter writing. Planting churches. Being very hard to understand.
Why does he matter? Defined many of the fundamental theological ideas of Christianity.
Could you have a drink with him down the pub? Definitely. Although he would probably try to convert someone, and there might be a fight.

The bandy-legged, monobrowed angel

Paul's life is a microcosm of the transformative power of early Christianity. He was born in Tarsus, a cosmopolitan city on the south coast of Cilicia in what is today Turkey. He was a Roman citizen by birth, and a tent-maker or leather-worker by trade. His family were orthodox Jews, and Paul went to Jerusalem and studied under rabbi Gamaliel. (Not *literally*, obviously. Although, having said which, the life of rabbinic students did involve copying their teacher closely: there is an account of one rabbinical student who followed his master so closely that he actually hid under the bed of the rabbi and his wife. When the rabbi protested, the student said, 'But this is Torah [the law] and I must learn it.' It's certainly an approach that would make the TV show *The Apprentice* a lot more interesting.)

Anyway, soon after the Pentecost experience the Jewish authorities lost patience with this new sect. Riots broke out and one of their number – a Greek-speaking Jew called Stephen – was killed. Paul was part of this persecution. But then his life changed. On the way to Damascus to close down a new Christian group there, he was hit by a kind of spiritual speed camera: a light flashed around him and he heard the risen Jesus saying, 'Why do you persecute me?' This orthodox Jewish persecutor of Christians became the leading apostle to the Gentiles.

Fig. I. *On the Damascus Road, Paul initially mistakes the cause of the supernatural event*

His background fitted him perfectly for missionary work: he was a Roman citizen from a Greek city, who was trained as a Jewish Pharisee. His first language was Greek, but he spoke Hebrew and had studied Torah – the Jewish law. He had other important qualities as well, notably an irresistible passion, drive and sheer bloody-mindedness and an ability to endure a large amount of personal violence. He had the talent for getting into hot water that is the sign of the true radical. Unusually for these apostolic figures, we may even know what he looked like. An early church story called the *Acts of Paul and Thecla* is a made-up story, but it contains a portrait of Paul that is so unflattering it very well may be original: 'Paul . . . a man small in size, bald-headed, bandy-legged, well-built, with eyebrows meeting, rather long-nosed, full of grace. For sometimes he seemed like a man, and sometimes he had the countenance of an angel.'

After his conversion he didn't go to Jerusalem to consult any of the embryonic church leadership (probably because he realised that the authorities would not be hugely delighted that he had joined the enemy. Or maybe his bandy legs were giving him trouble). Instead, he went to Arabia for a few years – which means the region around Damascus, rather than somewhere on a great big sand dune eating Turkish Delight. We don't know much about what Saul got up to, but it seems to have made him some enemies. Because he was forced to flee Damascus in the night, escaping over the wall in a laundry basket.* After three years he finally went to Jerusalem where he met Peter, James and the other leaders of the church. Unsurprisingly, they were nervous – but Paul was vouched for by Barnabas.

Once this meeting was over he did what he did best: he got into trouble. Acts records that he went out from the meeting and started 'speaking boldly' with the Hellenists. These were Greek-speaking residents of Jerusalem: the immigrant community, in fact. It was not what you'd call a success: the Hellenists responded to Paul's message by trying to kill him. So Paul was 'encouraged' to leave Jerusalem by the rest of the apostles. He went north, back to Tarsus, for a while.

---

* Hence the origin of the phrase 'He got clean away.'

Death and life

Rewind a bit. The death of Stephen was the first salvo in an outbreak of violence against the Greek-speaking Christians in Jerusalem. Christianity had been making inroads among this community – indeed there had been some friction internally between the two groups – but when the violence broke out it seems from the biblical accounts that the Jewish Christians – including leaders such as James and Peter – managed to remain in the city, while the Greek-speaking 'Hellenists' had to leave.

One of them, Philip, took the gospel north to Samaria, a radical move, considering that most Jews hated the Samaritans as half-breeds and heretics. Then he went south of Jerusalem and converted an Ethiopian eunuch he met on the road. Although eunuchs could hold responsible, even powerful, positions, they were nevertheless viewed with a kind of disgust by both Romans and Jews. Jewish law made it clear that no man with damaged tackle would be allowed in the temple.* So the significance of these events is profound: no one is outside the kingdom of God. It doesn't matter how strange and exotic your nationality, or even what bits you are missing: you can still come in.

The eunuch was baptised in some water near to the road on which he was travelling. Baptism was the other distinctive practice of the Christian community. It probably originated in Jewish ritual bathing, but Christians adopted it from John the Baptist, the 'herald' of Jesus. Jesus, after all, was baptised. And if it was good enough for him . . .

Along with the thanksgiving meal, baptism was the other sacred rite of the early church. Effected in the name of 'the Father, the Son, and the Holy Spirit', Paul describes baptism as symbolising death and resurrection. You are buried in the water and then you come back to life. In later versions of the rituals dating from the third century AD new members of the church would take off all their old clothes, go down into the water, come up the other side and be given a new set of clothes.† They would also be given a drink of milk and honey – symbols of the promised land.

* Leviticus 21.18–20 in case you're interested. Which, let's face it, you are. As well as banning anyone who has 'crushed testicles' it also excludes the blind, the lame, hunchbacks, dwarfs, anyone with a rash and 'one who has a mutilated face or a limb too long'. In your face, equal opportunities!

† Men and women were segregated, of course. Just making that clear, in case anyone suggests going back to 'Early Church Baptismal Practices'.

Then, and only then, would they be allowed to take part in the Eucharist. When architects started designing custom-made baptistries, they made them to resemble sarcophagi to emphasise the point.*

I say ekklēsia; you say kuriakē

Judea, of course, was a province in the Mighty Roman Empire™. And soon the message of Jesus spread beyond its Jewish origins. Acts emphasises this in another tale, of the conversion of the Roman centurion Cornelius, this time through the work of Peter. In the Acts account this is explicitly tied in with an understanding of the purity regulations between Jew and Gentile. Peter receives a vision of pure and impure food descending from heaven in a sheet. And when the spirit descends on Cornelius and his household he sees it as proof that 'God has given even to the Gentiles the repentance that leads to life.'

Not everyone was convinced. The issue was not whether Gentiles could become Christians, but whether being a Christian meant becoming a Jew. Peter interpreted his vision as being about people, not food. He did not rush out and eat a pork pie. But as more Gentiles came to the faith the question arose as to whether they had to be circumcised and honour Jewish cleanliness laws.

Some time in the forties AD Christianity established itself in Antioch, the third biggest city of the Mighty Roman Empire™ and a crucial cultural and trading centre. Antioch had a reputation for tolerating many different faiths and practices. This was down to its diverse, cosmopolitan nature: Greeks, Syrians, Jews, Arabs, Phoenicians, Persians, Egyptians, Indians, Romans and many more rubbed shoulders. (And they rubbed other things as well: the city also had a reputation for loose morals.)

Antioch was a *proper* Graeco-Roman city. And like all such civilised places at the time, it was crowded and filthy. The quality of most housing was more like what we would associate with slums. Walking the streets of the cities of the Roman Empire meant dodging the human waste thrown from the Roman apartment blocks – known as *insulae*

---

* Some scholars suggest these baptistries also resemble a vulva, so the act is like emerging from the womb. Which goes to show how some scholars are *badly* in need of a girlfriend.

– or encountering the dead bodies of beggars. The emperor Vespasian was at a banquet once when a dog ran in with a human hand in its mouth, taken from a corpse in the street. The emperor, far from being shocked, thought it a good omen and carried on with the banquet. (I just hope it wasn't a finger buffet.)

Christianity offered a radical alternative to the dog-eat-dog (or dog-eat-beggar) world of the Graeco-Roman city. Indeed, one of the prime reasons that Christianity grew so fast and so far in the first few centuries was that it looked after people. Christianity not only promised eternal life after death for its believers; it also offered quite a bit of life *before* death as well. Christians fed the poor with a daily meal. They clothed widows. They visited those in prison. They healed the sick and cast out demons. Christians created a kind of miniature welfare state, only without the paperwork.

This lifestyle was, of course, modelled on the actions of their founder, who said that you should 'love your neighbour as yourself'. Christianity offered a distinctive way of life. And that, indeed, was how it was known in those first years: it was called simply 'the Way'.* But in Antioch it got a different name. The people of Antioch coined a mocking term for these wayfarers: they called them the *Christiani*, a conflation of the Greek word 'Christ', with a pun on the name *Chrēstos*, which means 'good' or 'useful' and was a common slave name. They were the *Christiani*, good little slaves, followers of Christ.

It was not what the Christians called themselves. Their chosen collective noun was the *ekklēsia*, a Greek word that means 'gathering'. This was a reference to the synagogue, which means 'assembly'. But it also references the society around them. In the cities of the Roman Empire the *ekklēsia* was a kind of local council, where the great and the good got together and decided what was best for everyone else. They were the local council of an alternative kingdom.

They certainly did not call themselves 'the church'. That comes from an entirely different Greek word – an adjective, *kuriakē*, which means 'belonging to the Lord'.† It's not a term that appears in the New Testament: in fact, it's not used of Christian groups or assemblies until some 250 years after Paul was writing.

---

* Another title might have been 'ebionites' – the poor. You can tell that no marketing executives were involved in that decision.
† You get a stronger hint of it in the Scottish word 'kirk'.

JAMES

James. From a Russian icon, so what you might call an 'artist's impression'

Name: Jacob of Nazareth.
Aka: James, brother of Jesus.
Nationality: Galilean Jew.
Dates: died c.62.
Appearance: Not known, but may have had misshapen knees.
Before he was famous: Probably carpenter/ builder. Brother of Jesus along with Jude, Simon and Joses.
Famous for: First leader of the church in Judea.
Why does he matter? He represents the earliest, Jewish, form of Christianity.
Could you have a drink with him down the pub? Maybe. But you would have had to have drunk from different vessels because of Jewish purity laws.

He ain't heavy. . .

In Judea the followers of Jesus weren't known as the *Christiani*, but as the Nazarenes.* This means, simply, 'from Nazareth'. The founder of the sect came from Nazareth, and his brother – also from Nazareth – was the man in charge.

Although we know him as James, that is the much later, westernised version of his name. His name was Jacob. The gospel accounts list several brothers of Jesus: Jacob, Joses, Judas and Simon. (He also had at least one sister, but the girls are never named.)† They were not

---

* Although the term occurs only once in Acts (24.5) it must be an early term, since it originates from Aramaic, not from Greek or Latin.

† Over the years there have been arguments as to the precise relationship of these 'brothers'. The Catholic Church, to support the doctrine of Mary's

supporters of Jesus while he was alive, but, according to the early church tradition, James was converted after an encounter with the risen Jesus. In a fragment from a now lost gospel, known as the Gospel of the Hebrews, there is an account of this meeting: Jesus appeared to James, who 'had sworn that he would not eat bread from that hour in which he had drunk the Lord's cup until he should see him risen from among them that sleep'. And they eat bread together.

With his fasting, the story reflects James' reputation in the early church for piety and asceticism. Hegesippus, one of the earliest historians of the early church, paints a portrait of James, as a righteous, orthodox Jew, whose life was such that he was known as 'James the Righteous', and who prayed so much that 'his knees became hard, like a camel's'. This reputation wasn't just among Christians: James is one of the few characters from early Christianity who is mentioned outside of the New Testament or Christian writings; he appears in the histories of Josephus.

But his leadership role was not, at the end of the day, due to his piety or his Jewish orthodoxy. It was down to one thing: family. He was the Lord's brother, part of the dynasty. And this family connection continued for some time in Judea and Galilee. Jesus' brother Judas (Jude) was also a well-known figure in the early church.

And when James died, the leadership of the church passed to Simeon, son of Joseph's brother Clopas and the cousin, therefore, of Jesus. Eusebius, who gives us this anecdote, wrote that 'He [Simeon] was a cousin – at any rate so it is said – of the Saviour; for indeed Hegesippus relates that Clopas was Joseph's brother.'* Simeon was executed in the reign of Trajan, some time after AD 100 – by which time the Christian community had left Jerusalem. There is also evidence that at the end of the first century two of the grandsons of Jude – Zoker and Jacob – were still farming the family smallholding in Nazareth, but were also leaders of the Palestinian Jewish Christian community. And taking the family connection even further, around AD 200 Julianus Africanus

---

perpetual virginity, argues they were cousins, while the Eastern Orthodox Church teaches that they were stepbrothers: children of Joseph from a previous marriage. However, the Greek word for cousin, *anepsios*, is never used of James and the others, either by the gospel writers or by early Christian writers.

* This is probably the same Clopas who saw the risen Jesus on the road to Emmaus. Indeed, the third-century scholar Origen identified the other, unnamed, disciple in that episode as Clopas's son, Simeon.

reported a tradition that the relatives of Jesus operated as missionaries, starting from Nazareth and Kochaba (a village near Nazareth) and taking the gospel throughout the land.

I believe the Lord is saying, 'Maketh mine a pepperoni'

The church in Antioch started to grow. So the HQ in Jerusalem sent Barnabas out to manage things. And he, in turn, recruited Paul to come to help. Then, around AD 47, Paul made a return visit to Jerusalem, accompanying Barnabas and taking a gift – some money to help the home church during a famine.

Paul, by now, was a man with a plan. Convinced of his special role to take the gospel to the Gentile world, he had a meeting with the 'acknowledged leaders' – James and Cephas and John – where he told them what he was intending to do. In a kind of 'here's one I prepared earlier' moment he took with him a Gentile convert from Antioch called Titus, who was later to be one of Paul's most trusted lieutenants.

No minutes are available from this meeting, and one imagines that the various parties may have had different impressions of what was agreed. Paul was the kind of man who, if you gave him an inch, would take a light year. He and Barnabas returned to Antioch, then embarked on a journey that was to last for most of the next two decades of his life.

Say what you like about the Romans – and you can say what you like because they're all dead – they were very good at infrastructure. I mean, yes, they were brutal, violent tyrants, but they made lovely roads. When Roman soldiers conquered a region, the first thing they did was to build bridges and roads and aqueducts so that trade could flourish. They were like stormtroopers with shovels. The result was that travel was easier in the time of the Mighty Roman Empire™ than at any time up until the nineteenth century. This enabled Paul, and people like him, to travel great distances to spread the word. Over the course of the next two decades Paul travelled to many of the major cities of the empire. He endured great hardship – but he took the gospel to many areas it had not reached before.

He was not always successful. In Corinth and Ephesus he was instrumental in establishing churches. But in Athens the philosophers there were pretty much baffled by what he had to say. Elsewhere Paul's teaching and speaking resulted in riots and violence. This was a man who could cause an argument in a phone box.

21

Paul, of course, was not the only Christian missionary trudging the roads of the Roman Empire. There were many itinerant preachers and teachers – and some of them had a 'flexible' approach to their expenses. A first-century discipleship training manual called the *Didache* gives instructions for congregations to help them work out if a visiting teacher was offering genuine spiritual food, or was just after free bed and board. The *Didache* states that a real apostle will stay in one place for only a maximum of two days. And 'if he asks for money, he is a false prophet'. It also gives a fine example of one of their tricks. It says that 'any prophet who orders a meal in the spirit shall not partake of it; if he does, he is a false prophet'. Quite how this worked we don't know. Maybe the false apostle spoke in tongues and then interpreted his own message as 'Thus saith the Lord: order a Four Seasons Pizza with extra garlic bread.' 'That's fine,' says the *Didache*, 'providing he doesn't take a slice for himself.'

Above all, in an instruction that, one thinks, later generations would have been wise to heed, the true teacher was to be shown by his actions: 'not everyone who speaks in the spirit is a prophet, but only if he exhibits the Lord's ways . . . if any prophet teaches the truth, yet does not practise what he teaches, he is a false prophet'.

Tenement church

Paul's letters, along with the *Didache*, tell us something of the style of early-church meetings. At this time there were no church buildings. (Still, on the plus side that means no bell ringers.) Christians had been exiled from synagogues; and they obviously could not use pagan temples, with their idols and immoral worship practices. So they met in domestic spaces: homes, flats, workshops, rented rooms. Sometimes these would have been sizeable dwellings. But just as often – maybe more often – they were small.

Indeed, the earliest description we have of a church meeting comes from the book of Acts, where Paul spends some time with the group of Christians at Troas. The meeting takes place on the first day of the week – literally 'the first of the sabbath'. So we are talking about a meeting on a Sunday evening. It has to be at night, because Sunday is just a working day at this time, and most of those involved had jobs to do. (And also, since the Christian meeting was on a Sunday it meant that if the synagogue was still open to them, they could also join the other Jews there on the day before.) It takes place on the third floor of a building. It's in an apartment, a room in one of the *insulae*, the first-century apartment blocks. Unlike today, where the penthouse suite is the most sought after, the upper floors of *insulae* were sought after only by people either with no money or with no wish to live very long. They were shoddily built with little ventilation.

The church was small enough to fit into this apartment, which is lit only by burning oil lamps. It grows hot and stuffy. Paul is not preaching – the word is *dialegomai*, which means 'discussion' and from which we get our word 'dialogue'. This is not some sermon, but a conversation. Perhaps not a riveting one, though, because a young slave, sitting at the window, literally drops off: he falls asleep and falls three floors to his death on the street below. Paul goes down and he is miraculously restored to life. His name is a slave's name – Eutychus. It means, ironically, 'lucky'.

After this they return to their discussion and to breaking the bread together.

So, small domestic spaces, sharing food, listening to teaching, holding discussions. Paul's letters tell us that there were also songs: psalms from the Old Testament, but also their own Christian songs. They also received prophecy. Two or three people might bring a message from God, and listeners would then ask questions. The *Didache* also includes a form of the Lord's Prayer, indicating that fairly early on there were simple liturgical elements.

The elements of this meeting, then, although different in style, would be much the same as found in many churches today. Only without the coffee afterwards.

Signs and wonders

'By the power of signs and wonders, by the power of the Spirit of God,' wrote Paul, 'from Jerusalem and as far around as Illyricum I have fully proclaimed the good news of Christ' (Rom. 15.19). He travelled by Spirit-power.

That meeting in Troas led to the miraculous healing of Eutychus. And one of the things that characterised the church is the miraculous power of the Holy Spirit. Historically, whether we like it or not, miracles are one of the key reasons why the church grew.

Christian communities were places of miracles. Of course, there are the accounts in Acts – Luke talks about people lying in the street so that Peter's shadow might fall on them. The sick are cured and those possessed by unclean spirits are freed from their torment. James reminds believers that 'the prayer of the righteous is powerful and effective' (Jas. 5.16). Paul talks about the miraculous in a similarly 'matter of fact' kind of way. To him it was a sign of apostleship: 'the signs of a true apostle were performed among you with utmost patience, signs and wonders and mighty works' he wrote to the church at Corinth (2 Cor. 12.12).

The miraculous tales of the early church – indeed, of the church of any era – make uncomfortable reading for many people today. Such things don't fit neatly into our world view. But we cannot understand the spread of the early church until we understand that they lived in a world where the supernatural was taken for granted and where they witnessed the miraculous. It was signs and wonders that proved to people that this movement was from God.

Some individuals might come to faith through discussion and argument, or by reading the Scriptures, but most people couldn't read. So those kinds of things weren't going to get you that far. Gregory, a pupil of the famous Christian scholar Origen, wrote a learned treatise on God. But what really made him famous was the miracles he worked among the populace of north-central Turkey. That is why he was known as Gregory the Wonderworker, rather than 'Gregory the Bloke Who Wrote That Really Clever Treatise'.

Tertullian (who we will meet soon) described Christians as being in 'touch with the miraculous'. He described how the name of Jesus can 'remove distractions from the minds of men and expel demons, and also take away diseases'. He goes on to give some specifically documented cases citing particularly how Severus, father of the emperor Antonine, was healed from sickness by a Christian with the rather medical sounding name of Proculus Torpacion.* 'How many men of rank', he writes, '(to say nothing of the common people) have been delivered from devils and healed of diseases!'

Even the enemies of Christianity agreed that something strange was going on. An opponent called Celsus (we'll meet him as well) claimed that 'it is by the names of certain demons, and by the use of incantations, that the Christians appear to be possessed of [miraculous] power'.

---

* 'Is it bad, doctor?' 'I'm sorry to say you've fractured your proculus. It's completely torpaciated.'

Celsus admitted Christians healed people; he just claimed they did it through magic.

Healing was evidence of power, of the presence of God, of resurrection. In the resonant phrase of Theophilus of Antioch (um, we probably *won't* meet him), healing was seen as 'the work of resurrection going on in yourself'.

Tent-making

Paul travelled around with a variety of companions, founding churches and teaching the gospel. In this he drew on the aid and support of a variety of other teachers and leaders. There was Timothy, his young protégé, from Lystra in Galatia; there was Barnabas, on the first journey – though they then argued and fell out. There was Luke the doctor and Silas the scribe.

Other evangelists were at work as well. Churches were established in places like Colossae and Laodicea, which Paul didn't visit. Paul didn't stop in Asia Minor, either; in one episode in Acts Paul has a vision of a man from Macedonia, who urges Paul to come to help the Christians there, so the faith spreads to what we today would call Europe.*

In fact, it had already reached further west. Paul met Priscilla and Aquila in Corinth and their lives show us something of the mobility – and uncertainty – of being a Christian in these early decades. They were tent-makers like Paul. And they were in exile.

Aquila was a diaspora Jew from Pontus, a region bordering the Black Sea. Born in the east, he went to Rome, presumably to work. The Roman satirist and early *Daily Mail* columnist Juvenal complained that '[The immigrants from the east are] doing everything . . . surveyor, painter, masseuse, doctor . . . he understands everything . . . the sailor's wind blows him to Rome together with plums and figs'.

They come over here, taking our jobs . . .

When Paul met Aquila and Priscilla, though, they were not in Rome, but in Corinth. They had been expelled from Rome because they were Christians: 'Claudius had ordered all Jews to leave Rome' (Acts 18.2). The Roman historian Suetonius gives us a glimpse of what caused this

---

* In later, less authentic manuscripts, he has a vision of the man from Del Monte® but all he does is give Paul a tin of pineapple chunks.

expulsion: 'Since the Jews constantly made disturbances at the instigation of Chrestus, [Claudius] expelled them from Rome' (Suetonius, *Claudius* 25.4). The most plausible explanation of this is that Suetonius has misspelt the name of Christ. This probably took place in AD 49. And Dio Cassius says that 'the Jews' were not allowed back until the beginning of Nero's reign in AD 54.

Since there were thousands of Jews in Rome, it's not likely that all of them could be expelled. For a start it would have decimated the Roman Salt Beef industry. So probably what is being referred to here is the expulsion of all the Jewish Christians. Christianity was probably founded in Rome soon after Claudius' reign began, planted there by anonymous Christian missionaries who brought it into the synagogues. And it began to cause fights and disputes. So Claudius banned all the Jewish Christians, all the followers of Chrestus.

Priscilla and Aquila moved to Corinth, found work, and, with Paul, founded a church. Most likely it met in the tent-making workshop that would also have served as Priscilla and Aquila's home.

One of the interesting things is that in four out of the six mentions of the couple in the New Testament, Priscilla is mentioned first. This is unusual: the ancient world was patriarchal to a degree that would make the average Saudi Arabian husband look like a raving feminist. So why does her name come first? It's possibly to do with her status: she was the teacher. Indeed, when the text is talking about their ministry, it is always 'Priscilla and Aquila'. The fourth-century cleric John Chrysostom, who was not what you'd call a big fan of women, noted the order of the names 'seems to acknowledge a greater godliness for her than for her husband'. In fact, given the low status of women in the cultures of the time, it is remarkable how many women feature in the letters of Paul, either teamed with their husbands or working alone. It cannot be denied that they held positions of authority and responsibility – despite later attempts by male theologians to edit them out.

Oriental menace

Later, Priscilla and Aquila went to Ephesus, returning eventually to Rome in AD 54. In Ephesus one of the people whom Priscilla and Aquila taught was a gifted speaker called Apollos. He was a native of Alexandria, the city in Egypt that was the second biggest in the Mighty

Roman Empire™. We don't know if that was where he encountered Christianity, but certainly Christianity had spread into Africa during the first century. We have already encountered the Ethiopian eunuch, but there were other Africans mentioned in the Bible. Simon, who carried the cross of Jesus, came from Cyrene – modern Libya. There are other people from Cyrene mentioned in the text too.

By the fifties Christianity had spread to Greece and Italy, along the shores of the Black Sea in Asia, throughout Syria and into Arabia, and along the great coastal cities of Africa. The cities in these tales would become the great centres of Christianity for the first three centuries: Rome, Ephesus, Alexandria, Antioch.

They remind us of something that is often forgotten: that Christianity is an Asian – or oriental – religion. Nowadays it's so associated with 'western values' – whatever they are – that we forget that it came from the far east of the Roman Empire. Jesus died in Judea. They were called 'Christians' in Antioch, the capital of Asia. The heartland of the faith in the first centuries was in Asia Minor (modern-day Turkey). And much of what we take for granted in Christianity – the New Testament, monasteries, church buildings, liturgy, eccentric Christians in Fair Isle jumpers, arguments about infinitesimally small differences of theology, even church music – all began in what the Romans termed 'Syria'.

This, indeed, is one of the reasons why the Romans started viewing Christianity with suspicion. They associated it with the east, which in their eyes meant loose morals, debauchery and general un-Romanness. One of Juvenal's characters complains about the dregs of the Orontes – the river running through Antioch – being emptied into Rome. Rome distrusted oriental excesses, and Christianity was numbered among these. And it wasn't long before Christianity was associated with all kinds of immoral behaviour.

You want to cut off my WHAT?

Paul developed a three-step approach to evangelising a new city:

1. Go to the synagogue.
2. Start a ~~fight~~ debate.
3. Get kicked out of the synagogue. Or the city. Or both.

Despite this, he planted churches, which, along with music, prayers and teaching, soon exhibit many other features common to churches through the ages, that is, forming cliques, arguing, calling each other names and bitching about the church leadership.

This meant Paul had to solve a number of pastoral issues. In Corinth the church was deeply split over a number of issues, including the observance of the Lord's Supper and an instance of sexual sin in the congregation. In Colossae there were issues about observing different customs and various local superstitions. But *the* key issue, the one that really got everyone wildly excited, was the thorny question of Christianity's relationship to Judaism.

It is this issue that inspired Paul's first letter, written around AD 48 to the churches he had founded on his first trip to Galatia.* On a return visit he discovered something that must have made him raise an eyebrow in surprise: Jews had been to these churches and insisted that they observe Jewish customs, including the dietary laws and circumcision. What is more, the same kinds of issues were cropping up in Antioch. Peter had visited and had been persuaded by 'some men from James' not to eat at the same table as Gentiles. Even Barnabas had done the same. Paul went ballistic.

Paul was capable of writing the most sublime prose and the most outrageous polemic. In his letter to the Galatians, for example, Paul recommended that if the Judaisers were so keen on circumcision, they should cut the whole lot off. Writing to the Philippians about the same issue, he says, 'Beware of the dogs, beware of the evil workers, beware of those who mutilate the flesh!' (Phil. 3.2). These three Greek nouns – *kunas, kakous ergatas, katatomēn* – all begin with the same explosive 'k'. It is as though Paul spits the words out. When he talks of his previous righteousness as a Jew, he says it is nothing but rubbish. He counts it as rubbish – and the word here is *skubalon*, which means 'excrement, manure, garbage, kitchen scraps'. It is, in fact, a pile of crap.

This is grievous bodily theology. But Paul was never what you'd call diplomatic. During the argument over how far Christians should observe Jewish purity laws, he publicly upbraided Peter – Peter! – for his behaviour. But unity, based on equality before God, was one of Paul's most

---

* Some scholars argue that the letter was written a lot later. They are wrong. I've written a whole book on Acts, so, you know, come and have a debate if you think you're hard enough.

important beliefs. In one of the most radical statements of the ancient world Paul said that Christ makes everyone equal: 'There is no longer Jew or Greek,' he says, 'there is no longer slave or free, there is no longer male and female; for all of you are one in Christ Jesus' (Gal. 3.28). Nowadays we pass over that with barely a hesitation. Of *course* all are equal. We live in a democracy. But in the ancient world there was a massive difference between 'slave' and 'free'. Slaves were owned objects. Free men, were, well . . . *free*.

If Jewish Christians could not eat with Gentile Christians, then there could be no true unity. So Paul argued that it was not necessary for Gentile converts to obey the Jewish law, that what mattered was not outward ritual, but faith in Jesus, the Christ, the Messiah. It was not the observance of the law that reconciled you to God, but grace.

At times, it has to be admitted, this leads him into some eye-wateringly complex theological gymnastics. In Romans, for example, he states that the Law is holy, but also that it leads inexorably to sin. Work that one out.* Nevertheless, this idea came to be crucial to Christianity. Later expressions of Christianity all said that Christians were freed from the requirement of obeying Jewish law. (And to demonstrate that freedom they fasted, did penance, paid their church tithes, went to church on pain of arrest . . . Er. I'll get back to you.)

The book of Acts describes a crisis meeting of the different sides in Jerusalem at which it was decided that Gentile Christians would not be asked to observe Jewish laws. But like all church councils before and since, the decision was widely ignored on both sides, and the debate about Christianity's relationship with Judaism was to go on for a long time. Despite the strong arguments in his letters, Paul actually went out of his way to reassure the Jerusalem church of his Jewish orthodoxy, taking up offerings for the poor in the city and even, at one point, having Timothy circumcised. How Timothy felt about this piece of diplomacy is not recorded.

Paul's arguments were all well and good. But theology is often driven by pragmatism – far more often than it cares to admit, in fact. And, in the end, two factors decided the issue. The first was the sheer numbers of Gentile converts. The second – the thing that tipped the balance

---

* Reading Romans, I take comfort in the words of the famous Pauline expert Bernard Green: 'Paul can contrive to be a very unclear writer at the best of times but he surpasses himself in the Letter to the Romans.'

decisively – was that Jerusalem itself, the centre of Jewish Christianity, where the family of Jesus himself were still in charge, was about to come to an end.

It's not the end of the world, you know

Jesus had promised his followers that he would return. Several times, Paul wrote in expectation of his imminent return: the understanding that 'the days were short' was one reason why he travelled so ceaselessly and worked so zealously.

But Jesus *didn't* return. And as the years ticked by many Christians started metaphorically looking at their watches and realising that, clearly, they were going to be here for a while. And that meant changes had to be made. They had to get organised. Gradually, Christianity began to develop its own sense of order and structure. And that took three forms. First, as the original witnesses of the events died they had to make sure that the official story was written down. Second, as churches continued to spread they had to develop some kind of organisation and leadership. Third, they had to find ways to express their shared beliefs through creeds and official statements.

So around AD 60 the stories of the church were gathered and edited together to form the Gospels. Mark's is generally agreed to be the earliest. Luke and Matthew probably used it as a basis for theirs, along with material from other sources – in particular a collection of Jesus' sayings. John was written later and comes from a different perspective – that of a Jerusalem-based disciple of Jesus. These were not yet the 'New Testament': that would take centuries to come together. But they were to be accepted as the most reliable accounts.

Second, the church developed a (kind of) leadership structure. It took the titles for its leaders from the world around it. Just as the church had repurposed the word *ekklēsia*, it took other titles from the culture surrounding it. The three titles used for leaders in the early church are *episkopos* (which we have turned into the term 'bishop'), *diakonos* (deacon) and *presbuteros* (elder). The titles all sound ecclesiastical today, but they were very mundane at the time. *Episkopos* just meant 'foreman' or 'overseer'. A *presbuteros*, or 'elder', was a man of standing in the community. And *diakonos* just meant 'servant'.

The first bishops were definitely nothing like the blokes in pointy hats we have today. A local bishop would oversee, at the most, a few congregations, which might only be twenty or thirty people in all. Far from holding positions of power, many local church leaders had trouble making anyone take notice of them at all. (How times have changed . . .) The *Didache* urges Christians not to despise the bishops, 'for they are your honourable men along with the prophets and teachers'. It was to be a long time before becoming a bishop was seen as a good career move. Even in the second century, when we have a single 'bishop' overseeing several churches in a city, those churches would only have numbered a few hundred Christians at most.

Part of the bishop's role was to make sure that the poor and needy had somewhere to sit – especially if they were elderly. And, according to one early church document, if no place was available, then the bishop had to give up his seat.* And while the church later developed specific roles for bishops and deacons, in the early church they were pretty much interchangeable.†

Eventually this structure would solidify with the local church network leader – the bishop – supported by a group of elders and deacons. But that was decades away.

The third task – that of developing liturgy and creeds – happened more slowly. We have already seen that some common Christian sayings were present in Paul's letters written in the fifties. The Lord's Prayer seems to have been widely used (although it wasn't called that – the title wasn't given to it until the mid-third century). But the sheer geographic spread of the churches must have delayed the development of a central liturgy. And the church had not yet got the benefit of that key invention, the photocopier – so the sharing of service sheets was pretty limited.

And anyway, by the mid-sixties the church had a more crucial task on its mind: survival.

---

* Nowadays, many Anglican churches have bishop's chairs, which are supposed to be used only by visiting bishops. This would have been anathema to the early church.
† Paul talks to the elders (*presbuteroi*) of Ephesus but tells them that the Holy Spirit has made them overseers (*episkopoi*) of their church. And Paul's letters show quite clearly that gifts were exercised by all of the members of the church, not just by the officially sanctioned few.

The counter-imagined empire

Christianity saw itself as an alternative kingdom; as a 'counter-imagined world'.* The world around it was greedy, violent, repressive, uncaring. But Christians responded by redefining the cosmos. Their songs and creeds were statements of an alternative reality. They saw the world as it was, but pledged allegiance to the world as it should be.

Few documents express this as well as a wonderful piece of writing called the *Epistle to Diognetus*. Written about AD 150, it talks about how Christians 'live in their own countries, but only as nonresidents; they participate in everything as citizens, and endure everything as foreigners. Every foreign country is their fatherland, and every fatherland is foreign . . . They live on earth, but their citizenship is in heaven.'

It goes on to observe that Christians 'love everyone, and by everyone they are persecuted. They are unknown, yet they are condemned; they are put to death, yet they are brought to life. By the Jews they are assaulted as foreigners, and by the Greeks they are persecuted, yet those who hate them are unable to give a reason for their hostility.' That was written in the mid second century. So what had happened? How come Christianity had got so dangerous in a single century? The answer was simple: the Romans woke up to the threat of Christianity.

In the Mighty Roman Empire™ the emperor was revered as a god. Sacrifices were made in his honour, temples erected to his name. Emperor Augustus, for example, was the 'divine Augustus'. An inscription from Halicarnassus (now Bodrum in south-west Turkey) describes him as 'saviour of the common race of men, whose providence has not only fulfilled but actually exceeded the prayers of all'. Numerous inscriptions throughout the empire talked of his mighty deeds, how he was the answer to the prayers of his people, how he was the bringer of peace and lord of all. Stories were created which claimed that he wasn't, in fact, mortal, but that he was the offspring of his mother and the god Apollo. Let's just say he had a fantastic PR department.

But Christians said exactly the same thing about *their* leader. Only their leader wasn't a Roman aristocrat, but a Galilean peasant. Now, many of the Christian terms come from the Hebrew Scriptures, but they were also used in a deliberate undermining of the claims of the

---

* A phrase, I think, from, Walter Brueggemann. No idea where I got it from. Probably the internet.

empire. When Christians call Jesus prince of peace, saviour, or
God, they are using the very same terms that Romans used
emperor.

It wasn't just the emperors, either. To the utter bemusement
Romans, Christians refused to recognise the entire pantheon of k
gods. The Romans were only too happy to add foreign gods to the
– so much so that Hesiod reckoned that there were over 30,000 diffe
gods. They differed from city to city and region to region, a rich
heady brew of Greek, Roman, Egyptian and Syrian anywhere-else-yc
can-think-of gods. There were the premier-league gods Zeus, Artem
Apollo. There were ones slightly lower such as Nikē, god of victory anc
unfairly traded sportswear. And there were purely local gods or ones with
very specific remits, such as Clivicola, goddess of roads that went uphill.*

But Christians refused to attend the banquets, or make the sacrifices.
And it was this that turned them into targets.

Caught in the crossfire

Paul eventually made it to Rome. But first, according to the account
in Acts, in 57 he returned to Jerusalem and – surprise, surprise – became
embroiled in a riot. (Admittedly not of his own making. Well, not *just*
of his own making.) Arrested by the Romans, he appealed, as a Roman
citizen, to have his case heard by the emperor. After two years in a
Caesarean jail cell he was eventually put on a ship and sent to Rome.
After an eventful voyage (storms, shipwreck, no duty free) he arrived
in Rome in the spring of 60. And that's where Acts ends. We don't
know of his fate for sure. But later tradition – strong tradition – has
it that both Paul and Peter were executed in Rome.

And the man ultimately responsible for their fate was the emperor,
Nero.

In 64 a fire broke out in Rome. It spread rapidly, destroying homes
and buildings and burning for five-and-a-half days. Of the fourteen
districts of Rome, three were completely destroyed and only four escaped

---

* Later the job descriptions of these numerous gods would be handed on to
equally numerous saints. I don't know who took on Clivicola's department
in the early days, but the patron saint of road builders is Sebastian de
Aparicio, a sixteenth-century Franciscan who built roads in Mexico and
miraculously lifted a hay wagon on his own at the age of 95.

some kind of destruction. There was widespread looting and gangs were even reported as preventing people from fighting the flames. This led to conspiracy theories and ugly rumours. There were claims that 'Someone I know had seen people actually setting light to buildings. No, really. They were clearly acting under orders. It was all a government conspiracy, man.' And for *government*, read Nero.

The myth that Nero fiddled while Rome burns is wrong, and not only because the violin hadn't been invented.* But he was deeply unpopular because of his conspicuous wealth and scandalous lifestyle. He had, after all, killed his own mother.† Rumours spread like, well, wildfire, that the blaze was started on his orders to clear the way for a new city to be built named after himself. So Nero did what leaders always do in such circumstances: he found someone else to pin the blame on. He found the Christians. The Roman historian Tacitus recorded that

> an immense multitude [of Christians] was convicted, not so much on the charge of arson as because of hatred of the human race. Beside being put to death they were made to serve as objects of amusement; they were clad in the hides of beasts and torn to death by dogs; others were crucified, others set on fire to serve to illuminate the night when daylight failed.

The main accusation against the Christians was based on their 'hatred of the [rest of the] human race'. They were burned and savaged and crucified because they were different.

An immense multitude, and among them, probably, was Peter, the über-apostle. We don't know when he had arrived at Rome – in fact we can't be certain he was in Rome at all. But there is a famous story, the 'Quo vadis?' legend, where Peter is urged by his fellow-Christians to flee from Rome. On his way out of the city he sees the figure of Jesus walking in the opposite direction. 'Quo vadis?' Peter asks, which is Latin for 'where are you going?' Jesus – who, surprisingly, turns out to speak Latin – replies that he is going into Rome to be crucified again. So Peter turns around and follows his master to his death.

---

* The first stringed instruments played with a bow originated at least six centuries later – in Mongolia. Just a free bonus fact for you there.
† Allegedly. Oh, all right, almost definitely.

Fig. II. *Nero identifies those responsible for the fire of Rome*

It's a famous story and has made for a couple of extremely ropey Hollywood films, but the story comes from a thoroughly unreliable source called *The Acts of Peter*, which was written sometime between 180 and 225. The book is more like Harry Potter than Simon Peter. There is a running battle between the apostle and a character called Simon Magus, which features, among other things, a talking dog and the amazing resurrection of a herring. At the end of it Simon tries to fly and gets quite a long way up before the prayers of Peter bring him crashing to earth, breaking his leg in three places.

Not *sober* history, then. However, the story of Peter's death in Rome probably does have a strong historical basis. There were shrines to him and to Paul in the city from very early on, indicating that Paul too was executed, although whether as part of this persecution or later we don't know. Although a later tradition has Paul leaving the city after his trial and going to Spain, there's no real evidence that he ever left the city. According to the legends, he was beheaded.*

(In AD 67, just to compound his sins, Nero introduced the organ to Rome. There were public organ-playing competitions. The organ was played in the arenas too. So at least Paul was spared listening to that.)

The persecution in Rome shattered the church in the city. Those who could escape did. Those who couldn't kept their heads down. Evidence of their suppression comes in the fact that we hear nothing more from the church at Rome for another fifty years or so.

Things weren't much better in Jerusalem. Rising nationalism, combined with the actions of a series of completely inept Roman officials, meant that the situation in Judea was getting more and more tense. And in 62, during a power vacuum when the province was between Roman governors, the high priest took a cheap shot to get his revenge. The high priest's name was Ananus and his father, Ananus, or Annas, had judged Jesus. His brother-in-law was Caiaphas, and he was the man who had engineered the execution of Jesus. An old vendetta. So, while the Romans were looking the other way Ananus Jr took the opportunity to kill, according to Josephus, 'a man named Jacob, the brother of Jesus who was called the Christ, and certain others. He accused them of having acted illegally and delivered them up to be stoned.'

It was a deeply unpopular move and the incoming Roman Procurator Albinus saw that Ananus was removed from his post. Ananus died at the hands of his own people – assassinated by a group of Jewish assassins, the Zealots – in 68. But by that time he was no longer the high priest, but commander-in-chief. He was leading the Jewish rebels – because by that time Judea was in revolt.

---

* According to later legends his head bounced three times, and at each bounce a fountain sprouted up, which is why the traditional site of his death is called *Tre fontane*. There is a church there now. Presumably, if we were able to measure the distance between the fountains we could work out just how strong the executioner was. Just a thought . . .

PETER

Peter, from a third-century medallion. Fine head of hair for a man of his age

Name: Cephas.
Aka: Simon, Peter, Simon Peter.
Nationality: Galilean Jew.
Dates: died c.65.
Appearance: Not known. Traditionally quite a big bloke.
Before he was famous: Fisherman. Disciple.
Famous for: Following Jesus. Not following Jesus. Following Jesus again. Leading the church in the first few months after the resurrection.
Why does he matter? He's the über-disciple. The heart and soul of early Christianity. Passionate, determined, occasionally wrong-headed. Jesus said he was the rock on which the church would be built, although people have argued for years about what exactly that means.
Could you have a drink with him down the pub? Yes. But he might want to sit at a different table to you, depending on how Jewish he was feeling at the time.

Rome 1, Jerusalem 0

The flashpoint came in AD 66. In Caesarea, Syrian Gentiles provoked Jewish rage by sacrificing a chicken in the alleyway outside a synagogue. It's not clear why this was such an insult. It was probably a pagan sacrifice. Or maybe they were Jewish vegetarians. Anyway, it's probably the first time in history that a chicken has led to a mass uprising.

The procurator, Florus, refused to punish the chicken-murderers, and then he began to help himself to money from the treasury in the temple in Jerusalem. This was seen as sacrilege and when Florus next appeared in the city, a hostile, jeering, mocking crowd was waiting. Possibly waving chickens. Maybe even making clucking noises. Although probably not.

Florus let loose his troops and thousands of people were butchered. The city exploded into violence. The Roman garrison was routed, the rebels took control of Jerusalem and the Sadducean aristocracy were massacred. Judea was in revolt. In response Nero sent one of his best generals, Vespasian, with 60,000 troops, to regain the province. But in 68 Nero committed suicide, so Vespasian returned to Rome to restore order, which he duly did by becoming emperor himself. It was left to his son, Titus, to finish the job of controlling Judea.

In the meantime the Christians left Jerusalem. Christians were not interested in Jewish nationalism and even if they had been, as a pacifist organisation the church was not much use in a fight. According to early tradition, the Christians went to a town called Pella in the upper Jordan valley (although this may have been a later invention by the first-century equivalent of the Pella tourist board), where they were led by Jesus' cousin Simeon.

The Romans recaptured Jerusalem in AD 70, by which time many of the rebels had killed each other during months of internecine conflict. The city was destroyed, largely demolished. Hundreds of thousands of Jews were taken to Rome to become slaves or to provide entertainment in the circuses of the empire. Worst of all, the temple was destroyed, burned to the ground in the course of the final assault. This was the 9/11 of the ancient Jewish world. An unimaginable terror in which the impure Gentiles had struck at the very heart of their world and destroyed their most precious building. There was never to be a temple in Jerusalem again.

Josephus claimed that Titus wanted to preserve the temple as an act of moderation, but a later writer called Sulpicius Severus claimed that Titus was determined to destroy the temple 'in order that the Jewish and Christian religions might be more completely abolished; for although these religions were mutually hostile, they had nevertheless sprung from the same founders: the Christians were an offshoot of the Jew, and if the root were taken away the stock would easily perish.'

Funny how things work out. Two thousand years on, Judaism and Christianity are still around. The Roman Empire, on the other hand . . .

Judaism in Jamnia

The destruction of the temple changed the relationship between Judaism and Christianity. For the Christians it meant that the centre of Christianity shifted. While Jerusalem and the temple still stood they acted as the HQ, and tied Christianity to its roots. But once they were gone, other cities – notably Antioch, Alexandria and, eventually, Rome – became more prominent. And although that particularly Jewish style of Christianity survived for some time, it was Paul's Gentile-friendly brand that triumphed.

Judaism underwent a similar transformation. The Sadducees – the party of the aristocracy and the temple – were completely wiped out. But the Pharisees escaped the siege and settled in the coastal city of Jamnia (modern Joppa) where they effectively became the last Jews standing. They got to write the future. The Orthodox Judaism we have today, therefore, is the offspring of the Pharisees, just as the Christianity we have is the offspring of Gentile Christianity. Jews throughout the empire held out hopes for the rebuilding of the temple, but with time those hopes began to fade. So Jewish faith moved to being centred around the synagogue.

In Jamnia the rabbis kept themselves busy compiling the Old Testament. Well, obviously *they* didn't think it was 'the Old Testament' – but the Hebrew Scriptures. Up to then there had been disagreement as to what, exactly, the scriptures of the Jewish faith were. Everyone agreed on the Torah – aka the Law, the books of Moses, later known as the Pentateuch. All forms of Judaism agreed that these books were the foundation of the Jewish faith. But there were many other books: histories and poetry, philosophical books of wisdom, love poetry and many books of prophets. And different flavours of Judaism had different views as to the authority of those books, and even which books should be included in the canon. For example, the Dead Sea Scrolls, which represent the library of an unidentified Jewish sect (possibly, but not definitely, the Essenes), had copies of every book of the Hebrew Scriptures, except the book of Esther. Clearly they did not think that Esther was proper Scripture.

In fact, it was not until Jamnia, around AD 90, that the Hebrew Scriptures were absolutely defined.

Meanwhile, the antagonism between the two faiths increased. Some Christians began to express the thought that the destruction was a punishment on the Jews for their rejection of Jesus as the Messiah. And in their synagogues Jews began to introduce into their prayers curses against Christians, to ensure that no Christians could take part in their worship.

It was a parting of the ways.

Apocalypse now

Towards the end of the first century an emperor called Domitian (81–96) launched a wave of persecution against Christians. Domitian, the son of Vespasian and brother of Titus, was big on the whole emperor worship thing and, in the fine tradition of Roman emperors, as mad as a bag of monkeys.

One of those caught up in this persecution was a church leader in Asia Minor called John. He was sent to the island of Patmos – probably as a punishment.* There, one Sunday morning, he had a vision of Jesus that he captured in a strange book known as Revelation.

The final book of the New Testament is a work of apocalyptic literature. Apocalyptic does not mean 'end of the world', despite its slang use, but 'revelation'. Apocalyptic literature shows you the bigger picture of what's going on – it's the religious equivalent of conspiracy theory: the truth is out there.

This book, with its outlandish imagery and cosmic struggles, was to exert a huge influence over the church in the subsequent centuries. Today the internet is full of websites claiming to have cracked the code of Revelation, and to have worked out the timetable of the End of the World. But the message of Revelation is much more about its time than we recognise today. Revelation is, in fact, mostly a picture of the Mighty Roman Empire™ in all its brutality. It describes Rome as Babylon – a Jewish shorthand for tyranny and destruction, harping back to the Babylonians who destroyed Jerusalem in the sixth century BC. It portrays Roman power and propaganda as horrific, rapacious beasts, and the city of Rome itself as a whore.

---

* The Bible never actually explicitly states why John was on Patmos, but later tradition assumes he was sent there as a form of punishment by the authorities in Ephesus. There is also a question as to the date. Most scholars go for the reign of Domitian, but it could have been earlier.

Revelation is a hugely subversive book, the most overtly and obviously revolutionary book of the Bible. John saw, from his rocky outcrop in the Aegean Sea, that the emperor of the world and the prince of peace could never really mix. To be a true Christian was to be inescapably engaged in confrontation with empire.

In its first sixty years of life Christianity began by annoying the Jewish aristocracy in Jerusalem, moved on to annoying many Jews in other cities, and ended up by annoying the Mighty Roman Empire™.

'Prince of Peace.' Are you having a laugh?

THINGS YOU LEARN FROM CHRISTIAN HISTORY

NO. 2
All traditions have to start somewhere

Here is a list of a few words not mentioned in the Bible: Lent, purgatory, penance, heresy, Trinity, evangelical, fundamentalist, predestination, confirmation, church, Christmas, Advent, Easter, madonna, pope, archbishop, cardinal, transubstantiation, diocese, cathedral, Catholic, Orthodox, Anglican, ordination, monk, nun, abbot, mass . . . oh, and Christianity.

Just because they're not in the Bible doesn't make them wrong, or unimportant. But it does mean that, at some point in the history of the church, they were new.

2 Marcion, Montanism and Monks

Lions 1, Christians 0

Around AD 100 a letter was sent from the church in Rome to the church in Corinth. The Corinthian church had (not for the first time) fallen out spectacularly with its leaders and replaced them with new ones. Clement, a church leader in Rome, wrote a letter urging them to rescind this decision. His argument was that by removing the officially ordained leaders the Corinthians were breaking a direct line of authority stretching back through the apostles to Jesus himself.

In a rather dodgy piece of translation he quotes a line from Isaiah: 'I will establish their bishops in righteousness and their deacons in faith.' This is the first mention of the idea of apostolic succession, the idea that Jesus had appointed the apostles, who had then appointed church leaders, who then appointed other church leaders . . . and so on, and so on. Only this idea, says Clement, ensures that leaders carry on the true, orthodox teaching. It also shows that a leader in Rome was assumed – if only by himself – to have a say in matters hundreds of miles away in Greece. Somehow, although they were miles apart, they were part of the same organisation. Both the Christians in Corinth and those in Rome – not to mention others scattered around in Syria, Palestine and Asia Minor – were 'the church'.

It was a leader from Antioch who put a name to this concept. His name was Ignatius of Antioch (c.35–107) and in a letter he uses a particular word to describe this organisation. He calls it *katholikos*, the Greek word for 'whole' or 'universal', to refer to the church 'where Jesus is'. The word isn't found anywhere in the Bible, but Ignatius clearly assumes that his readers were familiar with the term: he doesn't bother to explain it. This became the word 'catholic', the term today still widely used in our creeds – generally much to the confusion of various church-goers who confuse the term with 'Roman Catholic'. Given the number of splits, schisms, excommunications and general differences of opinion on virtually everything, when standing and saying the phrase in the creed 'we believe in one holy, catholic and apostolic church', this has always struck me as rather a triumph of optimism. But this is where it starts: with leaders like Clement and Ignatius.

Ignatius was the Bishop of Antioch, and he wrote this letter – and others – while he was on death row. A very long death row . . . he was being taken from Antioch to Rome to be martyred. He was a dead man walking, and walking a very long way. He talked of his journey in terms of being thrown to wild beasts in the circus: 'From Syria even to Rome I fight with wild beasts, by land and sea, by night and by day, being bound amidst ten leopards, even a company of soldiers, who only grow worse when they are kindly treated.' In one memorable phrase he described himself as 'God's wheat . . . to be ground by the teeth of wild beasts, so that I may become the pure bread of Christ'. But he was not going to the mill against his will. On the contrary, Ignatius saw martyrdom as the crowning point of his Christian life. Nor was he the first to make the journey. He says that others had 'preceded him in martyrdom . . . from Syria to Rome for the glory of God'.

This was literally a farewell tour. Along the way he had the opportunity to meet many church leaders from the districts through which he was taken. And he wrote several letters to other churches, which he sent out via a network of runners. We see in the letters of Ignatius a church whose separate groups are always writing letters to each other, sending visitors from one church to another, keeping in touch. This is a man who would have *loved* email.

Ignatius' letters show that the church now had a much more developed leadership structure. He urges Christians in one church to follow their bishops 'as Jesus Christ does the Father', and their elders 'as you would the apostles' and to revere the deacons 'as being the institutions of God'.* For Ignatius, a Eucharist is now only 'proper' if administered by a bishop. Baptisms are unlawful, he says, if they are not overseen by the bishop. (The fact that Ignatius has to argue for this, though, shows clearly that other churches disagreed.)

* As opposed to putting them in an institution. Although with many of them that wouldn't have been a bad idea.

But they were 'bishops' rather than 'THE bishop'. Ignatius writes to Polycarp, Bishop of Smyrna, but he appears to be one of a collegiate group of bishops in the city. Less like a CEO and more like a board of directors. And while Ignatius admires the high standards of doctrine held in Rome, he doesn't mention any single Roman leader, certainly not a single 'Bishop of Rome'.

This was not some power trip. The authority of these people was important, because it was the only way, as far as Ignatius was concerned, to ensure proper teaching. Ignatius addresses an idea called Docetism that has crept into some church teaching. The term comes from the Greek word *dokein*, meaning 'to seem'. Docetists claimed that Jesus was not a real man: he only seemed that way. What he really was, was a mystical spirit.

Fig. III. *In the arena, Ignatius of Antioch puts on a show*

The idea originates in Greek philosophy. Jews believed that since God was good and since God had created the world, then the world was pretty good, at least in the beginning. But Plato, the Greek brainbox, had suggested that matter and the body were intrinsically bad. More, that they were a secondary reality. There was a higher, purer reality, an *ideal*, of which this world was just a reflection.

To Docetists it was impossible that God should sweat and bleed and cry and urinate and do all the other stuff that normal bodies require. Divine beings don't do that kind of thing – they just waft around looking gorgeous. Ignatius utterly refuted this. Jesus could be touched, he said. He became flesh, a man, who 'might be touched and handled in the body . . . and who in every kind of way suffered for our sakes'. He was a real man, and really God.

Ignatius died around AD 108, killed by the wild animals in the games. According to tradition, his remains were carried back to Antioch by his companions and interred outside the city gates.

That was real enough, all right.

Hidden gnowledge

Docetism was one example of a form of thinking that came to be known as Gnosticism. The term was coined by a seventeenth-century academic, but he based it on a much earlier phrase used by Irenaeus, Bishop of Lyons, who talked about a whole range of 'alternative' Christianities as being *gnōstikē hairesis* – 'a choice to claim knowledge'. From this phrase we get two powerful and potent terms: 'Gnostics' and 'heresy'.

As more people explored Christianity they asked some searching questions: 'How can a world with so much suffering be created by a good God?' 'How could the all-powerful God also be a crucified Jewish peasant?' And 'How can I make money out of this thing?'

Sometimes, these questions led to different versions of Christianity. Irenaeus listed 217 of these variant Christian splinter groups. Although they get lumped together under the title 'gnostic', they were very different in outlook. For a long time all that scholars had to hand in examining the Gnostics were the writings of their opponents. Then, in 1945, in the Egyptian desert, a man went digging for *sabakh*, a kind of fertiliser, and he found a red earthenware jar containing thirteen leather-bound, papyrus books, containing fifty-two Gnostic texts. The books became known as the Nag Hammadi library, after the place in which they were found.

These books show that Gnosticism had many different expressions. However, among the different groups there are some frequently recurring ideas.

1. *The world is really bad.* Many Gnostic sects believed the material world to be evil. And if that were the case, it could not have been created by a perfect God. So the creator God of the Old Testament must be a lower-division god – a 'demiurge' (an idea they nicked from Plato: the word means 'craftsman').

2. *The human body is really,* really *bad.* Gnostics show a distaste for the human body. In the Docetists' case this led to the idea that Jesus wasn't a real man. Others suggested that Jesus merely moved into a body for a bit. His spirit joined the human Jesus but left just before the crucifixion, thus avoiding all that messy blood and inconvenient pain stuff. (This is called Cerinthianism, after Cerinthus, its most prominent spokesman.) Gnostic writings in this form sometimes have the spirit Jesus sitting on a tree nearby, laughing while the human Jesus goes through agonies. This seems rather unchristian behaviour on the part of . . . er . . . Christ.* Because flesh was sinful, Gnostics treated it harshly and were often ascetics. But this contempt did not extend so far as to actually *losing* the flesh. There are no accounts of Gnostic martyrs; indeed, they were rather sniffy about Christians who embraced martyrdom. They might have considered the flesh disgusting, but they clearly had their limits.

   Others took this disdain for the flesh in the opposite direction. The father-and-son team of Carpocrates (*c.*145) and Epiphanes argued that God's law actually commanded promiscuity. They believed that in order to progress from this world you had to experience absolutely everything. So they indulged in every sin, up to and including Morris dancing.†

3. *The universe is really bad and really good.* Many Gnostic sects believed in a kind of dualism: an endless cosmic battle between dark and light, good and evil, the Dark and Light Side of the

---

* One particularly famous Gnostic was a teacher called Valentinus, who taught at Rome sometime before the middle of the second century. He solved what we might call the 'toilet problem' by claiming that while Jesus ate and drank nothing ever came out: 'he ate and drank in a peculiar way and did not evacuate his food'.

† They were also proto-Communists, claiming that all class differences were wrong and that all property, and women, should be held in common. Clement of Alexandria claimed that at their services they 'have intercourse where they will and with whom they will'. A whole new light on 'sharing the peace'.

Force, etc. This might be because they had some contact with Persian Zoroastrianism. Or it might be because they could see things only in black and white.

4. *Anything Jewish is really, really, really bad.* Gnostics, mainly being Greek, found it deeply embarrassing that the early church relied so much upon the Hebrew Scriptures, with their ridiculous accounts of creation.

5. *Women are really unspeakably bad.* You sometimes hear claims that Gnostic teaching represents a milder, kinder, more hypo-allergenic Christianity, which is heavily feminist and that would appeal to the third-century equivalent of *Guardian* readers. In fact, Gnostic texts abound in misogyny. Women were rubbish, basically.

6. *The enlightened, on the other hand, are tremendously good.* Much of their teaching was reserved for enlightened, superior believers known as 'spirituals'. True wisdom was not for the plebs. The doors of perception opened only to those with an invite.

All Gnostic groups had a problem, though. And that was that pretty much everything in the Gospels was exactly the opposite of their enlightened, 'hidden' ideas. Evidently the truth was so deep that it had been hidden from those who actually knew and saw Jesus. The Gnostic sects solved this problem with a masterstroke of lateral thinking: they invented their own gospels.

But here they came up against the same issue facing Ignatius and Clement: How do you give authority to your ideas? The Gnostics did it by attributing their gospels to various characters in the New Testament narratives. There were gospels attributed to Philip, to Thomas and Mary; there were apocryphal visions attributed to John, Paul, Adam, and three to James.

Claims that these gospels tell us stuff about Jesus are almost always a load of *sabakh*. For one thing, they were written between 150 and 200 years after Christ. To take perhaps the most famous, the *Gospel of Thomas* dates from AD 150 to 200, at the earliest. (The first known reference to it comes from between 225 and 235.) Some may contain nuggets of truth, or genuine memories, or even (as is the case with Thomas) some genuine sayings of Jesus among the welter of invention. But they are not eyewitness documents. Anyone who tries to tell you that the *Gospel of Judas* was really by Judas, or the *Gospel of Philip* was written by Philip, or that Paul had anything to do with the *Apocalypse of Paul* is trying to sell you something. A documentary, normally. Or a terribly written novel.

Pliny and persecution

Around AD 110, three years after Ignatius died in Rome, Pliny the Younger, governor of Bithynia-Pontus, wrote to the emperor Trajan regarding the Christians that he found in his region. He dragged some in, interrogated them, sent them off to punishment. His activities set off a torrent of accusations. Some who were arrested denied being Christian. Others said they had been in the past but weren't any longer. Others claimed they had never been a Christian: 'Oh, no, not me, Guv. I swear I don't know how that hymnbook fell into the folds of my toga.'

Their 'crime' was familiar: the refusal to worship the traditional Roman gods, in particular, the emperor. By now the cult of emperor worship had become a fundamental test of civic loyalty throughout the Mighty Roman Empire™. Sacrificing to the emperor showed that you were a loyal, obedient Roman subject. It was like singing the national anthem or saluting the flag.

Trajan instructed Pliny not to go looking for Christians, but that if he found them he should punish them, unless they 'deny being Christians, and make it plain that they are not, by worshipping our gods'. Pliny even devised a three-part test to determine whether someone was guilty of being a Christian: first they had to worship Roman gods, repeating after him a simple invocation. Secondly they had to make a sacrifice of frankincense and wine to the gods; and thirdly, they had to curse the name of Christ.

And if they refused, they were killed.

In Smyrna Polycarp failed the test.* The aged Bishop of Smyrna – to whom Ignatius had written and who, as a young man, had listened to the apostle John – was offered the chance to save himself. All he had to do was perform the sacrifice to the emperor and he would be freed. He refused. As he was dragged into the arena the crowd yelled,

---

* 'Polycarp' is Greek for 'a lot of ornamental fish'.

'This is the teacher of Asia, the father of the Christians, and the overthrower of our gods, he who has been teaching many not to sacrifice or to worship the gods.' And on 22 February AD 156, he was burned at the stake. The church collected his bones and gathered every year at the tomb to celebrate what they liked to think of as his real birthday.

Martyrdom was seen as the ultimate for Christians. The bones of the martyrs were treasured and their example seen as inspirational. Martyrdom was the ultimate imitation of Jesus – so much so that sometimes the desire to follow their leader got out of hand and Christian leaders had to discourage wannabe martyrs. In the 150s a group of Christians from Smyrna handed themselves in to the authorities, in a zealous desire for martyrdom, only to find that their leader ended up making a sacrifice to Caesar to save his life. 'That is the reason, brothers,' said the church, patiently, 'why we do not approve of men offering themselves spontaneously.'

Increasingly, Christians saw themselves as different to the rest of the Roman world. In the third century Christians even invented their own term for the non-believers: *pagani* (the word actually means 'country-folk'). They were the yokels, the 'pagans', people who still believed in the old gods.

Fig. IV. *In the arena, Christians have mixed luck*

Rome 2, Jerusalem 0

In 132 the Jews revolted. Again. Fury had been growing since the destruction of the temple in 70, and this time they were inflamed by a man called Simon Bar Kochba. The end result was the same as before, only more so: the Romans crushed the revolt and exiled the Jews from their own country.

The emperor and famous wall-builder Hadrian turned Jerusalem into a Roman camp called Aelia Capitolina. The very name of Jerusalem was erased from the Roman world. With deliberate offensiveness Hadrian built a temple to Jupiter in the city. (By coincidence this was built over the traditional site of Jesus' death and resurrection and ironically enabled the Christians – some of whom returned to the city – to remember the site. When other Christians came and asked where it had happened, they could point to the temple and say, 'It's under that ugly big temple over there.')

For the Jews this was final. Now there was no hope of rebuilding the temple. And it made them suspicious of any more would-be messiahs. Rabbi Akiba – who had proclaimed Bar Kochba to be the Messiah – was flayed alive for his part in the revolt. And the rabbi Johanan ben Zakkai, who had survived the first destruction of Jerusalem, advised his followers to finish what they were doing before rushing out to meet the next messiah.

But the second revolt also had a marked effect on Christianity. It cost the Jewish strand of the faith dear. They refused to engage with the revolt, which led to violent reprisals and accusations of betrayal from their fellow-Jews. After the revolt they no longer had the prestige associated with Jerusalem to rely on.*

Christians elsewhere distanced themselves even more from that heritage. They had enough problems without being linked to rebels. The Romans imposed a punitive tax on the Jews, and Christians were keen to avoid that as well. But that made Christianity more visible. And, for all these troubles, Judaism was still a *religio licita*, an officially approved Roman religion. Christianity didn't have any such protected status.

---

* Jewish Christianity limped on for a few centuries. In the 380s, when the scholar Jerome moved to Bethlehem to work on his Bible translation, he encountered surviving Jewish-Christian communities even then.

The destruction of Jerusalem had one final effect. Leaving Christianity without a central 'holy city' as it did, other candidate cities started to jostle for that position.

The shorter version

Utterly severing the relationship between Judaism and Christianity was something that was very important to a man called Marcion.

He was born around AD 100 in Sinope, in the Roman province of Pontus, on the south shore of the Black Sea. When he was just a young man, he was banished for heretical opinions by the local bishop. Given that the bishop was also Marcion's own father, you might argue this did not bode well.*

He made a lot of money in shipping – enough to retire and spend his life in theological study and in annoying people. Sometime around 140 he went to Rome and made a big impact, not least because he made a massive donation to the church. They even let him preach. Then they heard what he had to say, expelled him and gave him his money back.

Marcion loved the teachings of Jesus, was a big fan of Paul and preached a God of love and forgiveness. It was just the rest of it he had a problem with. He decided that Christianity was just too Jewish, so he rejected, well, the entire Old Testament. He was not the only one to feel uncomfortable about some parts of the Hebrew Scriptures, but where other Christians read these stories symbolically or allegorically, Marcion took the text at face value. For him, allegory was for wimps. The only thing suitable for these unhealthy books was amputation. So he cut out any text that clashed with his own sense of good religion.

The problem was that it wasn't just the Old Testament that was a bit Jewish. There was a lot of similar stuff in the New Testament. So he cut that out as well. This basically left him with ten letters of Paul, a truncated version of the gospel of Luke and a work of his

---

* We have to be careful with some of the details of Marcion's life, which were all transmitted via his enemies. These enemies are, therefore, not without their own agendas. And they are fabulously rude. Tertullian called him 'fouler than any Scythian. . .' not to mention a monster, a savage beast, a 'gnawing beaver' and, oddly, 'a Pontic mouse'. So there.

own, called the *Antitheses*, which made clear the difference between his Scriptures and the Jewish version.*

But even that didn't solve the problem – Paul was full of Old Testament ideas and references and Jesus was a Torah-observant Jew. So Marcion had to find more and more labyrinthine ways of explaining these ideas away. They were forgeries, interpolations. They weren't original. (In many ways you might say he is the father of modern biblical scholarship.)

He created his own organisation, the 'true church'. It had a lot in common with the church that had rejected him: they baptised people, they prayed and worshipped and they even celebrated the Eucharist (only with water instead of wine). But it was thoroughly un-Jewish.

True to his entrepreneurial roots, though, Marcion was successful in franchising his ideas. There were Marcionite congregations as far afield as France and Syria. Some scholars believe that Marcionites even outnumbered non-Marcionites in the 160s and 170s. It was not until the third century that Marcionism began to decline in the west, but it persevered in the east a great deal longer.† In the fifth century Marcionite congregations and churches are known to have existed side by side with their orthodox brethren. It was so confusing that Cyril of Jerusalem warned orthodox Christians to be careful lest they accidentally enter a Marcionite church. You couldn't be too careful.

You, me and Irenaeus

Persecution was sporadic, but it was real. It spiked in certain areas at certain times. In 177 there was a pogrom against the Christians in the town of Lyons, and among the victims was the bishop, Pothinus. A young man called Irenaeus (*c*.130–*c*.200) was chosen to take his place.

Irenaeus had been born in Asia Minor but, following the age-old

---

* Tertullian mocked Marcion's god as being like a woolly liberal: 'A better God has been discovered who never takes offence, is never angry, never inflicts punishment . . . He is purely and simply good.'
† Some scholars have suggested that Marcionite congregations were still around in the tenth century, in what is now Iran and Afghanistan.

principle 'Go west, young man', he travelled to Rome and then to Lyons to be a kind of missionary among the Celts in Gaul. Hardly surprisingly, given the circumstances, Irenaeus was a strong defender of the faith. His flock were attacked on two fronts: physically, through officially sanctioned persecution and harassment; and spiritually, through the increasing influence of gnostic thinking. His great work *Against Heresies* discusses all manner of divergent beliefs, from Gnostic mystical hoo-hah to ascetic Judaistic Christianity. (It's ironic that a man who had seen so much persecution himself popularised a term, 'heresy', that was to be used to justify so much killing in the future.)

Irenaeus also emphasised the importance of strongly shared practices and beliefs and the transmission of orthodox teaching. As a young man he had sat and listened to Polycarp, who, in turn, had listened to apostles – people who had seen the Lord: 'I distinctly recall the events of that time better than those of recent years . . . I can tell the very place where the blessed Polycarp used to sit . . . how he would tell of his conversations with John and the others who had seen the Lord, his mighty work and teachings.'

These accounts could also be found in the Christian Scriptures. Irenaeus was the first writer to promote the four Gospels explicitly as canonical, as 'true and reliable'. He may also have been the first person to describe the Hebrew and Christian Scriptures as the 'New' and 'Old' Testaments.*

Ignatius also introduces a new emphasis: the leadership of Rome. He calls it 'the great and illustrious Church, to which, by reason of its supreme status, every church, which is to say the faithful wherever they may be, must turn'.

---

* The other candidate for this is a man called Melito of Sardis. I thought Melito was a kind of ice cream, but there you go.

JUSTIN

Justin Martyr. Either he's counting or he's really not pleased to see us

Name: Justin.
Aka: Justin Martyr.
Nationality: Came from Nablus, in Samaria.
Dates: c.110–65.
Appearance: Wore a philosopher's cloak.
Before he was famous: Seeker after truth.
Famous for: Philosophising. Teaching. Apologising, in the old sense.
Why does he matter? First apologist of the Christian church. Sought to explain Christianity through the culture around him.
Could you have a drink with him down the pub? Probably. There would have been an inn or two close to the bath house where he lived.

Justin would like to apologise . . .

Around the same time that Marcion was arriving in Rome another major figure was also settling there. He is known as Justin Martyr – although 'martyr' is not his surname: it's what happened to him.

Justin (*c.*110–165) was born in Flavia Neapolis (modern-day Nablus) in Palestine and became a Christian around 130. Before that he tried various teachers: a Stoic, an Aristotelian, a Pythagorean and a Platonist. The stoic couldn't explain anything real about God to him; the Pythagorean insisted that he had to learn music, astronomy and geometry before he could discuss the meaning of life; and the Aristotelian seemed mainly interested in what kind of fee he was going to get. (Justin quite liked the Platonist, though.)

Frustrated, he went for a walk near the beach. It was there that he encountered an otherwise unremarkable old man, a Jewish Christian, who simply began to talk to him. As Justin listened, he became awestruck, more and more convinced of the power and truth of what the old man was saying. He had come to the end of one journey, and a new one was about to start.

He moved to Rome where, wearing the *pallium* – the cloak worn by philosophers – he started his own Christian philosophy classes, in a room above the Timotinian Baths. Well, I suppose it saved on central heating costs. To Justin, Jesus was the culmination of all the world's philosophies. All of them were a bit right, but only Christ was entirely right. But this wasn't just 'philosophy': it made a real difference to people's lives:

> we who formerly delighted in fornication, but now embrace chastity alone; we who formerly used magical arts, dedicate ourselves to the good and unbegotten God; we who valued above all things the acquisition of wealth and possessions, now bring what we have into a common stock, and communicate to every one in need; we who hated and destroyed one another . . . now, since the coming of Christ, live familiarly with them, and pray for our enemies . . .

Justin was an apologist – a word that actually means someone who is emphatically *not* sorry for what he believes. An apologist offers a defence of a viewpoint. Justin engaged with the culture around him, explaining God the Father using an idea from Plato – the idea of the one, supreme being. To explain Jesus, Justin used another Greek concept, the *Logos*, the word. In the past 'the Word' gave wisdom and understanding to Greek philosophers; but Jesus didn't just hear 'the word', he *was* the word. Justin described Jesus as being separate from the Father, but derived from him – like a flame passed from one torch to another. Jesus is light from light: as Christians still declare as part of their creed today.

From Justin we also have the earliest description of a church service:

> And on the day called Sunday all who live in cities or in the country gather together to one place, and the memoirs of the apostles or the writings of the prophets are read, as long as time permits; then, when the reader has ceased, the president verbally instructs, and exhorts to the imitation of these good things. Then we all rise together and pray, and, as we before said, when our

prayer is ended, bread and wine and water are brought, and the president in like manner offers prayers and thanksgivings, according to his ability, and the people assent, saying Amen and there is a distribution to each, and a participation of that over which thanks have been given, and to those who are absent a portion is sent by the deacons.

After that a collection is taken for the orphans, the widows and the sick. Throw in a photocopied service sheet and some dodgy coffee and biscuits and you've basically got a modern service.

Justin was a fan of Socrates (not the Brazilian footballer), but he saw Jesus as vastly superior. No one, he pointed out, trusted so much in Socrates that they died for his belief; but in Christ 'not only have philosophers and scholars believed, but also artisans and entirely uneducated people have despised glory, fear and death'.

Justin followed in their path. Ironically, this foremost among Christian thinkers was killed by the orders of Marcus Aurelius, a fellow-philosopher – and emperor of Rome. Justin was tried together with six companions and beheaded, probably in 165. And that is how he got his nickname.

The single version

Other people were also having issues with the Scriptures, and resolving them in various ways. In Antioch, around 170, a former pupil of Justin's called Tatian created a mash-up of the four Gospels, called the *Diatesseron*. The name means 'one through four' and that is what Tatian (d. *c*.185) did: he wove together one gospel from the four. He did this by removing any repetitions, harmonising discrepancies, and even 'correcting' what he considered omissions.* (He was a strict vegetarian, so he also cut out the bit about John the Baptist eating locusts, and just left in the honey.)

His work proved hugely popular. A synopsis was much easier to use than four separate books, and people could more easily grasp one story.

---

* The name is a bit wrong, because scholars have been able to reconstruct the *Diatesseron*, and it turns out that some readings within it actually come from the *Gospel of the Hebrews*. Tatian was not the only harmoniser, for that matter. Other Gospel harmonies were available. Justin actually used one.

The *Diatesseron* was probably the first ever gospel translation, since it was written in Syriac, and it became the official Syriac Gospel for some three hundred years. It was not until 423 that Theodoret, Bishop of Cyrrhus in upper Syria, impounded some two hundred copies and 'introduced instead of them the Gospels of the four evangelists'. But the influence of Tatian's mash-up gospel had in the meantime spread all the way into India, China and even as far away as Mongolia.

Bringing up baby

Some people, though, wanted more, not fewer, gospels. So they created a range of forged 'Acts', which attempted to tell more of the stories of various apostles. These, unlike the Gnostic gospels, were intended either to fill in the gaps, or to give expression to orthodox ideas which were not overtly stated in the Gospels themselves.

One of the most famous of these was *The Acts of Paul and Thecla*, which is a kind of early Christian romantic novel, telling of the relationship between Paul and a female convert called Thecla. The man who wrote it was an elder in Asia, who was sacked for this fraud. But he claimed that he wrote it in honour of Paul, like loyal fans of *Star Wars* or *Twilight* today who create their own original tales based on the characters from the show. The story features, among other things, Thecla being thrown to the animals in the circus – including, apparently, a pair of carnivorous seals.

Some were motivated by less noble considerations. The *Gospel of Peter* (of which we have only fragments) comes from around AD 200 and shows the passion narrative of Jesus. But it entirely exonerates Pilate and pins the blame squarely on the Jews.

Another popular genre was of infancy gospels, 'prequels' to the Gospels proper, filling in the gap between Jesus' birth and the start of his ministry. They show Jesus as a schoolboy, playing miraculous tricks on errant schoolmates or nasty teachers, turning them into birds, or killing them and then bringing them back to life. Of these, the most influential was *The Infancy Gospel of James*, written sometime in the late second century.* This helpfully ~~invents~~ fills in some details missing from the Gospels, such as the name of Mary's mother (Anna or Anne),

---

* Its posh name is *The Protevangelium of James*.

the real status of Jesus' brothers (step-brothers from Joseph's previous marriage). The book was written to support an idea that was now growing in popularity: the perpetual virginity of Mary.

The longer version

These books were able to gain traction because the official list of what constituted Christian scripture had still not been finalised. And that same problem lies behind the next 'heresy', which started around 160 in a small village in Phrygia (modern-day central Turkey).

There a Christian called Montanus fell into a trance and began to speak in tongues. Montanus had been a priest of the mystery cult of Cybele.* Then he converted to Christ and came over all spiritual. He attracted two female followers, Priscilla and Maximilla, who abandoned their husbands to join him. Hmmm. Anyway, the group of them relocated to the little town of Pepuza, some twenty miles north-east of Hierapolis, which is where, based on their reading of Revelation, they believed the New Jerusalem was going to descend and Christ would return to start his 1,000-year rule.

These were no wild, abandoned cult leaders: they obeyed a strict moral code. The movement became known as the New Prophecy. (Opponents called it Montanism.) Many people were soon attracted to what they saw as a return to the raw excitement of the early days of the church; in particular, the ecstatic trances, during which they received messages from God. These pronouncements were written down and – here is where others started to get worried – treated as Scripture. One leader called Themiso even dared to write a general epistle to the church. As if that were not bad enough, women were appointed to leadership. *Women!* I ask you. As one Victorian reference book put it, 'If Montanism had triumphed, Christian doctrine would have been developed, not under the superintendence of church teachers, most esteemed for wisdom, but usually of wild and excitable women.'† I don't know about you, but I quite like the sound of that.

* Don't ask: it's a mystery.
† The quote comes from an endlessly fascinating book called *A Dictionary of Early Christian Biography and Literature to the End of the Sixth Century A.D., with an Account of the Principal Sects and Heresies*, by Henry Wace, vol. 4. 'Naamanes – Zuntfredus' is particularly entertaining. Actually, it's a very good resource, if you like that sort of thing. Which, obviously, I do.

The bishops of Asia Minor declared this new prophecy to be the work of demons. Their decision was upheld by the bishops of Rome, Carthage and elsewhere in North Africa, none of whom had ever managed to attract any women to follow them, and were therefore *very annoyed*. Plus, these people were nobodies. If the Holy Spirit wanted to send a new message or two, why didn't he talk to the bishops who stood in the properly ordained line of apostolic succession?*

But the Montanists had a point. If John, on Patmos, could experience a divine revelation, why couldn't someone else? And it wasn't as if the Holy Spirit was saying anything particularly controversial. (Or even, frankly, that interesting.) On the other hand, if anyone could create Scripture, then Scripture itself lost its meaning. How would the church be able to combat falsehoods?

The Montanists' revelations were inspired by the book of Revelation. This led to a general distrust of apocalyptic literature in general, and anyone who was keen to see Jesus return in particular. The Montanists were looking forward to the second coming, but, by and large, the rest of the church had given up waiting.†

From now on, really, the church got suspicious of enthusiasts. Montanism was a forerunner of many revival and Pentecostal movements to come – movements of the Holy Spirit to which the authorities never know quite how to react. When the Holy Spirit starts to speak through ordinary people, the authorities don't know whether to be pleased people are taking an interest, or annoyed that God has not seen fit to speak through the proper channels.

Despite being officially proscribed, Montanism survived around Pepuza for another four hundred years. Eventually, in AD 550, the emperor Justinian sent the squaddies to destroy the shrine of the

---

* The leaders of the New Prophecy claimed that their three founders had received their prophetic gifts from other prophets, in a line stretching back to Agabus and the daughters of Philip the Evangelist. Thus they were asserting an alternative apostolic line of succession.

† The only figure of any note who still showed any enthusiasm for the return of Jesus was Irenaeus of Lyons. And his comments proved so embarrassing to the church that they were later censored out of his works. We know only that he was looking forward to it because some of the lost passages of his work turned up again in the sixteenth century, which was a bit embarrassing to the Roman Catholic Church, because he was saying the same kinds of things as some of the more radical Protestants.

founders. The Montanist city was destroyed and lost for 1,500 years, until an archaeological expedition in 2001 rediscovered a 'church in a cave', a huge 'rock-carved monastery with Byzantine graffiti' and a nearby settlement and burial ground. Pepuza, home of the Montanists and breeding ground of radical spiritualism, had been rediscovered.

But it also spread further afield. Notably to North Africa, which always liked a bit of wildness, where it gained perhaps its most famous follower: Tertullian.

TERTULLIAN

Tertullian. Looking annoyed as usual. Perhaps something in that telegram he's just received

Name: Quintus Septimius Florens Tertullianus.
Aka: Tertullian.
Nationality: Born in Carthage, North Africa.
Dates: c.160–225.
Appearance: Not known. Probably grumpy-looking.
Before he was famous: Not known. May have been studying for the law.
Famous for: Writing. Polemics. Outspoken style. Montanist.
Why does he matter? He is called the Father of Theology. First major Latin-writing historian. First person to use the term 'Trinity'.
Could you have a drink with him down the pub? Yes, but not to excess. And don't mention the Greeks.

Three in one

Often called the Father of Theology, Tertullian (*c.*160–225) was an African, born and educated in Carthage, a Roman colony in what is today Tunisia. That part of the world did not speak much Greek, so

Tertullian was the first major theologian to write in Latin.*

Which was OK by Tertullian, who was no fan of either the Greek language or of Greek philosophy. He wasn't interested in making links between Christianity and Greek philosophy, such as those made by Justin. 'What has Athens to do with Jerusalem?' he wrote, booting the whole concept into touch.

He was a good booter. His writing is powerful, angry, outspoken. Church historian Philip Schaff said, 'His polemics everywhere leave marks of blood. It is a wonder that he was not killed by the heathens, or excommunicated by the Catholics.' He was a professional rebel. Perhaps that explains why, in the end, he rebelled even against the orthodox church itself, becoming a champion of Montanism. We don't know when this happened. One account has it that he was present at the council where Montanism was condemned, and was so angry at the decision he walked out and signed up with the Montanists straight away. It sounds like Tertullian.

He was the kind of writer who really needs an opponent. His writing takes on a range of 'enemies', including supporters of Marcion, advocates of infant baptism and, in general, anyone he suspected of collaborating with the empire.

Perhaps his most influential idea occurs in a typically abusive pamphlet, where he is laying into a Christian from Asia Minor called Praxeas – whom Tertullian describes as being 'inflated with pride' simply because he's spent a bit of time in prison. Praxeas was proposing an idea known as monarchianism. Praxeas saw no division between the Father, Son and Holy Spirit: they were all essentially one being. God was like a Greek or Roman actor. He might appear on stage wearing a different mask – Jesus, God, the Holy Spirit – but it was still the same actor. The Latin word for the actor's mask was *persona* and from this we get our word 'person'. Thus the godhead was one being wearing three 'personas': three masks.

Tertullian argued that the Father, Son and Holy Spirit were distinct from each other, although they shared the same substance: 'these three are one substance, not one person; and it is said, "I and my Father are one" in respect not of the singularity of number but the unity of the

---

* It's probable that the first Latin-speaking church was in Carthage, rather than in Rome. Rome, after all, was a city with high immigration and Greek was still widely spoken. Whereas Cyprian of Carthage (c.200–258) was the first to quote a Latin text.

substance. The very names "Father" and "Son" indicate the distinction of personality. The Father is one, the Son is one, and the Spirit is one.' In arguing this he is the first person to use the term *trinitas*, 'threeness', from which we get our concept of the Trinity.

Tertullian was a stern, even conservative, thinker. But he had real issues to engage with. In 202 there were anti-Christian riots in Carthage and some Christians were imprisoned. These included a young noblewoman called Vibia Perpetua, and her slave Felicitas.

Perpetua had a baby, whom she was forced to abandon. But then the jailer relented and she was allowed the baby with her in prison. Her father begged her to renounce the faith but she refused. Felicitas was pregnant – and even the Romans baulked at executing a pregnant woman. But once she delivered her child, the two women were taken out into the arena. They were gored by bulls, and in the end had to be dispatched by gladiators. But what struck the crowd was that, before their deaths, the two women, from different social classes, embraced like sisters.

In the face of such persecution Tertullian wrote a passionate defence of Christian belief and conduct. And he warned that Christianity could not be defeated in this way: 'Your cruelty, however great, is a better advertisement for us than for you. The more you mow us down, the more we grow. The blood of Christians is seed.'*

Plague town

In Carthage martyrdom drew people to Jesus. Another factor was the radical lifestyle of the early church. When the plague of Galen hit the empire in 165, the pagans left town as fast as their flappy little sandals could carry them. But the Christians stayed behind and tended to the sick. A century later when another plague hit North Africa, Dionysus of Alexandria wrote, 'Certainly very many of our brethren, while, in their exceeding love and brotherly-kindness, they did not spare themselves, but kept by each other, and visited the sick without thought of their own peril, and ministered to them assiduously, and treated them for their healing in Christ . . .'

---

* As well as his writings, Tertullian left another legacy in the form of a tiny Christian sect who called themselves the Tertullianistae. They lasted about a hundred years after his death before being quietly absorbed back into the church in Carthage in the late fourth century. They were probably a pretty grumpy little group. In many ways I'd have felt at home among them.

The church gave the dead a decent burial, 'laying them out decently, they clung to them, and embraced them, and prepared them duly with washing and with attire'. This contrasts with the pagans among whom

> all was the very reverse. For they thrust aside any who began to be sick, and kept aloof even from their dearest friends, and cast the sufferers out upon the public roads half dead, and left them unburied, and treated them with utter contempt when they died, steadily avoiding any kind of communication and intercourse with death; which, however, it was not easy for them altogether to escape, in spite of the many precautions they employed.

Ha. In your face, pagans. And don't think that Dionysius is bigging up the Christians, either. He's writing about the plague in Alexandria to people who had actually been through it. This is not some kind of PR spin. His correspondents are people who had seen this behaviour for themselves.

And those who were cared for by Christians and survived – to whom would they give their allegiance? Not to the pagans who left them to die, but to the Christians who stayed with them.

Give peace a chance

Another way in which the Christians distinguished themselves from their contemporaries was in their attitude to war. Christians were pacifists. Soldiers killed people. And Christians didn't. 'We who were filled with war and mutual slaughter and every wickedness have each of us in all the world changed our weapons of war – swords into ploughs and spears into agricultural implements,' wrote Justin Martyr. Tertullian put it with typical force: 'But how will a Christian man war, nay, how will he serve even in peace, without a sword, which the Lord has taken away? . . . Christ, in disarming Peter, unbelted every soldier.'

Another Carthaginian Christian, Cyprian, remarked that homicide is considered a crime when committed by individuals, a virtue when carried on publicly. He was martyred in AD 258; close to his grave was the tomb of the youth Maximillianus, executed for being a conscientious objector.

Their enemies certainly knew that Christians hated violence.

Athenagoras mocked Christian softies who could not 'endure to see a man being put to death even justly'. He pointed out that Christians turned away from all forms of killing, including gladiator fights, abortion and infanticide. Around AD 248 Celsus felt able to level the accusation at Christians that 'If all men were to do the same as you, there would be nothing to prevent the king from being left in utter solitude and desertion and the forces of the empire would fall into the hands of the wildest and most lawless barbarians.' To which Origen replied tersely that 'We do not fight under the emperor, although he require it.'

Christians were told to love their enemies. 'Rome grew great', Tertullian said, 'not by religion, but by wars which always injure religion.' To him, the laurel crown, the Roman symbol of high honour and victory, was smeared with blood. 'Is the laurel of the triumph made of leaves, or of corpses? Is it adorned with ribbons, or with tombs? Is it bedewed with ointments, or with the tears of wives and mothers?'

For similar reasons Christians also refused to serve as magistrates. 'We have no pressing inducement to take part in your public meetings,' wrote Tertullian, 'nor is there anything more entirely foreign to us than affairs of state.' Magistrates were the method by which Rome enforced its power. And they did that, mostly, by sentencing people to death.*

The early church was not going to do the empire's dirty work.

Clement from Greeksville

In Carthage Tertullian was not a big fan of Greek philosophy. But further along the coast, in Alexandria, some Christians certainly were.

Alexandria was the intellectual capital of the empire. You could find schools of every major philosophy in the city, and it had at one time been home to the biggest library in the ancient world: some 70,000 scrolls. Greek was widely spoken here. Welcome to Greeksville, North Africa. You probably couldn't move for hummus.

It was also the home of the first Christian Bible college, as it were: the catechetical school. The man who was head of the school was Titus

---

* The first Christian bishop to hold the post of civil magistrate was Paul of Samosata, in Palmyra in AD 268. But he was a rogue bishop. He had furniture designers design a special throne for him and went around accompanied by a bodyguard. Unsurprisingly, perhaps, he was later sacked for misconduct.

Flavius Clemens – Clement of Alexandria, as he became known. In a town like Alexandria Clement needed to demonstrate that Christianity did apply to the educated as well as the uneducated. So his writings adopted the philosophical style of the city. He stuffed in quotations from pagan authors to demonstrate his wide reading. He argued that Christianity was the culmination of Greek philosophy. The work of philosophers like Plato was, for Greeks, the equivalent of the Law for Jews – the philosophers were schoolteachers, designed 'to bring Greek culture to Christ'.

Many Alexandrians certainly didn't think much of what they saw as the crude and vulgar stories of the Jews. (Alexandria had a strong history of anti-Semitism, despite having the biggest diaspora Jewish community in the Roman Empire.) Clement's approach, therefore, was to interpret the Old Testament in deeply symbolic, allegorical terms. These obscure, odd writings held hidden truths – but you had to decode it. This, of course, is worryingly close to Gnosticism. And Clement was pretty friendly to the Gnostics. For Clement, in fact, Christians were the 'true gnostics'. This made him suspect in some eyes and is probably the reason why hardly any of his writing survives. ('That Clement, he's a little too keen on the Gnostics, if you ask me.')

For Clement, like candidates in the X Factor, we are all on a journey. And that journey continues after death, where, he believed, the soul would be purged by a fire of wisdom. Later ages would rediscover this idea of Clement's and turn his purgation into the concept of purgatory.

It all sounds very other-worldly. But Clement wrote about a lot of other, ordinary things, from sex to table manners. (Most importantly: don't talk with your mouth full.) He argued for sensible stewardship of money and resources, rather than a literal obedience to Jesus' injunction to 'sell all you have'. And he had a positive view of sex. He did not see it, as many Gnostics (and, indeed, many Christians) did, as innately sinful. But he did believe that it was unnatural to have sex for any other reason than to produce children. So, along with purgatory he also paved the way for a view of sex that is still current in many Christian circles – notably Roman Catholic – today.

And as if that wasn't enough invention, Clement of Alexandria was the first person to call the Scriptures 'the Bible'. Well, he didn't actually call them that. The title he used was *ta biblia* – Greek for 'the books'. He was talking about the Hebrew Scriptures, but by 223 his pupil Origen was using the word for both the Hebrew and Christian Scriptures. So from *ta biblia* we get to 'the Bible'.

ORIGEN

Origen. He wrote a lot more books than that

Name: Origenes Adamantius.
Aka: Origen.
Nationality: Born in Alexandria, Egypt. Possibly of Greek descent.
Dates: 185–254.
Appearance: Not known. But may have walked with a limp. Or two limps.
Before he was famous: Zealous, eccentric boy genius.
Famous for: Theology. Biblical criticism. Mastery of languages. Brainbox.
Why does he matter? Invented the field of biblical criticism. Promoted the symbolic reading of the text.
Could you have a drink with him down the pub? Maybe. Although heaven knows what theories he would have come up with once he had a drink or two inside him.

A true origenal

In 202 a bout of persecution hit Alexandria, and Clement was forced to leave the city and move to Capadoccia. He was succeeded as head of the catechetical school by an eighteen-year-old called Origen. He was only in his late teens, but he had boy genius written all over him. (Not literally. Obviously. Although if he had, he could have written it in several languages.)

Origen had a brain the size of a planet, albeit a planet in a seriously eccentric orbit. He nearly didn't make it to take up his new post: during the persecution his mother had to hide all his clothes to prevent him from running out into the street and declaring himself a Christian. His zeal was such that it threatened to tip him over the edge at points. In his early reading of the Bible he read Jesus' apparent commendation of 'eunuchs who have made themselves eunuchs for the sake of the kingdom of heaven' (Matt. 19.12). So he castrated himself.

After this, not surprisingly, he abandoned a literal approach to the Bible and started reading it more as allegory. Of Genesis, for example, he wrote, 'Who is so silly as to believe that God, after the manner of a farmer, planted a paradise eastward of Eden, and set in it a visible and palpable tree of life, of such a sort that anyone who tasted its fruit with his bodily teeth would gain life?'

Origen was the prime exponent of a style of biblical interpretation that has become known as the Alexandrian school. He argued that there are three levels of biblical meaning: literal, moral and spiritual. And these corresponded to the three levels of human existence: body, soul and spirit or intelligence. Naturally Origen believed that this three-level thing required an intelligent and spiritually advanced person to interpret it – someone like, oh, I don't know, Origen, perhaps.

There were areas where such readings of the text were heavily resisted, not least at Antioch, where theologians argued for a simpler, more literal, reading. The Antioch school and the Alexandrian school ended up having a lot of fights over this one . . .

And, just as there was a hierarchy of meanings in the text, Origen believed there was a hierarchy in the Trinity: God at the top, then Jesus, then the Holy Spirit. They were all God, but some of them were more God than the others. But he rejected the idea that the Son was created: instead the Son was timelessly, eternally, begotten of the Father.

All of which shows that he wasn't an orthodox thinker. He was a theological *enfant terrible*: restlessly, relentlessly independent minded, endlessly thirsty for knowledge.

Almost inevitably this attitude brought him into conflict with the church authorities. He was eventually banned from preaching in Alexandria by the bishop, and moved to Caesarea (a move aided by a large dollop of funding from a rich admirer).

In Caesarea Origen virtually invented the discipline of biblical textual scholarship. He had come to realise that even someone as clever as, oh, I don't know, Origen, didn't necessarily know all that they thought they did. When he engaged in debate with Jewish teachers, the Jews used the Hebrew Scriptures. Origen, like all Christians, used a Greek translation called the Septuagint. And the

Septuagint, while undeniably popular, had some serious mistranslations. The result was that when Christians quoted some of their favourite proof texts from the Old Testament, their Jewish adversaries would torpedo their argument by pointing out either that the verse was a mistranslation, or that it was in fact completely missing from the original Hebrew.

Origen concluded that the Christians needed better tools. So he compiled the Hexapla – the first 'scientific' version of the Bible. Written in six parallel columns, it gave the Hebrew text, a transliteration of the Hebrew text into Greek, then the Septuagint, and next to that a variety of Greek translations. It took him fifteen years to complete and ran to over 6,500 pages, in 15 volumes. All written, of course, by hand.*

As if that wasn't enough, Origen wrote commentaries on nearly all the books of the Bible, and there is also a large collection of his sermons. It is in the writings of Origen that we first find the phrase 'New Testament' to describe the Christian Scriptures, although it was clearly in common usage at the time.

For all his braininess, though, there are times when his attempts to solve such issues as the fall of humanity, and the incarnation of Jesus, lead to fairly wild speculative theology. He was, for example, a universalist: he believed that at the end all would be saved. If the fall was universal, then its reversal – salvation – must also be universal.

For these reasons Origen's work may have been widely admired, but was also viewed with suspicion. Eventually, what was called Origenism was condemned at a council in Alexandria in AD 400. His writings were deemed heretical and many of them were burned, meaning that most of his work is preserved only in fragments.

Mind you, for all his theorising, Origen was no ivory-tower scholar. Throughout his life he visited prisoners in jail and supported the poor. His early desire to be identified publicly for Christ came to fruition in 250 when he was imprisoned, subsequently dying as a result of the brutal treatment he received in prison.

He was brave, as well as brilliant. Whatever else you might say of Origen, this was a man with cojones. (Not literally. Obviously.)

---

* It was never copied, and was probably destroyed in the seventh century, when the library of Caesarea was burned during the Arab invasion.

The excommunicator

Origen's clashes with his bishop show how the church was developing its internal discipline. But who watches the watchmen? Who bishops the bishops? That was a tricky question. For Irenaeus of Lyons, the answer was clear: 'The faithful everywhere must agree with the church at Rome.'

Since re-establishing itself after the Neronian persecution, the Roman churches had been led by a collegiate group of bishops. An early Christian visionary dream-story called the *Shepherd of Hermas* was written in Rome, and implies that there was a group of presbyter-bishops in charge. This is significant, because the author's brother, Pius, was Bishop of Rome and if he'd been the head honcho, his brother would have said so. Possibly the first solo Bishop of Rome was Anicetus (*c.*155–166), but it was probably one of his successors, Victor, who was the first 'proper' Bishop of Rome, in the sense of someone who was Really In Charge.

It was Victor who invented *the* main sanction of the church: excommunication.

He was chosen as Bishop of Rome around 189 and held the post for ten years. By that time it had become the custom for the bishop to bless the Eucharistic bread and wine and then send it out to churches throughout the city in a kind of divine pizza-delivery service. The consecrated bread and wine went to a wide variety of churches, some of which were decidedly unorthodox. (Imagine today if the Anglican church in your town had consecrated bread and wine delivered to the other churches by courier. Unthinkable.) Anyway, Victor decided that must stop. He refused to have it delivered to Montanist or other 'dodgy' churches. It meant they could no longer receive the 'official' communion. They were excommunicated.

It was probably Victor who made the switch from Greek to Latin for the language of worship in Rome as well. By now the influence of Greek was waning everywhere. Only one Greek prayer remained in the Latin liturgy: the *Kyrie.**

Victor was a monarchical bishop: a single leader over the whole church. But he wasn't 'the pope'. The earliest mention of that title

---

* Not to be confused with the *Kylie*, which is an Australian prayer. The ancient Greek *Kyrie* runs *Kyrie Eleison, Christe Eleison, Kyrie Eleison*: 'Lord have mercy, Christ have mercy, Lord have mercy.'

doesn't occur until a hundred years after his time. It comes from the Greek *pappas*, meaning 'little father'. And then it is applied not to the Bishop of Rome, but to a deacon in the city. Up until the 800s the title of Pope could be applied to any senior member of the Christian community.

Madmen

Rome, of course, had one thing the other cities did not have: the emperor, at this time a man called Commodus. He kept a harem of 300 beautiful women, and another of 300 boys. He was a man of eclectic tastes. Not to mention stamina. Intriguingly, the administrator of his harem – a eunuch named Hyacinthus – was also a cleric in his local church. Not many people in history have managed to combine two such different jobs.* But Commodus went mad: he became convinced that he was Hercules and started to perform, in character, in the arena, fighting both against wild animals and as a gladiator. According to the records, he entered 735 fights and was victorious in every single one of them. Then again, he was the emperor.

Nonetheless, all winning streaks must come to an end. On 31 December 192 he was strangled in his bath by a man who had been a champion wrestler. What this wrestler was doing in his bath or how he was hidden we don't know. Perhaps he used a snorkel. Or disguised himself as a particularly large rubber duck. Anyway, according to the histories, the wrestler was working for the emperor's favourite concubine, a woman called Marcia, who was *also* alleged to be a Christian. Now, we do have to take this claim with rather a large chunk of bath salts. Given that she was involved with at least one judicial execution before the assassination of Commodus, she's what you'd call a fringe Christian.† But she was sympathetic, at least. And she knew Victor: it was through her influence that he managed to gain the release of a group of Christians who were being forced to work in a Sardinian copper mine.

Anyway, after a brief civil war a new emperor arose; from North

---

* Some medieval popes would give such a job-share a go. But that's for later.
† She also poisoned the emperor's food, but he vomited it up. So they had to switch to plan B. That's B as in 'Bath'.

Africa, this time. His name was Septimus Severus. He died in York in 211. (His last words were, 'Ee by gum.' Possibly.) Here is his advice to his successors: 'Be united, enrich the soldiers and scorn the rest.' From now on, even more than before, being an emperor was not about legitimacy and birth, but about the support of the army. But that cost money. Taxes were hiked to raise funds. To avoid paying the punitive taxes, many people fled the towns and turned to banditry. The rise in banditry meant you needed more soldiers. And that meant more taxes and . . . well, you get the idea.

The currency collapsed. Many Romans turned to barter. Even the soldiers demanded to be given their pay in kind. It was all a bit of a decline.

Degrees of Celsus

One of Origen's most famous books is useful, not only for his own arguments, but because it shows just what non-Christians thought of Christians. A Roman aristocrat called Celsus wrote a savage attack on Christianity, excerpts of which are preserved in a book called *Contra Celsus* by Origen, which rebuts the accusations.

Celsus was a traditionalist. He loved the old gods of Rome, who had majesty and grandeur and who had been around a long time. The Christians' worship of an executed Palestinian workman was worse than stupid: it was vulgar. Tasteless. Christianity, he wrote, attracted only those of low intelligence and with low social status. Most often both. Celsus paints a picture of a church that is full of 'the silly, and the mean, and the stupid, with women and children'.

His social prejudice shows. But Origen does not dispute this. What he challenges is the idea that these people had nothing to offer. He focuses on the value of what those lowly folk had found.

By now Christians were an easy group to target with accusations regarding all kinds of calumnies. They met before dawn (suspicious); they allowed men and women to mingle together (very suspicious); they shared in something called 'a love feast'. (That's it – they're perverts!)

Around 200 a North African Christian called Minutius Felix wrote a book called *The Octavius*, which is an argument between a pagan called Caecilius and a Christian called Octavius, with Minutius acting as the referee. Caecilius throws all kinds of accusations at Christians: they are 'an unlawful and dangerous faction . . . which is leagued together by nightly meetings . . . a people skulking and shunning the light'. And then he goes all *Daily Mail* on us, with lurid accounts of what the Christians get up to in their meetings: 'They know one another by secret marks and insignia, and they love one another almost before they know one another. Everywhere also there is mingled among them a certain religion of lust, and they call one another promiscuously brothers and sisters . . . I hear that they adore the head of an ass, that basest of creatures.'

It gets worse. They're accused of killing (and eating) babies, drunken orgies where they tie a dog to a lampstand and then encourage it to pull over the light. The moment it goes dark, he alleges, 'in the shameless darkness, the connections of abominable lust involve them in the uncertainty of fate'.

Blimey. Those all-age services in Carthage really were a bit wild.

Top Mani

Christianity was attacked because it was growing. But it was not the only growing religion. There was an increased interest in the magical and the mystical across the empire, while long-established philosophies like Stoicism died a death. (Presumably stoically.) In the third century several new religions appeared – or new expressions of old religions, anyway.

Manichaeism emerged in Parthia – a once-powerful kingdom, outside the empire and situated in modern-day north-east Iran. Its originator, Mani (b. *c*.216), went on a Persian gap year, travelling as far as India, where he encountered what so many hippies have encountered down the centuries since: Buddhism, Hinduism and dysentery. He merged that lot (apart from the dysentery) with Christianity to create Manichaeism, a dualistic religion that saw the cosmos as an unending struggle between good and evil. Mani called himself an 'apostle of Jesus Christ' and saw Jesus as judge, healer, teacher. But he rejected the idea that Jesus had a human body: he was definitely a spirit.

Zoroastrianism, meanwhile, saw a revival. It was resurrected by Ardeshir I (ruled 226–241), founder of the Sassanid Dynasty that took over Parthia. Zoroastrianism had been an ancient religion, but it had gone into a bit of a decline. Ardeshir ordered that the special sacred fires be relit.* This revival later led to persecution of Christians. On Good Friday 344 the accounts tell of believers being forced to watch the execution of 100 Christian leaders, before they themselves were killed. Thousands of Christians lost their lives in the 'Great Persecution' between 339 and 348.

Within the empire, meanwhile, Neoplatonism, or Plato 2.0, was the latest religious fashion. This was launched by a man called Plotinus, a contemporary of Origen. This promoted the idea of the supreme being. There were thousands of gods and goddesses in the Roman pantheon, but Plotinus suggested that there was one God to rule them all. He didn't do away with the other gods, but held that they were merely platonic reflections of the ultimate one.†

The Edessa files

By now Christianity had spread east as well as west. It moved through Syria and then beyond, to Edessa, a cosmopolitan trading city under the protection of the Romans. Or the Parthians. Or whoever was more powerful at that particular time. The church in Edessa claimed descent from the apostle Thaddeus – and, who knows, they may be right. It's certainly possible.

In Edessa Christians found freedom. While Christians in the Mighty Roman Empire™ were gathering in homes and shops and tenements, Christians in Edessa were able to build proper public church buildings. The earliest public church building in the world is recorded here. It was destroyed in a flood in 201.

The Christians in Edessa were very hot on the interfaith thing. They are recorded as being on good terms with the Jews, even studying the Bible together. It was probably Abgar IX ('the Great') who officially adopted Christianity around 222. But legends grew up about his ancestor, King Abgar V, who, it was claimed, had a correspondence with Jesus

* An act celebrated by Dan Hartman's 1979 hit single 'Relight My Fire'. The cover version by Take That features Lulu, who is rumoured to be a Zoroastrian high priest. Or not.
† Descriptions of Plotinus make it clear that he was the first identifiable dyslexic in history. So he never wrote much.

himself – there were even some (forged) letters. Jesus helpfully sent Abgar a picture of himself. This portrait later became the first of the miraculously imprinted cloth pictures of Jesus. It was known as the Towel of Edessa (the Greek word is *mandylion*) and it had impressive healing powers. Not only that, but if you draped the holy towel over your sun lounger, you were guaranteed a good tan. It later became linked with the Turin shroud.*

Hymns of praise

Music has always had a special relationship with worship. 'With gratitude in your hearts', Paul wrote to Christians in Colossae, 'sing psalms, hymns, and spiritual songs to God.' And Christians seem to have made up songs from his time onwards.

We tend to think of church music in western terms – Bach, choirs in robes, perhaps a few brother monks breaking it down in the Gregorian stylee. But the real source of western church music probably lies (where else?) in Syria.

The earliest known collection of Christian hymns, the *Odes of Solomon*, comes from Syria.† Hymn writers flourished there: around 200 a Gnostic leader called Bardaisan of Edessa promoted his message through popular hymns and songs. He was countered by church leaders like Ephrem of Edessa, who wrote hymns and liturgy in metrical verse and even put new, orthodox lyrics to older popular melodies. (This was an approach used much, much later by the Salvation Army, who wrote Christian lyrics to well-known music-hall tunes.)

Eastern popes in Rome imported these practices. Western Christians who sing the *Agnus Dei*, 'Lamb of God, who takes away the sins of the world', are using a Syrian form of words imported by Pope Sergius. And English church music followed suit: there was a Syrian Archbishop of Canterbury, Theodore of Tarsus, of whom Bede says that after he arrived on English shores, 'they began in all the churches of the English to learn Church music'.

The oldest known hymn with both lyrics and music is the so-called

---

* Tatian – he of *Diatesseron* fame – came from this region.
† One of the hymns in the *Odes of Solomon* contains the first reference outside the Bible to Mary as a virgin. These hymns also refer to the Holy Spirit as female.

Oxyrhynchus hymn, which was found in an Egyptian rubbish dump, and dates from around 290.*

Up until recently at least, what is probably the earliest known liturgical music was still being sung in the church of St George in Aleppo. But Aleppo has suffered terribly in the recent Syrian conflict. I hope and pray they are still singing.

Lapsed Christians

In the west, meanwhile, there were churches in Gaul, in Africa, even in the chilly climes of Britannia. Emperor Alexander Severus (208–235) incorporated Christ into his pantheon of gods.† He had staff who were Christians and, unusually, he allowed Christians to hold property. Persecution had quietened down, even if it hadn't entirely St Petered out. It wasn't that Christians were respectable, but they were tolerated to some extent.

The early church historian Eusebius claimed that another emperor, Philip the Arab, was a Christian. Well, sort of. It was reported that he went to celebrate Easter with Christians in Antioch – but Bishop Babylas made him stand with the penitents. Philip and his wife also received letters from Origen. However, the coins from his reign show the usual emphasis on the state religion, centred on the emperor. So he may have been sympathetic, rather than a full convert.

But then the clouds turned dark again. Whatever Philip the Arab thought, his successor was most definitely *not* a Christian. On Philip's death, an emperor called Trajan Decius seized power. A conservative traditionalist, he had a strong concept of 'the good old days' and the way in which Rome was no longer what it was. He blamed all the evils of the modern world on the Christians. Ye olde gods were annoyed with Rome for permitting Christians to ignore them and refuse to sacrifice. Decius believed that the empire would be restored only if everyone started worshipping properly again. So he ordered that

---

* You can hear versions on various recordings. Type 'Oxyrhynchus' into iTunes. Go on. I dare you.

† He was the last of the Severan dynasty, begun by Septimus, who was his great-great-uncle. Or possibly a cousin, several times removed. Anyway, the dynasty included Septimus, Caracalla, Geta, Heliogabalus, not forgetting Dumbledore, Giantortus, Toysarus and many others.

throughout the empire everyone had to offer sacrifices to the gods. Those who did so received a certificate (some of these have been found in Egypt). Those who did not were thrown into prison (Origen, for example, who died during this period).

One of Decius' first acts was to order the arrest of church leaders. The bishops of Rome, Antioch and Jerusalem were killed; others, like Cyprian, Bishop of Carthage, went into hiding.

The effect on the church was devastating. There had been a period of relative peace and many people had become Christians. These new converts had no idea that persecution might be part of the deal. So many Christians pitched up to offer the prescribed sacrifices that the Roman authorities had to turn away the crowds. Others bought certificates if they could – including a number of bishops. These fallen Christians were known as the *lapsi* – the lapsed. Those who held firm even unto death were known as the confessors – they had 'confessed' their faith.

The persecution was terrible enough. But in many ways the real problems started when the persecution stopped.

There was widespread condemnation of people like the bishops of Carthage and Alexandria who had gone into hiding instead of staying to face the music. When these bishops returned to their churches, they faced a frosty reception. Some of the confessors even elected their own 'true' bishops, rather than accept the authority of those who had run away.

And now many of the *lapsi* wanted re-admittance. But they looked to the confessors for forgiveness and reintegration, not the official bishops. Some confessors took a hard line on this and told them to get lost. Others were prepared to admit those who had simply purchased their certificates, after they had done suitable penance. Those who had sacrificed would be admitted, but only at their deaths. (The confessors even started issuing their own anti-certificates of forgiveness for those whose courage had failed them.)

But the majority of bishops decided to absolve the penitents and welcome them back. This outraged one of the confessors at Rome, a man called Novatian. He declared that the church had lost its way. It had become corrupt – and he would purify it. He managed to have himself consecrated Bishop of Rome; which would have been OK, had there not already been a Bishop of Rome, Cornelius. He established a separate church, a group of hardliners called the Pure. And he started ordaining his own bishops.

Cyprian

Meanwhile, in Carthage, Cyprian (*c.*200–258) was fighting hard to keep the church together. Originally from a wealthy aristocratic Roman family in North Africa, he had thrown that aside to become a Christian. His talents were such that he was made a bishop almost immediately, around 250.

In a pamphlet called *On the Unity of the Catholic Church* Cyprian argued that 'no one can have God as Father who does not have the church as mother'. There could be no true spiritual life outside the one, catholic church. This cut no ice with the Novatianists, the 'Pure', who saw Cyprian as a cowardy-custard who had run away and hidden, and who believed that *theirs* was the true church. So you had the Novatianists who thought themselves the true church, and then the official church, which also thought itself the true church.

Then it got even more confusing. The Novatianists started sending out missionaries. They made and baptised converts in North Africa and Rome. But then some of these converts wanted to leave Novatian's church and rejoin the proper one. So the official church was faced with a big decision. Was the Novatian baptism valid? Stephen, Bishop of Rome, took a conciliatory line and accepted their baptism as valid. Cyprian argued vehemently that it wasn't. Stephen was arguing that baptism was valid if done properly and with the right motives; Cyprian was arguing that it could be valid only if done within the orthodox community of the church.

So Stephen called Cyprian a false Christ and excommunicated him. Cyprian argued that every bishop had the right to his own opinion, but Stephen argued that it was only the opinion of the Bishop of Rome that really counted. In an attempt to clinch the matter he played the St Peter card, citing Matthew 16.18: 'on this rock I will build my church'. Stephen claimed that this meant Jesus based the entire church on Peter and, by extension, on the Bishop of Rome, his successor. This claim was something new: in over two hundred years no one had ever dreamed this statement had anything to do with the Bishop of Rome.

It's bizarre, in a way, that so much of the prestige of Rome and what became the papacy is based on Peter, a man who, as far as the New Testament shows, was never a bishop of anywhere, never mind Rome. Paul has a much stronger connection, but Paul makes an uncomfortable role model: it's not easy to base your authority on someone who spent his whole life getting up the nose of the church leaders.

And that, indeed, was what Novatian had done: he had challenged the 'accepted leaders'. But at the root of this argument was a clash of views about what the church was. Cyprian's view was an expansionist one; Novatian's was idealist. Novatian viewed the church as a place for the pure, Cyprian as a place for sinners.*

And then, in 258, Emperor Valerian brought some much-needed unity back to the bishops – by ordering that they should all be killed. Persecution was back. Putting aside all their differences, Stephen, Cyprian and Novatian shared the same fate: they were martyred. In Rome Stephen and his successor Sixtus II were both martyred. In Carthage Cyprian was hauled before the authorities and offered the chance to make a pagan sacrifice. He refused. Initially he was only banished, to Curubis.† But when a new edict came round he was brought back to Carthage, interrogated and sentenced to die by the sword. He was beheaded on 13 September AD 258. No hiding now.

Things didn't go well for Valerian, as it turned out. He was captured in battle by the Persian king Shaphur I and for the rest of his life when Shaphur wanted to mount his horse, he used Valerian as a mounting block.

* The Novatianists did not die away quickly. Their church survived well into the fifth century.
† Modern Korba in Tunisia. Apparently it is famous today among birdwatchers. Cyprian's biographer recorded that it was 'a sunny and appropriate place . . . a refuge secluded as he wished' along with a more uncertain passage that may read 'he also ticked off 53 new species including a rare spotted egret'.

> ## ANTHONY
>
> *Name:* Antonius.
> *Aka:* Saint Anthony.
> *Nationality:* Egyptian.
> *Dates:* c.250–356.
> *Appearance:* Thin. Very thin. Very, very thin. And leathery, probably.
> *Before he was famous:* Not known. His parents were wealthy, apparently.
> *Famous for:* The most well known of the desert fathers.
> *Why does he matter?* He defined the ideal of the ascetic solitary monk, living in a cell, fighting temptation, having visions, etc.
> *Could you have a drink with him down the pub?* Not really, given the fact he lived in the desert.

Monk

The 'Pure' episode raised the issue of whether all Christians are the same, or whether some are more Christian than others. As soon as any movement gathers members there arise those old hands who tell the newbies that they are not doing it right and complaining that the movement has 'gone soft'. But it is clear that some had already started to think that Christianity had rather lost its way.

Somewhere around 270 a young man called Anthony walked into a church in Egypt and heard the following words from Matthew's Gospel: 'If you wish to be perfect, go, sell your possessions, and give the money to the poor, and you will have treasure in heaven; then come, follow me' (Matt. 19.21).

Anthony *did* wish to be perfect. And, not being someone who embraced Origen's allegorical reading of Scripture, he left the church, sold all his possessions, put his sister into care and went to live in the desert. There he lived in solitude, devoting himself to prayer and eating only bread and salt. His only companions were enemies: demons, who assailed him with lurid sexual temptations and appeared as wild beasts. Anthony spent his time conquering all his fleshly desires, so much so that when he emerged from the desert twenty years later he was, according to his biographer, 'ashamed to be seen eating'.

Fig. V. *Saint Anthony fights with his temptations*

Anthony wasn't the first desert monk.* But he was the most famous. And he thrived on it. He was a simple man, who may even have been illiterate, and he had an almost pathological dislike of human company. So the desert rather suited him. He lived to 105 in the midst of a land where the normal male life expectancy was about 35.† He was martyred by the Romans, which seems a bit of a waste of effort given that he was already 105 years old. They could just have waited a bit.

---

* The first we know of is Paul of Thebes. He left for the desert in 250 and lived in a grotto near a palm tree and a spring for ninety years. He was so fond of solitude that when Anthony discovered him, he let Anthony knock on his door for an hour before letting him in. During the visit, Paul asked Anthony 'whether there were any more idolaters in the world, whether new houses were built in ancient cities and by whom the world was governed'.
† Someone should really start marketing the Saint Anthony diet.

Armenian rhapsody

These were dangerous times. At some point in the third century in Colonia Aquincum (modern Budapest) someone built an organ of four rows and thirteen pipes made of bronze. Thankfully it was destroyed in a fire. But it was a clear sign: no one was safe.

Despite the persecutions, Christianity continued to expand. In the late third century it crossed into Armenia, with the conversion of King Tiridates III of Armenia. He was converted by Gregory the Illuminator (c.257–331), the inventor of the lightbulb.* Gregory was allowed to build a church and he oversaw the construction of the Holy Mother of God Church in a place called Vagharshapat in Armenia (modern-day Ejmiatsin). It still stands today, the oldest state-built church in the world.

Armenia, then, is the oldest Christian state. And of course, being in a hard-to-find place full of people with strange names, it has been pretty much ignored in the history of Christianity. Nonetheless, the fact is that it was the first country to declare Christianity its official religion. Many Armenians went to Jerusalem and settled there. In the eleventh century they bought the church on Mount Sion and dedicated it to Saint James, or *Surp Hagop* as he's called in Armenian. (I *love* the names!) It became the centre of the Armenian community and they've been there, living in the Armenian quarter, ever since. In fact, there have been Armenians in Jerusalem continuously since the fourth century, which is longer, in fact, than the Jews and the Arabs can claim. If anyone has a right to Jerusalem, it might just be the Armenians.

The Bible was translated into Armenian in the fifth century and the story of its translation is not only interesting, but includes the best names in the history of the world. Ever. The account crops up in the writings of the brilliantly named historian Lazar of Pharb (c.500). He writes how a soldier called Mesrop Mashtotz (died c.439) became a Christian missionary, created a new alphabet and then translated the Greek text into Armenian with the help of someone called Catholicus Sahak (aka Isaac the Great, 390–439). See what I mean about the names?

* Actually, that's Illuminator as in 'enlightener'. Gregory the light-shedder. His relics are all over the place. His head is in Armenia, his right hand in Lebanon and his left hand in Ejmiatsin Cathedral. (The whereabouts of the lightbulb are not known.) His life was written by people with brilliant names, including Moses of Chorene, Symeon the Metaphrast and a being called the Vartabed Matthew.

All we're missing is a giant slug called something like Babba the Kutt and we'd be halfway to a *Star Wars* film.

Diocletian

In the Roman Empire, though, Christians remained an easy target. You could pin anything you liked on these Christians; they were the sect everyone loved to hate. Such rumours fuelled violence, but it was mostly very localised. However, all that changed in 303 when the emperor Diocletian launched an empire-wide assault intended to wipe out Christianity for ever.

Diocletian was a glory boy. Specifically a glory-of-Rome boy. He had a vision of the old empire and he wanted to restore it.

But the empire was old. Inefficient. It needed modernising. So Diocletian introduced an efficient (many would say oppressive) bureaucracy. There were so many government bureaucrats that people complained there were more men using tax money than there were paying it. He's the European Union's favourite Roman emperor. And – in a move that was to have enormous long-term consequences – he divided the empire into two, creating a western and eastern empire, each with an emperor and a deputy emperor – a management team of four. Further, the empire was divided into twelve subsections, which Diocletian called 'dioceses'.

Christianity later took this name for its own administrative districts. Which is ironic, because Diocletian was one of the church's greatest enemies. At first he was not hostile to Christianity. For the first two decades of his reign he tolerated Christians and his wife and daughter may even have been baptised. But then something changed. One story tells how, during a religious ceremony, one of his priests entirely failed to give an accurate prediction based on careful inspection of the liver of a chicken. When his failure was investigated it was discovered that the fault was not in the priest, nor in the liver, but in the fact that some Christians nearby had crossed themselves rather than take part.

Initially Diocletian was inclined to believe that it was enough simply to ban Christians from public service and official positions. But his deputy Galerius insisted they must be exterminated.

It started in Nicomedia (Diocletian's eastern capital), on 23 February 303, with the destruction of church buildings and the confiscation of copies of the Scriptures. The next day Diocletian issued his first 'Edict against the Christians', banning Christians from gathering for worship and ordering the burning of all Christian Scriptures. A few weeks later there was a fire in the imperial palace, which Galerius pinned on Christian conspirators. The executions culminated in the beheading of Anthimus, Bishop of Nicomedia.

From 303 onwards there began a full-scale assault on Christianity. Churches were destroyed. Clergy were killed. Sacred Scriptures and church vessels were confiscated and destroyed. Many Christians chose to protect the Scriptures with their lives. In Thessalonica a woman called Irene was found to have kept many 'parchments, books, tablets, small codices and pages' hidden in cupboards and chests in her house. Her punishment was brutally Roman: she was placed naked in the public brothel and the writings she had kept were ordered to be publicly burned. Eventually she and two companions were burned at the stake in the spring of 304.

Not everywhere saw such suffering. In Gaul, Spain and Britain Diocletian's appointed ruler Constantius didn't really enforce the edict. He demolished a few church buildings just to show willing, but after that did nothing. His colleagues in the east were not so lenient. Maximinus, ruler of Palestine, Syria and Egypt, was ferociously anti-Christian.* Eusebius, who was living in Caesarea at the time, wrote a book describing the dreadful events. He claimed that in some areas so many were killed that the executioners were worn out and had to work in shifts.

In Numidia, in Africa, the bishops were forced to surrender the church's sacred vessels (although one got out of it by pretending to be blind and claiming he couldn't find them). When the Bishop of Carthage was ordered to hand over sacred writings he gave the soldiers the work of heretics. Since the soldiers were illiterate, they seemed happy enough with this. (Of course, what the bishop was doing with heretical writings in the first place is an interesting question.) Marcellinus, Bishop of Rome, seems to have made a sacrifice to the emperor to escape punishment. (Despite this, he is still called Saint Marcellinus. Not sure how he got away with that one.)

---

* The effects of this persecution in the east can be seen in the fact that in Serbian folk mythology, Diocletian is remembered as Dukljan, the enemy of God.

A two-year reign of terror started to slow only when, in May 305, Diocletian took early retirement, moved to Dalmatia and grew cabbages.*

In the end even the thug Galerius had a change of mind – when he contracted bowel cancer. Realising that Christianity was not going to go away, he ordered that the persecution stop and that the Christians pray for him. I can't help but think that, despite Jesus' injunction to love their enemies, many Christians in the empire might have struggled just a bit with that request.

The great persecution was the last attempt to wipe out Christianity by the empire. By the end of the third century Christianity had withstood many challenges. It had faced ridicule, discrimination and persecution, but it had survived. It had dealt with heresy and schism, but it had held together. The Romans had made it illegal, but still it continued to grow.

However, in the fourth century AD Christianity was to face its deadliest enemy of all: popularity.

* He retired to his palace at modern-day Split. Hence the famous Latin phrase 'Let's split.'

Hibernia

Eboracum
(York)

Britannia

Milton Keynes

Londinium

Belgica

BIG HAIRY

Gallia

Raetia

P

Aquitania

Lugdunum
(Lyons)

Liguria

Mediolanum
(Milan)

D

Ravenna

Italia

Hispania

ROME

Sicilia

Hippo

Carthage

Numidia

Africa

Mauretania

WEST OF THIS
LINE PEOPLE
MAINLY
SPOKE LATIN

EAST
PEOP
SPOK

NOT SURE WHO LIVES DOWN HERE BUT
THEY'RE PROBABLY BIG AND HAIRY

THE MIGHTY ROMAN EMPIRE™

Around the end of the third century

BARBARIANS

Moesia
Dacia
Thracia
Macedonia
Achaia
Athens
Corinth

CONSTANTINOPLE
Chalcedon
Nicea

Scythia

Pontus

Galatia

Cappadocia

Armenia

BIG HAIRY PERSIANS

Edessa

Asia
Ephesus
Pisidia
Tarsus
Antioch
Syria

Damascus

Arabia

Jerusalem
Palaestrina

Alexandria
Aegyptus

Libya

LINE
NLY

THINGS YOU LEARN FROM CHRISTIAN HISTORY

NO. 3
Christianity and power do not mix

When Jesus wanted to illustrate power and status he chose a child as his example. He told his disciples not to lord it over one another like the Gentiles (Luke 22.25-26). Hmmmm.

3 Constantine, Councils and Creeds

Here comes the Sun King

Diocletian handed over the empire to his senior management team of four emperors. They showed their sense of responsibility by immediately launching a series of attacks on each other. In the west, Britain was under the command of Constantius I. He died in 306 at Eburacum (York) and was succeeded by his son Constantine.

Six years later Constantine's army faced one of his rivals, Maxentius, in a winner-takes-all bout for control of the western half of the empire. The battle took place at the Milvian Bridge, just outside Rome. According to Constantine's own account, the evening before the battle, he saw a vision, a cross of light that shone amid the rays of the sun, and in it the words 'Under this sign, conquer.'* The sign was a combination of two Greek letters, Chi and Rho – the first two letters of the word 'Christ' in Greek – formed into the shape of a cross. The next day his troops destroyed their old pagan imagery, marched to battle under this new, Christian, symbol, and cut their enemy to pieces. Jesus must have been so proud.

Fig. VI. *Constantine sees the light*

* He claimed that all his soldiers saw this vision as well. Although, strangely, not one of the 40,000 said anything about it at the time.

Constantine duly established himself as the emperor of the west, halted the persecution of Christians and ordered the return of any confiscated property. The following year – only ten years since the start of Diocletian's great persecution – he had a meeting with Licinius, emperor of the east (not to mention Nanook of the North, the Queen of the South, Scott of the Antarctic and the Wicked Witch of the West), and issued the Edict of Milan, which proclaimed toleration for all faiths. Two years later crucifixion was abolished (you could hardly continue to use a method of punishment that had been used to kill your God). And in 321 Sunday was given the legal status of a sabbath.

Now you might take from all this that Constantine was a Christian. But you'd be wrong. That is to say, he wasn't a Christian in any sense we would understand. The coins of Constantine – and Roman coins were always the medium for state propaganda – never actually carried any Christian symbols. Instead, they were adorned by images of Mars, the god of war (and of those nourishing chocolate bars). And of the sun.

Yes. There were a *lot* with symbols of the sun.

Constantine worshipped the sun just as much as he worshipped the Son of God. By the end of the third century the 'ultimate being' touted by the Neoplatonists had become identified with the sun. The worship of the sun god became popular in the Roman Empire. (Hardly surprising in the Mediterranean, although evidence shows it never caught on in Manchester.) Constantine seems to have combined Christianity with his own worship of the sun god. Jesus had, after all, spoken to him from the sun. This is the real reason why he declared Sunday a sabbath: 'It seems to us improper', he said, 'that the Day of the Sun, which is kept for its veneration, should be spent in legal disputes.'

Christian leaders, who now had a powerful, wealthy supporter, certainly weren't inclined to worry too much about his orthodoxy. He was, after all, giving them safety, security and a lot of money for really big churches and really posh clothes. After all, as it surely ought to say in the Bible somewhere, 'Don't look a gift horse in the mouth.' In fact, they appear to have slavishly followed the emperor's interfaith approach: when they got their calendars together to arrange a date to celebrate Christ's birth, they chose 25 December: same day as the Roman feast of the Birth of the Unconquered Sun. Coincidence? You decide.

All Donatists welcome

So why did Constantine support the Christians? Christians were more numerous than in the past, but still formed only maybe 10 per cent of the population. They had no real power, not much wealth and were no good in a fight. Well it's possible that what Constantine valued in Christianity was its emphasis on unity. This was a man who fought all his life to unify the empire. A religion based on unity could be a handy weapon in such a fight.

All of which might have worked had the Christians actually been, you know, *unified*. But throughout his reign this not-very-Christian emperor found himself embroiled in endless theological rows. The first of these broke out the year after the Edict of Milan declared toleration and peace for all.

During Diocletian's persecution many clerics had surrendered their copies of the Scriptures or had even gone back to worshipping the pagan gods. They became known as *traditores*, from the Latin *traditio*, meaning to 'hand over'.* An argument arose over whether the *traditores* should be allowed to continue as bishops and priests.

The debate focused around a man called Caecilian, who in 313 was consecrated Bishop of Carthage by a cleric with the brilliant name of Felix of Apthungi. Felix was accused of being a *traditor*. The accusation was false, but that didn't stop the hardliners, who declared the consecration invalid and put forward their own, alternative, bishop, a man called Donatus. The movement that he formed became known as Donatists. This was really Novatian 2.0. The Donatists claimed – as the Novatians had – that they were the one true church.

Donatism gained a lot of followers, partly because everyone really disliked Caecilian, whom they considered a Roman toff. The Donatists, on the other hand, were mostly from local farming stock and they spoke the vernacular, rather than the Latin of Rome.

The churches in Rome, though, recognised Caecilian as bishop. So they called on their new patron, Constantine, to settle the issue. He called a council of bishops, which decided that the Donatists were in the wrong. The Donatists promptly ignored the result and carried on.

* The word is the origin of our word 'traitor'. But it's also the origin of the word 'tradition'. It all depends on what is being passed over, and to whom.

This baffled the emperor, who was not used to subjects appealing to a higher power than, well, him. So he called for another council – a bigger one – to be held in Arles in 314.* But things didn't go smoothly there either. The Donatists refused to rejoin the church. Frustrated, the emperor did what emperors do: he called in the troops. The Donatists were given a choice: rush back into the loving arms of the church – or face the consequences. A mere three years after the final ending of their persecution by pagans, Christians started persecuting each other. Brilliant. In November 316 Constantine ordered that the churches of the Donatists should be confiscated. During the ensuing riot several Donatists were killed, by a mixture of soldiers and an angry mob.

It couldn't work, anyway. The Donatists had been born in persecution: that was what the whole row was about in the first place. Enduring persecution was the Donatists' USP. The Donatists became the majority in North Africa and Donatus even had the temerity to appoint their own Bishop of Rome to rival the 'proper' one.

Constantine tried for four years to get them to give in, but then gave up. As a general he knew an unwinnable war when he was in one.

Rome from Rome

In 324 Constantine defeated Licinius, the emperor of the east, and took over the whole of the Mighty Roman Empire™. And he decided it needed a new start. Rebranding. He chose a new capital, a little, ancient city called Byzantion.

It was in a strategically brilliant position, on the entrance to the Black Sea, commanding the trade routes to the east and to the west, and poised perfectly between the two halves of the empire. He renamed the city Constantinopolis – the city of Constantine, or, as we call it, Constantinople. Its old name lingered, though, eventually becoming, in its Latin form of Byzantium, the name for the eastern empire itself. Constantinople was to become such an archetype that for millions of people it was simply *the* city. In medieval times Greeks spoke of going

* For the first time three British bishops are recorded among their number. Their names are Eborius of York, Restitutus of London and Adelphius, from . . . well, no one's quite sure. Lincoln, possibly. Or Colchester. Or Milton Keynes. Anyway, they were British. Hip-hip-hooray.

eis tēn polin – to the city. And when the Turks captured it in 1453 they turned that into its new name: *Istanbul*.

It was also known as New Rome. Yes, the empire had moved east: behold the *new* Mighty Roman Empire™. Same classic product, but with a shiny new package. All the brutal violence and military repression you've grown to love, but with a tantalising hint of eastern exoticism. (And talking of brutal violence, some believe that Constantine imported the organ to the Byzantine Empire. In the imperial palace they even had organs with golden pipes ornamented with precious stones.)

Constantinople, though, was a Christian city. It was even dedicated to the Virgin Mary. Constantine oversaw a magnificent church-building programme. In Constantinople he planned a magnificent church to hold the bodies of the twelve apostles. (Oh, and his corpse as well.) The only problem with that, though, was that they didn't have the bodies. But they had some other stuff. Because Constantine's mother had been off exploring.

The cross woman

She was serving as a waitress at a cocktail bar when Constantius met her.

Well, sort of. Her name was Helena and, according to a man we shall shortly meet, Ambrose of Milan, she was a *stabularia*, which means 'stable-maid' or 'innkeeper'. Barmaid seems close enough.* Despite this lowly background, she became a partner of Constantius (though they were probably never actually married) and gave birth to Constantine.

Somewhere along the line she became a Christian. And when Constantine became sole emperor, he gave her unlimited funds to go to Jerusalem to find the relics of this faith.

She had some get up and go, the old girl. And she got up and went – at the age of seventy-eight. It has to be said that, as archaeological trips go, it was quite successful. As so many zealous Christians (mainly Americans) have done since, Helena went to Jerusalem to search for

---

* He wasn't being rude. He said she was a *bona stabularia*, and *bona* means good.

proof. And as so many zealous Christians (almost exclusively Americans) have done since, she found it. Her archaeological expedition miraculously discovered the one true cross on which Jesus had died some three centuries earlier. They also found the nails of the crucifixion, the ropes used to tie Jesus to the cross and the robe for which the soldiers gambled. Frankly, Helena makes Indiana Jones look positively incompetent.*

Fig. VII. *Helena discovers the true cross*

Perhaps more substantially she also founded several churches in Jerusalem and elsewhere in Palestine. According to Eusebius, she was responsible for the building of the Church of the Anastasis (i.e. 'Resurrection') on the traditional site covering both the place of Jesus' crucifixion and tomb where he lay. She also built the Church of the

---

* She is not the best 'pseudoarchaeologist', as they are known. That honour has to go to the late Ron Wyatt, an American whose discoveries apparently include Noah's Ark, Sodom and Gomorrah, Egyptian chariot wheels in the Red Sea, the site of Mount Sinai, a sword (possibly Goliath's), relics from Solomon's temple and the Ark of the Covenant. Not bad for a former nurse-anaesthetist with no archaeological training.

Nativity in Bethlehem and a huge church called the Nea on the Mount of Olives. She may also have been responsible for the building of Saint Catherine's Monastery.

Returning from her archaeological dig in 326, she stopped at Constantinople, where she was involved in something a lot less pious. Between 15 May and 17 June 326 Constantine had his eldest son, Crispus, arrested, interrogated and then executed by poison. A month later, for reasons that are not clear, Helena urged her son to kill his wife, the empress Fausta. She was left to die in an overheated bath and their names were expunged from inscriptions and from the official histories. Helena, it seems, was good at both discoveries and disappearances. Astonishingly, despite this skulduggery, she was still made into a saint.

She eventually moved to Rome, taking with her significant chunks of the cross. These were stored in the chapel of her private palace, and when she died the building was converted by her son into a church: the Basilica of the Holy Cross in Jerusalem. Which is actually in Rome. It gets its name from the fact that the floor of the church was covered with soil from Jerusalem. So, a little bit of Jerusalem set down in Rome.

Anyway, talking of churches . . .

The house of God

Constantine's support of Christianity meant that, within the Roman Empire, the church could move out of people's houses and into proper buildings.

In some parts of the empire large houses had already been converted into churches. One such building, which was destroyed around 256–257, has been discovered in the frontier town of Dura Europos, on the banks of the Euphrates. That was a conversion, not a purpose-built structure, but it does have some of the features that were common once Christianity got proper planning permission. There were separate rooms for worship and for baptism, and a schoolroom for trainee Christians.

But there was no special area for the Eucharist to be celebrated – no altar. And that is because the church imported that concept only in the time of Constantine. Now the church could build from scratch.

The template it chose was the basilica – based on the Roman building where the ruler held his audiences. Usually this was a long, rectangular room, with an entrance on one of the long sides and a semi-circular apse where the ruler sat on a raised platform. Christians made some alterations. First, wherever possible, they made the building run east–west. At the east end they put the semi-circular space, into which they put a table for the Eucharist and a chair on which the bishop could sit. Second, they moved the entrance to the opposite end, the western end. So if you entered one of these basilicas, your eyes were immediately drawn along the space stretched out ahead, to the table at the end and the bishop's throne.

This was the most common form. And it demonstrates the enormous, seismic change that had come over Christianity in the early fourth century. The faith had moved out of the home and into the judgement hall. In the house churches the bishop had a chair, which he had to give up for the poor, but in Constantinople he had a throne.

ARIUS

Name: Arius.

Aka: None.

Nationality: Born in Libya.

Dates: c.256–336.

Appearance: Tall, 'with downcast countenance'; wearing a short cloak and sleeveless tunic; quietly spoken but persuasive, or, according to his opponents, 'counterfeited like a guileful serpent'.

Before he was famous: Student. Church elder.

Famous for: Inventing Arianism.

Why does he matter? Because he argued that Christ was created. It forced Constantine to call the first church council at Nicea to resolve the matter.

Could you have a drink with him down the pub? Definitely. And he would lead a singalong as well.

The man who wasn't there

Meanwhile, there was trouble brewing in North Africa. Again.

It began, as so many heresies do, with a simple question: Who is Jesus? The answer seems obvious: teacher, miracle-worker, ex-carpenter, bloke with a beard, you know – walks on water. Oh, and he's God.

But *how* was he God? Tertullian had come to the conclusion that each part of the Trinity was distinct and yet the same. But in Alexandria a man called Arius (*c.*256–336) couldn't see how this made sense. The more he thought about it, the more he came to the conclusion that if Jesus was 'the son', then he had to be younger than the father. That, after all, was one thing all sons had in common: they were younger than their dads. After all, didn't Paul describe Jesus as 'the firstborn of all creation'? Didn't that mean he was created? Great, glorious, perfect, and all that – but definitely created.

And *that* meant there had to have been a time when Christ wasn't around. Arius decided there must have been a time when Jesus wasn't. In fact, 'there was when he was not' became Arius' slogan. He taught his ideas through simple songs.* He probably had t-shirts done and everything.

And soon he had a following. A persuasive speaker, his ideas made Jesus more accessible to the everyday person. Jesus was part of the created order, like them. Arius wasn't saying that Jesus wasn't God. He just wasn't quite as 'Goddy' as God was.

But the other aspect of this was that it made Christ inferior to the Father, even if it made him superior to everything else. And this made many bishops annoyed, not least because they hadn't thought up any songs of their own. In 320 Arius was hauled before a synod of nearly a hundred bishops from Egypt, Libya and Tripolitania, where his teachings were condemned and he was sacked from his post. Leading the counter-charge against Arius was Athanasius, a young Alexandrian theologian. Only twenty-two, he already had his own big hit – a pamphlet called *The Incarnation*, which explored the idea that humanity was saved by uniting with the divine in Christ. In Athanasius' eyes a *created* Jesus simply wasn't good enough to

---

* One of his big hits was a song called 'The essence of the Father is foreign to the Son'. All together now . . .

reunite God and humankind. Only the creator could recreate humanity.

Arius fought back. He found support from Eusebius, Bishop of Nicomedia,* who rallied more support for Arius, and soon the eastern part of the church was in turmoil. Arius appeared before two further synods in Asia, where clerics overwhelmingly supported his view. Two years after fleeing Alexandria he had enough support to enable him to march back into the city in triumph and demand his job back.

The argument grew so intense that in 324 the emperor himself decided to sort it out.

Nicea to see you, to see you, Nicea

After a few delays, a council gathered in Nicea in May and June 325. It was intended as the first ever ecumenical – which means worldwide – council of bishops. It would be so high-powered that no one would be able to dispute its rulings. And Constantine, the undisputed one and only emperor, would chair it. You can't get more high-powered than that.

It was certainly impressive. The emperor and his officials were there in all their finery; but just as impressive, in a different way, were those clergy who had survived the great persecution, many of whom proudly bore their scars.

But it wasn't exactly 'worldwide' because, as it turned out, the western clergy didn't show up. Over 300 bishops from the east attended; the western regions sent 5. And the most important western cleric, Bishop Sylvester of Rome, couldn't make it. He was washing his hair, or something. He just sent two priests as observers. The fact is that his nose was put out of joint. If anyone called a council, he felt it ought to have been the top bishop, whom he considered to be . . . er . . . Sylvester, Bishop of Rome. It's also likely that the western clerics really didn't get what all the fuss was about. Latin didn't even have words for most of the technical terms that so agitated the Greek-speaking church. But this non-attendance could not have gone down well in the eyes of the emperor.

* Not to be confused with the historian Eusebius, who was Bishop of Caesarea. Nor with Eusebio, who played centre forward for Portugal during the 1960s. (Eusebios means 'pious', by the way.)

The verdict of the council was plain: Arius and his followers were condemned, and Arius' writings were ordered to be burnt. Just to make things absolutely clear, the council composed an official statement of faith, a creed. There had been creeds before, but they varied from region to region and were usually spoken by converts at their baptism. This one, however, was for everyone, not just newbies. Anyone in a position of responsibility who didn't sign up to it would be deposed. It was the Christian version of Diocletian's official certificates of emperor worship.

All around the world today Christians still recite the Nicene Creed. But the interesting thing is that the creed recited today *isn't* the one agreed at Nicea. The original, authentic, Nicene Creed has some major differences from our modern versions. First, it's a lot shorter. Second, it merely mentions the Holy Spirit and then moves straight on. (With Montanism still fresh in the memory, everyone agreed not to talk too much about the Holy Spirit.) Third, it doesn't say anything about baptism or the resurrection of the dead, or Mary, or the crucifixion, or the prophets or . . . well, you get the point. Finally, and most noticeably, the original Nicene Creed ends with some very specific anti-Arian clauses. See for yourself:

> We believe in one God, the Father All-sovereign, Maker of all things visible and invisible.
>
> And in one Lord Jesus Christ, the Son of God, begotten of the Father, only-begotten; that is, of the substance of the Father, God of God, Light of Light, true God of true God; begotten, not made, of one substance with the Father through whom all things were made, things in heaven and things on earth; who for us men and for our salvation, came down and was made flesh, and became man; he suffered, and the third day he rose again, ascended into heaven; is coming to judge living and dead.
>
> And in the Holy Spirit.
>
> And those that say: 'there was when he was not;' and 'Before he was begotten he was not;' and that 'He came into being from what-is-not' or those who allege that the Son of God is 'Of another substance or essence' or 'created,' or 'changeable,' or 'alterable' – these the catholic and apostolic church condemns.

The creed that Christians recite as the Nicene Creed actually comes from another council, held over a century later at Chalcedon. We recite the Chalcedonian Creed. Still, on the plus side, at least we don't have to waste time cursing any Arians lurking in the congregation.

Obviously much of this creed is concerned with making absolutely clear the relationship between Jesus and the Father. That is why it seems so repetitive: it was making sure ABSOLUTELY EVERYBODY GOT THE POINT. But there is one very significant word in there that, according to the imperial press office (or its ancient equivalent), was proposed by the emperor himself.* He suggested that the Son was 'of one substance' with the father. The Greek word is *homoousios*.

This suggestion was welcomed by everyone, mainly because when the emperor suggests something you'd be an idiot *not* to welcome it. The only tiny problem with Constantine's suggestion was that, frankly, not many people understood it. It sounded, in one way, suspiciously like that modalism stuff, where the Father, the Son and the Holy Spirit were the same person wearing different masks. However, it was the best they could do. Two bishops didn't sign up – which took some chutzpah, given who was chairing the meeting – but the rest signed on the dotted line, and everyone went home.

(Some other things were agreed at Nicea too. One main thing was the date of Easter, the most important Christian festival and the time when most catechumens were baptised. Easter was always preceded by a period of fasting. In fact, the council of Nicea is the first mention we get of fasting for forty days and forty nights before Easter – what Christians call Lent.)†

Of course, coming up with a nice form of words didn't solve the problem. Arius was exiled to Illyricum (the area roughly covered by modern Albania/Croatia) and forbidden from returning to Alexandria, but within a few years he was back in Nicomedia, preaching and campaigning just as hard as before. Finally, in 336, Constantine ordered him to Constantinople to account for himself and he died while there. According to his enemies, he died while answering a 'call of nature'. But this story comes from his old foe Bishop Athanasius, so it's on the 'spiteful' side of biased.

* This is imperial spin. Constantine was no theologian. It was probably the suggestion of his Spanish adviser, Bishop Hosius of Cordova.
† Ash Wednesday, on the other hand, dates back only to AD 960. And really became official only in the eleventh century. Pancakes aren't mentioned at all.

Fig. VIII. *At the Council of Nicea, Constantine comes up with a solution*

Arianism went on to survive in several different flavours. There were the extra-strong Arians who went as far as saying the Son is *unlike* the Father. There were the much more mild, vanilla-flavour, Arians who backed creeds that merely said the Son is *like* the Father. (This party later won the support of Constantinius II, who imposed this formula on both the western and eastern churches.) And then there are the low-fat Arians, whose leaders backed a statement which said that the Father and Son are *similar* in substance.

Talking of which . . .

Divine Constantine

Appropriately enough for this 'Christian' emperor, Constantine died on Pentecost in 337. For years he had styled himself a bishop of the church, but he was never ordained and received baptism only in the nick of time on his deathbed. He was baptised by Bishop Eusebius of Caesarea (who was an Arian, btw; in his later years Constantine himself seems to have moved towards adopting Arianism). As to how Christianised he left the empire, it's worth noting that on his death he was declared a god by the Roman senate after the usual fashion.

Perhaps his most lasting legacy was that Christianity developed a theology of power. In this view of things the emperor was the earthly representative of God and any church councils derived their power not from a shared understanding of the will of God, but from the approval of the emperor.

The organisation that from its start had provided a home for the outcast, the ostracised and the hopeless of all sorts suddenly had its own seat at the table. Joining the church became a Good Career Move. Clerics could now expect their rise through the ranks to end in a blessed retirement, rather than martyrdom.

Mary's song about sending the rich away empty must have seemed pretty ironic to those now looking on from outside at gold-laden basilicas and priests in fine robes. From its roots as a religion for poor people, slaves and women, Christianity was itself becoming a faith that spent its time carefully threading camels through needles. It had won. It had gained the whole world.

Hmm. I'm *sure* Jesus had something to say about that.

Deserters

Other Christians decided that worldly wealth and power, far from being something to be embraced, was to be avoided at all costs. So they ran away, into the desert, to follow Anthony's example and become monks. Some were motivated by a desire to spend a life in prayer; some were refugees from the persecutions of the third and early fourth centuries; some were simply escaping from the taxman.* But they were all, in some way, avoiding the Roman Empire. Their approach is summed up by one of their number, Abba Chomas, who, as he lay dying said to his 'sons', 'Do not have anything to do with rulers, then your hands will not be opened to gather together, but open to give.'

---

* So many people in third-century Egypt moved out of the cities into smaller settlements to escape taxes and bureaucracy that in the end Diocletian was forced to reform the tax system.

They took their name from their surroundings: the word hermit comes from *erēmos*, the Greek word for wilderness. They were, quite literally, deserters. Early monasticism was a protest movement, the first dissenting church, the first Separatists. Egypt made this easy. It has a narrow, fertile strip along the Nile, but beyond that huge stretches of desert. It was easy to retreat into the desert: first you had to walk away from the town and then . . . er . . . well, there you were. No satnav required. 'You know the Nile? Well, just walk away from it and you'll be fine.'

The increase in the numbers of monks made Anthony, never the cheeriest of blokes, extremely grumpy. He never wanted to be famous; he just wanted to be left alone. But followers crowded around him. Not that he was the only one. There were other well-known spiritual leaders in the desert as well. Their sayings and deeds were later collected together and they make inspiring – often amazing – reading.

Monasteries are so much a part of Christian history now that we forget how truly independent and revolutionary they were. Monks like Anthony had surgically removed themselves from the authority of the church.

They came from a wide variety of backgrounds. The African desert father Abba Moses, for example, was a black African who was a former slave and then a robber in the hills of Egypt. He is known either as Moses the Robber or Moses the Negro. When a brother came to him for advice, he replied, 'Go, sit in your cell and the cell will teach you everything.' There were monks who were former camel drivers, ex-slaves and even murderers.

The authorities were never quite sure about them. Yes, they were holy men, but they were also outside the system. They were, literally, out of control. This was OK when there were just a few old blokes sitting and scratching themselves in the desert, but when there were lots of them, authority and control became a more pressing problem.

The solution was devised by a man called Pachomius. When he was a young man, he was forcibly conscripted by the imperial army and taken down the Nile. That night he was locked in a cell, standard practice with all new conscripts to stop them running away, and during the night some local Christians came and gave him food and blankets. He was so impressed by this that, when he was released from the army a short time later, he went straight to the nearest village, found a nearby

Christian hermit, became a Christian himself and headed straight into the desert.

He quickly attracted a bunch of disciples of his own, whom he organised into nine, self-sufficient communities. He invented, in fact, the monastery. Monks in these communities renounced their possessions and vowed obedience to their *abba*, 'father'.* Pachomius' sister followed his example and founded female communities of nuns, one of which had four hundred members. (Again, they had varied reasons for joining. For some it was an escape from oppressive husbands.) Pachomius created a rule for his monks to follow: manual labour, reading of Scripture and, above all, prayer. Monks ate together, but in silence, and every weekend they shared the Eucharist. They were egalitarian organisations: in Pachomius' communities seniority was derived from the date you joined the foundation, so no one could claim higher status because of age, birth or background.

Holy fools

Pachomius was no fan of excessive self-denial. 'Excessive abstinence is worse for us than overindulgence,' he wrote, but, over time, the asceticism practised by those who came after him got more and more extreme. Poverty and celibacy? That was for lightweights. Monks began to live lives of almost grotesque hardship. They lived up trees, or in caves so low that they couldn't ever stand up properly. They tied weights to their necks and other parts of their body (don't ask, and, for pity's sake, don't try it at home). They whipped themselves, each other and anything else that moved.

They lived on starvation rations. In Gaza, Hilarion reportedly ate nothing but dry lentils for three years. No wonder people chose to let him live in solitude. For ten years John the Dwarf watered a stick stuck in the ground, to teach himself obedience.* Thalelaeus of Cilicia spent ten years in a barrel, crying most of the time. Mother Sarah lived by an Egyptian river for sixty years, but as an act of discipline never even looked at it. Macarius the Alexandrian felt so guilty about swatting a mosquito that, as penance, he moved to a mosquito-infested swamp for six months. His diet consisted of nothing but raw vegetables and

---

* In Europe *abba* becomes 'abbot'. And later, a Swedish rock band.

a bit of bread, but for some bizarre reason he is now the patron saint of pastry chefs. If you'd given him an éclair, he would have died of shame.

Why were they doing this? One reason was to show up those at the other end of the scale. Basil the Great, a theologian who began his career in the church as a monk, wrote that 'While we try to amass wealth, make piles of money, get hold of the land as our real property, overtop one another in riches, we have palpably cast off justice, and lost the common good.'

Monks were not necessarily respected. They didn't have the power of bishops. When the monk Hypatius went to Chalcedon to protest against the games being held in the city, the Bishop of Chalcedon told him to 'go and sit in your cell and keep quiet. This is my affair.' On the few occasions they went near 'civilisation' many of these low-class, unsettling strangers were beaten and thrown out of town. And quite often the person ordering the beating was the local bishop.

To be fair, sometimes the bishop had a point. Some hermits did not live as solitaries, but as a kind of combative, unsettling, performance artist. Simeon 'the holy fool' reportedly simulated madness so that no one would realise that he was secretly doing charitable acts. His 'crazy' act was very convincing. It involved dragging a dead dog around, then going into church, putting out all the lights and throwing nuts at the women. On the way out of church he turned over all the stalls selling cakes and pastries, which would have annoyed their patron, Saint Macarius. According to his biographer, Leontios of Neapolis, he was trying to imitate Jesus. (I must have missed the bit in the Gospels where Jesus rushes into a woman's bathhouse with nothing on.)

The most famous of these hermit types, though, was Simeon the Stylite ('pillar-dweller'). For years, Simeon lived on top of a sixty-foot column, situated on a main road outside Antioch in Syria. He lived in a kind of wicker basket, like a nest.* There he acted as a kind of local religious leadership. Bedouin tribesmen came and burned their idols below his pillar. One entire village converted to Christianity under his

---

* Archaeological investigations have shown that the pillar had en suite facilities. I'm not sure *how* the archaeologists have proved that, and, frankly, I don't want to find out.

influence, and placed stones carved with crosses around their village to protect themselves from werewolves. And field mice.

He was widely imitated throughout the eastern Mediterranean by monks living atop ever more vertiginous pillars. It wasn't simply an attempt to be the fifth-century David Blaine; they were sending out a message. First, the pillars they used were taken from old pagan temples. They were living in the ruins of paganism. Second, they wanted to be seen and heard. Simeon's pillar was right by a main road and he would bellow down his sermons to his many fans. Unlike more traditional hermits, they did not retreat into distant caves in the desert. They *wanted* to make an exhibition of themselves. They were potent, visible rebukes to the society around them.

It was an eastern phenomenon. Attempts to imitate Simeon in the west were scuppered by the climate. In fact, we know of only one western pillar-percher: a hermit called Wulflaic who lived atop a pillar at what is now Carignan in the Ardennes in AD 585. This was a symbolic protest gesture: there was an old temple of Diana there, and from the top of his pillar Wulflaic preached rousing sermons against paganism. But the weather was harsh. He lost his toenails in the harsh winter and icicles formed in his beard. In the end some passing bishops encouraged Wulflaic to come down for a chat, and one of them broke up his pillar while he wasn't watching.

St Martin's cloak

Like Pachomius, Martin of Tours (c.316–c.400) was an ex-soldier who became a monk. In 354, while in the army, he converted to Christianity. One day his regiment were on patrol near the city of Amiens when he passed a naked beggar on the road. Martin immediately took off his cloak, tore it in half, and gave half to the beggar. He had read Christ's injunction to give your coat to the poor, so that's what he did. Even if it was army property.

Then Martin realised that you had to obey Christ's other commands as well. Such as not killing people. So he resigned. 'I am Christ's soldier,' he said. 'I am not allowed to fight.' He left the army, studied theology and became a monk.

His piety soon attracted attention, and in 372 he was pressurised into becoming the bishop of his home town, Tours. He established a monastery there and rejected any kind of finery or other bishopy bling, choosing to dress as one of the poor. He was a great church planter and, although he was active in destroying pagan shrines, he also allowed some compromises, allowing simple folk customs to be observed, even if sometimes they clashed with Christian claims.

In the end he moved out of the city to Marmoutier, where he founded probably the first Egyptian-style monastic community in the western empire.*

He was renowned for his miraculous powers of healing. Martin was probably the first western Christian to be recognised as a saint without being martyred. Previously that was the qualifying process for saint-hood: you had to be martyred. But monasticism was perhaps its own kind of martyrdom.

Martin spoke truth unto power. Later, though, power, in a textbook example of Completely Missing the Point, claimed him for its own. After his death, Frankish kings claimed that they had found the actual cloak he had given the beggar, and they carried it into battle as a kind of charm to confer divine protection.

And now it gets really interesting. In Latin the cloak is called the *cappa Sancti Martini*, the 'cloak of St Martin'. It first appears in the royal treasury of the Frankish kings in 679. Later, a special priest was appointed to look after the relic when it was on military service, as it were, and he was called a *cappellanu*. Eventually all priests who served the military were called *cappellani*, which in French becomes *chapelains*, and in English, 'chaplain'. Yes, it's irony overload: all clergy in the military are named after the cloak of a conscientious objector.†

So Martin left us a relic. But he was really a relic himself. He was a throwback to the days of Tertullian, Origen and Hippolytus, when it was blindingly obvious that you could not be both a soldier and a Christian. But now things were different.

---

* John Cassian is often credited with founding the first monastery in western Europe, the Abbey of St Victor, in southern Gaul, near Marseilles. But he didn't arrive there until around 415, forty years after Martin had been made Bishop of Tours.

† Similarly, there were temporary churches built to house the relic on its journey, and they were called *capella*. That's where we get the word 'chapel' from.

Athanasius against the world

Anthony, the über-hermit, was a great friend of Athanasius, Bishop of Alexandria. (Athanasius wrote the monk's official biography.) A secretary at Nicea and vehement opponent of Arius, Athanasius' epitaph was *Athanasius contra mundum*, 'Athanasius against the world', which tells you most of what you need to know about his career.*

Athanasius, who became Bishop of Alexandria at the age of thirty, saw himself very much as the champion of Nicea. But his anti-Arianism got him into trouble. In 335, ten years after Nicea, Athanasius was accused of mistreating Arians. Constantine exiled him to Trier in Germany.

When Constantine died, Athanasius returned to Alexandria. But Constantine's son, Constantius, was an Arian, so he exiled Athanasius again. (This time to Rome.) He was allowed back to Alexandria in 346, but then in 350 Constantius banished him for a third time.

Constantius was an Arian of the hardcore, Jesus-is-unlike-the-father variety. Where his father had sought agreement and consensus, Constantius simply banned people from disagreeing. In 357 he issued what is known as the Declaration of Sirmium, which not only banned the idea that the Son was 'of the same substance' as the Father, but forbade any further discussion of the issue. And to back this up Athanasius (who had snuck back into Alexandria through the back door) was exiled for the fourth time.

He went to the Egyptian desert and moved around various monasteries there. During this time he wrote many of his major works, including *Apology Against the Arians*, *Four Orations against the Arians*, *History of the Arians*.† Thankfully, he never got around to writing *Arians are Smelly*, *Why I Really Hate the Arians*, or *101 Things to do with a Dead Arian*.

But Constantius was so fanatically Arian that even some of the Arians got fed up. The eastern bishops were moderate Arians and they resented being lumped in with these extremists. So they came up with a possible compromise. They talked of the Son being 'of similar substance' to the Father. Athanasius, adamant in his exile, still thought it was substance abuse, but the two sides were moving closer.

* Athanasius had a creed named after him. Twice as long as the Nicene Creed, it was not actually written by Athanasius, or even during his lifetime.
† In which, with typical tact, he described Constantius as a precursor of the Antichrist.

Constantius died in 361 and Athanasius returned to his post in Alexandria. Fifth time lucky.

Fig. IX. *In Alexandria, Athanasius is exiled. Again*

Pagan reformer

Alas not. Constantius was succeeded by his nephew Julian.* The good news was that Julian wasn't an Arian. The bad news was that Julian wasn't a Christian.

He was a pagan. And an evangelistic pagan, at that. Julian was a brilliant, determined individual and a big adherent of Neoplatonism. Before he came to power he pretended to be interested in Christianity, but once he gained the throne he set out to return the entire empire to the one true path of paganism.

To be fair, he didn't declare war on the Christians. But nor did he do anything to stop pagan mobs from exacting revenge for what they saw as decades of Christian aggression. And he did continue the

---

* Despite being family, there had been no love lost between the two – largely because Constantius had previously had most of Julian's family butchered.

honourable family tradition of exiling Athanasius, who was kicked out of Alexandria for a fifth time.

Julian was the Martin Luther of paganism. He reorganised the religion into a more coherent whole and, in effect, tried to set up what was essentially a pagan church. Priests were recruited on the basis of merit (skill at sacrificing goats, looks good in a laurel wreath, etc.) rather than whether they came from good families. He even went on one-man preaching tours, proclaiming the virtues of the old gods. You can't help thinking that 'Julian the Apostate', as he became known, would have made a *brilliant* Christian emperor.

But he was fighting a losing battle. The pagan priests just didn't get it. In a famous letter Julian complained that his priests didn't help the poor like the Christians did: 'The impious Galileans support not only their poor but ours as well,' he complained. 'Everyone can see that our poor lack aid from us.'

Julian's career lasted only three years: he was struck down by an arrow during a battle against Persian troops on the eastern frontier. Many Christians saw his death as divine punishment.

The talk of the town

Julian's successor, a general called Jovian, re-established Christianity as the empire's *religion du jour*, and then promptly died from fumes given off by the charcoal fire in his tent, making him among the earliest known victims of carbon monoxide poisoning. Before he died, though, he managed to reinstate Athanasius as Bishop of Alexandria. His sixth time in the post.

Jovian was succeeded by another general, Valens. And he was, guess what? That's right, an Arian! So, he exiled Athanasius again. This time though, Athanasius had learned from experience and didn't bother moving very far – just to the outskirts of Alexandria. (Some reports indicate that he spent this time living in his family tomb.)

Valens was persuaded, fairly swiftly, to rescind the order and Athanasius returned. Fortunately for this sixty-seven-year-old, seven times Bishop of Alexandria, the power and influence of Arianism was waning. In 378 Valens was killed during a battle. At this time the empire was in two bits – the western and the eastern halves. The western emperor, Gratian, sent a retired Spanish general to assume the throne.

He became emperor Theodosius I, and had absolutely no time for the intricacies of Arianism. He reflects a general attitude in the west, which saw a lot of this theological argument as just namby-pamby mucking about with words. To Theodosius those who rejected Nicea were simply 'demented and insane'.

Theologically, much work had also been done by the work of three clerics known as the Cappodocian Fathers: Basil of Caesarea (c.329–379, aka Basil the Great), his brother Gregory of Nyssa (c.330–c.395) and their friend Gregory of Nazianzus (330–389).* These three managed to rally most of the churches around a compromise. They accepted the Nicene idea that the Father and Son share one substance. But they also agreed with what Tertullian had proposed two centuries earlier: that Jesus and the Father were of 'one substance', but that they were three distinct 'persons' – Father, Son and Spirit.

Now to modern readers this might all sound like some kind of esoteric argument between clergy, but actually everyone was talking about it. Gregory of Nyssa complained that

> [Constantinople] is full of it, the squares, the market places, the crossroads, the alleyways; old-clothes men, money changers, food sellers: they are all busy arguing. If you ask someone to give you change, he philosophises about the Begotten and the Unbegotten; if you enquire about the price of a loaf, you are told by way of reply that the Father is greater and the Son inferior; if you ask 'Is my bath ready?' the attendant answers that 'the Son was made out of nothing'.

Constantinople was clearly 'full of it' in a number of ways. The city talked theology like modern cities talk football. And what is interesting – and, frankly, depressing – about the debate over Arianism is that it is the first major example of theology turning into brain surgery: one tiny slip, and you're dead. With Novatian and Donatus at least the arguments had been about real things, stuff that you did. It was about whether or not you had

---

* Macrina (c.327–380), Basil and Gregory's sister, was also a renowned leader and founder of an important nunnery. Today she is celebrated in the famous liturgical dance the Macarena. Basil got his nickname 'the Great' from his actions. He used nearly all his family's fortune to create a food bank for the poor during a famine in Cappadocia. He also built one of the first Christian hospitals and a hospice.

made a sacrifice to the emperor. Marcion and Montanus? That was about big stuff as well, huge chunks removed from, or added to, Scripture. But this? This seems about playing with words. No, *less* than words: *letters*. At one stage the debate becomes between two Greek words: *homoiousios*, which means 'similar essence', and *homoousios*, which means 'same essence'. The difference between them is the Greek letter 'i': one iota. Talk about jots and tittles.

And because Christianity was now part of the imperial structure it became possible to properly punish those who disagreed with you. Theodosius decided to put a stop to all this nonsense. In 381 he summoned a council – the second ecumenical council – at Constantinople. Arianism was once again outlawed. And, significantly, Theodosius declared that from that time onwards heresy would henceforth be a crime against the state. All heretics would be fined the enormous sum of ten pounds of gold, and any laymen who allowed heretical rites to happen on their land could find all their property confiscated.

For the first time heresy was enshrined in criminal law. For the first time in the history of Christianity there was thought-crime. Jesus had argued with people who disagreed with him. He had made fun of them. But he had also shared meat and drink with them and, on the cross, forgave them. Now his followers were prosecuting them and locking them up. No wonder so many of his followers ran away into the desert.

The Council of Constantinople also declared that since Constantinople was the 'new Rome' it should have an appropriate status. So it was declared the number two bishopric in the empire, second only to Rome. This annoyed the clergy in Rome, who thought of themselves as above such things as needing a number two. And it *really* annoyed Alexandria and Antioch, who thought of themselves as much more historic and worthy of such status (not without reason).

Basil was dead by the time of the council. Which is probably just as well. It would only have upset him: it was riddled with politics. Many people could see the trajectory that Christianity was on, and they didn't like it. Gregory of Nazianzus was so angry he walked out of the council, resigned the bishopric of Constantinople, to which he had only just been appointed, and returned to his monastery.

When he was invited to another council at a later date, he utterly refused to attend. 'Synods and councils I salute from a distance,' he said. 'Never again will I sit in those gatherings of cranes and geese.'

His farewell sermon, delivered at Constantinople, is perhaps the most magnificently sarcastic sermon ever preached. He painted a picture of what the higher echelons of the clergy had become: 'I was not aware that we ought to rival the consuls, the governors, the most illustrious generals,' he said. 'I didn't know we were supposed to ride on splendid horses, and drive in magnificent carriages, and be preceded by a procession and surrounded by applause, and have everyone make way for us.' And with that he left.

Theodosius had reunited the Not So Mighty Roman Empire™ under one ruler, but he was the last emperor to rule over both the eastern and western halves. On his deathbed he left the eastern empire to his elder son, Arcadius, and the western to his younger son, Honorius. For the west it was the beginning of a run of thirteen emperors, each more hopeless than the one before, and an eighty-year descent into oblivion.

Papa Damasus

The decision to promote Constantinople to second-in-command status did not go down well in Rome. For the Bishop of Rome, increasingly, it felt like his world was under attack. The empire was weak. Barbarian tribes were threatening the borders, moving south from Germany, even heading towards Rome.* And now this so-called council, under this upstart eastern emperor, had declared that Constantinople was second only to Rome? Nonsense.

Rome, of course, was the *former* capital of the empire. Purely symbolic. It was occasionally visited by emperors, sure, but they didn't stay there. This meant that the top dog in the city was the Bishop of Rome.

And no one was more top-doggy than Damasus.

Damasus is an example of how, suddenly, being a Christian leader

---

* Interestingly, they were Arian barbarians. Arian missionaries had been active among the barbarian tribes. For barbarians interested in Christianity, one of the attractive things about Arianism was that it *wasn't* the official belief of the empire.

had become a prize worth fighting for. Literally, in fact. He became Bishop of Rome in a most unholy way: he hired a gang of thugs to stone the church where his rival, Ursinus, had his headquarters. Some 137 people died in the resulting fight. He was the Bishop of Rome when Theodosius called the second ecumenical council at Constantinople in 381, but like his predecessor during the Council of Nicea, he refused to attend. Nor did any other western bishops.* He thought that Constantinople's new status threatened the historical pre-eminence of Rome.

Rome was, after all, the only western city mentioned in the Bible.† Damasus knew that Rome was pre-eminent not because the emperor lived there, but because it was the resting place of the bones of Peter (and Paul). So Damasus started bigging up the connection with Peter (and Paul). He named Rome 'the Apostolic See'. He had a tablet set over the spot where it was believed Peter (and Paul) lay buried, which read, 'The east may have sent the Apostles, but because of the merit of their martyrdom Rome has acquired a superior right to claim them as citizens.'

He also started a much more overt use of the name 'Papa'. Whereas the name 'Papa' (father) had previously been used in the west for any bishop, after Damasus it was to become a distinct, unique title for the Bishop of Rome.

He encouraged rich people (notably women, according to the gossip) to donate large sums to the church. His enemies accused him of riding in gilded carriages and serving banquets 'so lavish that their dinner parties outdo the feasts of kings'.‡

To be fair, Damasus wasn't just about self-aggrandisement. He wanted to establish the unity of the church, and to emphasise that, by now, Christianity had a grand history. The relics of the martyrs and their shrines were to be a match for any of the grand buildings of pagan antiquity. But perhaps he is best summed up by the words of Basil of Caesarea: 'the man is arrogant'.

---

* Sometimes not many bishops attended from either east or west. The low point was the third ecumenical council at Ephesus in 431, which attracted a measly fifty bishops. The rest sent notes from their mums.

† Unless Paul's missing letter to the Mancunians turns up one day.

‡ Damasus' success with the ladies earned him the nickname Matronarum Auriscalpius, the ladies' ear-tickler. It refers to his habit of whispering in their ears. At least I *hope* it refers to that.

He needed help at times, though. Rome still had a significant number of pagans. And when the senate tried to preserve the pagan Altar of Victory from destruction, Damasus called in the big guns. He called in fellow-bishop Ambrose.

The fast-track bishop

Ambrose of Milan (*c*.330–397) is notable for a number of things, not least being the first bishop with a name that sounds like a menswear shop. (Unless there was one called Bishop Trousers of Chelsea.) The son of a Roman prefect whose province included modern France, England and Spain, he followed his dad into a military career, becoming governor of the area that included Milan, which is where he accidentally got elected bishop.

The Christian population had to elect a new bishop, but were bitterly divided over whom to choose. At this time bishops were elected by the people of the city.* Ambrose was attending with a few troops, just in case any unchristian fisticuffs broke out. The crowd, seeing him there, dismissed the two candidates and chose Ambrose instead. He wasn't even a baptised Christian at the time, which meant that he had to be baptised, ordained and then consecrated as Bishop. It was the ultimate fast-track promotion and it shows an assumption that would have astonished and even repelled the early church: that someone with secular power would naturally be a good choice as a church leader. For the early church fathers Ambrose's position as a Roman military official would have made it impossible for him to be a Christian, let alone a bishop. But to the people in Milan, at this point in time, he was the obvious candidate.

Ambrose, as you might expect, proved to be very good at managing such power. He understood the minds of ordinary people. He promoted the relics of the martyrs and built new churches to house them. He composed music and songs. He fed the poor. He also recognised that, even at this stage, not all churches followed the same customs. 'When I am here [in Milan],' he wrote, 'I do not fast

---

* Even as late as the fifth century, Pope Celestine I insisted that 'no bishop be given to a community against its will; the consent and desire of the clergy, people, and nobility is required'. Hmm. Note that 'nobility' bit at the end.

on a Saturday; and when I am at Rome, I do. If you do not wish to cause scandal, observe the local practice of any church you might visit.'

But he brought with him all the character traits of a member of the Roman upper classes. His social position gave him huge influence with Theodosius, whom he persuaded to root out the last vestiges of paganism. Temples were demolished or converted to churches. The most famous example is the Parthenon in Athens, which transferred its allegiance from the goddess Athene to the Virgin Mary.

Anti-pagan, then. But also anti-Semitic. When rioters in Thessalonica murdered the governor, Theodosius sent in troops who massacred seven thousand of them. Ambrose was outraged and excommunicated the emperor until he repented. But in 388 Christian rioters attacked a synagogue in Callinicum, Mesopotamia, which they burnt to the ground. Theodosius ordered that the rioters should pay to rebuild it, but Ambrose bullied the emperor into cancelling the compensation owed to the Jewish community. 'What real wrong is there, after all, in destroying a synagogue,' he wrote, 'a home of perfidy, a home of impiety, in which Christ is daily blasphemed?' Ambrose actually halted a mass the emperor was attending, and refused to continue the service until Theodosius revoked the order. He's sometimes praised as a bishop who stood up to the emperor; but the effect of this protest was to get a load of anti-Semitic arsonists off scot-free.

Ambrose grudgingly admitted that 'some Jews exhibit purity of life and much diligence and love of study', but attitudes such as his were becoming more and more common.

The vulgar tongue

Damasus was keen on Rome. And Rome spoke Latin. But one of the things that was bothering him was the state of the Latin Bible. By now the Bible was available in a number of Latin translations (now known as 'Old Latin' versions). Probably originating in North Africa, they were colloquial, even slangy at times.* Damasus felt that for the west to compete with the east, they needed a proper, grand, grown-up Bible.

* The Old Latin translation of *Luke* 13.8 for example has the vineyard keeper declaring 'I will chuck on a basket of dung.' Only in Latin. Obviously.

And there was only one man for the task: his personal secretary, Jerome (c.347–420).

Jerome's real name was Sophronius Eusebius Hieronymus. (You can see why people preferred to use 'Jerome'.) He was a clever child and when only twelve he was sent to Rome to study rhetoric, philosophy and classical literature. In 373 he nearly lost his life when he fell ill during a journey into northern Syria. During this illness he had a vision calling him to put aside his study of secular, pagan literature and devote himself to God – and to the Bible.

So that's what he did. When he recovered, he headed for the desert, where he became a hermit. Well, sort of, since he records that apparently he 'was often present at dances with girls'. But in between doing the samba, he had the time and solitude to study and, in particular, he started to learn Hebrew from a converted Jew. Jerome became a talented linguist. Augustine (whom we'll meet in a minute)* called him a 'three language man', on the basis of his knowledge of Greek, Latin and Hebrew. It's a sign of how far Christianity had come since the days of the New Testament writers that hardly any of its adherents in the west spoke Greek any more, let alone Hebrew.†

Jerome eventually returned to Rome, where he became secretary to Damasus. It was then that Damasus suggested Jerome should work on a kind of 'Revised Latin Version', which would then become the standard.

Jerome set to work and published his revision of the Gospels in 383, followed by his correction of the Old Latin book of Psalms, which had become known as the Roman Psalter. In his preface to Damasus, written to accompany the revision of the Gospels, he wrote, 'You urge me . . . to sit in judgement on the copies of the Scriptures which are now scattered throughout the whole world . . . how can I dare to change the language of the world in its hoary old age, and carry it back to the early days of its infancy?' He put his finger on a real issue. The Old Latin Bibles may have been slangy, error-prone and just plain wrong as translations, but they were familiar, much-loved, slangy, error-prone and just plain wrong translations. So Jerome faced some opposition. Things weren't made any easier by his complete lack of tact. His

* Depending on the speed of your reading. Or whether you take a break in the meantime. Look, just don't hold me to it, OK.

† Augustine himself knew only a few fragments of Greek and hardly any Hebrew.

polemical writings are always on the abusive side of outspoken. He called those opposing his changes, for example, 'two-legged donkeys'. And that was one of the milder insults.

His outspokenness rebounded on him when Damasus died. Without a high-level protector, Jerome's opponents rounded on him. He was accused of having an improper relationship with a widow and caught up in the Roman equivalent of a tabloid scandal. He was forced to flee the city, accompanied by his brother, a priest and some other monks.

He eventually settled in Bethlehem, where he continued his revision of the Bible. But after a visit to Caesarea to consult Origen's famous *Hexapla* he became convinced that what was actually needed was to start again from scratch and retranslate the Old Testament from the Hebrew.

This was a radical move. The Septuagint – the Greek translation of the Hebrew Scriptures – was the Bible of the Greek-speaking east. For both Jews and Christians it had attained the status of a divinely inspired translation: the legend said that God had inspired seventy translators to come up with the same text independently. Jerome was having none of it. He went back to the Hebrew. And then he found another problem: the Septuagint had more books than the Hebrew Scriptures. So Jerome reclassified these books and gave them the group title *apocrypha*, 'hidden'.*

He finished his work around 406 and it was published to immediate and widespread apathy. It took a long time for Jerome's work to gain traction. In fact, it wasn't until some 400 years later that it became the *de facto* Latin version used by the Catholic Church. And it took a further 700 years or so before it was given the name by which it is still known: the Vulgate – from the Latin word for 'common', meaning 'used by everyone', not 'coarse and vulgar', obviously. At the Council of Trent in 1545, nearly 1,200 years after the work was commissioned, the Catholic Church finally declared Jerome's Vulgate to be the author-ised Bible of the Catholic Church.

Well, you don't want to rush these things, do you?

---

* Most of them he didn't even translate. He did Esdras and the Greek parts of Daniel, Tobit and Judith, but left all the others.

Fig. X. *In his study, Jerome finds his translation hard going*

Spanish rigorism

It might come as some surprise to realise that even by this time, the contents of the New Testament had not been officially agreed. In fact, it is not until AD 367, in a kind of annual church newsletter from Athanasius (during one of his many brief spells as Bishop of

Alexandria) that we first see the full list in the order that we know them.

Around the same time as that list – or perhaps even earlier – some scribes in Alexandria produced the first proper Bibles – in the sense of books with the entire contents of the Bible bound within the covers. But even these great codices, known as Codex Sinaiticus, Codex Alexandrinus and Codex Vaticanus, have some variance: Sinaiticus and Alexandrinus both have extra books in their New Testament section.

There was still plenty of debate, particularly over the status of the book of Revelation. When Eusebius of Caesarea wrote about the Christian Scriptures in his *Church History* he listed Revelation as being 'canonical and recognised' by some churches, but in other places as 'spurious', that is, popular, and not anti-Christian, but not actually canonical. Eusebius clearly has reservations. He has to include it in the first group, because by the time he is writing it is widely accepted, but you sense that if he had a choice he would not include it at all.

Indeed, this distrust of Revelation was widespread in the east. Partly it must have been a hangover of the Montanist controversy, which gave the very idea of 'enthusiastic' apocalyptic writings a bad name. But it must also have been to do with the contents of the book itself. Because no book in the Bible is more vehemently anti-imperial than Revelation. It can't have been top of the bestseller list in Constantine's local book-shop. Even today there is still something of a tight-lipped silence about Revelation in the Greek church. (It's the only book of the Bible that does not feature in the official Greek lectionary.)

Nevertheless, it did make it into the final list of Bible books. In the end a consensus had emerged. Damasus hosted a synod at Rome in 382 which agreed with Athanasius' list; ten years later in 393 a Synod of North African churches at Hippo Regius agreed. The New Testament was agreed, and it, along with the Hebrew Scriptures, was the Bible. And reading it – or listening to it, at any rate – was officially a good thing.

Or not.

Sometimes, reading the Bible could get you into trouble. Priscillian, Bishop of Avila, was a devoted Bible scholar and pioneering monk in Spain. He was writing a commentary on Paul's letters when he was struck by Paul's instruction to make the body 'a temple of the Holy Spirit within you' (1 Cor. 6.19). Priscillian took this to mean that

Christians should reject wealth and earthly honour and embrace a life of humility, discipline and chastity.

Priscillian was accused of Manichaeism. There was gossip that he was so keen on the Bible that he was allowing mixed groups of men and women to meet, pray and study the Scriptures. At a synod held at Saragossa in 380 Priscillian's teachings were condemned.

Despite this condemnation by the synod, Priscillian's supporters succeeded in having him made Bishop of Avila. But in 383 the western emperor, Gratianus, was murdered in Lyons and a general called Magnus Maximus (Big Max) took control of Britain, Gaul, Spain and Africa. (This was before Theodosius reunified the empire.) Maximus was keen to curry favour with the church and gain support of various church leaders, so he reopened the trial of Priscillian, and brought trumped-up charges of sorcery and holding licentious orgies against him (ridiculous, given his insistence on celibacy). At Trier in 386 Priscillian and six others were executed: the first heretics ever executed by Christian authorities.

The seriousness of this step was recognised immediately. Ambrose of Milan, Martin of Tours and even Pope Siricius protested against the execution, arguing that an ecclesiastical case should not be decided by civil powers. But it was too late.

The action taken against Priscillian reflects an anxiety in the church against what is called rigorism: that is, taking the whole thing far too seriously. Such a concern would have been unthinkable in the times of Peter (and Paul) for whom the question was really 'How can you NOT take this thing too seriously?' But the church grew increasingly suspicious of such people, not least because the commitment of such groups tends to throw the behaviour of the official church leadership into a rather bad light.

Priscillian's influence in Spain endured for quite some time. His supporters in the region honoured him as a martyr. They retrieved his remains from Trier, buried them carefully, and revered him as a martyr and saint.

Some five hundred years later a hermit discovered a monumental grave. It was decided that this was the tomb of James, the apostle, whom the stories said had come to Spain to be a missionary. So a big church was built over the site – and many thousands of pilgrims still make their way every year to Santiago de Compostela. The problem is that no story linking James with Spain exists before the ninth century.

And the stories telling of his bones being taken to Spain in a miraculously guided, unmanned boat made of stone come from three centuries later.

If it is true that there was a big tomb containing the saint's bones, then it's possible that it is not James but Priscillian to whom thousands of visitors pay homage each year.

As they should.

Bachelor boys

From the start, Christianity had embraced – to use an inappropriate word – a conservative view of sex. Paul had strong words to say about fornicators, and the Christian lifestyle stood out against the more permissive lifestyles of some sections of Roman society. As the *Epistle to Diognetus* put it bluntly, 'Christians share their food but not their wives.'

But gradually an idea began to take hold that all sex was a bit – you know – impure. That if you were really serious about this Christianity lark, you stopped embracing the opposite sex and started embracing chastity. This idea was deliberately spread by people like Tertullian, who believed in the absolute necessity of sexual abstinence. But then, Tertullian was scared of women. He called them 'the gateway to the devil' and stated that they should dress themselves in the 'silk of modesty, with the linen of holiness, and with the purple of chastity'. He's only missed out 'the cotton of doing your hair nicely, and the polyester of knowing your place'.

From the middle of the second century onwards the idea of celibacy as a higher calling took hold. Biblically there was little evidence for this.* The apostles had wives. It took some creative theology to airbrush Mary and Joseph's sex life from Matthew 1 verse 25. In 1 Timothy Paul says that a bishop should not have more than one wife. And Peter, the über-apostle, was married – a fact that should have proved a *tad* inconvenient to anyone who wanted to call him the first pope of Rome.†

---

* The much-cited passage from Matthew 19 is actually about divorce, not celibacy as such. When Jesus says 'Not everyone can accept this word', the word he's referring to is his teaching on divorce given a few sentences earlier.

† It's likely that the church leaders were influenced less by the Bible and more by pagan ascetics. First- and second-century Stoic philosophers taught that

In the east things were more relaxed. Chrysostom argued that sex between husbands and wives was important for 'the sole purpose of fleeing sin and freeing oneself from every sort of lewdness'. It was perfectly permissible for priests to have wives. And sex lives.

But in the west celibacy became the ideal. In the fourth and fifth centuries it found some of its most eloquent spokesmen. Ambrose, Jerome and especially Augustine all had a high view of chastity. Ambrose demanded that priests should stop having sex with their wives.

Then, in the 390s, the great men of the western church joined forces against a man called Jovinian. Jovinian was a monk who argued that virginity was, frankly, not the marvellous state it was cracked up to be. A fairly *liberal* monk, then. We know his writings only from that of his chief opponent, Jerome, not the most unbiased reporter, but he argued that virgins, widows and married women were all equal in the sight of God. Jovinian wasn't saying chastity was bad, just that married people could be equally holy. 'If the Lord had commanded virginity,' he wrote, 'he would have seemed to condemn marriage, and to do away with the seed-plot of mankind, of which virginity itself is a growth.' He argued that there was only one future punishment and reward, not different grades for different people. For Jovinian all sins were equal.

Jovinian also denied the perpetual virginity of Mary. Mary, famously, had been a virgin when Jesus was born. But in the second century she became the poster girl for celibacy and the idea grew up that she had remained a virgin. As we've seen, works like the fictional *Infancy Gospel of James* sought to explain Jesus' brothers and sisters away by claiming that these were actually Jesus' step-brothers and sisters: the children of Joseph by a previous marriage. This is why in Renaissance pictures of Joseph he's always portrayed as a very, very old hairy bloke.

Jerome was one of those who chose to rebrand Jesus' siblings in this way. When he found out about Jovinian, he went ballistic. His writing seethes with the anger of someone who has given something up only to be told he was wasting his time. He wrote two treatises

---

sex was intended only for procreation. They may even have been influenced by Gnosticism, which, with its contempt for the flesh, tended to idealise virginity.

against Jovinian, one of which was so abusive that some Christian leaders in Rome tried to have it suppressed.

Jerome had support, though, from the Bishop of Rome himself. Damasus' successor, Siricius, had the haughty, arrogant nature of a man with nothing to be arrogant about. He was the first Bishop of Rome to use the title Pope in the modern sense. Siricius was a huge fan of (a) celibacy and (b) the *Virgin* Mary. He argued strongly for the perpetual virginity of Mary, arguing that Jesus would never have allowed himself to be born in Mary's womb had she at any point allowed that lodging 'to be stained by the presence of male seed'. Siricius said it was a 'crime' for priests to continue to have sex with their wives after they were ordained.

In the end Jovinian was excommunicated. Ambrose called in another favour, upon which Theodosius had Jovinian scourged with a lead-tipped whip and exiled to the island of Boa. It was to take a long time to become universally acknowledged, and it was never uniformly enforced, but, in the west, clerical celibacy became the official line.

Increasingly it was urged on the laity as well. So much so that, by the early Middle Ages, there was hardly any legitimate opportunity for a bit of 'it'. Around 585 the church ruled that there should be neither rumpy nor pumpy for the forty days before Christmas. Nor for forty days before Easter. Nor the eight days after Pentecost. Nor on the nights before the great feast days of the church. Nor on Sundays. Or Wednesdays. Or Fridays. And not for thirty days after your wife gave birth to a boy, or forty days if she gave birth to a girl. Nor for five days before Communion. By my calculations that means Christians of this period were allowed sex on second Thursdays in October.

No, really, it cuts out around 40 per cent of the year. Given the high mortality rate at the time, people could not possibly have obeyed this. Otherwise, the human race in the west would have died out.

The problem with all of this holy holy stuff is that it reinforced the idea of a two-track holiness: that some were Christians while others were *Christians*. Married laity were second-class, while monks, priests, nuns – the clergy generally – were literally holier than thou.

> ### JOHN CHRYSOSTOM
>
> *Name:* John of Antioch.
> *Aka:* John Chrysostom.
> *Nationality:* Syrian Greek.
> *Dates: c.*347–407.
> *Appearance:* Short, long-limbed, thin to the point of emaciation, high forehead, bald with a short beard. He compared himself to a spider.
> *Before he was famous:* Law student.
> *Famous for:* The greatest preacher of the Greek world.
> *Why does he matter?* He showed the power of what preaching can do. He spoke truth to power.
> *Could you have a drink with him down the pub?* No. I'm pretty sure he'd given all that up. But he could be good fun in the company of friends. Apparently.

The man with the golden tongue

Some people – like Damasus – really, really, *really* wanted to be a bishop. But often at this time one reads of people being elected bishops very reluctantly. One of those was a man called John of Antioch. Or, as he is better known, John Chrysostom (*c.*347–407).

'Chrysostom' is a later nickname. It means 'golden-mouthed' and is testimony to the thing for which John was – and is – most famous: he was the first of the star preachers. During his sermons, congregations frequently broke out into applause and cheers (much to his irritation). He had trained as a lawyer, where he saw first-hand how the power of rhetoric could be used and abused.* He left the law and became a monk. After six years of studying Scripture (two of them spent alone in a cave) he had to return to his home in Antioch following a bout of ill health. His preaching there attracted a lot of attention and when, in September 387, Nectarius, Bishop of Constantinople, died, John was 'recruited' from

---

* He once quoted the example of Jacob as someone who told a lie 'which was not a deceit, but an economy'. Yes, this man invented the phrase 'economical with the truth'.

Antioch. The imperial troops feared a riot in Antioch if the people knew their star preacher was being transferred.* So the imperial emissaries called him to a Really Very Important Secret Meeting, outside the city walls. When John turned up, the imperial guards kidnapped him and took him 800 miles to Constantinople as a prisoner. The Constantinople church took its head-hunting very seriously.

The high-ups in Constantinople thought they were getting a great entertainer. What they got was a curmudgeonly old radical. John hated the lavish pomp of the court. 'The desire to rule', he proclaimed, 'is the mother of all heresies.' He argued for the social redistribution of wealth. He even suggested that all private property should be abolished, as it was in the days of the apostles. He threw all the ornate luxury furniture out of the bishop's residence, sold all the gold plate and gave the money to the poor. He cancelled the lavish catering contracts and ate alone in his own room. And he attacked women who had chamber pots made out of silver: 'What then can be more senseless than the wealthy? . . . Do you pay such honour to your excrements, as to receive them in silver? I know that you are shocked at hearing this; but those women that make such things ought to be shocked . . .' Great stuff. And to any readers who have gold-plated in their bathrooms . . . well, you know what to do.

The people liked him. They liked that he was so rude about the clergy and the aristocracy. The clergy and the aristocracy were not quite so keen. They thought he was stuck up. And his clergy disliked him, because he began to purge the church of inefficient priests. He made them work harder as well, reintroducing night-time services for those who couldn't make it to church during the day.

Things didn't start to unravel, though, until he began to criticise the behaviour of the empress. (Eudoxia had left her husband, Emperor Arcadius, and taken a string of lovers.) While Chrysostom was absent from the city, she had him deposed and replaced with the man he had left in charge: Severian, Bishop of Gabala.

When Chrysostom returned, he headed straight to church and preached a sermon during which he called the empress 'Jezebel'. His enemies, led by Theophilus, Bishop of Alexandria, had him put on

---

* Some of them might have been happy. He told his flock off in Antioch for skipping church in order to see strip shows put on by a local pagan cult, featuring 'women swimming and revealing all their physical attributes'. I suppose that's one strategy for evangelism.

trial, accused of misuse of church funds, of violent and tyrannical behaviour towards his clergy, of having 'private interviews with women' and of being a glutton in private. In short, pretty much everything they could think of. The emperor banished the bishop for life.

When the people found out, they rioted in protest. Constantinople was in revolt. And then there was an earthquake, which the empress, scared stupid, believed had been caused by the banishment of John. So he was recalled, and carried into the city on the shoulders of the adoring people. Theophilus fled to Alexandria.

Things settled down to an uneasy truce, until the empress decided to have a statue of herself made and put on a column in front of the church of St Sophia. Its unveiling was accompanied by 'boisterous and licentious revelry', which interrupted the church services inside. This time John didn't call the empress Jezebel. Instead he called her Herodias – a reference to the scheming, manipulative, murderous wife of Herod Antipas.

He was deposed and the emperor sent troops to drag him away. For the greater part of Easter week Constantinople was like a city that had been stormed. Private dwellings were invaded to root out clandestine assemblies. Supporters of Chrysostom – the Joannites, as they were called – were thrown into prison on the slightest suspicion, and scourged and tortured to compel them to implicate others.*

On 5 June 404 John surrendered of his own accord to avoid any further bloodshed. He was exiled to Cucusus, a remote village in the Taurus Mountains. After some time there he was ordered to the appropriately named town of Pityus, 'the most ungenial and inhospitable spot in the whole empire, and therefore the most certain to rid them quickly of his hated existence'. It was this final journey that killed him. His guards were instructed to force him to march, regardless of the weather or his health. If he died on the way, it was hinted, they might gain a promotion.

The journey was a slow martyrdom. One account describes his body, wizened and browned by the sun, as being like a ripe apple ready to fall from the tree. He died just outside the town of Comana on 14 September 407, aged sixty. It is not known if the guards were promoted.

Thirty-one years later his body was taken and reinterred with great pomp right next to the altar in the Church of the Holy Apostles, the

---

* In subsequent interrogations two clerics were tortured to death. Others barely escaped with their lives.

burial place of the imperial family and of the bishops of Constantinople. The young emperor Theodosius II assisted at the ceremony and asked pardon for the way his parents had treated John.

Let's be clear: John was no saint. (That is, he *is* a saint, now. But he wasn't then, if you see what I mean.*) He was irascible, intemperate, angry. It is easy to applaud his stinging rhetoric against those with wealth and power, but he had a nastier side. He was virulently anti-Semitic. 'The Jew will live under the yoke of slavery for ever,' he said. 'God hates the Jews, and on judgement day, he will tell their sympathisers, "Depart from me, friends of my murderers!"'

He was equally pro-slavery (he was the first to suggest that Onesimus in Paul's letter of Philemon is a runaway slave, something the letter itself never says). In this he is similar to many we shall meet along the course of Christian history to come: great men in many ways, but seriously flawed.

Talking of whom . . .

AUGUSTINE

Name: Aurelius Augustinus.
Aka: Augustine of Hippo.
Nationality: North African. Born in Tagaste, Numidia.
Dates: 354–430.
Appearance: Not known, but he was probably black.
Before he was famous: Student. Rhetorician.
Famous for: Writing. Theology. Author of *Confessions* and *City of God* among tons of other stuff.

Why does he matter? Shaped the thinking of the western church more than any other theologian save Paul. Shaped ideas on original sin, just war, salvation by grace through faith, even predestination.

Could you have a drink with him down the pub? Oh I think so. Just don't get him started on his mother.

* He's the patron saint of education, lecturers, orators and preachers and, less obviously, Constantinople and epilepsy.

Confessions of a church father

One of the churchmen who condemned Priscillian as a heretic and Manichaean was the greatest theologian of his time: Augustine of Hippo.

'Hippo', I should point out, is not a reference to his size, but to Hippo Regius, a Roman city in what is now Algeria, the place where, eventually, he ended up as bishop.

Augustine's life was one of conflict and turmoil. In the background to his writing is the slow, messy spectacle of the decline of the western Roman Empire. While in the foreground is the slow, messy spectacle of Augustine's struggles with himself. Because he spoke no Greek, his ideas have had virtually no impact on the eastern church. But possibly only Paul himself has had more influence on the western church.

He was raised in a small town in North Africa. His father, Patricius, was a pagan; his mother, Monica, a devout Christian. She was the most important influence in his life, but at first Augustine dismissed her simple Christianity. His parents saved all they could in order to send their gifted boy to university at Carthage.

And, typically, the freedom and irresponsibility of university living led him astray (at least in his mother's eyes). He began to paddle in what he later rather sensationally called 'hell's black river of lust'. He did try to read the Bible, but he found its contents truly appalling: full of villainous kings, foolish superstitions and silly fairy-tales. These were not for Augustine. As a sophisticated, cosmopolitan Roman he studied the great pagan philosophers. And he did other sophisticatedly Roman things as well, like taking a mistress (who bore him a son) and becoming a well-known teacher of rhetoric.

Everything was going swimmingly. But he was tormented by inner anxieties. In particular, he looked at the world and wondered where all the evil came from. Since this was 1500 years before Simon Cowell, he couldn't come to the same conclusion that most of us do, so he looked around for another explanation. For nine years he was a Manichee.* But this too began to wane. He moved to Rome and then Milan, and dabbled in Neoplatonism.† And then he met Ambrose.

* As in the Persian dualistic sect. As opposed to a manatee, which is a large aquatic mammal. He was not a large aquatic mammal. Even though he came from Hippo.
† He moved to Rome against his mother's wishes. On the quayside she clung

Augustine had not been much impressed by the Bible, which he thought crude and simplistic. Ambrose's sermons, on the other hand, were rich and deep. Gradually, Augustine felt himself pulled towards Christianity.

He was pushed as well. In Milan his mother caught up with him. Augustine was always tied to her apron strings (not literally, obviously) and she now took him in hand. She persuaded him to find himself a proper wife, which meant sending away the woman he had been living with for twelve years, and the mother of his son. (The son stayed with them.) He was devastated by this. But even so, when he writes about her in his autobiography, *Confessions*, he doesn't even tell us her name. They found a suitable candidate from a nice family, but she was under age, so he had to wait until the engagement could be announced. In the meantime he found another mistress and had, in effect, a breakdown.

One day he was sitting in the garden, wracked by guilt, beating himself up (literally, actually – he was tearing his hair and punching himself in the head), when he heard a child's voice singing, *Tolle, lege. Tolle, lege* (Take, read. Take, read). It was the voice of God. A command. He rushed to a copy of the letters of Paul, which he had placed on a nearby bench, opened it and began to read, 'let us live honourably as in the day, not in revelling and drunkenness, not in debauchery and licentiousness, not in quarrelling and jealousy' (Rom. 13.13–14). The command struck home. Augustine was converted. He resigned his teaching post and decided to become a monk. He and his son were baptized by Ambrose and his mother died, happy that her life's work was complete. Few mothers have had a more profound effect on theology than Augustine's mum, Monica. She was later canonised, but today Santa Monica is better known as a suburb of Los Angeles. Somehow I don't feel this is quite what she would have wanted as a memorial.

Augustine returned to North Africa to set up a Christian community. In 391 he visited a town called Hippo Regius and found the church there struggling. He was persuaded to be ordained priest,

---

to him and refused to let him go, hoping that 'I would either come home or take her with me'. Augustine convinced her that the boat was not due to sail until the next day, so she went off to visit the nearby tomb of St Cyprian. He and his mistress then immediately got on to a boat and left.

and soon became Bishop, remaining in post until his death in 430.*

For the rest of his life he battled with the guilt of his past. He became ashamed, not only of his mistress and his lusts, but of sex itself. We've seen already how the church had begun to prize celibacy. This was given a further boost by Augustine's theology of original sin, which he saw as completely bound up with sex. For Augustine, original sin was a sexually transmitted disease. In this, as is so often the case, Augustine's personal problems shaped his theology – and proved hugely influential.

In Hippo, though, there were other battles. He discovered that the Donatists were still around. Augustus, along with Aurelian, Bishop of Carthage, tried to persuade the Donatists to return to the fold. But the grievance was too old, and too bitter. They started out talking, but these talks soon descended into violence in an ancient equivalent of religious terrorism. More or less exactly the kind of sectarian violence we have seen in recent years in Lebanon, or Ulster, or Nigeria.

Augustine lost patience. He backed the most extreme government intervention. He became, in fact, an apologist for persecution, providing theological justification that he based on a deliberate, terrible misreading of one of the parables of Jesus. Jesus told a story in which a king holding a banquet ordered his slave to 'Go out into the roads and lanes, and *compel* people to come in, so that my house may be filled' (Luke 14.23). The feast was the church. The king was Jesus. It was the duty of the Christian imperial regime to punish heresy and recruit people to the church. By force if necessary.

The problem was that Augustine didn't speak Greek. While the Latin text has 'compel', the Greek originals read 'Bring them in'. Mind you, he came up with other examples too. God had violently converted Paul, he said. It is not loving to someone to tolerate wickedness, he claimed. He did not approve of execution, of course, but a bit of violence is OK. And in justifying this he uses a phrase that becomes rather chilling in this context: 'Love and do what you will.' Nothing wrong, for Augustine, with a bit of tough love.

---

* He was never tempted to leave, partly because Rome was increasingly chaotic, and partly because he suffered terrible seasickness.

Fig. XI. *In Hippo, Augustine takes questions*

Decline and fall

By now, though, the Roman imperial machine wasn't in a particularly good state to compel anyone to do anything. Italy in 401 had something in common with modern-day Reading: in the summer a lot of Goths came to have a good time. Admittedly these were more the hairy, sword-wielding, blood-and-violence kind of Goths than the black-eyeliner-wearing soft-rockers. But to be fair to King Alaric the Visigoth, he and his people were just seeking a place to call home. And they quite fancied Italy.

It would have been possible to accommodate them quite easily, but the emperor of the west at the time was a dimwit called Honorius who was more interested in raising poultry. When Alaric first besieged Rome in 408, Honorius decided the best course of action was to hide in a marsh. It was left to Pope Innocent, the Bishop of Rome, to negotiate with Alaric. In the end Alaric made his demand: large quantities of gold

137

and silver, and also 3,000 pounds of pepper.* Thanks to the negotiating skills of the pope, his demands were met, and when the Visigoths entered Rome they did not attack church property. (He might not have attacked it anyway, because Alaric was a Christian, albeit an Arian.)

But nature abhors a vacuum, especially if that vacuum is called Honorius, and, in the absence of strong leadership, it was up to the next Bishop of Rome to step in. Innocent I (401–417) was in fact a generally good egg. He has been called the first really great pope. He was a man of high ability and impeccable morality, and he was determined to preserve the status and power of the 'papacy' as best he could. As part of this he proclaimed that all matters discussed at synods should come to him for a final decision (a proclamation completely ignored in the east, where they still had an emperor for that sort of thing).

In 410, though, the Goths attacked again, and this time they were not to be bought off with gold, silver and large quantities of seasoning. In an event that sent shockwaves through the empire, the Goths took over Rome.

'If Rome can fall,' wrote Jerome from distant Bethlehem, 'what can be safe?'

Back to Hippo

Well, North Africa for one. Or *safer*, at any rate, and thousands of Romans fled across the Mediterranean to Hippo, where Augustine had the unenviable task of holding them together, cheering them up, and providing them with answers. He did so in his masterwork *The City of God*. It took him thirteen years to write and is an attempt to place the sack of Rome in a much wider, cosmic context.

In the book Augustine imagines two metaphorical cities: one on earth and one in heaven. These two kingdoms are entangled, enmeshed, sometimes even at war with each other. Christians needed to grasp that they were not citizens of the earthly city, but of the heavenly one. Rome was great, but it was the city of man and any peace and happiness found there was therefore transitory. In contrast, the city of God 'possesses peace by faith; and by this faith it lives'. But if Rome was

* Perhaps he was working on a really big steak *au poivre*.

the earthly city, where was the heavenly city to be found? Augustine sometimes seems to identify it with the church. (Certainly over the next thousand years that's how the medieval church saw it. They were always happy to equate their opponents with citizens of the earthly city.)

Augustine argued that believers are saved by grace through faith in Jesus Christ, but that such grace can be found only within the church. But who made up 'the church'? Augustine developed the idea of the 'invisible church'. Not all within the visible church are Christians – only God knows truly who is or isn't. And he knows who will become a Christian, because they have been called by God before all of time. 'Many who seem to be outside the church are really inside,' he said, 'and many who seem to be inside are really outside.' It's only in retrospect, therefore, that we shall know who the true church was. This is not a blanket inclusion – there are some people who are obviously not chosen. But we can't just exclude people from the church because they seem to be horrendous sinners: in Augustine's theology we're all born sinners. That, in turn, is why you have to baptise babies. And that is why – in Catholic and mainline Protestant theology – everyone is born into the church.

He also had a very western take on the Trinity. He used the analogy of the human mind, defining its three activities as memory, understanding and will (or love). Different tasks, but one mind doing all of them. He almost seemed, though, to relegate the Spirit to third place. In the eastern creeds the Spirit proceeded from the Father, but Augustine talked of the Spirit proceeding from the Father *and* the Son. It may not sound like much, but it was going to cause a *lot* of rows later on.

A very British heresy

Augustine's arguments about original sin were responsible, albeit unintentionally, for a new heresy that arrived in Rome in the last decades of the fourth century. And this is a proper, well-made heresy. Because it's the first heresy from Britain. Oh, it makes you proud.

Pelagius was a British monk who was working in Rome as a kind of spiritual director to a number of high-born Roman converts. In the time-honoured tradition of virtually any Briton on coming into contact with Johnny Foreigner, he was pretty unimpressed. These people weren't serious about Christianity: they had no real intent to change their lives. They weren't, in fact, making any attempt to try not to sin.

One day Pelagius heard a public reading of Augustine's *Confessions*, where Augustine was talking about his struggles with chastity. Augustine seemed to be saying that he couldn't possibly fight this sin in his own strength: he could do it only if God gave him the strength to do it. Augustine's concept of original, inherited sin seemed to imply that we can do nothing about sin ourselves. You could not overcome sin except through God's Spirit. It's all up to God.

To Pelagius it seemed that Augustine just wasn't making an effort. He argued that humans were not so fallen, so corrupt that they could do nothing towards their own salvation. Pelagianism, the doctrine that developed from his works, argued that Adam's sin was not an infection, but an example, a warning; just as Christ's goodness is an example to us all. We aren't born either damned or saved. We have free will. It's up to us.

It was not that he didn't believe in grace. In the few pieces of his writing that have survived censorship and destruction he made it clear that all good works are done only with the grace of God. But he did not see this grace as overpowering us, but enabling us. God wasn't pulling our strings like a puppet master: he was helping us along. 'In all men free will exists equally by nature,' he wrote, 'but in Christians alone it is assisted by grace.'

Pelagius gathered followers in Rome, but when the city fell in 410 his disciples scattered throughout the rapidly diminishing empire. One of them – Celestius – arrived in Augustine's backyard, in North Africa. Celestius took Pelagianism to the extreme, arguing that, since there was no original sin, there was no need for infant baptism. There was nothing, in fact, to forgive.

Augustine led the fight against these ideas. And he recruited Jerome as well, who helped out in his own uniquely tactful way by calling Pelagius 'a hound of Albion, who is like a mountain of fat'.

Eventually all the supporters of this extreme Pelagianism were dismissed from their posts. But the fight – as fights always do – pushed Augustine into ever more extreme positions. He almost certainly accused Pelagius of saying things Pelagius never actually said. Augustine declared that the sin of Adam had made it *impossible* for human beings not to sin (*non posse non peccare* in Latin). If you do good deeds, that's just because God has enabled you to be good. But then he argued that not only were all human impulses to do good a result of God's grace, but that God predetermines who should receive this grace in an entirely arbitrary way. God had chosen, before time, who would be foreordained to be saved through grace. It was, in fact, predestination, 1,000 years BC (Before Calvin).

The strength of opposition from bishops in Africa, and from the western emperor, Honorius, forced Pope Zosimus to excommunicate both Celestius and Pelagius in 418. But they were long gone by then, living in the east, where their opinions caused much less bother. Unlike Augustine, Pelagius was fluent in both Greek and Latin. He was never condemned as a heretic in the east.

Augustine, more than any other theologian, shaped the thinking of the church in the west for the next thousand years. And he was a western, Latin-speaking theologian. In some ways you might say he got (himself) lost in translation. His theory of original sin, for example, was partly based on a faulty Latin translation of Romans. Theologians in the east didn't proclaim either original sin or predestination as part of the faith. 'God wishes all to be saved,' said John Chrysostom, 'but forces no one.'

Anyway, there were more pressing problems for the church in the west. By the time Augustine died in Hippo in 430 the Franks were rampaging in Gaul, the Lombards in North Italy, the Angles and the Jutes in Britain. Even Augustine was living in a city under siege. Hippo was being attacked by the Vandals, who were tired, presumably, of simply destroying bus stops throughout the empire. They would go on to capture all of North Africa and persecute the church, the city of God that Augustine had done so much to define.

There's something about Mary

Rome – and much of the western empire – was occupied territory. But in the east things were going on as normal: people were fighting, clerics were arguing and heresy was breaking out left, right and centre.

In 428 Nestorius, a cleric from Antioch, was elected Bishop of Constantinople. Bishop Cyril of Alexandria was outraged by this appointment, partly because Nestorius hailed from that great rival city, Antioch, but mainly because Nestorius started attacking one of the Alexandrians' favourite titles for Mary: *theotokos*, 'God-bearer'.

By the fifth century Mary had been transformed from a fourteen-year-old peasant girl into a queen mother figure. Nestorius hated this. 'Don't make the virgin a goddess!' he cried. And you can see why he was concerned. In Luke's Gospel Mary sings a song when she is told she is pregnant. Known as the Magnificat it has, for many centuries, been embedded in the liturgical language of the church. But it seems at odds with such a setting. It throbs with the language of class war. It talks of the poor being lifted up and the hungry filled, while the powerful are torn from their thrones and the rich are sent away empty. This is emphatically not the song of the mother of an emperor.

Devotion to Mary, though, had been steadily growing for decades. Centuries, even. Much of the initial impetus came from the churches of the east, in Syria and Asia. The feasts associated with Mary – the Purification and the Annunciation, as well as the commemorations of her birth and passing, or Dormition – would be popularised in Rome by Pope Sergius at the end of the seventh century. And Sergius' family came from Antioch.

Mary began to accumulate titles. Like *theotokos*. God-bearer. The title *theotokos* had been encouraged in some quarters because it was another way of ensuring that Jesus was seen as fully divine. Nestorius, however, thought it was stupid: How could an earthly woman be the bearer of God? 'Mary did not give birth to God,' he said, 'A creature cannot deliver her Creator.' So he preferred the title of *Christotokos*, 'Christ-bearer'. Nestorius insisted that Mary was the mother of the human Jesus, not the divine God.

His opponents sensed an opening: Was he saying that Jesus was *just* a man? In Alexandria Cyril (who had never got over the fact that the council of Constantinople had, unsurprisingly, declared Constantinople to be the leading church in the east) claimed that Nestorius was dividing the two natures of Jesus. Cyril was an uncompromising, ruthless operator who ruled Alexandria like a mob boss. He had been installed as Bishop with the help of a rent-a-thug mob of rioters, and one of his first acts was to burn all the synagogues and expel all the Jews.

A council was called in Ephesus in 431, in St Mary's church, appropriately enough. Nestorius had supporters in Antioch, but they were late arriving. And Cyril had the support of the emperor's sister, the empress Pulcheria. She was a self-styled virgin empress, so she felt like, you know, she really *got* Mary. Nestorius made the mistake of engaging in a smear campaign against her and she therefore made sure that Cyril won the battle: Nestorius was condemned and deposed. Undaunted, when Nestorius' supporters eventually made it through the roadworks and arrived at the venue, they held their own council next door and deposed Cyril.

The emperor was at least even-handed. Although he ratified the title *theotokos*, he arrested both bishops. They then adopted significantly different strategies: Nestorius spent his time in prison regretting that he had ever left the monastery, while Cyril busied himself bribing top figures in the imperial court. So Nestorius was, in the end, condemned.

When Cyril died, one bishop predicted that the dead would hate his company so much that they would return him to the land of the living.

Three-way split

Despite the condemnation of Nestorius, the row simmered on. The emperor had condemned Nestorius, sure, but he hadn't exactly endorsed the Alexandrians. So, typically, everyone overreacted and went to the other extreme – as represented by an archimandrite in Constantinople called Eutyches.* The problem with the Nestorians was the idea that in the incarnate Christ there were two distinct Persons, one divine and the other human. Mary was, in a way, giving birth to twins, just in one body. Christ had, therefore, two natures. Eutyches countered with the idea that Christ had a *single* nature: that his human nature was utterly absorbed in the divine. His followers became known as Monophysites, from the Greek: *mono* + *physis* = 'single nature'.†

This was felt to be as heretical as Nestorius' view, just in the opposite direction. The new Bishop of Constantinople, Flavian, accused Eutyches of heresy and had him removed from his post. Eutyches – perhaps following the honourable example of Chrysostom – appealed to the emperor and to his fellow-monks; to anyone who would listen, frankly. The row unleashed chaos. There was council after council, bishops were sacked and unsacked, there were massive rows between Rome, Constantinople and Alexandria.

A council was arranged in Ephesus in 449. Eutyches appealed to

---

* An archimandrite is a leader of several monasteries, not a fossil. Although, frankly, he was getting on a bit. 'Archi' means 'to lead'. So archbishop – leader of a group of bishops – and architect – leader of a group of, er, tects.
† However, both the two-nature and the single-nature Christians simply prefer to call themselves orthodox. In their eyes it is the other lot who are heretics.

Pope Leo I (440–461), who saw this as a chance to establish papal supremacy in matters of theology. Leo was rather keen on supremacy. Indeed, as the Roman Empire crumbled around him, Leo resurrected an old title, *pontifex maximus*, 'high priest', a title that had once been used by emperors such as Augustus. Now Leo took it for the pope.

This was an eastern problem, and Leo certainly wasn't going to travel all the way to Constantinople, but he sent a written judgement, known simply as the *Tome* (Latin for text or letter), which he confidently believed would sort the whole thing out. Perhaps it might have, if it hadn't been completely ignored. (It may not even have been read out.)* Instead, the Monophysites were victorious, largely because they had the backing of the emperor, his soldiers and a group of incongruously armed monks. Bishop Flavian was not only deposed, but was, apparently, beaten to death by Egyptian clergy.

The situation changed, though, when the emperor died in a riding accident and his sister, Pulcheria, took over. She was an enemy of the Monophysites in Constantinople. Being a girl, of course (albeit a sixty-year-old one), she wasn't allowed actually to rule, but she armed herself with a thoroughly house-trained husband, and through him called a further council at Chalcedon, in 451.

At Chalcedon Leo's *Tome* had its delayed premiere. According to the suspiciously fulsome official account, it was met with rapturous approval. The assembled bishops cried out, 'This is the faith of the fathers, this is the faith of the Apostles. So we all believe, thus the orthodox believe. Peter has spoken thus through Leo', before continuing, 'Leo, Leo he's the man, if he can't do it, no pope can', etc.†

The council decided that both extremes – Nestorius and Eutyches – were wrong and they endorsed the teachings of Leo, Cyril and the late Flavian. But the empress pushed for more. She wanted them to come up with a definitive, watertight statement about Jesus. So they produced what has been known as the 'Definition of Chalcedon'. This

---

* The only western representatives were an otherwise unknown bishop called Julius and a deacon called Hilarius, who, hilariously, later became Pope. These represented Pope Leo I. Originally there was a third member of their team – a priest called Renatus, but he died on the way. Honestly, the lengths some people will go to to get out of a meeting . . .

† Once again, Leo didn't attend in person. He sent a five-man delegation, none of whom died on the way. There were also two bishops from North Africa. Apart from that, the rest of the some 600 delegates were from the east.

stated that Jesus was 'perfect in divinity and also perfect in humanity; truly God and truly man, of a rational soul and body; consubstantial with the Father according to his divinity, and consubstantial with us according to his humanity'.

It went on to state that 'the distinction of natures being by no means taken away by the union, but rather the property of each nature being preserved'. I hope you've got that. No? Me neither. But let's just say that Chalcedon stated that Christ is entirely God and entirely man, and that his humanity and divinity are neither separate nor completely merged. Having established that to everyone's satisfaction, they went on to make some other decisions, notably that bishops were not allowed to sell ordinations, and that the clergy should not form lynch mobs, carry off women or loot the houses of bishops after their death. I must remind my vicar of this.

They also took the opportunity to further condemn Nestorius, who had by now died in his remote, high-security Egyptian prison. The puppet emperor ordered Nestorius' writings burned, and any children bearing his name were to be renamed and rebaptised.

And that was that. Game over.

Oh, for heaven's sake, of course it wasn't. Many sections of the eastern church simply refused to sign up to what they saw as a fudged compromise. And Chalcedon didn't actually answer any of the questions: it just booted the questions into touch. Which is the problem with such councils, of whatever flavour: you cannot force people to be moderate. You can aim for the middle of the road, but that leaves plenty of room in the outside lanes for people to race away in some other direction. That's what happened at Chalcedon. Those who believed differently went on believing differently.

The Nestorians packed their bags and left. They went further east, into the Persian Empire, where they formed one of the longest-lasting and most neglected branches of the church, a church that was active for centuries and that even sent missionaries to Arabia, China and India. They were, in fact, much more successful in these areas than their western colleagues.

Other churches also refused to sign up. In Egypt the church split into two branches, a minority who accepted Chalcedon and the majority who remained Monophysite. The Armenian and Georgian churches, who had not been represented in the council's discussions, also dissented. (And in 450 there were still Donatists, Novatians, Arians, Montanists, and even Marcionites, around.) These churches simply withdrew from the imperial faith.*

Convinced that (from their point of view) heresy was endemic in the empire, they moved to the margins, to Persia, Syria, to the Coptic-speaking areas of Egypt. This had two effects. The first was that the centre of orthodox Christianity – the children of Chalcedon – shifted a bit to the west. The second was that two centuries later, when Islamic Arabs started attacking the empire, these branches of Christianity refused to fight for what they saw as a heretical empire.

Chalcedon, historically depicted as a triumph of orthodoxy, actually left Christianity split into three and seriously weakened the empire in the east.

The man in a field-mouse suit

Leo's *Tome* had carried the day, even though he hadn't got entirely the respect he thought he deserved. Back at home, though, he had more pressing problems. Big problems. Problems riding horses, problems wielding axes and swords. Problems heading for Rome.

The Huns were coming.

The Huns were a savage race who didn't bother with little distractions like houses or cooking or hygiene. They slept in the open, and wore clothing made from the skins of field mice – which must have needed a lot of stitching, one would have thought. Their leader was Attila, a swarthy, bearded man with beady little eyes. (Maybe that's why he liked wearing field-mice skins: he looked like one. A big one. A big scary one.)

In 452 this particular field mouse was on the rampage, heading for Rome, when he stopped. No one knows why Atilla the Hun stopped outside Rome, but Leo somehow persuaded Attila to halt. How he did it we don't know – the traditional story credits Leo with persuading him that terrible wrath-of-God style punishments would be visited on Atilla and his army. A more likely explanation involves a short

---

* Although, historically, these churches have been called 'Monophysite', they resented – and still resent – the label. They prefer the term Miaphysite, which also means 'one nature' but in the sense of one united nature. In Christ the divine and the human nature are united in one. It's still a compound nature, but mixed up into one.

conversation and a huge amount of money. Maybe their supply lines were seriously overstretched. Maybe Leo threatened to read Atilla his *Tome* if he didn't behave. Or maybe the Huns had heard of a large number of troops from Constantinople who were heading their way.

Whatever the case, Attila turned back. He died a year later, following a particularly strenuous wedding night with one of his many brides. He was buried inside three coffins, one of lead, one of silver and one of gold, and all those who witnessed his burial were killed. As a security strategy it was highly successful: his tomb has never been found.

Fig. XII. *Outside Rome, Leo threatens Attila with the wrath of God*

But you know how it is with barbarians. You wait for ages and then they all come along at once. Three years later Gaiseric and his Vandals arrived and they did *not* turn back. Leo met with them outside the walls and, again, pleaded for moderation. He managed to persuade them only to sack and loot the city, but not to burn it to the ground.

Leo may not have got the respect he deserved in Chalcedon, but he was widely respected in Rome. And that is why he is one of only two popes known as 'the Great'. When he died, he was buried in the porch of St Peter's, but two hundred years later he was reburied inside the basilica of St Peter's itself – the first pope to be accorded this honour.

By the time of his death, however, the decline and fall of the Roman Empire was complete. Rome was a shadow of its former self. The buildings were ruined and the glory long gone.

Yes, there was no doubt about it. The Mighty Roman Empire™ had definitely both declined and fallen.

THINGS YOU LEARN FROM CHRISTIAN HISTORY

NO. 4

Sometimes it's hard to work out who the barbarians are

Sometimes the man to be scared of is not the hairy, grunting bloke with the axe, but the one in silk speaking Latin.

4 Barbarians, Byzantium and Benedict

Now who's wearing the trousers?

Empires are like relationships. When they fall apart, they rarely do so in a neat and orderly fashion. There are rows, tears, drunken abuse, the lawyers get called in and there are massive arguments over who gets custody of the provinces.

Certainly the decline and fall of the Formerly Mighty Roman Empire™ was a long drawn-out and messy affair.

The last emperor of the west was named Romulus Augustus. Perhaps he was named in the hope that combining the name of the founder of Rome and its greatest emperor could restore the old magic. For all the good it did, they might as well have called him Kevin. He paid barbarian troops to fight for him, and was quite surprised when, in 476, they turned round and deposed him.

It didn't make much difference. By then most of the west was already under the control of various barbarian tribes. Some of these had even arrived in Italy on the suggestion of the emperor in Constantinople. He was a man with the rather sci-fi name of Emperor Zeno and for a long time he had been fighting the Ostrogoths, a semi-nomadic people who lived in the lands north of the Black Sea. Zeno suggested that what the Ostrogoths really needed was a place to live where it was warmer, had great pasta and was ruled by an idiot called Kevin Romulus. So, in 488, Theodoric and his Ostrogoths set out on one of the great package holidays of history. Five years later they ruled Italy.

Theodoric was an Arian Christian.* And he turned Ravenna into his

---

* Nominally at least. He had agreed to rule jointly with a rival barbarian leader, Odoacer. At the official banquet to celebrate the agreement Theodoric

capital, building not only magnificent palaces, but wonderful churches. They might have been barbarians, but they were not barbaric. Part of what made them such an effective fighting force was that they had invented trousers, which meant that they could ride fast around Europe on horseback, engage in widespread carnage *and* look good in nightclubs.

And Theodoric was generally tolerant of other religions. He allowed the Jews of Genoa to rebuild their synagogue. When Christians attacked Jews in Ravenna, Theodoric fined them all and made them pay damages.

At this point things could have gone a number of ways for the western church.* They could have sought help from their family in the east, but they didn't. They could have made accommodation with the Arian faith of their conquerors, but they didn't. They could have disappeared entirely, but they didn't.

Instead they started to steer their own course, to seek their own allies. It was time for independence.

Frankly speaking

Despite the collapse of the old kingdom, the kingdom of God was growing. One of the many warring tribes in Europe was the Franks.† Their rather spicy leader, Clovis, married a Burgundian princess called Clotilda. The Burgundian tribe were orthodox Latin Christians, and Clotilda recommended that Clovis apply immediately. Clovis refused, but then, like soldiers before and since, he found himself in the middle of a battle that was not going well. So he prayed: 'O Jesus Christ, Clotilda tells me you're the son of the Living God. If you give me victory I will be baptised and follow you. Terms and conditions apply.' Or words to that effect.

Jesus – who by now appears to have become a huge fan of warfare – answered his prayer and the Franks won. So, on Christmas Day 499, Clovis was baptised along with all his three thousand soldiers, thus establishing the French military principle 'all for one and one for all' so beloved of the later musketeers. He took to wearing something he called 'a

---

came up behind Odoacer and sliced him in half, top to bottom.

* All right, I accept that at any point things could go a number of ways. But let's leave the multiverse speculation for the moment.

† If you think that name is rather mundane, there was a barbarian tribe near the Black Sea called the Alans.

salvation-giving war-helmet' and went on to take the whole of Gaul. The Franks had arrived.

Fig. XIII. *At the baptism of Clovis, not everyone is happy*

The emerald isle

The church was expanding, penetrating into the most savage, marshy, boggy wastes. Or, as we call it today, Ireland. Ireland was never part of the Roman Empire; even the Romans weren't *that* desperate for territory. But Christianity went where Romans feared to squelch.

The evangelisation of Ireland was the work of, ironically, an Englishman. Or a Welshman. Or at least a Romano-Briton. OK, whatever else he may have been, Patrick wasn't Irish. He was born in Britain at *Bannavem Taberniae*. Sadly, we have no idea where this actually was. It was probably in the south of Britain, somewhere like Somerset, since that was where the more heavily populated Romano-British settlements were to be found. His family were Christian: his father was a deacon and his grandfather a priest.*

---

* He describes his father as a Decurion, which indicates some kind of local town official.

When he was sixteen, Patrick was captured by a raiding party and taken into slavery in Ireland, where he worked as a herdsman. Eventually he escaped and made his way home. And there he became a priest. Many years later he had a vision of a man coming from Ireland with letters, and he seemed to hear Irish voices appealing to Patrick to come to help them. So he returned, this time of his own accord.

He converted various tribal kings and established monasteries that became the hub of Christian mission in the country. 'Those who never knew God, worshipping impure idols, have become a people of the Lord and are called sons of God,' he said. 'The sons and daughters of Irish kings are now monks and virgins of Christ.'

The church in Ireland was different to the rest of Europe. It was not centred on major cities and towns, for the simple reason that there weren't any. So it never developed a major emphasis on bishops. Instead, the significant figures in Irish Christianity were abbots and abbesses, and Christianity in Ireland was driven by the monasteries.

They exported this monastery-based model when Irish monks took Christianity into northern climes. An ex-prince named Columba (521–597) sailed to a little island off Scotland called Iona. Others took it to northern England, Cornwall, Brittany, Denmark, Germany . . .

Fig. XIV. *Columba looks out towards Scotland*

The city of God

While the western empire was busy falling, the eastern empire was rising to its greatest heights.

On 1 August 527 Justinian I ascended to the throne in Constantinople. Justinian (*c.*482–565) was a man with outstanding administrative skills, vaunting ambition and the temper of a bull hippo with a migraine. His big dream was to restore a united empire, stretching from Spain to Syria. Determined to bring the Italian peninsula back into this empire, he oversaw a series of military campaigns that vanquished the Vandals in Africa and ousted the Ostrogoths from Italy. He reconquered Illyria and southern Spain, and, in 540, Rome.*

Justinian redefined the empire. A natural organiser, he codified imperial law. As part of this, Justinian renegotiated the relationship between the emperor, the empire and . . . er . . . God. The empire was declared to be the earthly manifestation of the kingdom of heaven. And that meant that the emperor was God's representative, God's living icon, in fact. Church and state were a single entity.

It sounds a bit over the top, but if you entered Constantinople you would have seen this represented in physical form. The churches were filled with icons and were beautifully decorated. Beautiful music filled the air. On the great feast days the streets of the cities were filled with richly adorned processions, heading to churches designed to represent the kingdom of God.†

This was Augustine's city of God made visible.

Well, in some ways. Scratch a bit under the surface and it wasn't hard to find the same old violence and intolerance. Jews were forbidden to build synagogues, read their Hebrew Scriptures or testify in court against Christians. And when, in 532, rioters attempted to remove Justinian from the throne, he sent in the troops, leading to the deaths

---

* I say 'he', but the campaigns were mainly carried out by his brilliant general Belisarius, perhaps the greatest military commander in history. Justinian was always jealous of Belisarius, who he secretly thought had ambitions for the throne. In fact, Belisarius was unswervingly loyal.

† The display of beauty was helped by the addition of silk. Silk had been jealously guarded by the Chinese for centuries, but in 552 some traders smuggled silkworms out of China hidden in bamboo tubes. The cat (or in this case the worm) was out of the bag.

of thirty thousand people.* According to his adviser Procopius – not, it has to be admitted, the most unbiased observer – Justinian's actions were those of the devil: 'Sooner one could number the sands of the sea than the men this Emperor murdered,' Procopius said. In the riots the church of Hagia Sophia was burned down. Justinian replaced it with a new, even more magnificent, building which still stands there today (though it is no longer a church).

In the east the church and empire were inextricably mixed. While the pope operated largely independently of direct political influence from the emperor, the Bishop of Constantinople lived above the shop. (Not literally. He had a palace.) The emperor was his line manager. And the emperor's line manager? Well, that would be God. This managerial structure was outlined by Justinian in an edict of 535. He described how God had given two great blessings to humanity: priest and emperor. God was the ultimate source of law, but he had delegated earthly authority to the divinely ordained emperor. And the emperor was therefore the source for all earthly laws. The priests, meanwhile, had, according to Justinian, responsibility for 'matters divine'.

Justinian's Constantinople gave physical form to this relationship, and from the sixth century onwards court ceremonial incorporated an increasing amount of liturgy. Emperors were crowned in churches from 602 onwards. But there was bound to be tension, not least because of the somewhat blurry line between matters divine and matters secular. Many emperors took a deep interest in theological matters and expected to overrule the patriarchs, as they became known.† From the sixth century to the fall of Constantinople in the fifteenth century (we'll come to that in . . . well a few hours, probably) over 30 per cent of all

---

* The rival clans of rioters were grouped around two rival chariot racing teams: the Blues and the Greens. They were split along political and theological lines. Emperor Justinian I was a supporter of the Blues. It was a bit like the association of Catholics and Protestants with Celtic and Rangers football clubs. Only with horses. And a lot more death.

† Around this time the bishops of the five main administrative centres of the Christian world started calling themselves 'Patriarch' – they were the 'leading fathers' of the church. We think of it as a title used solely in the eastern church, but it first appears applied to Pope Leo I. Like the word 'pope', it began as an honorific title for any venerable bishop. In the fifth and sixth centuries the bishops of Besançon and Lyons, for example, were called patriarchs.

patriarchs were either deposed or forced to resign because of fallings out with the emperor.

The man who consecrated the new building in 562 was Eutychius, Bishop of Constantinople, and his story illustrates these tensions only too well. Two years after his starring role in opening the new building, he fell out with the emperor over a theological issue (of course) and was charged with using ointments, eating delicate meats, and praying for too long. He was exiled to Amaseia where he settled down in a monastery and gained a reputation for healing. He healed a blind man and restored a mother's milk so effectively that she ended up acting as a wet-nurse to the entire neighbourhood. He was never that holy in office. Turns out people got more saintly the further they moved from Constantinople.

Despite Justinian's desire for uniformity, the cracks in Christianity that Chalcedon had attempted to paper over were still evident. Since Chalcedon the orthodox view had been that Christ possessed two natures in one person. He was both divine and human. The Monophysites, of course, had never accepted this. To them – and they were numerous – Christ was God in the shape of a man. Egypt was pretty much completely Monophysite, Syria and Palestine were also heavily in favour. The Monophysites had friends in high places too. Justinian's powerful, strong-willed empress, Theodora (500–548), was a devout Monophysite and began to alter the liturgy to reflect her own theological convictions. She even managed to install a new pope – a man called Vigilius, who was made Pope by Belisarius. In return for the favour Vigilius promised to reject the principles laid down at Chalcedon and adopt the Monophysite creed.

Things weren't helped by the arrival of a fanatical, charismatic Monophysite evangelist called Jacob Baradaeus. His surname means 'the man who has a horse-cloth' and refers either to his widespread travelling or the fact that he had a My Little Pony blanket. Jacob was the Bishop of Edessa, and he decided that he would win the east for Monophysitism. Often in disguise, he rode through Syria and Palestine, creating, effectively, an organised Monophysite church, ordaining several thousand priests and even consecrating some bishops. This church, the Syriac Orthodox church, is known by his name: the Jacobites. The name is also a nod to James/Jacob of Jerusalem, brother of Jesus.

Justinian was forced into action. He had to do something that looked

(a) decisive and (b) orthodox. But he couldn't afford to alienate Egypt, because that was where most of the empire's grain supplies came from. Plus he was scared of his wife. Not to mention that he couldn't get his hands on Jacob.

So, in the hope that people weren't paying attention, he condemned someone else instead: the Nestorians. Which was a bit of a left-field choice, because they had already been condemned in 431 at Ephesus, and most of them had fled to Persia and were outside the empire. But Justinian thought that maybe he could unite the Monophysites and the orthodox if he found a common enemy.

The plan failed, for one simple reason: it was stupid. The Monophysites were angry because they'd hoped for some recognition and they didn't get any. The orthodox were furious because the emperor wasn't attacking the Monophysites.

Things descended into farce. At one point even the pope was kidnapped to ensure that he took the correct side. He was taken to Constantinople where, although under house arrest, he refused to endorse Justinian's decision and issued his own pamphlets. But eventually he surrendered, admitted all his past errors, signed anything they wanted him to sign, and was released. He died during the journey home.

In the end the Definition of Chalcedon became the official statement of faith of Justinian's empire. And after Theodora's death, he jettisoned the Monophysites, who went off to form their own churches (including the Coptic church of Egypt and Ethiopia).

Meanwhile, outside the empire the Nestorians carried on with their missionary endeavours. Nestorian beliefs were taken into China by a missionary called Alopen. (He later invented muesli. Probably.) There, with a nod to its origins, it was known as 'the religion of Syria' and was given official recognition by the Emperor T'ai-Tsung in 638. Alongside his pioneering work with breakfast cereal, Alopen wrote a kind of Chinese-friendly version of the Christian story, which was engraved on a monument in China. The story tells how 'Aloha, the Three-One, the mysterious unbegotten person, seeing that confused humanity was incapable of finding the road to return home, decided to intervene.'

Ah, so.

BENEDICT

Name: Benedictus of Nursia.
Aka: Benedict, Scholastica's brother.
Nationality: Roman, born in Umbria.
Dates: c.480–c.547.
Appearance: Not known. But probably somewhat scratched.
Before he was famous: Student in Rome.
Famous for: The father of western monasticism.
Why does he matter? Wrote the Benedictine rule, which became the pattern for western monks to follow.
Could you have a drink with him down the pub? No. But you might be able to share a sip of water with him in his grotto.

A night at the Cassino

In Egypt the monastic movement had been kickstarted by Christians who saw how evil the world had become and wanted no part of it. In Italy very much the same thing happened. Benedict of Nursia (*c*.480–*c*.547) was an Italian who, while studying in Rome, was appalled to find that the Holy City was very unholy indeed. So he decided to run away from all that as far as he could.

He fled to the Italian countryside where he lived for three years in a cave and spent many happy hours overcoming temptation by repeatedly throwing himself naked into thorn bushes. By now the works of Pachomius and Basil of Caesarea, with their monastic rules, had been translated into Latin and, at least during the times he wasn't picking thorns out of himself, Benedict decided to follow their example. In 529, accompanied by his sister Scholastica, he founded a monastery at Monte Cassino designed to offer a home for those who were looking for something different to the way of life being offered by the church of the west. And you can't get much more different than flinging yourself into thorn bushes.

CELTIC
CHURCH

CELTIC
CHURCH

Milton
Keynes

Cantuaria

THE

In the six

FRANKS

Parisi

Lugdunum
(Lyons)

Mediolanum
(Milan)

RAVENNA

Italy

VISIGOTHS

ROME

BYZA

Sicilia

Carthage

Mauretania

Africa

MAINLY
WESTERN
OR LATIN
CHURCH

MAIN
OR GE

Several miracles are attributed to him – including miraculously surviving three attempts to poison him by other monks who were annoyed that he refused to become their abbot. Might be a clue as to why he turned them down, really.

Benedict himself is a shadowy figure. We may in fact be talking about several Benedicts: there are suggestions that the ideas attributed to him come from a number of individuals. But the rule attributed to him/them was simple and straightforward, meaning that it could be replicated and adapted by monks wherever they set up. And so the Benedictine rule became the template for monastic life in Europe. Benedict is, indeed, the patron saint of monks. Not to mention cavers, Italian architects and people suffering from nettle rash.

From the earliest days Christians had followed a pattern of fixed-hour prayer. Benedict used this kind of pattern for his rule. To gather the community to prayer from wherever they were in the monastery, Benedictine monks eventually invented machines that rang the bells – or *clocca*, in Latin. And the whole world came to rely on the descendants of these machines: the *clocca*, or, as we know them, clocks.

His monks took vows of poverty, celibacy and obedience. Silence was also encouraged: monks were not allowed to talk too much, or to laugh. It was disciplined, but not harsh: despite Benedict's adventures in the thorn bush, he thought that 'nothing too harsh, nothing too burdensome' should be demanded of the community. Benedictines were expected to remain in their community for life. Their motto was *ora et labora* – 'prayer and work'. They were to work to support themselves and benefit the economy around them. The rest of the time was to be spent praying or studying the Bible. Study was immensely important. Benedictine houses were places of learning, and in the west they preserved and copied many scrolls and books.

GREGORY

Gregory. Here he's wearing designer stubble, in real life he had a beard.

Name: Gregorius.
Aka: Gregory I 'the Great'.
Nationality: Roman.
Dates: c.540–604 (pope from 590 to 604).
Appearance: Medium height. Bearded. Face 'most becomingly prolonged with a certain rotundity'. Dark complexion. In later life he suffered a lot of ill health.

Before he was famous: Civil servant. Imperial prefect in Rome. Benedictine monk.

Famous for: Reorganising the papacy; sending a mission to Britain; first monk to become Pope.

Why does he matter? He reformed the church and brought administrative skill to the papacy. Set a template for the role of the pope for centuries to come.

Could you have a drink with him down the pub? Yep. Although he would probably give your drink away to the poor.

Under new management

The only ancient account of Benedict is found in a four-volume work written around 593. Its author was the next major figure in western Christendom: Pope Gregory I, or, as his fans call him, Gregory the Great.

In 552 Justinian's forces had finally driven the Goths out of Italy. But their 'outstanding success' (official line © Press Office of Justinian I) left the region utterly desolated. The Byzantine forces took over the capital at Ravenna, but were never really strong enough to gain much control. So, when the Goths left, a tribe called the Lombards, led by King Alboin, crossed the Alps and established themselves in the plain that today we still call Lombardy. They marched on Rome, and, with no help forth-coming from the Byzantines, once again it was left to the pope to rescue the city.

Gregory (c.540–604) was the son of a wealthy Roman family. At least one of his relatives had been a pope.* In 573, though, Gregory threw away his successful career as Prefect of Rome, turned the huge family palace on the Caelian Hill into a Benedictine monastery and became a monk himself. (He also founded six more monasteries on family lands throughout Italy and gave away the rest of the family fortune to the poor.)

Why? He thought the end was nigh. The world was 'growing old and hoary, hastening to its approaching death'. What with the Goths, Justinian's army and now the Lombards, Italy was a place of squalor, poverty and disease. 'Everywhere we see mourning,' he wrote, 'from all sides we hear lamentation. Cities are destroyed, military camps are over-turned, fields are laid waste.' Rome was, 'abundantly afflicted with tremendous misfortunes'.

Might as well be a monk, then. But after three happy years in the monastery Gregory was headhunted and sent to Constantinople for six years as a kind of ambassador from the western church. (He lived in the same palace that had been Vigilius' prison.) He didn't enjoy himself, didn't like the eastern empire, and utterly refused to learn Greek, hated the food, moaned about the weather, etc., etc.

After his allotted time in Constantinople he returned to his monas-tery, but when the plague saw off Pope Pelagius I (no, not the heretic), it was obvious to everyone that the next pope should be Gregory. Well, I say obvious; obvious to everyone except Gregory. He was so appalled at the prospect that he fled the city, hidden in a basket. But he was caught, returned to Rome and in 590 became the first monk – and the first of many basket cases – to be elected Pope.†

It was a city in crisis. The Lombards were looming. Rome was full of refugees who had fled from the advancing hordes, including 3,000 nuns. (The nuns weren't part of the hordes: they were part of the refugees. Do keep up.) The Byzantine official in charge of Ravenna was no help whatsoever. It was all up to Gregory. He raided the papal

* His Auntie Doris. No, my mistake; it was Felix III (483–492).

† Popes were elected, at this time, by nineteen deacons who were in charge of Rome. Although they were occasionally referred to as Cardinal, the title wasn't properly used until 100 years later.

treasury to pay them off, but in 598, with no help forthcoming from the east, he negotiated a peace agreement with the Lombards himself.

Then he set about the task of rebuilding Rome. Rome, as everyone knows, wasn't built in a day. More to the point, it wasn't built without paying the builders. Gregory didn't have much ready cash, but he did have a lot of land. The church was by the largest landowner in the west, but a lot of the income from this land was siphoned off by local rulers and rich bishops. Gregory reorganised the administration and ensured not only the collection of rents, but accurate accounts. He established, in fact, a rival to the imperial civil service. Bishops became responsible for keeping things 'straight' in their cities: Gregory refers to them as 'rectors', from the Latin *rectus*, meaning 'straight'.*

At heart Gregory always remained a monk. He argued passionately that the wealth of the church belonged to the poor. Every day twelve paupers joined him for dinner. But he also reformed church practices. He began the Roman Schola Cantorum, the progenitor of the modern cathedral choir school. The style of traditional plainsong that developed in his time is still known as Gregorian chant. He was the first major preacher and teacher to systematically use non-scriptural religious anecdotes and stories to aid his sermons.

What he was, in short, was the Roman church's first great chief executive. He cracked down on the abuses of clerical power, including the sale of bishoprics. He banned clerical marriage and his office manual, a book called *Pastoral Care*, remained the standard instruction manual for clergy for many centuries.

Gregory is responsible for the seven deadly sins. (Not literally responsible. Obviously.) I mean, he invented the list. Or, more properly (and fittingly, given his love of administration), he reorganised them into the final seven we know today. It was the monk Evagrius of Pontus who first drew up a list of eight 'evil thoughts'. They were gluttony, lust, avarice, sadness, anger, acedia (from the Greek word meaning 'not to care', a kind of spiritual can't-be-arsed-ness), vainglory and pride. Evagrius ranked them in order of increasing severity. In the 590s Gregory reorganised the list into seven. He combined vainglory and pride, and acedia and sadness, and brought in envy. Here's his list then: pride, envy, anger, sadness, avarice,

---

* Hence 'correct', 'rectify' and, of course, 'rectum'. Which comes from intestinum rectum, the 'straight intestine'. You see? *This* is the stuff other church histories don't give you.

gluttony and lust. (Later theologians replaced 'sadness' with sloth. And in some lists covetousness replaces avarice.)*

Gregory also put the idea of purgatory squarely at the heart of Catholic theology. Unheard of in the east, he made it part of official dogma, and with it the idea of getting time off in purgatory for doing penance. (Again, his successors were to abuse this idea dreadfully.)

Gregory was truly an excellent leader, and if any pope deserves the epithet 'the great' it would be him. Not that he would have enjoyed the title. He preferred to be known as the 'servant of the servants of the Lord'.

Talking of titles and self-aggrandisement . . . In 588, two years before Gregory became Pope, the Patriarch of Constantinople decided to adopt the title of 'Ecumenical Patriarch'.† Since ecumenical, as we've seen, means 'the whole church', the implication was clear: he was Top of the Popes. His name was John IV 'the Faster', which came from his habit of fasting, rather than his victories in the annual Eastern Patriarchs Half Marathon. Despite complaints from western church leaders the title stuck, and to this day the eastern orthodox leader is still the Ecumenical Patriarch of Constantinople.

Saints alive!

Gregory was a man of simple faith. It was Gregory, as much as anyone, who encouraged a belief in miracles and prophecies and in the relics of the saints, and who kicked off the popular idea of saints as almost magical, folktale heroes and heroines.

Belief in saints had been steadily growing. Since the early days of the church the bones of the martyrs had been venerated. But two things changed when Constantine became (almost) Christian.

First, the shrines of these saints were blinged up to the max. We've seen how he built St Peter's Basilica over the traditional site of St Peter's grave in Rome. But other saints got the full VIC treatment.‡ At the shrine of St Lawrence at Rome Constantine installed flights of stairs leading

---

* The eighth deadly sin – playing your MP3 player too loudly in a train carriage – was put on hold until such a time as it became necessary.
† Actually, other prelates had used the title before, but no one had noticed. John IV was the first one to make a big thing about it.
‡ Very Important Corpse.

up and down from the grave, which he covered with a 'grille of solid silver weighing a thousand pounds'. This restricted access to only the most faithful. While at St Peter's shrine, according to Gregory of Tours, 'Whoever wishes to pray there must unlock the gates which encircle the spot, pass to where he is above the grave and, opening a little window, push his head through and there make supplication that he needs.'

Some people were allowed golden keys that opened these gates, the ecclesiastical equivalent of an Access All Areas backstage pass. Ordinary pilgrims would lower cloths on to the grave below and 'draw them up heavy with the blessing of St Peter'.*

The second major development was that the supply of martyrs dried up. Christians weren't being killed for their faith any more. (At least not proper, orthodox Christians. And the others didn't count.) So more saints had to be found. Some were new saints – one of the earliest 'non-Martyr' saints was Martin of Tours. Elsewhere the bones of famous Christians were miraculously happened upon. St Stephen's bones, for example, were discovered in a field some twenty miles from Jerusalem in 415. The priest who found them was guided by a vision of Rabbi Gamaliel, who, along with Nicodemus, had apparently been buried there. The identification of the bones was confirmed because, on the opening of the coffin, the earth trembled, and the air was filled with 'a smell of sweet perfume . . . such as no man had ever known'. And seventy-three people were healed immediately. Why had this grave not been discovered before? Timing. Augustine said, 'His body lay hidden for so long a time. It came forth when God wished it.'

Once the bones were discovered they might stay in that place with a shiny new church built over the top – or be transferred to more important cities. (Stephen's went to Jerusalem, and others' to Rome.) And there people would visit them. Saints were assumed to be present, somehow, at their shrines. The inscription on the shrine of Martin of Tours ran, 'Here lies Martin the bishop, of holy memory, whose soul is in the hand of God; but he is fully here, present and made plain in miracles of every kind.'

The veneration of saints basically filled a gap. First, saints' days helped to replace the many pagan festivals and feast days that had

---

* Justinian later wrote to Rome requesting some bones of Peter. His request was flatly refused; instead, they sent him one of these cloths. I imagine he was not best pleased.

previously been celebrated. When the fifth-century Bishop of Javols went on a missionary journey into the Auvergne in France, he found peasants celebrating a three-day festival where they would trek to the top of a mountain to make sacrifices to the old gods. He told them to 'acknowledge God and give veneration to his friends'. After that they carried on making the trek up the mountain, but this time to venerate Saint Hilarius, some of whose bones were installed in a shrine there.

Second, saints were people with influence. They were, in the Bishop of Javols' words, 'God's friends'. In Roman society – and especially in court – everything depended on personal contacts and influence. As the church became more and more like the imperial court, cosying up to a pet saint gave people a way of 'having a word' with the right person. Now you could know someone at the heavenly court.

In the heavenly court, as in its earthly counterpart, it's not what you know, but who you know.

A Canterbury tale

Like all great CEOs, though, Gregory was good at spotting opportunities to expand. The Ecumenical Patriarch business had convinced him that there was no point seeking to try to gain influence in Byzantium. So he went in the opposite direction: north and west, to Visigoth Spain and Frankish Gaul and remote Anglo-Saxon Britain.

King Recared, Spain's Visigoth ruler, converted to Catholicism. The Frankish kingdoms (which encompassed modern France, Belgium, the Netherlands, north-west Germany and Switzerland) proved harder – mainly because they were a mass of brutal anarchies and, although theoretically Christian, what clergy there were in those places were usually corrupt and useless.

But Britain . . . Britain had possibilities. So in 597 Gregory sent a man called Augustine to the north.

Augustine was a Benedictine monk, the Prior of St Andrew's Monastery in Rome, where Gregory himself had been a monk. Gregory put him in charge of forty or so brothers and sent them on a mission to England, to rescue Kent from paganism. And if you've been to Gillingham, you'll know what a big ask that was.*

---

* Bede, the eighth-century monk who wrote a history of the English church,

Kent was probably chosen for a couple of reasons: (a) it was convenient for the cross-Channel ferries; and (b) King Aethelbert of Kent had recently married Bertha, daughter of Charibert I the king of Paris, and she was a Christian. So Christianity had what you might call an intro.

Augustine wasn't particularly keen. He was more what you might call terrified. He and his group had only just left Rome when they started to hear terrible stories about the barbarian Angles. Some said they were cannibals. Maybe they mentioned Margate. And winkles. Augustine was sent back to Rome to ask Gregory to call the whole thing off. Gregory refused and sent Augustine back with letters encouraging them to persevere.

In 597 they landed on the Isle of Thanet, which, frankly, is not a good start for any trip. But, according to Bede, King Aethelbert came to meet them and gave them lands to build a monastery near Canterbury. Aethelbert was converted, and Augustine became the first Bishop of Canterbury.

There was a mass baptism of the king's subjects on Christmas Day 597. Hardy folk, these Angles.* Bishops were established at London and Rochester in 604.

The event has been called the conversion of England, but that rather ignores the fact that good chunks of Britain were already converted, thank you very much. We know that British bishops were present at the Council of Arles in 314. Celtic missionaries had done much to establish Christianity in Wales and the north. Mind you, the withdrawal of the Roman legions in 410 led to an upsurge in paganism in the southern parts. If you've ever had paganism in the southern parts you will know how nasty that can be. The invading Anglo-Saxons – themselves pagan – drove the Celtic Christians west. But these western regions, beyond the Anglo-Saxon kingdoms, stayed largely Christian. So what we're talking about at this point was rather the conversion of Anglo-Saxon Britain.†

---

tells a (probably made-up) story in which Gregory saw fair-haired Saxon slaves in the Roman markets and asked where they were from. When told they were 'Angles' Gregory uttered the worst pun in Ecclesiastical History: 'Non Angli sed angeli' – 'Not Angles but Angels'. He really hadn't been to Gillingham.

* Gregory claimed to the Patriarch of Alexandria that over 10,000 people were baptised, but he was probably showing off a bit.

† It may come as a shock to certain political parties who like to tout their Anglo-Saxon roots that the Anglo-Saxons were German immigrants. And weren't Christian.

Fig. XV. *Gregory meets Anglo-Saxons in the slave market*

Gregory, typically, had already made plans for organising the church in Britain. He instructed Augustine to set up two Archbishoprics, in London and York. Gregory probably intended for London to become the centre, but Augustine never transferred there. This may have been because London was not part of Aethelbert's kingdom. Or it may have been the cost of train tickets. Whatever the case, he stayed in Canterbury and when he died, around 604, he was succeeded by Laurence, one of the monks who had come with him from Rome. And that's how Canterbury, not London, became the HQ of English Christianity.

The key issues

Gregory intended for the Celtic branch of the western church to rush joyfully into his organisational chart and come singing and dancing to sit under the central control of Canterbury. But, the native, Celtic church had other ideas. They were based in the north, on the Holy Island, Lindisfarne. And they did things their own way. They set their own date for Easter and the monks even had different hair-cuts.*

Frankly, Augustine played his hand badly. He called a council in 602, at which he failed to show the Celtic contingent enough respect, remaining seated when they entered the room. In return they refused point blank to accept his authority. (Thus began the long British tradition of completely ignoring the Archbishop of Canterbury, which endures to this very day.)

The conflict between the Celtic and Roman church came to a head at a synod in Whitby in 664. It was hosted in part by Hilda, a converted noblewoman, who had become the abbess of a unisex monastery.† The meeting was convened by King Oswy of Northumbria, with the aim of reconciling some of the conflicts between the Celtic and Roman versions of Christianity. The Romans considered the northern Christians uncouth and uncivilised. Meanwhile, the Celts considered the southerners patronising, arrogant, imperialistic, southern softies.

In the argument over the date of Easter one monk compared the two sides thus: 'the Hebrews, Greeks, Latins and Egyptians who are united in their observance of the principal solemnities' versus 'an insignificant group of Britons and Irish' who are 'pimples on the face of the earth'.

This, though, was the key issue. The whole Christian year was centred on the great feast of *Pascha*, or Easter, as it became known. This was the most sacred festival of the Christian year – far more important than Christmas. Ambrose called the three days of Good Friday to Easter

---

* The Roman style was to shave the top of the head, in the form of tonsure that we know today. It's not certain how the Celts did theirs, but they may have shaved in front of a line running from ear to ear. Gothic German monks no doubt kept to the traditional mullet.

† Caedmon, one of the earliest known English poets, who also wrote a verse translation of the Bible, was one of Hilda's monks.

Sunday 'the three most sacred days' of the Christian year. On the Saturday Christians would walk, carrying candles, to the church where, after an all-night vigil, the bishop would baptise new Christians. Then the congregation would celebrate the first Eucharist of Easter.

But the Celts held it at a different time to everyone else. The Celts claimed tradition: their church was founded by saints like Columba, who established the monastery at Iona.* He had performed miracles. The Catholics trumped that with the Damasus defence, i.e. *their* church was founded by Peter. And *he* had been given the keys of heaven. This, apparently, was news to King Oswy. He asked if Columba had also been given a spare set of these keys. When they answered no, he decided that Peter was his man.

Oswy may not have been the sharpest knife in the box, but he was bright enough to know that if you wanted to get into heaven, it paid to be nice to the bloke who had the keys. So after that, British Christianity increasingly came under control of the successor of Peter, the Bishop of Rome.

Evidence that the clergy really didn't understand the local culture can be found in a decision from a local church council in 787, in Calcuth, Northumbria. This banned all pagan tattoos. As far as I know it's never been rescinded, so Geordies – take note.†

Submission

The Byzantine Empire had been fighting the Persian kingdoms for centuries. But in the seventh century a new force emerged from Arabia, a region that hitherto had been known only for tribal conflict. And camels. And sand.

In 610, in a cave near the city of Mecca, a man called Muhammad had a vision. He became a prophet, and, over the next twelve years, gathered many followers. But he also made enemies, and in 622 he was forced out of Mecca to find refuge in the city of Medina. This was the *hegira*, and it marks the beginning of the Muslim era.

---

* Sometimes they were called Ioanan Christians, as in 'from Iona'.
† Tattooing remained popular among royalty, though. After the Battle of Hastings in 1066 one of the ways troops identified Harold's body was because of its tattoos, including the name of his wife, Edith, tattooed over his heart.

LACK OF HUMOUR ALERT: Readers should note that, for obvious reasons, there are no jokes in this section.

Muhammad was sternly monotheistic. He was familiar with both Jewish and Christian religions, but he believed that both had deviated from the true path. He proclaimed one, unified faith under 'the God' (Arabic, *al-ilah*; later shortened to Allah). This faith was Islam, which means 'submission'.

Islam rejected the divinity and resurrection of Jesus, although it recognised both Jesus and Moses as prophets. At the start Muhammad instructed his followers to pray facing Jerusalem, but after violent conflict with the Jews in Medina he changed the direction to be towards Mecca. Despite the conflict with Jews, Islam endorsed circumcision and dietary laws as well as other aspects of Judaism.

But Islam also seems to have adapted some of the practices of early Christianity. Ramadan may come from early Christian observance of Lent: prayer mats and prostrating yourself in prayer were the norm among Christians in the Middle East. In fact, prayer mats were used by Christian monks from Syria to Ireland. You can even see them in the 'carpet' pages of the illuminated Celtic manuscripts.*

One thing it definitely *didn't* adopt was early Christian pacifism. Islam was avowedly militaristic. Muhammad himself returned to Mecca with an army and captured the city in 630. When he died two years later, he left behind a large group of well-armed, highly motivated followers. In 634 an Arab army defeated the Byzantine emperor Heraclius. Twelve years after Muhammad had fled for his life from Mecca the whole of Arabia was Muslim. In the decade following they took all of Syria, Palestine and Egypt.

Most significantly, in February 638, Jerusalem was captured by Muslim forces after a year's siege. The victorious Caliph, Umar, rode into the city in a dignified way. Or as dignified as anyone can be when they are riding a camel. Alone and dressed in the plain robes of a pilgrim, he received the surrender from Sophronius, Patriarch of Jerusalem. He refused to enter the Church of the Anastasis, but went to the Temple Mount, which he found in a ruinous state. He subsequently built a mosque on the ruins.†

* It's even been suggested that the familiar minaret towers of the mosques may have been inspired by the pillars of monks like Simeon.

† In the early 690s, this original building was replaced with what is now known as the Dome of the Rock, a building that bears in the writing on its walls

By the end of the century, Muslim forces had spread west along North Africa to the Atlantic. They even arrived at the walls of Constantinople in 672, but were repulsed.* By 711 the Arabs had conquered North Africa and crossed the straits of Gibraltar into Spain.† Twenty years later they crossed the Pyrenees into France, where, at Poitiers, only 150 miles from Paris, their advance was finally halted by the Frankish ruler Charles Martel.

The effect of all this conquering was devastating for the church. The North African church – the church of Tertullian and Cyprian and Origen and Augustine – was effectively wiped out. Some communities survived, by rather devious means. The St Catherine Monastery below Mount Sinai managed to find a document in its archives in which Muhammad guaranteed protection to the community. (He'd even 'autographed' it with a picture of his own hand.) Just to make sure, they also built a mosque inside the walls, complete with minaret. (It was facing the wrong way, but no one seems to have spotted this.)

Christians were expelled from Arabia itself; in other regions, Christians and Jews were organised into separate communities where they were free to practise their religion in private. But they had to pay special taxes and were allotted second-class status.

Three of the five historic centres of the church – Alexandria, Antioch and Jerusalem – had fallen. The historic homelands of Christianity, its countries of origin, were lost to Christianity. Such Christians as remained had to live with the reality that they were no longer in charge. And barring a brief few decades, they have remained no longer in charge ever since.

---

the earliest datable use of the word 'Muslim'. Perhaps the most famous Islamic building in the world, it was actually built by Greek Christian craftsmen from Byzantium. The Arabs of the time were jolly good at tents, but not so hot on intricate octagonal architecture.

* The Greeks used something called 'Greek fire' to destroy the Arab ships – a mix of petrol, sulphur and pitch fired from a copper tube. It was the seventh-century equivalent of napalm.

† Gibraltar is actually an Arabic name: it comes from Jabal-ı Tārıq – 'the mountain of Tariq'. The famous rock of Gibraltar was named after the general Tariq ibn-Ziyad, who led the first invasion.

Nothing to see here

One of the tenets Islam copied from Judaism was an abhorrence of images. In 722 Caliph Yazid ordered the destruction of all Christian icons in Syria. Surprisingly, four years later a Christian emperor did exactly the same thing on his home turf. In 726 Emperor Leo III sent soldiers to destroy the huge, golden statue of Jesus that stood at the gateway of his palace. He then sent orders to his bishops that all icons should be destroyed and soldiers were sent out into the city to carry out his commands.

There was a riot. Devout women attacked the soldiers. Mobs filled the streets. The patriarch denounced the emperor. The church was split between the iconoclasts (those who destroyed images) and the iconodules (who 'served' images).

For many people the icons were a way in which they could glimpse some of the glory of heaven. For people who couldn't read, these pictures were immensely important and had a mysterious power. So this dispute was a class struggle: the elite – those who could read and make fancy speeches – were discarding one of the key means of worship for the poorer, illiterate masses. No wonder the poor revolted. There was nothing for them to look at.

Support for their position came from the theologian John of Damascus (c.655–750) who argued that the icon was merely an aid to worship. And he pointed out that Jesus was a kind of 'icon' of God. John said things like 'the image is one thing, the person represented another', and 'Icons are not idols but symbols,' not forgetting, 'You can't touch me because I'm in Syria.' He probably didn't say the latter, but it was true. Leo called for John's arrest, but John was in Damascus, which had been captured by the Arabs. Ironically, the pro-icon John was protected by the very anti-Icon Caliph.

Leo, as you'd expect from any good emperor, called a council in 730, which pushed through a ban on icons and sacked the Patriarch of Constantinople. In Rome, meanwhile, the pope excommunicated the iconoclasts. Leo responded by seizing control of churches in Byzantine-controlled territory in southern Italy, and attempting to have the pope assassinated. That, my friends, is *seriously* robust theology.

The argument was to rumble on inside Byzantium for centuries. In 780 Empress Irene restored icons to the churches and called her own council in Nicea in 787, to discuss and debate – and then decide that she was right. And so it went on.

Hammer time

Leo had managed to grab wealth from churches in Italy because the Byzantine Empire still held on to some territory there that they had taken during Justinian's day. But in 751 the Lombards conquered Ravenna, the Byzantine capital of Italy. They had already taken Rome, looting the city while Pope Gregory III looked on, powerless to stop them. But now they were dominant in all of Italy. For the pope this posed a problem. Should he side with the Lombards or with the Byzantines?

In the end he went for 'None of the above' and allied himself with the Franks, under their leader Charles Martel. Martel means 'the hammer' and, as we've seen, he hammered the Arabs at Poitiers and drove them back into Spain.*

When Charles died, his son Pepin the Short was elected by his peers to be king. 'How short was Pepin?' I hear you cry. And the answer is, we don't know. The name may have nothing to do with his height; it may refer to the length of his hair, which he wore cut short, in contrast to the long, flowing locks of his father. Anyway in 754 Pope Stephen II travelled to Pepin's court, where he anointed the king and his two sons, Carloman and Charles, and declared Pepin king 'by the grace of God'. Stephen gave the king the title of Patrician of the Romans. It had been hundreds of years since the last Roman emperor was seen in those parts but, you know, tradition and all that.

In return for this endorsement Pepin became the official defender of the papacy. He went south, defeated the Lombards and gave the pope a load of territory covering Ravenna, Perugia and indeed Rome itself. These states – known as the Papal States – would continue as such for another 1,100 years.

(The Byzantine emperor Constantine V, nicknamed 'Copronymus', sent Pepin an organ in 757, thus reintroducing the instrument to the western world, where it had been happily absent since the fall of Rome. Copronymus means 'dung-named'. He was not, as perhaps you can tell, the most popular of emperors. Hardly surprising, if you go around giving people organs.)

---

* Charles is responsible for the invention – or the widespread implementation, anyway – of two things that were to have a huge effect on European history. The first was the heavily armoured knight. And the second was stirrups, which meant that heavily armoured knights could actually stay on their horses.

When Pepin died, his kingdom was divided between his two sons. But then Carloman, the eldest, died, so Charles became the sole ruler of the Franks. At Easter 774 he decided to visit Rome. From the start he showed proper devotion. He is said to have ascended the steps of St Peter's on his knees. To the pope he was everything that you could wish for: a Christian king who showed proper respect for the papacy. It was as if all the pope's Christmases had come at once. Only at Easter.

Charles went on to conquer the Saxons in Germany and to annex Bavaria, Hungary and much of Austria. (He failed to get Spain, but you can't win them all.) I've called him Charles so far, on the logical grounds that that was his name. But his exploits earned him the title Charles the Great, and it is the Latin version of this, *Carolus Magnus*, that got transmuted through Old French into the better known name of Charlemagne.

And so, as the eighth century drew to a close, there was a proper empire in the west once more. It was *almost* like the good old days.

What it needed, of course, was an emperor.

THINGS YOU LEARN FROM CHRISTIAN HISTORY

NO. 5

Always be suspicious of really virtuous-sounding names and titles

Variant: Never trust anyone called Innocent.

Pope Innocent III launched the crusade against the Cathars. The Tribunal of the Holy Office of the Inquisition turned out to be not very holy at all. The Holy Roman Empire™ was always an oxymoron. (Some of its leaders were actual morons as well.)*

* This rule remains very much in force. The highly dubious Vatican bank is called The Institute for the Works of Religion. The same rule also applies to other faiths: the much-feared Saudi Arabian religious police are called the Committee for the Promotion of Virtue and the Prevention of Vice.

5 Dark Ages, Dating and Divorce

Kid Charlemagne

Charlemagne was the top man in Europe. And it was to him that the church turned when, in 799, the pope went on trial.

Pope Stephen III was succeeded by Pope Hadrian I, and when

Hadrian popped off he was succeeded by Pope Leo III.* His appointment outraged Hadrian's family, not only because Leo was common and possibly part Arab, but because they essentially viewed the papacy as a kingdom with a big church attached. And they expected the position to be inherited by another member of their family. On 25 April 799 Leo was attacked by a group led by Hadrian's nephew. They tried to blind him and cut out his tongue. He was rescued and taken to Charlemagne's court for protection. When he returned to Rome in November, he found himself assaulted in a different way: he was charged for simony (selling church positions for money), perjury and adultery.† For the first time in history a pope was put on trial.

Problem: who can judge the pope? The eastern emperor wasn't an option, for a number of reasons, but mainly because he was a she. At this time the emperor was an empress, Irene. Frankish law, known as the Salic law, excluded females from inheriting land or titles, or doing anything very much except simpering and looking feminine, so that ruled her out immediately. She wasn't a proper ruler.‡

Nope. There was only one man for the job: Charlemagne. So he went to Rome and on 23 December 799 the pope stood at the high altar of St Peter's and swore on the Gospels that he was innocent.§ And that was that. Sorted.

Two days later Charlemagne had his reward in the form of a Christmas present from the pope. On Christmas Day Charlemagne was praying at St Peter's tomb. As he rose from kneeling for prayer at the conclusion of the Christmas Day mass, the pope stepped forward and placed the imperial crown on Charles's head.

Leo proclaimed Charlemagne the first Holy Roman Emperor.

* Do not confuse with Emperor Leo III. Just don't. That's all.
† Simony gets its name from Simon, in the book of Acts, who tried to purchase the power of the Holy Spirit from Peter and John. Seems a bit unfair, really. Simon only wanted miraculous powers: he wasn't after becoming Archbishop of Samaria.
‡ To be fair, she did her best to act like the men. She had her own son blinded and murdered, and even dared to convene an ecumenical council, held at Nicea in 787. This is the last of the seven official 'ecumenical' councils and was the one where icons were agreed to be a Very Good Thing. But the council didn't bother to invite the bishops of the Franks or their king. Charlemagne dismissed it and called the eastern church 'a filthy pond of hell'.
§ Not Innocent, innocent. Innocent was another pope. Or a load of popes, actually. This one was Leo. Do try to stay focused.

The proceeding clause

Historians have long argued over whether Charlemagne knew this was coming. Apparently, he looked surprised, and his first biographer quoted Charlemagne as saying that he would never have set foot in the church had he known of the pope's intentions. But it's hardly likely that the pope wouldn't have discussed his idea with Charlemagne. And in any case it only legitimised what everyone knew: Charlemagne was the top man in the west.

Fig. XVI. *Leo gives Charlemagne his Christmas present*

From the pope's point of view the good thing was that *he* was the one doing the anointing bit. It established a precedent: if you wanted to be an emperor, you had to be anointed by the pope. And the title of Holy Roman Emperor was to endure for a thousand years, even though for much of that time the post-holder didn't have an empire to be Holy and Roman with.* At the time, though, it was more of a marketing ploy.

The reaction in Constantinople was furious. If any emperors were

---

* The title endured until 1806, becoming the hereditary title of the Hapsburgs in Austria.

holy and Roman it was them. There was one God in heaven; there could only be one emperor on earth; and he, she or it was always found in Constantinople.

Pope Leo III was nothing special in terms of popishness. But he was in the right place at the right time: the place being just by Charlemagne's head and the time being when the emperor was looking the other direction. But his action had profound consequences. Charlemagne took on the role of emperor with gusto. By the end of his reign he commanded an empire that included most of France, Belgium, Holland, Germany and Austria, and much of Italy.*

He embarked on an ambitious building programme: throughout his realm churches were consciously modelled on the forms of churches from long ago. (His private chapel at Aachen was a replica of one built for Justinian at Ravenna.) He took a real and personal interest in theological matters – his favourite bedtime reading was, apparently, Augustine's *City of God*.† He also reformed the liturgy and funded a massive programme of manuscript production, his scribes even developing a new 'typeface' named after him, Caroline minuscule, which is a direct ancestor of the western typefaces we use today.

He also reformed the church, putting in place the administrative system from which the idea of parishes evolved. He was particularly fond of the Benedictines, and gave them the responsibility of reforming a lot of the other monastic orders in his realm. He also gave them lots of land, which brought in a healthy income. This enabled the monasteries to employ peasants to run the estates, something Benedict had never foreseen. It also allowed the monasteries to get enormously rich, something else Benedict had never foreseen. They could now afford to build wonderful new abbeys. In

---

* Charlemagne never conquered Britain. But he did leave a number of legacies. Not least our currency: it was Charlemagne who invented the system of pounds, shillings and pence that Britain still uses today. (At least in part. We got rid of shillings in 1971. And florins. And threepenny bits. Sigh.) Anyway, the next time *The Sun* goes all mad about Europe trying to get rid of the pound, it might be fun to remind them that we got it only through monetary union in the first place.

† This is understandable. Parts of it are very good for insomnia. Charles could read a bit, but he couldn't write. He could sign his own name, but only using a stencil.

fact, they developed a standard design, with a church, dining hall, dormitories, a chapter house to serve as the community's meeting room, a central cloistered walkway, and buildings to serve the community.

With their monastery gardens, monasteries also preserved horticultural knowledge, which otherwise would have been lost to the west. Most importantly, they also began to produce beer. *Proper* beer, that is: beer made with hops. The monasteries developed brewing on a proper, industrial scale, and had high standards of production. Today beers in Europe are still associated with monasteries.

Charlemagne also made changes to the liturgy. The Nicene Creed declared that the Holy Spirit 'proceeds from the Father'. It was Augustine who suggested that the Spirit proceeds from the Father *and* the Son, and in the seventh century some Spanish churches took up this idea and added the Latin word *filioque* (and from the Son) to the creed. Charlemagne liked this amendment and used it during worship in his private chapel. In 809 a church council held in Aachen endorsed its use. Charlemagne wanted it adopted in Rome, but Pope Leo hesitated. It wasn't that he had deep theological objections, but he could see that the eastern church would not take kindly to tampering with a text that had been agreed by two ecumenical councils. Rome's nervousness about the word continued for a long time. The city was one of the last places to adopt the *filioque* clause, not using it until the eleventh century.

> **FILIOQUE**
>
> *Name:* The *filioque* clause.
> *Aka:* 'And from the Son'.
> *Nationality:* Latin. And Spanish.
> *Dates:* First spotted in the seventh century.
> *Appearance:* One word, added to the Nicene Creed.
> *Before he was famous:* From an original idea by Augustine of Hippo.
> *Famous for:* Annoying the Byzantines.
> *Why does he matter?* The *filioque* clause adds the idea that the Spirit proceeds from the Father *and* the Son. It meant that the western churches had a different creed from the east.
> *Could you have a drink with him down the pub?* Not really, on the grounds that he's an abstract concept. Still we could try, eh?

When good men go to war

When Charlemagne died in 814, he left the empire to his three sons. One got Germany, the other got France and the third got the short straw: that is, the bit in between Germany and France that the Germans and the French would spend the next 1,100 years fighting over. It didn't work out too well.

This was a difficult time for the church. In the east the emperor, Leo V, was assassinated. Iconoclasts took control and violently persecuted their opponents. In 827 Arab troops from North Africa invaded Sicily, gaining a foothold in Italy and even launching an attack on Rome, where they stripped the silver plate from the doors of St Peter's.

(And, if that wasn't bad enough, in Aachen a priest named Georgius constructed the first European-built organ.)

Something had to be done. So in 849 the pope went to war. (Literally. Obviously.) Pope Leo IV led a coalition naval force with ships drawn from Naples, Gaeta and Amalfi. Assuming the supreme command, he utterly destroyed the Arab fleet off Ostia. He captured hundreds of prisoners of war and set them to work reinforcing the defences of the Vatican with a huge, forty-foot-high rampart. Known as the Leonine Wall, it was completed in 852 and sections of it still stand today.

If you want a job to be done, sometimes you have to do it yourself. Even if you're the pope.

Great Danes

It was a time of invasion all round. A new power was rising: great hairy seafaring yobs called Vikings or 'Norsemen', men from the north. They had a special penchant for attacking monasteries, where the only people guarding the treasures were . . . er . . . monks. In 793 Vikings attacked the monastery at Lindisfarne in Northumbria, and within fifty years they had overrun most of Britain.

One of Lindisfarne's greatest treasures was the glorious, sumptuously bound Lindisfarne Gospels, perhaps the most beautiful book ever produced. Miraculously, they survived the Viking attack. They were hastily packed up and sent from the monastery, but the boat carrying them was shipwrecked. Fortunately, the gospels washed ashore and were taken to Durham.*

The Vikings exported their particular brand of terror throughout Europe, raping, looting and pillaging their way through Europe and expanding their rule in a manner that they were never going to achieve again – at least until their distant descendants invented Ikea. And like Ikea, what they were interested in was profit. They made money either by plundering (or by being paid not to plunder), and through trading in goods and slaves. The people of Europe were scared to death and a new prayer was added to the services: 'From the fury of the Norsemen, O Lord deliver us.'

In 850 they had their first British sleepover, over-wintering in the country for the first time. The next year they sacked Canterbury Cathedral. In 866 they captured York. Edmund of East Anglia was killed by the Vikings in 870; he was widely regarded as a martyr and a saint. (By sheer coincidence he was killed near Bury St Edmunds, so that made an obvious place for his shrine. What are the chances, eh?)

Over the next decades various kings of Wessex tried to stop the Vikings, including Ethelbald, Ethelbert, Ethelred. But none of these

---

* Despite their precious nature, the Lindisfarne Gospels were later written on by a priest, Aldred, who, sometime in the late tenth century, inserted a word-for-word Anglo-Saxon translation in the spaces between the lines of Latin text.

Ethels managed to halt their advance. Ethelred was killed in a battle in 871 and was succeeded by his brother Alfred.

Alfred was a Christian king. He oversaw a programme of religious reform and education, translated Latin texts into English and funded the churches. He believed the Viking invasions were punishments from God. 'Remember what punishments befell us in the world when we ourselves did not cherish learning nor transmit it to other men,' he later wrote. 'We were Christians in name alone, and very few of us possessed Christian virtues.'

Alfred managed to stop the Viking advance in three ways: (a) by paying them money, (b) by hiding in the marshes and engaging in guerrilla warfare, and (c) by routing the Viking army at the Battle of Edington in 878. After this defeat, Alfred made a treaty with Guthrum, the Viking leader. The Vikings took the north of the country, and Alfred retained the south. But Guthrum also converted to Christianity. He took the Christian name Ethelstan, and was baptised. Alfred was his godfather.*

The fact that the Vikings now had a settled base in northern England enabled them to think about travelling a bit further. Like to France. After a series of devastating attacks in 911 the French king followed Alfred and made a settlement with them, granting them a large chunk of northern France. There they put down some roots and adopted the language and culture of the lands. They even changed their name. These Norsemen – men from the North – became the Normans.†

To Russia with love

It wasn't just the Vikings who were marauding around. In 811 the Byzantine emperor Nicephorus I was killed in a battle with the Bulgars, a race so savage that they set the skulls of their enemies in silver and used them as cups.‡

---

* The little church at Aller in Somerset may well contain the baptismal font, with a simple limestone bowl, less than a metre tall. I think we can assume it wasn't total immersion baptism.

† It's important to remember that the Normans weren't French. For one thing, they conquered England – and we have *never* been defeated by the French.

‡ For centuries 'Bulgar' was used as a shorthand for a barbarian capable of any depravity. It's where the word 'bugger' comes from. Not that I would ever say such a thing . . .

Fig. XVII. *Out at sea, the Vikings work on their mission statement*

(As if that wasn't bad enough, the Utrecht Psalter, produced at Rheims in 832, includes the first known picture of a church organ. Oh the horror . . .)

So the empire tried a new policy, of turning these cheeky Bulgars into Christians. They would then be less likely to attack Constantinople, because (a) the emperor would be their Christian leader, and (b) they would be bored into inactivity by the church services.*

So the Byzantines invaded Bulgaria and forcibly baptised their king Boris. Boris was eventually given a patriarch of his very own – a patriarch for the Bulgarian church: the first new patriarch since Constantinople. Since all the other old patriarchies were now in Muslim territory, this was a significant development.

Other areas wanted the benefits of Christianity as well. In 862 the Slavs, under King Ratislav of Moravia, asked Constantinople to send priests to conduct the services and teach the people. Emperor Michael III sent two brothers, Methodius and Cyril, who had learned the Slavonic

---

* They had tried this tactic before with mixed results. The Khazars were so unimpressed by the Christian missionaries who went to them that, when the missionaries left, the tribe converted to Judaism.

language in Thessalonica. There was no written alphabet, so Cyril devised one, a kind of glammed-up Greek with some Latin, a bit of Hebrew (or possibly Samaritan) and quite a lot of symbols he just dreamed up. Cyril died during the translation, but his brother finished the job and the script they devised later became known as Cyrillic. Today it is used throughout Russia and eastern Europe. I suppose if it had been named after the other brother it might have been called Methodist.

Around the same time a group of Varangians, a Viking tribe, settled the very north of Europe, in Novgorod. They were also known as the 'Rus', a name that may be derived from *rods*, the Old Norse word for 'men who row'. And from Rus we get Russia.*

Vladimir I was the Varangian leader of Rus. His grandmother had been a Christian. But his father Sviatoslav refused baptism on the perfectly reasonable grounds that his soldiers would laugh at him. Then Vladimir converted to Christianity. According to the story, his emissaries came back from Constantinople and, overcome by the majesty and beauty of the services, told him, 'In that place God lives among men.'

There may have been a more mundane reason: a rebel army was on the point of seizing Constantinople, and the Byzantine emperor Basil needed Vladimir's rowing team, as it were. Vlad agreed, on one condition: he wanted to marry the emperor's sister. This was tricky. For one thing, Vladimir already had four wives, a reputed 800 concubines, and, presumably, a very bad back. But he was a pagan. Still, needs must. Vladimir got the girl, on condition he also got baptised.

Despite this unpromising start, his proved to be a genuine conversion. Following his baptism in 988 he dismissed his other women, and ordered the destruction of all pagan idols. (The idol of Perun was first beaten with sticks, then bound to a horse's tail and dragged into the river.) He built churches and monasteries and imported the Slavonic liturgy and scriptures, developed by Cyril and Methodius – which is how Russia got the Cyrillic alphabet. He fed the poor and needy, and abolished torture and the death penalty. Which makes tenth century Russia more liberal than many countries are today.

---

* They were fearsome warriors. From the early 900s groups of Varangians served as mercenaries in the Byzantine army. They eventually became the Varangian Guard, the personal bodyguard of the emperors.

And that is how Russia went Orthodox.

This was a time of relative strength in the Byzantine Empire. The church was so entwined with the state that all the significant church festivals required the presence of the emperor. And the wealth of the empire was lavished on the church, particularly on the monasteries. It was at this time that Mount Athos, the 'holy mountain', was colonised. It's the closest thing orthodoxy has to the Vatican – a Monastic republic built on a rocky peninsula in the Aegean Sea. It contains many communities, but its most important, The Great Lavra, was established in 963. Later groups from the Russian, Serbian and other orthodox churches established monasteries on the Mount. Now an autonomous state within Greece, it still follows the Julian calendar (so is thirteen days behind the rest of the world) and it maintains an absolute prohibition on women: only males are allowed on the mount, including livestock.

The Dark Ages

With the dissolution of Charlemagne's empire, the papacy became the plaything of a few aristocratic Italian families, notably the Crescentii and the Tusculani. The popes at this period were some of the worst in its history. Which is saying something. Here are a few of the lowlights . . .

John VIII (872–882) was the first pope to be assassinated. Which would be bad enough, but the people who killed him were his own priests. They poisoned him, but the poison was slow to work and they got bored and bashed in his skull.

In 896 Pope Formosus – the name means 'good looking' – was put on trial by his enemies. What made this unusual was that he had been dead for eight months. So he'd probably lost some of his looks by then. Anyway, he was a good, efficient pope and, naturally, that made him enemies among the not-so-good. He was succeeded by Boniface VI, who died fifteen days after his election. And then along came Stephen VI, who hated Formosus so much that he exhumed the late pope's body, dressed it in the official robes, sat him in a chair and accused him of perjury and of coveting the papacy. Formosus, who remained strangely silent during his trial, was found guilty and his body was flung into the Tiber (minus the three fingers of his right hand that he had used to give blessings). The trial became known as the 'Cadaver Synod'.* Immediately afterwards Rome was hit by an earthquake and Formosus' corpse resurfaced downriver and started performing miracles. God had passed judgement on Stephen's actions. Six months later a more permanent judgement was implemented: Stephen was deposed by an angry mob, thrown into prison and strangled.

Many popes lasted only a short time. Stephen's replacement, Romanus, was deposed after just four months. His successor, Theodore II, lasted only twenty days. (But at least he did have time to organise for the now rather damp corpse of Formosus to be reburied in St Peter's Basilica.) Leo V was Pope from July to September 903, making him the only pope who ever took on the papacy as a summer job.

Plenty of popes met violent deaths. John X was suffocated with pillows. Stephen VIII was brutally tortured and died of his injuries. There were also several 'antipopes' – upstarts, pretenders who grabbed the pontifical throne during a kind of coup. The aforementioned Leo V was deposed and imprisoned by an antipope called Christopher. Then both the antipope and the official pope, Leo, were killed by a man called Sergius – who then became Pope Sergius III.

He hung on to power for a few years, mainly through the support of a fearsome local warlord called Theophylact, and his even more fearsome wife, Theodora.† Sergius was another Formosus-hater, and so he annulled any ordinations performed by Formosus. This caused a chain reaction: if Formosus' ordinations were illegal, then anyone ordained by the people he ordained were also illegitimate. It was chaos. No one could work out who was an ordained priest and who wasn't.

This was a terrible, dark period. Which is why the sixteenth-century historian Caesar Baronius called it the *Saeculum obscurum*: the dark age.‡ The term was later applied more generally to the period by later historians. Hence: the Dark Ages. Protestant German theologians rather less charitably called it the pornocracy.

The popes' behaviour was so bad that even the wildest stories gained credibility. The most famous of these was the story of Pope Joan, a woman who disguised herself as a man, became Pope and was only

* The name of a Goth Rock band, if ever I heard one.
† Sergius was very close to the family of Theophylact. *Very* close. In fact, it was rumoured that he had an illegitimate child by Marioza, Theophylact's fifteen-year-old daughter.
‡ He might have called it this because of the paucity of written records. But it certainly works as a value judgement.

discovered when she somehow became pregnant. (I say 'somehow'. I do know how it happened. But I can't work out *how* it happened, if you see what I mean.) The story gained traction around Europe. In the Reformation Jan Hus even used it as part of his evidence of the corruption of the Catholic Church. But it just wasn't true. The story spawned another myth: that to avoid another 'Pope Joan' a new procedure was introduced whereby at the enthronement of a new pope, a cardinal had the specific responsibility of checking out the 'papal regalia', as it were. This story is recounted in a number of places, including the works of one Felix Haemmerlein who wrote in 1490, 'in order to demonstrate his [the pope's] worthiness, his testicles are felt by the junior cleric present as testimony of his male sex. When this is found to be so, the person who feels them shouts out in a loud voice, "He has testicles!" And all the clerics present reply, "God be praised!"'

This had never been part of the official liturgy. But they should really introduce it. It would liven up events no end.

Mass consumption

In 910 Duke William of Aquitaine donated his hunting lodge at Cluny for use as a new monastery. He was sick of church corruption and keen for people to recapture the spirit of Benedict's original rule of living. Not him, obviously. But other people. Holy people. Monks. What made his move different – in an era when bishops, archbishops and even popes were appointed by local rulers – was that he gave the monastery the independence to choose its own leader. He set up a charter, which, as well as protecting the monks' independence, ends with a magnificent array of colourful curses on anyone who should try to interfere with the abbey, including 'everlasting damnation . . . his members putrefying and swarming with vermin'.

Cluny gave hope – initially at least – to all those who still believed that the church was capable of more than politics, greed and murder. But William's grant made Cluny enormously wealthy – possibly the richest monastic house in the west. The church was adorned with solid and silver candelabras and chalices of gold. The monks ate roast meals and drank fine wines. Their vestments were made from the finest linen and silk. They subcontracted the running of the estates to employed servants and managers and, in effect, became professional prayers.

Monks – not just at Cluny – became a kind of spiritual service industry. Medieval society believed in prayer. But it didn't always have the time for it. And, even though the times were violent, there was still a strong sense that warfare and killing wasn't a particularly Christian thing to do. If you engaged in war, technically, you had to do penance in the form of prayer and fasting and the saying of the mass.* So what you did was outsource your penance to the professionals: endow a monastery to do your religious stuff, pay a priest to say a mass on your behalf. It sounds terribly cynical, but we should remember that this society didn't have our individualistic view of life. God was like the Inland Revenue: he didn't mind whose account the money came from as long as the tax was paid.†

This dependence on third-party service provision gave the church a lot of leverage. People *needed* monks and priests and churches and all that stuff; otherwise, they were headed straight to hell. So the abbots and monks gained a lot of prestige. Now, that wasn't necessarily a bad thing. Many women found that being an abbess gave them the chance to exercise gifts of leadership that would have been denied to them otherwise.

And it also meant that there was an increased demand for the Eucharist – which by now was being called the 'mass', from the Latin word *missio*, which is the dismissal at the end of the service.‡ Where, previously, it had been a weekly, sung service with lashings of ritual, now production had to be ramped up. So a simplified version was developed, a 'low mass' that was said as often as possible, with just a server in attendance to represent the congregation. Monks were now ordained priests in order to keep up with the demand. And side altars were added to churches, so that you didn't have to use the rest of the church.

It was the age of mass consumption.

---

* When, for example, William the Conqueror led his Norse troops across to conquer the plucky Anglo-Saxons, his leaders were actually given penances. It has been calculated that if they'd actually done these penances they would have been too weak to have conquered the rest of England. And we would now be eating cow instead of beef.

† They probably do mind, actually. But so far they apparently haven't spotted that my cheques come from the Bank of Toytown.

‡ It means 'dismissal' or 'sending' and has the same root as the word 'mission' and 'missionary'.

The empire strikes back

In Rome things hit an all-time low in the reign of John XII.* He was a young aristocrat, entirely uninterested in anything spiritual, who lived with several women and turned the Lateran palace into a brothel. His behaviour was so awful that female pilgrims stopped visiting the shrine of St Peter. His passion for gambling meant that he went through shedloads of cash, most of which came from the offerings of pilgrims.

By now the papal lands were weak and vulnerable. They were under attack from a local ruler called Berengar of Ivrea. Desperate for help, John kept his trousers on just long enough to act: he appealed to the German king, Otto of Saxony. If Otto would come to rescue Rome, John said, then the pope would crown him Emperor.

Otto was a man with a dream: he wanted to resurrect the empire. A big fan of Charlemagne, he had even staged his coronation in Charlemagne's church in Aachen. And he was a fine military leader. So, on receiving the pope's offer, he travelled to Italy, defeated Berengar and, in January 962, was crowned by the pope. Through his sin and stupidity John had actually restored the Holy Roman Empire.

But Otto wasn't content to leave it there. He made it clear that from now on he expected a veto over the choice of pope, and that every pope had to swear allegiance to the emperor. And he gave John a stern talking to about his behaviour.

John, meanwhile, was a man with his brain in his trousers. He now regretted calling Otto in, and the moment the new emperor left Rome Otto entered into negotiations with Berengar's son Adalbert and offered to make Adalbert Emperor instead of Otto. Otto got wind of this and was furious. He marched on Rome and John fled to Tivoli, stopping only to grab whatever ecclesiastical gold he hadn't already spent on prostitutes or gambled away on the 3.30 at Verona. When Otto discovered the sheer weight of people's grievances against John, he wrote to John offering him the chance to defend himself. John wrote back, in his own, ungrammatical hand, 'Bishop John to all the Bishops. We hear that you wish to make another pope. If you do, I excommunicate you

---

* His real name was Octavian, but he changed it. This wasn't common among the early popes. In fact, Octavian was only the second pope to change his name. The first had been John II in 533, whose original name had been Mercury. So you can see why he changed it. Pope Mercury is probably not a combination that makes for confidence in one's orthodoxy.

by almighty God, and you have no power to ordain no one, or celebrate mass.'

He clearly wrote that all himself. His mum must have been so proud.

Otto ignored the note and did appoint a replacement pope, Leo. And then he left. But now the people of Rome got all uppity. They hated John, but that didn't mean they wanted the German emperor sticking his nose in. John may have been a fornicating donkey of a pope, but he was *their* fornicating donkey of a pope. So they rebelled. And John found enough support to re-enter the city. Predictably, he took a horrible, vicious revenge on all those clerics who had spoken out to the emperor against him. The new Pope Leo was excommunicated and fled the city. But before Otto could return to the city, John died, either because of overexertion in bed, or because of revenge wrought by the husband of one of his mistresses. He was only in his mid-twenties.

Pope and antipope

From now on this became the pattern. The emperor would choose a pope, the Roman clergy and aristocracy tried to impose another one. These alternative pontiffs are known as antipopes. (One imagines that if an antipope and a pope ever touched, the whole fabric of space-time reality would unravel.) Certainly, working out who was and wasn't a *real* pope in this period is a bit of a hopeless task. The confusion is so intense that in the official list of 'All the popes called John' it hops from John XV to John XVII: John XVI is completely missing. (He was actually an antipope, but in the later records he somehow acquired an official number before being expunged from the record.) And anyway, in most cases the popes and the antipopes were as bad as each other.

The other issue was interference from the east, where the Byzantines were resurgent under the impressively named Emperor Basil II (the Bulgar-Slayer). Otto I was succeeded by the imaginatively named Otto II when, in 983, the Byzantines managed to get a foothold in southern Italy. Otto II marched against them, but the Byzantines allied with the Saracens and demolished Otto's army. Otto was forced to swim for his life. Seriously weakened, he died from malaria at the age of just twenty-eight. He was buried in St Peter's, the only emperor to be buried there.

Darling, you were wonderful . . .

Meanwhile, in England, some monks were busily inventing the theatre. After the fall of Rome classical theatre had pretty much disappeared. A German nun called Hrostwitha had adapted the ancient comedies of Terence to give them a more Christian spin, but they failed at the box office, largely because, well, there wasn't a box office. Then around 970–980 the Benedictines in England started to introduce a bit of drama into the service. At the feast of Corpus Christi a monk (or monks) playing the angel (or angels) would say *Quem quaeritis?*, 'Who do you seek?'

This would be answered by monks – presumably the ones with better legs – who were playing Mary(s): 'Jesus of Nazareth, the Crucified, O heavenly ones.' Then the angel(s) would say, 'He is not here; he is risen.' Curtain.

It's not exactly *Hamlet*, but it did lead in that direction. Because the enaction of this simple scene was the beginning of a tradition of church-based drama. Eventually, these dramas moved outside the church and became the medieval mystery plays, with biblical scenes written by clerics and performed by the guilds. And that, in turn, led to Shakespeare and Marlowe and . . . well, the whole of western theatre in fact.

(Less artistically, and more worryingly, in 951 some monks in Winchester built the biggest organ in England. It contained 400 pipes and had twenty-six bellows, which it took seventy men to pump, working in relays. The music was apparently so loud that it could be heard throughout the entire city. Terrifying.)

Anno Domini

Otto II's son, Otto III, was just three when he became king. But he grew into an extraordinary, visionary boy. Steeped in Scripture, he had a vision of a restored empire, under the rule of God, with the pope and the emperor as its joint figureheads. Otto III appointed the first German pope: Gregory V. (Who also happened to be his cousin. Coincidence? You decide.) Otto was finally crowned as Holy Roman Emperor in Rome on Ascension Day 996 and, though he lived in luxury in a magnificent new-build palace on the Aventine, he would, at times, shed his royal clothes and go on a pilgrimage. He was aware, as so many others were, that the times were getting short.

How short, no one quite knew. Part of the problem was working out which year you were in in the first place. In the Roman Empire the years were reckoned by the reigns of various Roman emperors and consuls, for example 'the sixteenth year of Augustus', 'the seventh year of that bloke, you know, wossisname, the one with the big nose and the laurel crown'. That sort of thing. But when Diocletian came along, no Christian wanted to date anything with his name. So they renamed that era 'the era of the martyrs'.

A monk called Dionysius Exiguus* thought that time should be recalibrated, to date from the arrival of the king of kings. So he restarted the numbering of years from the date of the incarnation of Jesus 'so that the beginning of our hope may be better known to us'.

Sadly, he got the dates wrong. In fact, no one knows how Dionysus came to the date that he chose for the birth of Jesus. But he was at least four years too late because Dionysus' year one was four years after the death of Herod the Great. So, historically, we get the curious anomaly that Jesus was actually born around five years 'before Christ'. The 'BC' option, though, was only added in the eighteenth century.†

Dionysus' system took a long time to catch on. In the eighth century, in Rome, the years were dated from the date of the resurrection, which they took as AD 33. But Bede chose to use Dionysus' system in his *Ecclesiastical History*, which was a huge hit on the Continent. And from then on it was dominant in dating. But the effect of adopting this new system meant that suddenly people realised that it was nearly the year 1000. And everyone knew what that meant: it meant that Jesus would return.

The return of the king

The idea came from the book of Revelation, of course. John on Patmos had seen the evil one thrown into a pit and sealed shut for a thousand years. Augustine had argued strongly that the whole thing was symbolic,

---

* That is, Dennis the Small, Dennis the Little. Or, you might say, Dennis the Dwarf.

† Which explains why 'AD' is Latin, *anno Domini*, and BC is English.

but how could you be sure? And the times were pretty terrible. There were marauding Hungarians riding around. At one point they even held the Frankish ruler, Louis IV, prisoner.

In Paris a priest preached a sermon to his startled congregation warning them that the Antichrist would arrive 'the moment that one thousand years had been completed'. He was quickly shouted down by one of his colleagues, but the damage was done. It was a conspiracy, man.

By New Year's Eve 999 expectation had reached a peak. A crowd gathered outside the papal palace in Rome. Usually when a crowd gathered there it was for the removal and expulsion of a pope, but this time they wanted him to pray, because the end was nigh.

Midnight came. Nothing happened. The end, apparently, was not so nigh after all. So the pope gave them a blessing and sent them home.

This failure did not put off the millennial prophets. They merely recalculated. Maybe the 1,000 years should be calculated from Christ's death and resurrection in AD 30? Certainly there were apocalyptic earth-shattering events. In 1010 news reached Europe of the destruction of the Church of the Holy Sepulchre in Jerusalem by the messianic Muslim caliph al-Hakim bi-Amr Allah, the so-called Mad Caliph.* The prophets made a new plan: they would regroup in 1030 and see if anything happened.

And, indeed, those expecting the end of the world have been gathering at regular intervals ever since.

The scientist

The pope who appeared on the balcony that night was a Frenchman. He was remarkable in many ways, not least for being one of the few popes in this period who wasn't a complete and utter tool.

Christened Gerbert, as a young man he showed an astonishing intelligence and gift for science. He travelled to Spain to study the mathematics of the Arabs and later became the tutor of both numbers two and three of the Otto variety.

---

* The caliph's behaviour grew more and more eccentric. Finally in February 1021, at the age of 36, he went out in the night to the hills outside Cairo and never returned. A search found only his donkey and bloodstained garments. The donkey refused to talk without a lawyer present.

He eventually became Archbishop of Ravenna and then, on the death of Gregory in 999, Otto III appointed him Pope. He took the name Pope Sylvester II. He was a passionate reformer of the church, taking action against offences such as simony, sacking clergy who had taken on concubines and generally trying to ensure that bishops should be people with, you know, actual *morals*.

He authored treatises on mathematics, medicine, geometry, music and astronomy, and, heavily influenced by Islamic scholarship, reintroduced to Europe such scientific tools as the abacus, on which he could execute speedy calculations, the armillary sphere, used for teaching mathematics and astronomy, and globes. It was Sylvester who made popular the use of Arabic numerals.

Sylvester was a scientist. Or, as the other clergy more commonly called him, a devil worshipper. Because everyone knew, right, that he had learned this stuff at places like Cordoba and Seville, and they were ruled by the Arabs, who were all magicians. And what's more it was widely known that Sylvester was in league with the devil and he possessed a magic book which showed him the future. And I heard he had this head of bronze that could answer questions. I mean, admittedly it could answer only yes or no, but it was the work of the devil.

Rumour swirled around him. He was forced to flee Rome and head to Ravenna, and when Otto III died of malaria in 1002, aged just twenty-one, Sylvester was left without supporters. He did make it back to Rome, briefly, but died on 13 May 1003 and is buried in St John Lateran. If they'd both lived, think what might have been. We might have had the pocket calculator *decades* earlier.

(Mind you, Sylvester also worked on a system of improving the organ, introducing brass pipes and hydraulic power. So maybe he was in league with the devil after all.)

The new boy

Just as in the west, there were those in the east who wanted reform.

One of the strongest voices was a monk known as Symeon the New Theologian (949–1022, so not *that* new). Historically, the eastern church has called very few people 'theologian'; just John of Patmos, Gregory Nazianus and Symeon, the new boy. Symeon may have been given this title by his opponents as a sarcastic jibe, but his brilliance meant that it stuck.

Symeon hated the dry, theoretical arguments about words and names that passed for theology in Constantinople. He believed that people needed – and could have – a direct, personal experience of God, a deep, mystical encounter that would completely transform their character. He claimed that people could experience an 'intoxication of light' and 'movements of fire'. (You can get tablets for that nowadays.)

For Symeon, then, you weren't a Christian because you happened to live in Byzantium. Nor because you were baptised and went to church. 'Truly, among thousands and tens of thousands you will scarcely find one who is a Christian in word and deed,' he said. You had to be born again. To be baptised in the Holy Spirit.

Symeon was very new, then. He was essentially a charismatic. Yes, there was the authority of the Scriptures and the church fathers, but it was only a direct experience of the Holy Spirit that gave monks the authority they needed to preach and absolve sins. They didn't need formal ordination for that.

He wanted a reformation of the Byzantine monasteries – which had become wealthy and politicised. Being a monk should mean adopting a life of simplicity, asceticism and prayer. (And vegetables – one of his reforms was the introduction of vegetarian meals in the monastery.) Naturally, such views saw him condemned as a heretic. His opponents managed to have Symeon sent into exile in January 1009. He didn't go far – just to a small village on the Asian side of the Bosphorus, a ferry ride from Constantinople. Accordingly, many of his followers joined him there, where they set up another monastery. He died there, sadly, a mere thirteen years later, from dysentery. I blame the vegetables.

He never backed down from his argument with the church authorities. One of his hymns has Christ ripping into the bishops:

They are seen to appear as brilliant and pure,
but their souls are worse than mud and dirt,
worse even than any kind of deadly poison,
these evil and perverse men!

Now that's what I call a hymn.

Onward Christian soldier

When Otto III died, Henry II, his cousin, became Emperor. He was crowned by a new pope, Benedict VIII. Benedict and Henry had some things in common, notably killing people. Benedict was a trained soldier and he took 'Onward Christian Soldiers' rather literally. Immediately after his ordination he led an army to crush Italian rebels in the mountains.

Benedict was responsible for a number of significant developments. First he insisted on including the *filioque* clause in the creed, putting yet more strain on relations with Constantinople. Then, in August 1022, he and Henry held a synod at Pavia where they decided that marriage was to be prohibited for all clergy, not just for monks. It was a portent of things to come, but at the time it doesn't seem to have made any difference at all.

The fact is that during this period popes were not anywhere near as powerful as they liked to make out. In theory, they were spiritual supremos with the right to anoint the emperor. But that was really a bit of PR to big themselves up. In practice, they were humiliatingly subject to the whims of the emperor or, just as often, the Roman aristocracy. Out of the twenty-five popes between 955 and 1057, thirteen were appointed by local aristocrats and twelve by German emperors (who also sacked five of them).

And that is why so many lowlifes became popes: it was either an imperial appointment, subject to the emperor's whim, or a commodity for sale.

The successors of Benedict VIII – who came from the ruling *Tusculani* clan – show this all too clearly. After he died in 1024 his brother, John XIX, bribed his way to the papal throne. He was a layman, so he had to be fast-tracked to popeness (i.e. tonsured, ordained and enthroned) on a single day. This utter nonentity was followed by another relative, Benedict IX, also a layman and only in his twenties. He was an appalling, immoral monster who was eventually thrown out of Rome and replaced by Sylvester III. But with the aid of Daddy's private army he returned to Rome and kicked Sylvester out. Then he abdicated the papacy in favour of his godfather, who became Gregory VI (1045–46). And when I say 'abdicated', I really mean 'sold it in return for a huge sum of money and an advantageous marriage'. But he never actually resigned the papacy. Later he decided that, actually, he wanted to be Pope again. The result was that in 1045 there were three popes knocking around.*

The situation was resolved by a new emperor, Henry III, who had come to Rome to be crowned Emperor. Henry III was a devout Christian and zealous reformer. He took a simple course to sort out the mess: he sacked the lot and replaced them with his own choice. Unsurprisingly, he chose a German; or a succession of Germans, actually, since the first few proved to be not terribly resistant to malaria. They fell like flies. Or mosquitoes. The first of Henry III's popes lasted ten months, the second twenty-three days.

By now people were starting to realise that being Pope was a bit like being the drummer in Spinal Tap. It brought with it a high fatality rate. So the third nominee, Bruno, Bishop of Toul, was extremely reluctant to take the post and agreed only if there was a miraculous sign. He would go to Rome in the guise of a simple pilgrim and, if the people spontaneously proclaimed him Pope, only then would he take it. He went, they proclaimed him, and he became Leo IX. It was a miracle!

On the other hand, Leo was a tall, red-haired German. So, maybe he wasn't *that* hard to spot.

Norse and south

This Leo really put the papacy on the map. And probably used an actual map as well, because he travelled widely: northern Italy, France, Germany, two weeks in Benidorm, arguing for reform, preaching to packed crowds, presiding at magnificent services and ceremonies. He was the first Euro-pope.

One of the first things he did was to call a synod. To the surprise of those who attended, the first item on the agenda was for everyone to give a personal statement of interests: every cleric there had to stand up and declare whether or not he had paid for his post. Five of them confessed, including the Bishop of Langres, who fled the meeting and was excommunicated. When the Archbishop of Besançon attempted to defend him, he was struck dumb halfway through his speech. It was another miracle.

---

* According to one folktale, the evil Benedict was condemned to wander the earth until the day of judgement as a monster – half-bear, half-donkey. A Bonkey, if you will.

Leo deposed bishops who had purchased their positions. Then he imported his own back-room staff: a whole tranche of new cardinals. He followed this up with a 'hearts and minds' tour through Europe, promoting his reformist agenda of chastity and integrity, and sacking any bishop who wouldn't sign up to the new code of conduct.

It was all going terribly well. Then Leo made a bit of a misjudgement.

Around 1015 twenty pilgrims from the North had made a visit to the shrine of the Archangel Michael on Monte Gargano in Puglia. They were big, for pilgrims. Scandinavian looking. And, unusually, carrying a range of heavy weaponry. They were, in fact, 'Normans' – men from the north, and the result of their 'pilgrimage' was that they liked the place so much that they decided to stay on.

Soon word got out that in Puglia there were jobs going for mercenaries, and weather that was heaps better than in Normandy. So loads of other Norman 'pilgrims' started arriving. Eventually they kicked the Muslims out of Sicily and then began to encroach into southern Italy. By 1050 they had gained a considerable amount of land, and had mutated from mercenaries into conquerors.

Fig. XVIII. *The Normans invade England. And Sicily. And France, etc.*

The Normans were Latin Christians. In fact, they started insisting – with papal approval – that all the churches in their region follow the western customs, including using unleavened bread and the hated-in-the-east *filioque* clause. But Leo decided that their power was growing too great. He raised an army, marched to battle and was humiliatingly defeated. The papal army was routed and the pope himself taken prisoner. The Normans weren't going anywhere: they were there to stay.

A load of bull

It was partly the Norman reign in Sicily that led to the second, and much greater problem of Leo's reign: what was known as the Great Schism between the western and eastern church.

For centuries the two churches had been growing apart. There were differences in their rituals. Byzantines hated the *filioque* clause, the western church widely used it. Whereas the western churches used unleavened bread in the Eucharist, the east didn't. In the east the clergy could keep their wives; in the west they were supposed to be celibate and unmarried.

But there were also fundamental differences in language and culture. The Byzantines believed that doctrine was best agreed by ecumenical councils. For them the pope was, at best, first among equals. To the Latins the Greeks' endless discussion over words and their meaning was infuriating and intolerable. They wanted decisions, not yet another debate.

The Patriarch of Constantinople at the time was Michael Cerularius, a man who proved that popes weren't the only church leaders who could be petty, narrow-minded bigots. Cerularius hated Rome and was determined that Rome should be brought down a peg or several. It was usual, on assuming the job of Patriarch, for the new man to write to Rome and assure the pope of his orthodoxy. Michael didn't bother. His motto was, 'I will not serve', though how he squared that with Jesus' commands to Christians to serve one another he never said.

He saw Leo's ill-fated military adventure in the south as an attempt to weaken the power of the Byzantine Empire. When he learned that, horror of horrors, the Normans were forcing the Greek churches on the island to use unleavened bread for the Eucharist, he retaliated by insisting that all the Latin churches in Constantinople use leavened bread. If they objected, he closed down the church.

Leo looked on in horror. There was an exchange of letters. The patriarch called the Latin customs 'sinful and Judaistic'. The pope countered that he wasn't a proper patriarch, so there.

To back up his claim for supremacy in the west Leo quoted from a document, found in the papal archives, which *proved* that Constantinople was subject to Rome. It was an ancient document, signed by Constantine the Great himself and dated from 313. Apparently, Pope Sylvester I had healed the emperor from leprosy, in gratitude for which the emperor had given the pope and his successors 'Rome and all the provinces, districts and cities of Italy and the west as subject to the Roman Church for ever'. And lest anyone accuse this letter of being a forgery, the document itself says that they should be 'burnt in the nethermost hell'.

The document – known, because of the amazing generosity of the emperor, as the Donation of Constantine – had been mislaid for, oh about 300 years or so, before being rediscovered in the eighth century.

Leo quoted great chunks of it in a letter to Michael Cerularius. Clearly he believed it to be genuine, but it is one of the most successful frauds in history, right up there with Bigfoot, Piltdown Man and the idea that sprouts are food. No one knows who made it up. It was probably written in the mid-eighth century when the popes were negotiating with the Franks. Popes carried on using it to support their claims of supremacy for the next two hundred years.*

Finally, in 1054, Leo sent three envoys to Constantinople to negotiate a truce. It was probably not a good thing that all three really hated the Greeks. Their names were Cardinal Humbert of Mourmoutiers, Cardinal Frederick of Lorraine and Archbishop Peter of Amalfi. They acted like boors.

The emperor was polite to them but the patriarch refused to recognise their authority. And then the three men heard the news that back in Italy Leo had died. At this point sensible envoys would have returned. Or, at the very least, simply waited for further instructions. But not Humbert and Co. Instead, they just carried on arguing. A monk from the Monastery of the Studium who had dared to politely disagree with the pope's claims was called a 'pestiferous pimp' and 'a disciple of the malignant Mahomet'.

Finally, in the face of such flagrant politeness, Humbert lost it. At

---

* Eventually it was exposed as a forgery by a scholar called Lorenzo Valla, who showed that the language it used couldn't possibly have been written in 313.

3 p.m., Saturday 16 July 1054, these non-papal representatives, dressed in all their finery, strode into the great church of Hagia Sophia and laid a bull of excommunication on the high altar. A papal bull is not a large religious animal.* It is a document, official letter or pronouncement and the name comes from the lead seal (Latin *bulla*) that was added to the letter to authenticate it. Anyway, this one excommunicated Patriarch Michael and all his followers. It also, rather bafflingly, excommunicated the devil, for good measure. Which rather assumes that, up to then, the devil had been a good, orthodox churchgoer.

That done, they turned on their heels and marched from the building, pausing only to shake the dust symbolically from their feet. Two days later they left for Rome.

Mostly, people took no notice. In Constantinople the bull was burned – barbecued, perhaps, – and everyone went to watch the races or eat feta or do something else Eastern and Greek. After all, only a handful of people – and Satan – had been excommunicated. And, anyway, the document was technically illegal, since there was no pope to issue it. You can't have a Papal Bull if there is no Pope. Not only that, but it was full of obvious mistakes.

But there was too much history. The bull was not rescinded in Rome for another 911 years, in 1965.

After all their trial separations, this was it: divorce.

* You're probably thinking of a sacred cow.

THINGS YOU LEARN FROM CHRISTIAN HISTORY

NO. 6

All reforming movements end up needing reform

Variant: Holy men are nearly always, in some way, betrayed by some of their followers.

Nearly all reforming movements end up as part of the establishment. The Benedictines became wealthy. Francis of Assisi was remembered in an enormous basilica erected by the Franciscans. The Puritans fled persecution and then ended up persecuting others.

6 Crusaders, Cathedrals and Cathars

Going medieval

Some rather smug seventeenth-century historians looked back on the period between the fall of Rome and the rediscovery of classical culture, and named it the 'Middle Ages'. A kind of pause. An interval. Marking time between, you know, the *real* action.*

But for all the mud and blood and superstition and squalor, the Middle Ages have a rich and unmistakably Christian culture. They invented the Crusades, yes, but they also built cathedrals. There were bad popes (and patriarchs) but some brilliant peasants. Because, for all the officially sanctioned nastiness and brutality, this was a time when ordinary men and women started to reclaim a bit of holiness for themselves.

By the middle of the eleventh century Christianity had spread from the Celts in the far north-west to the Nestorians in the far east. And, despite all the theological squabbles, there was a lot of common experience. A Christian from Britain who went to Constantinople would not have understood much of the language, and, in the long-standing tradition of his people, would certainly have complained about the weather and the food, but he would still have found a lot to recognise in the church.

There was the calendar: Advent and Lent and Easter and Christmas were common to all. The week had a common pattern too with fasting on Friday and Sabbath on Sunday.†

---

* The word medieval is even more recent: it was coined in the mid-nineteenth century, to make the phrase Middle Ages sound posher.

† In 1017 it was decreed that princes, nobles and knights were to desist from all warfare from Saturday to Monday and during the holy seasons of Lent and Advent. Any soldier who fought during these times would be denied the

There were feast days and holy days: celebrations of local saints or commemorating events – real or imagined – in the life of Jesus and Mary. Such holy days were important in lives that were, for the most part, sheer, unremitting hard grind. And some of these days adapted previous pagan festivals, which allowed the faithful to keep links with their past. Rogationtide is a Catholic day of prayer for a good harvest; it replaced the pagan festival of Robigalia, which was a fertility festival.

In church, though, things were slightly less accessible for the ordinary Christian. Everybody went to mass, but the mass wasn't given to everybody. Worshippers received the bread, but not the wine – a tradition stemming from a superstitious literalism. Since the wine was thought to become the blood of Christ, priests couldn't take the risk of spilling it. So only the priest drank the wine.

And there were barriers. The western liturgy was still in Latin, a language few people understood (sometimes not even the one saying the words). And in the churches there was a literal barrier – a screen that separated them from where the priests did their stuff. For the ordinary Christian it was definitely not 'access all areas'.

And there was a growing feeling that things should change.

The hinges

One of those who wanted change – albeit not perhaps of *quite* the same kind as your man in the pew (not that they had pews yet) – was a man called Hildebrand.

Hildebrand (?–1085) was a former Cluniac monk who, though from a humble background, became the most powerful and influential figure in the papal administration. He was behind the election of several popes whom he used to carry forward his plans for reform.

First up for reform was the manner of choosing a pope. In 1059 Hildebrand and his supporters pushed through reforms which meant that from then on the pope would be elected by the college of cardinals. The word 'cardinal' comes from the Latin *cardo*, 'hinge'. The name was first given to the parish priests of the twenty-eight significant churches in Rome who were 'pivotal'. Everything hinged around them. Gradually they formed a college, a group that soon ranked second in

---

last rites, Christian burial and forgiveness for his sins.

precedence to the pope himself. From now on the choice of a new pope would hinge on the hinges.

The western emperor was only nine when this decision was taken. Henry IV (1050–1106) grew into a wild, uncontrollable youth with a reputation for viciousness. A teenager, as we now call them. One thing he wasn't wild about was this method of choosing the pope. In Henry's eyes that was the job of the emperor, not the cardinals.

He decided to show the church who was boss by choosing the next Archbishop of Milan. At the time the city was in turmoil, because of the rise of a radical reforming party called the Patarines.

The name is a typically sneering elitist put-down: it means 'rag-pickers', the lowliest workers in the cloth trade. The Patarines were ordinary workers, lower-class laity who hated the wealth and privilege of the church. They wanted reform. One of their radically dangerous ideas was that archbishops should actually be *Christian*. The Archbishop of Milan, Guido da Velate, was illiterate, sold church positions to the highest bidder, and lived with a number of concubines. The Patarine leader, Ariald, formed a community, composed of 'independent' priests who were no longer going to obey such archbishops, as well as lay men and women. They gave away their possessions, lived under a common rule, and embraced chastity. Ariald even began appointing his own, alternative, clergy. The response was swift and brutal. In 1067 he was killed by thugs employed by the da Velate family and his body dumped in Lake Como.

His followers were enraged. When Guido died in 1071, they put forward their own candidate, who had the approval of Pope Alexander and, more importantly, of Cardinal Hildebrand – who was more or less operating the pope by remote control. Henry blocked their choice, and fighting broke out between the two sides. The cathedral of Milan was burnt down. Then, in the middle of all this kerfuffle, Pope Alexander died. Hildebrand had now run out of puppet popes, so was forced to do the job himself. So, in 1073, he changed his name (hardly surprising for someone called Hildebrand) and became Pope Gregory VII.

Before we charge on with Gregory it's worth pausing a moment for the Patarines. Here we see the first flowering of the 'heretic' reforming movements of the twelfth century. Because the Patarine movement didn't stick at Milan: a Patarine was burned as a heretic at Cambrai, France in 1077. Actually, the problem for the church was that the Patarine movement didn't stop at all. The Patarines wanted proper root and branch reform: a contemporary church that reflected the radical Christianity of the apostles.

They were Christians who wanted real Christianity.

GREGORY VII

Gregory VII. His head actually was that shape

Name: Hildebrand.
Aka: Gregory VII.
Nationality: German.
Dates: ?–1085 (Pope 1073–85).
Appearance: Short, fat and ungainly.
Before he was famous: Son of a peasant – possibly a goatherd. Monk.
Famous for: Reforming the church and papacy. The Papal Dictates. Controlled the papacy for thirty-six years; was Pope himself for twelve. Excommunicated the emperor.
Why does he matter? Established the idea of the Pope having authority over the secular world. Imposed clerical celibacy.
Could you have a drink with him down the pub? Maybe. But it would always be your round. He was the Pope, after all.

Dictatus Papae

Hildebrand – or Gregory VII, to give him his papal name – had come from humble roots. The son of a peasant from Tuscany, he was short, fat and his accent was so thick that a lot of the time his colleagues couldn't understand what he was saying. But he had a vision: he was a big thinker. And chief among the thinks he had thunked was that the pope should rule the world. (I *told* you he had a big vision.) Many of his predecessors thought highly of themselves, but Gregory was in a different league. He saw the pope as a kind of universal monarch, with the church reigning over all the kings of the earth.

And this wasn't just a pipe dream. Gregory gave it a real go. Other popes had excommunicated the Patriarch of Constantinople. But Gregory excommunicated the emperor. Twice.

He started in determined fashion. At a synod in 1074 Gregory made clerical celibacy compulsory. Any priest who did not conform to this would be excommunicated. As we've seen, a belief in the ideal of celibacy had been growing from the fourth century onwards. Monks had taken vows of celibacy – and in the western church it was the norm for those at the higher levels of the clergy to be unmarried – but everyday clergy were often married. In fact, in many places, the priesthood was hereditary – the post was passed from father to son. Not forgetting – and this is a major part of what Gregory was concerned with – any lands that were attached to the post.*

So marriage was banned for the clergy; and for the laity it had to require clerical approval. In the eleventh and twelfth centuries – for the first time – the western church began to promote the idea that marriage was a sacrament. A sacrament is defined in the Book of Common Prayer as 'an outward and visible sign of an inward and spiritual grace'. Put simply, the sacraments are the special, sacred acts of the church.

But if marriage was a sacrament, it had to be performed inside a church, and not as was usual, outside in the churchyard, which was seen as the community's domain, rather than the priest's. And that put the decision about who should marry whom under the control of the church.†

Gregory was a papal supremacist. In 1075 he made his most ambitious statement yet. This was the *Dictatus Papae*, 'the dictates of the pope' – twenty-seven statements that made it clear the pope was responsible to God and no one else. The pope's word was therefore

---

* Celibacy for all clergy was not officially enshrined in canon law until 1139 – it took a long time for the clergy to give in to this demand. In England the married clergy resisted fiercely. But then they had English wives. By the thirteenth century celibacy was the norm everywhere, in theory (if not actually in practice).

† Over the centuries, what was and wasn't a sacrament had changed. In the early church there were two: baptism and the eucharist. In the end, Catholic theology defined seven sacraments, adding Confirmation, Penance, taking Holy Orders, marriage and anointing for the last rites to the original couple. But this list only dates from around 1150, and was not formally adopted until 1439 at the Council of Florence. The Orthodox church calls these the seven major sacraments, but argues that everything the church does is sacramental. The Anglican church rejects this view, possibly on the grounds that you would then have to include such obviously unholy church activities such as flower arranging and drinking very bad coffee: they stick to the original two.

divine law and disobeying it was a sin. (Or near enough.) The Papal Dictates claimed enormous powers for the pope: only the Roman pontiff could be called universal (in your face, Constantinople); he could depose emperors; all princes should kiss his feet; he decided what books were canonical. A sentence passed by a pope could be retracted only by the pope. No one was in a position to judge a pope.

No. 22 says that 'the Roman church has never erred; nor will it err to all eternity, the Scripture bearing witness'. No. 23 says that all canonically ordained popes are automatically made saints.

It is the most self-confident – not to say eyebrow-raising – document in history. If you look up 'chutzpah' in a dictionary you'll find a copy of the *Dictatus Papae*. One of its most incendiary clauses was No. 12: that the pope could depose emperors.

The emperor responded immediately. He appointed two German bishops, and threw in a new Archbishop of Milan for free. Gregory summoned the emperor to Rome. The emperor summoned his own council at a place called Worms (file that away for future reference) where he called Gregory a 'false monk' and sacked him from the papacy.

Gregory responded in kind: in 1076 he excommunicated the emperor.

The effect was remarkable. The last reigning monarch to be excommunicated by the pope had been Theodosius the Great in 390. Excommunication, technically, meant that none of Henry's subjects owed him any allegiance. In fact, if they did obey him, then they too should be excommunicated.

Henry blinked first. He met with his 'shareholders' – the German princes – who gave him a year and a day to be absolved and sort the mess out. But by the end of 1076 nothing had happened. Henry was beaten. That winter, with his wife and son, he headed for the only open pass across the Alps. He found the pope at the fortress of Canossa. He asked for an audience. The pope left him waiting for three days. And then, finally, absolved him.

In later centuries this story – embroidered with the idea of Henry waiting shivering and barefoot in the cold outside the castle – appears as an improving-morality lesson in the subjection of temporal power to the spiritual realm. In fact, it was a blip, a temporary surrender.

Henry hadn't repented; he merely did what he had to do in order to keep his position. And the German nobles felt let down by Gregory: they gambled that he would uphold the excommunication and therefore allow them to choose a new emperor. So they tried to impose a new emperor by more traditional means, that is, civil war. In this conflict Gregory backed Henry's opponent, Rudolf, Duke of Swabia, but Henry easily beat Rudolf in battle, then marched to Rome, and (after three attempts) took the city. Gregory barricaded himself in the Castel Sant'Angelo and had to watch, helplessly, when on Palm Sunday Henry oversaw the enthronement of Guibert, Archbishop of Ravenna, as Pope Clement III. A week later, on Easter Day, Henry was crowned Emperor in Rome.

So much for the Papal Dictates.

Fig. XIX. *At Canossa, Henry II gets fed up with the papal answering machine*

But Gregory wasn't beaten yet. He called in the heavy mob to help him: Robert Guiscard, the leader of the Normans in the south of Italy. The Normans sent in 6,000 horses and 30,000 foot soldiers. Henry informed his supporters in Rome that he had – ahem – important business back home and that he was trusting them to fight valiantly and defend the city and all that. Then he legged it. Along with his wife, children and his replacement pope.

The Normans retook the city and restored Gregory. But using the Normans was like calling in a tiger to fight off a lion. Yes, the lion runs away, but now you've got a flipping great tiger to deal with. Gregory was forced to look on in helpless despair as his so-called rescuers rampaged through Rome in a three-day orgy of destruction, violence and rape. Eventually the beleaguered people rose in desperation and fought back with the savagery of those who had nothing to lose. This time, the Normans had to fight for their lives. And in doing so they set fire to the city. The devastation was appalling. Churches, palaces, ancient historic remnants of Rome's past were caught up in the flames. The riot was quelled, the people defeated, but at a terrible price.

So the outcome of Gregory's policy of papal superiority was a devastated city and thousands dead. Shamefully, his letters show no remorse for the destruction his pig-headed, arrogant policy had wrought on ordinary folk. It didn't trouble his conscience. Because he had a Vision. And the Vision was all that mattered.

The Roman citizens, understandably, no longer shared his vision of a brave new papal world. They threw Gregory out, vision and all. He died in Salerno, in 1085, effectively in exile. His last words were typically lacking in self-knowledge: 'I have loved righteousness and hated iniquity, therefore I die in exile.' Everyone hates me, so I must be right.

The inscription on his tomb says it was 'built by Robert Guiscard at his own expense'. So much for papal supremacy: Gregory couldn't even afford his own tomb.

Strict monks and loose women

Here's how a large chunk of Christian history works:

1. Devout Christians look at the church and see that it is wealthy/lax/ corrupt/irrelevant/dictatorial (delete any that do not apply).
2. They establish a new movement to take Christianity back to its roots.
3. The new movement is successful and becomes popular.
4. The movement becomes so popular that it grows wealthy/lax/corrupt/ irrelevant/dictatorial (delete any that do not apply).
5. Rinse and repeat.

Cluny is a perfect demonstration of this. By now this 'reforming' monastery was the most magnificent abbey in France, a monastic palace with magnificent buildings and hundreds of servants. It had gone native, turned into part of the very establishment it was set up to challenge. And so new monastic orders sprang up.

In 1084 the first Carthusian monastery was established in France.* Their motto was 'never knowingly reformed'. Actually it's 'never reformed because never in need of reform', which seems like a hostage to fortune to me. They insisted that all monks live as hermits, taking vows of silence, living in individual cells, and only ever meeting for worship. Their members – never numerous – retained a really strong sense of calling. The Carthusians were one of the few monastic orders to put up a fight when Henry VIII dissolved the monasteries. (Not literally. Obviously. Although, actually, he got pretty close.)

Seven years later the Cistercians came along.† Founded as a direct response to the perceived excesses of the Benedictines, they were a rigorous, ascetic order. Monks had no possessions, hardly any food, worked incredibly hard and were allowed a fire only once a year as a Christmas present. Cistercians wanted to return to the wilderness of the original monks, so they built their monasteries in remote spots. In some cases wildernesses were hard to find, so they made their own by destroying any nearby villages, as in the case of Fountains Abbey in Yorkshire.

No Cistercian embodies their aggressive and spiritually severe approach better than their leader, Bernard of Clairvaux (1090–1153). He was a charismatic preacher of such persuasive power that it was

---

* The name comes from their place of origin: the monastery of the Grande Chartreuse (Carthusium in Latin).
† The name comes from the original monastic house at Cîteaux, which is Cistercium in Latin.

said that parents hid their children when Bernard came to town for fear they would run away to become a monk. This zeal and persuasiveness was to have terrible consequences later on.

By the end of the twelfth century there were 530 Cistercian monasteries in Europe and a Cistercian had become Pope. All directed from the HQ at Citeaux. But, typically, they fell into exactly the same kind of trap that they had been created to avoid. Their energetic, aggressive approach to life brought with it a kind of Cistercian Work Ethic. They made advances in sheep farming in England, for instance, which brought in big profits. They were the first great European corporation. So, in time, they became as wealthy as the rest.

However, they understood one of the key social factors of the times: that the laity were interested in holiness. They employed a huge number of lay brothers to do the everyday tasks. These were sworn to a simpler, less demanding monastic rule than the fully fledged monks. Living in a monastery was one way in which ordinary people could engage deeply with religion.

And ordinary people *wanted* to do that. There was a rising religious fervour. Itinerant preachers started to wander the lanes of Europe, people like Robert of Arbrissel, who was a kind of eleventh-century hippy, barefoot, dressed in rags and with long hair, who called people to a life of apostolic poverty.

Robert had been a reforming archpriest,* active in suppressing clerical abuse of power. Naturally, for this he was forced out of his diocese. He became a hermit in a forest, and then established a monastery. His monks were known simply as 'the poor of Christ'. The number and diverse social backgrounds of his followers began to worry the authorities. In 1097 he resigned as abbot and founded a new house, Fontevrault.† This was what is known as a double house: one for both monks and nuns. Astonishingly for the time, Robert stipulated that the leader of this order should always be a woman.

It certainly seems to have attracted the women. Loose women. Or ex-loose women, at least: there is evidence that his disciples included

---

* A priest who supervised a number of parishes. It's really an Eastern Orthodox term. Compare the whole archimandrite thing.
† The abbey was dissolved in the French Revolution. It's the burial place of Henry II of England, his wife Eleanor of Aquitaine and Richard I of England, among other notables, absolutely none of whom espoused the ascetic principles of Robert.

former prostitutes. For the rest of his life he went on missionary journeys throughout Europe, calling everyone to a life of simplicity and poverty.

There was an increasing feeling that people did not necessarily need 'the professionals'. Everyone could be involved. And that factor is what lay behind the medieval passion for pilgrimage.

Pilgrim's progress

Relics had been popular since the fourth century, but in the medieval period they *really* took off. Every church needed a good relic.

Rome had Peter (and Paul). Santiago had discovered the bones of St James. Venice had St Mark. (He had originally been at Alexandria, but his bones had been 'removed for safekeeping' by Venetian tradesmen in 828, lest the Muslims desecrate the tomb.)*

Indeed, there was big competition for relics. Your church was nothing if you didn't have a relic.† Get a good first-class saint's relic and you were guaranteed prestige and increased tourism. If you removed a saint's relics from one place to another, it wasn't called 'theft', but 'translating': and it was often accompanied by tales of miracles at the new resting place to show that the saint had really wanted a bit of a change all along. Perhaps the most extreme example of this craving for relics is Bishop Hugh of Lincoln, who went to see the arm of Mary Magdalene at Fécamp. After having tried unsuccessfully to break off a piece of the arm, he attempted to bite off one of the index fingers. He went home with a few fragments, and probable toothache.

There were bits of the true cross all over the place and at least three heads of John the Baptist. One pilgrim was shown the skull of John the Baptist at two different places on two days running. And the treasury of Cologne Cathedral had, according to one list, the skull of John the Baptist at twelve years of age. I'm still trying to work that one out . . .

These treasuries were the forerunners of modern museums, since

---

* They were hidden in a barrel of pork to stop the Muslim customs officer finding them.
† In fact, the official definition of an altar, in Roman Catholic canon law, is still 'a sepulchre containing the relics of saints'.

they might include, among the relics, other objects of curiosity. The treasury of the Cathedral of St Guy in Prague had the following:

* the skulls of Saints Adalbert and Venceslas
* the sword of St Stephen
* the crown of thorns
* pieces of the true cross
* the tablecloth used at the Last Supper
* one of St Marguerite's teeth
* a shinbone of St Vitalis
* a rib from St Sophia
* the chin of St Eoban
* St Affia's shoulder blades

It's like a medieval game of *Operation*.*

But as we've seen, to visit and venerate and pray at the shrine of a saint was to touch salvation: if anyone was certain of a place in heaven, a 100 per cent bona fide saint surely was. And so people began to travel long distances to pray at the shrine of a particular saint. The age of pilgrimage had begun.

Medieval pilgrims believed they were heading for places where miracles happened. These miracles were carefully logged by the local monks; for instance the *Miraculi Sancti Wulstani* logs the miracles occurring in the thirteenth century at the shrine of Saint Wulstan in Worcester.

Sometimes only a specific shrine could give you the results you wanted. A weaver in Canterbury who was crippled with a 'bone ach' prayed for many years at the tomb of Saint Thomas with no effect. Then a passing pilgrim from Norfolk recommended the shrine of St Walstan in Bawburgh in Norfolk. The weaver made a vow to go there and immediately he was healed. In gratitude he walked – without crutches – to Bawburgh, where he left a wax model of his leg as a votive offering.†

---

* And I haven't even mentioned the ash-plant of Moses, some of Mary's clothes, an elephant's tusk and a whale's rib. Say what you like about St Guy's in Prague, it's got something for everybody.

† People often left wax, silver, or gold models of the relevant healed body part at the shrine where they'd been healed. These were hung around the shrine as a kind of advert of the healing powers of that saint. When said body parts got too numerous they were melted down. The wax ones were made into candles. I imagine you could get quite a number of candles from one leg.

Many shrines had pools associated with them in which the pilgrims would bathe. You could bring back a vial of holy water from the river or the well, either to be drunk or to anoint the sick.*

But pilgrimage was about more than just visiting the shrine. There were other reasons too.

Some pilgrims went out of gratitude. Sailors caught in a storm vowed that if God spared them, they would go on pilgrimage. A French woman, caught in the throes of a difficult birth, vowed with her husband that if she survived, they would go on pilgrimage together. (The vow was later commuted on the grounds that every year after that she was pregnant and couldn't travel. Apparently some people never learn.) Louis VII of France went on pilgrimage as an act of thanksgiving when he replaced a bad wife with a better one.

Although clearly some just viewed it as a bit of a jolly, like Chaucer's Wife of Bath who is on the trip to Canterbury 'for the sake of the voyage', pilgrimage was supposed to be difficult. Occasionally church leaders reminded their flocks that pilgrimage was not supposed to be a holiday.

Going barefoot was extremely popular. Some even went the entire distance on their knees. The suffering was supposed to add to the salvation. No pain, no (heavenly) gain. Their reward was, in the words of Bede, 'a warmer welcome from the saints in heaven'. If you went on pilgrimage it meant that you would be fast-tracked past the queues at the Pearly Gates and ushered into the VIP Lounge (Very Important Pilgrims), with the odd angel or two floating around with trays of canapés and a glass of sherry.

The penitential aspect of pilgrimage is reflected in the fact that wrongdoers could be sentenced to go on pilgrimage by the courts or by the local bishop. When Pecham, Archbishop of Canterbury, found the Rector of Hamme in the Diocese of Chichester guilty of continual 'incontinence and fornication with various women' he sentenced him to go on three pilgrimages: to Santiago, Rome and Cologne.†
Appropriately, given the nature of his crimes, the rector's name was Roger. Presumably the idea of the three long journeys was to wear Roger the Rector out.

* Even a cynical scholar like Erasmus claimed that the water from the Walsingham spring was 'efficacious in curing pains of the head and stomach'.
† Incontinence here means lack of self-control. Not the runs, which were more often a consequence of pilgrimage rather than a cause. Especially if you drank the Holy Water.

Such pilgrimages could be avoided if you paid a fine instead. A 1338 list of pilgrimages from the Flemish town of Oudenade lists various penitential pilgrimages, along with their monetary value. The most expensive was a trip to St Nicholas of Bari, which would cost you 20 pounds to get out of. Interestingly, there are three British shrines listed: St Andrew's in Scotland (8 pounds), Our Lady at Salisbury in England (6 pounds) and St Thomas of Canterbury in England (also 6 pounds). The cheapest was a pilgrimage to Our Lady of Aardenburg, which could be avoided for 12 shillings. Bargain.

And it was pilgrimage – or opposition to it – that was to be the ostensible cause for one of the biggest tragedies of the whole of church history.

Urban's army

In the east the Turks were definitely winning in the Best New Terrifying Power category. They had taken over from the Arabs as the main power in Islam and in 1071 they conquered Armenia, inflicting a terrible, brutal slaughter on the inhabitants. The Byzantine emperor, Romanus IV Diogenes, led an army against them.* But it was a disaster. The Battle of Manzikert in 1071 was the most humiliating military defeat in the history of the Byzantine Empire. The emperor was captured, the Byzantine army wiped out and almost all of Asia Minor became 'the lands of the Turks': Turkey, as we know it today.

For the Christians in the west, though, there was better news. In 1085 a Christian army recaptured the city of Toledo from the occupying Muslims. It was the first stage in a campaign that saw the end to 350 years of occupation. And it started to give people ideas. Because if you could drive the Muslims out of Spain, then maybe there were other places you could drive them out of as well . . .

At Easter 1094 a new pope assumed the throne.† His name was Urban II – which is probably the most hip-hop name of any pope, unless there is a Pope P-Diddy lurking somewhere.‡ And he had some big ideas.

---

* If you think his name is fancy, his wife was called Eudokia Makrembolitissa.
† He'd actually been appointed Pope seven years earlier, in 1087, but the anti-pope Clement was in command in the city and it took seven years before he could enter Rome.
‡ It comes from the Latin *urbanus*, meaning 'city dweller'.

First up was the reunification of the church. Urban sent emissaries to Constantinople to the emperor Alexius calling for a great council of the church. The emperor – desperate for western military aid against the Turks, who now controlled most of the area east of Constantinople – readily agreed.

When the council gathered in Piacenza, the emperor's emissaries told spine-chilling stories of Turkish atrocities visited upon innocent pilgrims. Asia Minor was now in the possession of Islam. Pope Urban was impressed. But he reckoned that the initial scheme – to undo the most recent Muslim landgrab – wasn't ambitious enough. Never mind driving the Saracens from Asia Minor, why not drive them out from *all* the holy places?

And thus he invented the Crusades.*

He called a further council at Clermont-Ferrand on 18 November. He let it be known that he was going to make a big statement at a public session, open to all. Urban was a pope who really understood marketing. The excitement generated by this teaser campaign was huge.†
The town was packed solid. The pope had a platform set up in a field, from which he called on princes, knights and assorted thugs-for-hire to rescue the Holy Land from the clutches of the infidel. He declared that there would be a crusade. He had his own version of the dodgy dossier – a catalogue of (apparently imaginary) abuses Muslims had performed on the Christians in Palestine. He urged his listeners to 'take up the cross' and to go and kill the infidel, which I can't help thinking is not what Jesus had in mind when he first used the phrase. There must be no delay. A task force must assemble. And it should be ready by the Feast of the Assumption, 15 August 1096.

And to make it better there were incentives, the spiritual equivalent of cash-back. The conquerors would be able to keep all the lands they conquered by the force of arms and any Crusader who died on the journey would get fast-tracked to heaven, with no time in purgatory, extra leg-room and a bonus packet of dry salted nuts. This is the first public appearance of what was to become known as an indulgence – a document that granted forgiveness for a certain amount of past sins, and that would

* © Pope Urban II, 1094. All rights reserved. The name comes from their emblem: the crux or cross.
† Experts maintain that the excitement level has not been rivalled by any meeting in history, with the possible exception of the average Apple product launch.

consequently reduce, or cut completely, time spent in purgatory. Later on such indulgences would be sold at pilgrimage sites and to raise church funds. You could buy them in days, months or years. They were like iTunes vouchers for Purgatory. Time off for holy behaviour.

Not only was there the promise of loot and adventure, but it was also spiritual reward as well. It was the ultimate win-win scenario. People went mad for the idea. Led by Bishop Adhemar of Le Puy, several hundred people – priests and monks, noblemen and peasants together – knelt before Urban's throne and pledged themselves to take the cross. The Crusades were under way.

Fig. XX. *Pope Urban II launches the First Crusade*

Wild-goose chase

From Clermont the word went out through Europe, carried back not only by the feudal lords who had signed up, but by wandering preachers too. Many people seemed gripped by the madness. One small army even headed off led only by a prophetic goose.*

One of the most successful salesmen for the Crusades was a wandering preacher called Peter the Hermit, who roamed the highways and byways of France and Germany riding a donkey and eating nothing but fish. Peter's preaching of the crusade worked like a kind of medieval Twitter, spreading the word far more quickly than the official announcements. There was something of the Old Testament prophet about this itinerant preacher. His sermons fired up the imagination of so many peasants that while the proper army was still being organised, forty thousand men, women and children gathered in the Rhineland in 1096, where they began warming up for their great, heroic adventure in the Holy Land by slaughtering thousands of Jews in Germany – the first large-scale massacre of Jews in Europe. Not a good omen.

This so-called People's Crusade soon lost all semblance of order. In Hungary they looted Belgrade, killing four thousand people. They were then attacked by Hungarian forces and some ten thousand of their number were killed. When they reached Constantinople, the emperor could scarcely believe his eyes. He was expecting a proper grown-up army: what he got was an early version of football hooligans, led by a filthy monk who smelt of fish. He suggested that they wait for the proper army, but they were too impatient. They headed across the Bosphorus and into Turkish territory, eager to fight the infidel.

The accounts are truly appalling. In Nicea they indulged in horrific barbarism, torturing and killing the citizens and, if the reports are true, even spit-roasting babies. And the worst of it was that the Niceans were actually Christians, who were simply living under Turkish rule. When the Turks arrived, they showed no mercy and the amateur army was massacred. In the end around 3,000 people made it back to Constantinople: over 90 per cent of those who had started out on this great pilgrimage-war lost their lives.

---

* The goose died in Lorraine, apparently worn out by its exertions. Whether it benefited from less time in purgatory we don't know.

Shock and awe

The People's Crusade was a disastrous failure. The knights, however, did eventually make it to their destination (slightly hampered by the fact that they could move only two spaces forward and one sideways). In 1097 the official army arrived at the walls of Antioch. They began the siege in fine form, by catapulting the heads of 200 Turkish soldiers over the wall. But the walls proved unbreachable and, as the weather grew colder, food grew short. Thousands starved to death. Matters were not helped by the arrival of a group of Flemish survivors from Peter's crusade, who, apparently, had developed a taste for human flesh. They were particularly keen on roasted Turk. Well, it was Christmas, after all.

Finally, though, the city capitulated and the exhausted Crusaders entered and gleefully looted the city. When they looked out again, they found that the Turkish reinforcements had arrived and now the Crusaders were the ones being besieged.

It was time for a miracle. And one duly arrived. Another Peter found a relic buried under the ancient cathedral in Antioch. It was none other than the holy lance – the spear that pierced the side of Christ himself. This was truly a miracle, not least because there was one already on display in Constantinople. But the people didn't care. Inspired by the relic, maddened by hunger, desperate like cornered rats, they burst out of the city, attacked the Turks and routed them.

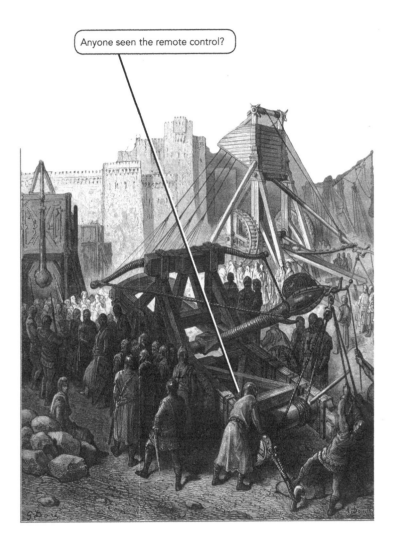

Fig. XXI. *Outside Jerusalem, the Crusading army hits a snag*

Many would have been happy to stop there. Apart from anything else, an Arab army had recaptured Jerusalem from the Turks, and thus one of the excuses for the Crusade – Turkish abuse of pilgrims – was no longer valid. But for others, Jerusalem remained the goal. Particularly for the sixty-year-old French count Raymond. He gathered together a group of zealous Crusaders and led them south, barefoot, to Jerusalem.

On Friday 15 July 1099, after a difficult and arduous siege, the Crusaders managed to capture Jerusalem. Their joy was expressed in widespread slaughter. Muslims in the city were massacred. Synagogues full of Jews were burnt to the ground in what Raymond's chaplain called 'a just and splendid judgement of God'. As one Crusader wrote home:

> If you had been there you would have seen our feet coloured to our ankles with the blood of the slain. But what more shall I relate? None of them were left alive; neither women nor children were spared. Afterward, all clergy, laymen went to the Sepulchre of the Lord and his glorious temple singing. With fitting humility, they repeated prayers and made their offering at the holy places they had long desired to visit.

The Crusaders went on to capture further territory in the area, and established the Crusader states of the Kingdom of Jerusalem, the County of Tripoli, the Principality of Antioch and the County of Edessa.

Militarily the operation was a success. Jerusalem had been recaptured. Many infidels were brutally slaughtered. It was a triumph for peace, justice and the European feudal way.

But the survival of the Crusader kingdoms was always precarious. Most of the Crusaders returned home in 1100, leaving only a few hundred knights in their newfound kingdom. The kingdom of Jerusalem was repeatedly under attack and none of the Crusader strongholds managed to hold off recapture for long.

And it did nothing for east–west unity, either. As Crusaders crossed Turkey they looted and burned many Byzantine cities that still had Christian inhabitants. Later eastern emperors grew to fear the advent of a crusade – and with good reason.

A knight at the Crusades

There were various crusading orders of knights founded during the conflicts and most of these exemplify the mixed morality of the Crusades.

The Knights Hospitallers were founded to care for the sick and the wounded, but eventually took up arms and started putting people *into* hospital. I suppose that's one form of alternative medicine. Another crusading order, the Teutonic Knights, started running a tent hospital for pilgrims at Acre in 1189 and ended up fighting in the Baltic and Russia where they 'encouraged' the pagan inhabitants to embrace Christ.

The most famous of these orders are the Knights Templar, founded in 1118 to protect pilgrims to Jerusalem. King Baldwin II of Jerusalem granted space for their headquarters in the captured Al-Aqsa Mosque on Temple Mount. The Templars believed this to be the temple of Herod the Great – a bit of a schoolboy error, since Herod's temple had been burned to the ground a thousand years earlier. But with a blissful stupidity they took their name from this 'temple'. They also took the building as a kind of ideal church pattern, and built a series of churches throughout Europe in this circular plan.*

They grew immensely wealthy and powerful, so much so that they too in the end were purged. The French king, Philip IV, in connivance with Pope Clement V, suppressed the order on a series of fabricated charges and false confessions extorted through torture. The leaders of the order were executed as heretics and their wealth and lands confiscated. The order disappeared, and today the only place it is found is in the pages of dubious thrillers where the Knights Templar are always depicted as a cunning, clever secret society in possession of mysterious secrets. In fact, they were a bunch of people so stupid that they built a series of churches based on the floorplan of a mosque.

Say what you like about the Crusades, they did bring us some benefits. Such as the apricot. And Saint George becoming patron saint of England. And . . . well, that's probably it.

Anselm and the God-man

In the eleventh century, schools of education had grown up around certain cathedrals and Benedictine monasteries. These developed into what were called cathedral schools.

Berengar, head of the Cathedral School of Tours, was a man

* Perhaps the best known of these is the twelfth-century Temple church in London.

renowned for his piety and asceticism. But – whisper it – there were rumours that he was not *entirely* orthodox. It was claimed he believed that the theory of transubstantiation – the idea that the bread and wine of the Eucharist actually turned into the body and blood of Jesus – could not be literally true.

He was opposed by Lanfranc of Normandy. God's truth, revealed by the church, is perfect, Lanfranc argued. The evidence of your own senses is not to be believed if it is contradicted by the authority of the church.

Berengar was excommunicated by Leo IX, and, in the end, was forced to submit to the traditional teaching. He never got over the way he was treated, and retreated to an island near Tours where he lived the rest of his life in solitude, silence and with a brooding sense of injustice.

Lanfranc was succeeded by Anselm (1033–1109), who later became Archbishop of Canterbury. He didn't believe that logic and reason were incompatible with the traditional teachings of the church. He used logic in his famous theory, which is called 'the ontological argument for the existence of God'.

It goes like this:

1. God can be defined as the greatest thing imaginable.
2. Things that really exist, by definition, are greater than things that are imagined.
3. Therefore, God must exist because otherwise he would not be the greatest thing imaginable.

It's an argument so circular you could use it as a hula hoop.

Anselm's most influential work, though, was *Cur Deus Homo?* Literally *Why God Man?* It was an attempt to work out why God had to become man and die on the cross. The traditional teaching had been the ransom theory: Satan held the human race captive and Jesus' blood paid the ransom price. But Anselm couldn't see how that worked at all. I mean, God is really big and powerful, right? More powerful than Satan, certainly. So if Satan kept humanity captive, surely God could just kick down the doors and release the prisoners by force.

Instead, Anselm suggested that everyone had dishonoured and disobeyed God. They had sinned. And God cannot just overlook this – otherwise there would be no difference between good and evil and no incentive to choose between the two. He had to receive satisfaction. But while humanity owes God satisfaction, none of us is good enough to pay it

– because all have been devalued by sin. Only God, in fact, is great enough to be able to pay this price. So God entered the world as Jesus and offered himself up to be killed. This made 'satisfaction' for the human race, of which he was a part and which he represented. It's a theory rooted in feudal society, where honour has to be restored by satisfaction. But it has proved to be the most influential of all theories of the atonement.

The unkindest cut of all

As well as the cathedral schools, the bigger of the Italian cities started developing their own schools as well, influenced by the Muslim schools of higher education, such as the school of Al-Azhar in Cairo, which had lectures, professors and degrees. (Being an Islamic country, though, the Students' Union bar was rubbish.) Out of these two types of education a new form emerged: the university.

These places became hotbeds of discourse, exploration and experimentation. They churned out new ideas. And old ideas rebranded as new ideas. This intellectual movement was named after these 'schools': Scholasticism. In Paris the university that emerged from the cathedral school of Notre Dame became the leading theological school in Europe. Indeed, it was a Paris scholar who popularised the term 'theology' when he called one of his books *Theologia Christiana*. His name was Peter Abelard (1079–1142).

He had come to Paris in 1100 as a student. Like many students he was rather unimpressed by his tutor. But unlike many students he made up for this disappointment, not by going on Facebook and moaning, but by giving rival lectures to correct his tutor's teaching. He eventually took over his tutor's students – and his job. Tact was never Peter's strong point.

Eventually students came from all over Europe to hear his teaching. He was now at the height of his fame, the undefeated heavyweight champion of philosophy. (At least according to Peter Abelard.)

And then he was asked by Fulbert, a canon of Notre Dame cathedral, to take on a bit of private tuition, teaching philosophy to Fulbert's beautiful young niece Heloise. And then philosophy went right out of the window and their lessons became more what you might call biology. Like all the greatest rom-coms, they defied convention, fell in love, got secretly married, and Peter was brutally castrated. OK, maybe not *quite* like the rom-coms then. I can't see Hugh Grant rushing to play that part.

Yes, Fulbert broke up their relationship in the most final of ways, by having Peter castrated. Heloise, who had given birth to their child (she called him Astrolabe, after the scientific instrument*), was forced to become a nun. She later founded a convent, one that became known for its tolerance and progressive approach.

Abelard became a monk, and later Abbot of the monastery, where his celebrated tact won him such respect that at one point his monks actually tried to kill him. But he was able to write and think. And, more to the point, encourage others to think. In one work, *Yes and No*, he juxtaposed 158 apparently contradictory passages from the church fathers and challenged readers to make up their own mind. He had no doubts about the power of . . . er . . . doubt. 'Through doubting we come to questioning and through questions we perceive the truth,' he wrote, 'we come to inquiry, by inquiry we come to truth.' It was daring stuff. Abelard was opening the way for a sceptical, questioning approach to church tradition.

In particular, Peter thought a lot about the suffering of Jesus. Abelard knew about 'justice' and vengeance, and came to reject completely Anselm's idea of the atoning satisfaction of Christ's death. For him the meaning of Christ's sacrifice was not payment for some kind of punishment, but the greatest act of sacrificial love. John 15.13 was the key verse: 'Greater love has no one than this, than to lay down one's life for one's friends.' For God to require the blood of an innocent man in payment of a debt seemed cruel and perverse. For Abelard, Christ's death was an example, a model of self-sacrificial love. Salvation was therefore found not in the payment of a debt, but in imitation of Christ and loving others in the way that he did.

He never fell out of love with Heloise, and they wrote to each other as long as they lived. They were buried together, achieving in death the closeness denied them in life.

Crossing out

Around 1130 a French preacher called Peter of Bruis also started to ask questions. We don't know a great deal about Peter – and what we do

---

* One wonders what they would have named their other children, had they had any. I'm thinking Compass, Abacus and Sinclair Scientific Calculator.

know comes from his opponents. But it seems that he and his followers apparently denied 'that children, before the age of understanding, can be saved by the baptism'. They were the first group since the days of the early church to argue for believer's baptism. Second, they believed that since God was everywhere, churches were pointless. Third, they didn't understand the veneration of the cross: 'because that form or instrument by which Christ was so dreadfully tortured, so cruelly slain, is not worthy of any adoration, or veneration or supplication'. They denied the theory of transubstantiation, and finally they derided 'sacrifices, prayers, alms, and other good works by the faithful living for the faithful dead, and say that these things cannot aid any of the dead even in the least'.

What these denials of key doctrinal points boiled down to was an attack on the authority – and wealth – of the church. It is likely that Peter and his followers were not opposed to churches per se, but to richly adorned and wealthy ones (hence also, perhaps, the attack on veneration of the cross as they saw it practised). And prayers and masses held for the dead brought in a lot of income for the church.

In or around the year 1126 Peter went to the town of St Gilles near Nîmes. There he built a fire and started throwing crosses into it as a protest. This was not the brightest idea since St Gilles was a centre for pilgrimage and therefore most people there were really rather keen on crosses and churches and all that kind of stuff. The mob turned on him and the unfortunate Peter was thrown into his own bonfire.

But Peter's teachings were not so easily disposed of. His ideas were adopted and, indeed, adapted by a former monk called Henry of Lausanne. Tall, bearded, bare-footed, a charismatic speaker, Henry lived by alms and slept on the ground. Henry incited the people to ignore ecclesiastical authority – which was pretty easy, since the ecclesiastical authorities were not tall, bearded charismatic figures who lived by alms and slept on the ground.

Henry argued that the gospel was the sole rule of faith. Like Peter he was against infant baptism, transubstantiation, prayers for the dead, and . . . well, you name it, he was probably against it. His preaching achieved rapid success in the south of France, so much so in fact that it attracted the attention of the most powerful Catholic orator of his age: Bernard of Clairvaux.

BERNARD

Bernard of Clairvaux, a man on a mission

Name: Bernard Sorrel.
Aka: Bernard of Clairvaux.
Nationality: French.
Dates: 1090–1153.
Appearance: Tall, gaunt, with a bad back.
Before he was famous: Monk.
Famous for: Preaching. Heretic hunting. Founding monasteries.
Why does he matter? He shows what happens when zeal gets turned up to eleven.
Could you have a drink with him down the pub? No. Just no.

'You do not love'

Few men have been more driven in their life than Bernard Sorrel, better known as Bernard of Clairvaux, after the monastery he had founded aged just twenty-five. He was tall, gaunt, austere. In near permanent pain from the severe lifestyle he had adopted. Burning with righteous zeal and dismissive of those who thought differently, Bernard was the most influential churchman of his generation – far more so than any of the popes (or antipopes) of the time.

He had massive reserves of energy. He was perpetually on the move, cajoling, arguing, bullying people into following his line. A compulsive letter writer, he had a finger in virtually every religious controversy of the time.

He had to travel so much because heresy was everywhere. When he went to hunt down the followers of Henry of Lausanne, he found an entire region full of heresy: towns like Bergerac, Périgueux, Sarlat, Cahors and Toulouse. At Bernard's approach Henry departed Toulouse, but he left behind many adherents, especially among the ordinary people. Bernard called heretics 'the little foxes that spoil the vines'. He loathed the idea of these little people, these nobodies, daring to attack the rooted, historical church. And they were *everywhere*. Hidden, of course, secret. They didn't wear 'I ♥ Peter de Bruis' t-shirts. They talked and discussed and thought their own thoughts. And the church was pushed to ever more extreme acts of fox hunting. Henry was still actively preaching in 1145, by the way, but when he was caught he ended up in jail for the rest of his life.

Famous people could be heretics as well. Bernard loathed Abelard and, in 1140, managed to get Abelard condemned at Rome as a heretic – an act that inspired Peter the Venerable, Abbot of Cluny, to write to Bernard with these quietly devastating words: 'You perform all the difficult religious duties: you fast, you watch, you suffer; but you will not endure the easy ones – you do not love.'

He was wrong, though. Bernard *was* in love. He was in love with the church. And he loved it with the pure, blind, chilling passion of the fanatic. In later times he would have been a fantastic KGB officer. He was incorruptible and unimpeachable. He was pure. Adamantine. Flintlike. He walked the talk, certainly. But it was a walk across coals of fire.

Bernard had the true, restless hatred of a fanatic. When there was a conflict between Innocent and Anacletus, two rival popes, Bernard campaigned ceaselessly for Innocent. Anacletus was from Cluny, a monastery Bernard loathed on account of its worldiness and greed. Worse, he had Jewish forebears. Bernard wrote that 'it is to the injury of Christ that the offspring of a Jew should have seized for himself the throne of St Peter'. Quite how Christ – himself a Jew – should have been injured by this he never made clear.

Bernard founded new communities throughout Europe, including several in England, Wales and Ireland. By the time of his death, in 1153, Clairvaux proper had grown to a community of some 700 monks.

His interference in church politics brought him the support of several popes. Not that he was always supportive of them. When Eugenius III was elected, Bernard wrote to those who had made the choice, 'May God forgive you what you have done! . . . What reason or counsel, when the Supreme Pontiff was dead, made you rush upon a mere rustic, lay hands on him in his refuge, wrest from his hands the axe, pick or hoe, and lift him to a throne?'

To Eugenius he wrote, 'Thus does the finger of God raise up the poor out of the dust and lift up the beggar from the dunghill, that he may sit with princes and inherit the throne of glory.'

And what is remarkable about this is that Eugenius was one of his friends! He was a former monk of Clairvaux and one of Bernard's disciples.

As Pope, though, Eugenius faced a problem. Several Christian states had been established as kinds of spin-offs from the First Crusade. One of these was the Christian County of Edessa, established by Baldwin of Boulogne in 1098. It was the most easterly – and therefore the most vulnerable – of the Crusader states and on Christmas Eve 1144 it was conquered by an Arab army under the brilliantly named Imad ad-Din Zengi, Atabeg of Mosul. Try saying that three times really fast.

The news was a stunning surprise back in the west, where people believed the Crusader states would be permanent. Eugenius, who was a mild-mannered, quiet man, asked Louis VII of France to put together a task force.* Louis agreed, for a number of reasons. First, he was a pious man, although some might have called him dull. Second, he thought the journey might bring a sense of seriousness to his rather flighty wife, Eleanor of Aquitaine. Third, he had recently been involved in some atrocious massacres for which he wished to atone with a visit to Jerusalem.

But when Louis tried to rally the troops, they showed a marked lack of enthusiasm for the whole thing. So Louis called in his master motivator. He unleashed Bernard.

Bernard addressed the crowds at an assembly at Vézelay. Not for nothing was he called 'Doctor Honeytongue'. He was magnificent, eloquent, forceful. He was wearing a palm cross that the pope had sent him, and, just by purest coincidence, he had prepared bundles of them in readiness for all the volunteers. As he spoke, people started to cry out for these crosses – and when the supply ran out, Bernard ripped his own clothes up to provide more.

He talked thousands of his listeners into signing up and cheerily going to their deaths in a welter of blood and stupidity.

Personally, it could have gone better for Louis. Eleanor accompanied him on the crusade but was deeply bored by him. When they eventually reached Antioch, she hooked up with her uncle, Prince Raymond of Antioch. It was widely rumoured that she and Uncle Ray got on very

---

* Whatever his faults, Eugenius was a man of integrity. From the day of his enthronement to his death, he always wore his white Cistercian habit under his papal robes. He was also a confirmed Anglophile; he once told John of Salisbury he thought the English were the best of all races (apart from when frivolity got the better of them).

well. Too well. Meanwhile, a huge Turkish force was marching towards them, and the only possible support the Crusaders had were the Muslims of Damascus, whose ruler was hostile to Imad ed-Din, the Turkish leader. Only an idiot would launch an attack on the only possible allies he might have in the region. So that's what Louis did.

He compounded this idiocy by failing to conquer the city and just five days after the siege began his forces were forced to retreat. Across the Syrian desert. At the height of summer. Attacked every step of the way by Arab archers. Thousands died – of sickness, starvation and Arab arrows.

Back in Europe, Bernard, when he heard the news, far from admitting any liability, decided that it was all the fault of the Byzantines. He even suggested they should launch a Crusade against Constantinople. As Peter Levi wrote, 'If ever a saint spent time in purgatory it must have been Bernard. He may be said to have invented the Christian European God of 1914.'

The English pontiff

Back in Rome Eugenius had other problems.

Or problem, singular. In the form of an agitator and revolutionary called Arnold of Brescia (1100–1155). Arnold was an Augustinian monk. The Augustinians took their name from Augustine of Hippo. They deliberately lived and worked in cities and towns. They were monks for the people and their accessibility made them very popular and valued by ordinary lay worshippers.

Arnold had studied under Peter Abelard. (Not literally, obviously. That position had been reserved for Heloise.) Arnold had come to detest the worldly power of the church. He did not mince his words. The cardinals were full of 'pride, avarice, hypocrisy, and shame'. The pope himself was 'a man of blood who maintained his authority by fire and sword, a tormentor of churches and oppressor of the innocent whose only actions were for the gratification of his lust and for the emptying of other men's coffers in order that his own might be filled'.

Go on, Arnold, tell us what you *really* think.

In the towns and cities of Europe there was a steadily growing class of tradesmen and labourers and artisans who simply could not understand what the wealthy, luxury-loving, political animals of the church had in common with Jesus and his fishermen-friends. These were not stupid people. They made things. And many of them became followers of Arnold. Arnold was no saint – later on he seems to have sanctioned violence – but he did reflect the times.

Bernard, of course, hated him. At the same synod where Bernard had Abelard condemned, Arnold was condemned as well. But, while Abelard submitted to his rebuke and kept his head down, Arnold didn't. When he was expelled from France, he went straight to Rome.

He arrived to find a city in turmoil. Some agitators within the city had attacked the papal guards and established a republic. Arnold joined them and soon rose to leadership. And the Roman populace *loved* him. Such was his popularity in the city that Eugenius offered to reverse the excommunication as long as Arnold was really, really sorry. But Arnold wasn't sorry. And such was the strength of opposition that it was the pope who had to leave the city.

Eugenius died before he could solve the Arnold-problem. It was left to one of his successors, the first and only English pope, Hadrian IV née Nicholas Breakspear, from St Albans. Other boys run away to join the circus: Nicholas ran away as a boy to join the monastery. He was refused admission in St Albans, so he went to France. After some time in Rome he went and reorganised the church in Scandanavia. Then he returned to Rome, presumably to thaw out. And became Pope.

Hadrian took action. First he had to do something about the unrest in Rome. So he went big. It was no use excommunicating Arnold; that had already been done. Hadrian excommunicated the entire city. In 1155 he closed all the churches in Rome. They could open only for the baptism of infants and the absolution of the dying; otherwise nothing. Nada. Lockdown. It was a papal curfew. There were bodies piling up. Easter was approaching. The Romans were beaten.

Hadrian regained the city with the aid of a new emperor, Frederick Barbarossa. Frederick was tall, powerful, charismatic, with a steely determination to restore the empire to the glory days of Charlemagne, and a big ginger beard.* He had come to Rome to be crowned, and Hadrian used him to mop up any resistance.

Arnold was captured by the imperial troops and found guilty of treason. He walked calmly to the scaffold and was hanged. His executioners were,

---

* Barbarossa is Italian for 'red beard'. In Germany, he was known as Kaiser Rotbart, Rotbart being German for, er, 'red beard'.

apparently, in tears. His body was cut down and burned, to ensure that no relics remained. And the ashes were scattered in the Tiber.

He was not accused of heresy. Heresy was not, at this time, a capital offence.

But all that was going to change.

Illegal immigrants

In May 1163 a church council in Tours addressed a 'damnable heresy' that had spread throughout a number of French provinces. Like a biological infection it was undermining the 'vineyard of the Lord'. The council ordered that heretics and their followers should be expelled from the community, that no one should trade with them, that their goods should be confiscated. They should be hunted out of their lairs, and imprisoned.

Heresy had been around a long time. Civil powers had been invoked, albeit sporadically. A few had been executed. But this was taking things up a notch.

Now both the heretics and their followers were to be targeted. And the hunt was to be proactive. No more waiting for heresy to show itself. Search and destroy.

Welcome to the War on Heresy.*

The council had been held under the patronage of King Henry II of England – and also the Duke of Aquitaine. Two years later he had the opportunity to demonstrate his orthodoxy when some Germans were found wandering around in Worcestershire. When questioned, they exhibited signs that they had been infected with heresy. They claimed to be Christians who believed in the apostolic teaching. But they 'attacked holy baptism, communion and matrimony, and wickedly dared to belittle the Catholic unity which is fostered by these divine aids'.

They were tried in Oxford over New Year 1165/1166. King Henry II took charge of the hearing himself. In accordance with the stipulations of the council – and a new royal ordinance declared by Henry himself – the poor Germans were stripped of their clothing and driven out into

* I haven't cited sources in this book for reasons of readability, space and applied laziness, but this phrase and much of the material on the twelfth-century heretics comes from R. I. Moore's brilliant, seminal book *The War on Heresy*.

the snow. According to a later report from a monk, 'Nobody showed the slightest mercy towards them, and they died in misery.'

And as they went to their fate they chanted, 'Blessed are they which are persecuted for righteousness' sake, for theirs is the kingdom of Heaven.'

Where's Waldo?

And still the interest in religion continued to rise.

'Everywhere in our cities and villages, not only in our schools but at the street corners, learned and ignorant, great and small, are discussing the gravest mysteries,' wrote the bishops of France to the pope in 1140. Crikey. People discussing religion. The nerve.

One of those taking an interest was Peter Valdes. An early biographer, Stephen of Bourbon,* described Valdes as someone who was 'not well-educated, but on hearing the gospels was anxious to learn more precisely what was in them'. And when, around 1170, he learned what was in them, he took it literally. Leaving enough money to care for his wife and family, he sold whatever else he owned and gave the money to the poor.

Valdes took the Bible to the people. He commissioned Bible translations into French and went out preaching to whoever would listen to the need for purity and holiness and generally doing what Jesus said. Naturally, the authorities ordered him to shut up. Valdes took his case to the pope, who approved of his voluntary poverty but banned him and his followers from speaking anywhere but in church. Since no clergy were ever going to invite him in, this amounted to a complete ban. Valdes refused. He and his followers carried on their unofficial preaching, with the result that they were excommunicated and driven out of Lyons. They became known as the Waldensians.

The Waldensians were eventually driven from France, but far from being destroyed they went underground and spread, establishing centres in Germany and central Europe. By the time they emerged again they found that the Protestant Reformation had nicked most of their best ideas. But they established the Chiesa Evangelica (Evangelical Church) in Piedmont and even travelled to America, where in the late nineteenth century some Italian Waldensians established the town of Valdese, North Carolina.

---

* That's a place, not a reference to Stephen's drinking habits.

Redbeards and Lionhearts

In 1187 a Kurdish Muslim called Salah al-Din Yusuf ibn Ayyub (better known in Europe as Saladin) surrounded Jerusalem with his troops. The Crusaders held out as long as they could, but in the end they were forced to negotiate a surrender and the Muslims re-entered Jerusalem.

Naturally, they looted and pillaged and raped . . . oh, hang on, no, they didn't. Sorry. Force of habit. Saladin ensured that not a house was looted and not a single inhabitant killed. He offered Frankish Christians their freedom at ten pence a shot (and there was even a special bulk buy offer for a group of peasants). And then, against the advice of his treasurers, he let a load of poor families leave anyway. Most of the soldiers were sold into slavery. Having reclaimed the Dome of the Rock, he allowed the church to reopen for pilgrimage and even invited Jews from Ashkelon to return to the city.

The western church was outraged. If there's one thing worse than an intolerant Muslim, it's a tolerant one.

The pope was so shocked by events that he promptly died. His successor launched an immediate crusade and a truly awe-inspiring force was assembled, an all-star cast, featuring Emperor Frederick Barbarossa of the Holy Roman Empire, King Philip of France and Richard the Lionheart of England – a man who has had probably the greatest PR in all British royal history.

Frederick, showing that tenacious inability to learn that always characterised the Crusades, led his army through Byzantium and into Asia Minor, where the heat and drought were so intense that the German soldiers were reduced to making a drink out of horse manure.* Finally they came upon a great river, which Frederick plunged into in order to lead his horse across. And drowned. In hindsight, it may have been a mistake trying to cross the river with his armour on.

Frederick's corpse was preserved in a large barrel of vinegar, making him more gherkin than German. (Nor was he the last Holy Roman Emperor to be pickled.) Most of the army went home. The rest continued to fight their way across Anatolia and then into Syria, where they were joined by Richard and Philip, who had selected to travel business class (i.e. by boat). They took the port of Acre, but then Saladin started to cheat in the battles

---

* Later on, of course, the Germans perfected this method and successfully marketed it as Liebfraumilch.

by being A Very Good General, which is not cricket. Richard won some victories, but despite the fact that the Crusaders had heavy armour and hearts of oak and all that sort of stuff, they could never hold on. In the end Richard signed a truce with Saladin, left the keys of Jerusalem under the mat and went home. The Third Crusade was over.

Richard actually never returned to England. He was captured in Austria, then ransomed, and subsequently spent the rest of his life in Normandy fighting the French. Despite being born in Oxford he spoke no English. That's why his motto – *Dieu et mon droit*, which is still the motto of the British royal family – is in French. In the entire ten years of his reign he was probably only in England for six months. A true English hero.*

Palaces of God

In 1194 there was a fire in a small town in northern France. The church had started in Roman times. Originally it commemorated some martyrs who had been thrown down a well. Then, five hundred years later, it acquired a notable relic, Mary's birthing gown, the very tunic she had worn while giving birth to Jesus. No, seriously, it had her NHS number on it and everything. Anyway, so many pilgrims came to see this they had to build a bigger church to accommodate all the visitors.

And then it burned down.

So they built a bigger one. A *really* big one. One of the biggest, most beautiful churches in the world. They built the astonishing, profligate wonder of stone and glass that is Chartres Cathedral.

It took about twenty-five years, but the result was staggering: the grandest and tallest structure in western Europe. Of the 176 stained glass windows 43 were donated by the guilds in the town, but it was the work of the people, for the people.† This was not a palace for the monarchy:

---

* He has featured in many films and even in computer games, such as Assassin's Creed, where he speaks English wiz a French accent. Perhaps the best film portrayal is by George Sanders in *King Richard and the Crusaders* which includes Virginia Mayo as Lady Edith delivering the historically authentic line, 'War! War! That's all you ever think of, Dick Plantagenet!'

† The windows contain messages from their 'sponsors': the window donated by the Shoemakers guild, which depicts the story of the Good Samaritan, begins with a picture of the Shoemakers at work, and then a picture of their offering the window to the cathedral.

it was palatial, certainly, but it was intended for everyone in the town.

This, indeed, was the age of the great cathedrals. Between 1050 and 1350, in France alone, they built 80 cathedrals, 500 large churches and many thousands of small parish churches.

Fig. XXII. *Work on the new cathedral is going well*

Some churchmen were singularly unimpressed by these buildings. Bernard of Clairvaux took one look at the Abbey of St Denis in Paris and declared it nothing but vanity. 'The walls of the church are ablaze with light and colour, while the poor of the church go hungry,' he moaned. Old grumpy-pants did have a point. They were fabulously expensive to build. Sometimes the money ran out. Beauvais, for example, began its cathedral the year Chartres was completed, and planned to go bigger and better. They completed the vaulted roof of the choir but then the money ran out and in 1284 it collapsed, leaving just the eastern end of the church still standing.*

* If it had been completed it would have been the biggest church in Europe.

These churches were dripping with decoration and overdosed on symbolism. The doorways would be filled with sculptures of all the great figures of church history: figures from the Bible, saints and church fathers, local kings and queens. There were the symbols of the four evangelists, taken from Revelation 4.7: Matthew was a man, because his Gospel opens with the human lineage of Christ; Mark was a lion, because his Gospel begins with a creature roaring in the wilderness (admittedly the creature in question was John the Baptist, but you get the idea); Luke was an ox, because his Gospel opens with the sacrifice of Zecharias, and everyone knew if you wanted to sacrifice anything properly it had to be an ox; and John was an eagle, because eagles were the only animal that could look at the sun, and John's Gospel was dazzling. Or sunny. Or something like that.

OK, so the symbols are complex. But then the whole church was a symbol. In 1286, just after the collapse of Beauvais, a monk called Guilleme Durand wrote a long treatise on how to 'read' a church building. The four walls were 'built on the doctrine of the Four Evangelists'; the foundation was faith; the door, obedience; the floor, humility. Some churches 'are built in the shape of a cross, to signify, that we are crucified to the world, and should tread in the steps of the Crucified'; others are circular, 'to signify that the Church hath been extended throughout the circle of the world' or maybe 'the crown of eternity which shall encircle our brows'. The apse 'so called because it projecteth a little from the wall . . . signifieth the lay portion of the faithful joined to Christ and the Church'. The crypts represent 'hermits who are devoted to a solitary life'. The 'gurgoyles' represent evil spirits 'as flying from the holy walls'.

And so it goes on, towers, windows, even the weather vane shaped like a cockerel, they all represent some aspect of faith: 'the cock at the summit of the church . . . is the preacher, who preacheth boldly, and exciteth the sleepers to cast away the works of darkness'.*

The point is that, when you went into a medieval church or cathedral, you weren't just entering a building: you were going through the wardrobe into another world. Cathedrals and churches were outposts of the kingdom of God. They were, in the powerful phrase of the Celts, 'thin places', where heaven seemed to break through to earth.

You could have put a fourteen-storey office block in the nave and it still wouldn't have touched the ceiling.

* This means that it's perfectly OK to describe the contents of a sermon as a load of cock.

The heady smell of incense filled the air, music was played (in 1287, in an act of blatant anti-bagpipe discrimination, the Council of Milan agreed that the organ 'should be the only musical instrument that may be used in church services'), songs were sung. The priests wore colourful and often sumptuous robes. There might even be the bones of a martyr nearby to add to the general numinousness. Or numinosity. Anyway, this was what holiness was supposed to look like.

CHARTRES

Chartres Cathedral. It's slightly more touristy these days . . .

Name: The Cathedral of Our Lady of Chartres.
Aka: Chartres Cathedral or 'Will you look at that'.
Nationality: French.
Dates: 1194 to present.
Appearance: Oh gosh. Enormous towers, astonishing sculpture, ravishingly beautiful stained glass. Plus a lot of annoying plastic and scaffolding (at least when I went).
Before it was famous: A small Roman church.
Famous for: Symbolising the glories of the medieval cathedrals.
Why does it matter? Because it's the greatest Gothic-style building ever built? Because it remains one of the architectural wonders of the world? Because it represents the astonishing skill and craftsmanship of an entire community directed towards the glory of God?
Could you have a drink with it down the pub? No, but raise your glass in honour of the amazing craftsmen who created it.

The law of the land

The other great edifice of this time, though not in a physical sense, was church law. Centralising power in the pope, it meant that, legally speaking, all roads led to Rome. If you wanted plans approved, proposals rubber-stamped, or to be appointed emperor, you had to go to Rome and fill in the forms, as it were. Monastery being interfered with by your bishop? Go to Rome. Want your marriage annulled? Go to Rome. Have you been involved in some kind of ecclesiastical accident? Call Pope Direct.

As the church gained more and more secular power its law became more and more important. In the twelfth century the church's law was codified and organised by a monk called Gratian. And it's no coincidence that all the popes between 1159 and 1303 were experts in Canon Law.

This meant increased bureaucracy. In Rome there was a large staff of functionaries, and the same form of centralised administration was replicated further down, with bishops having their own administrators and civil service. And this, in turn, meant that the emphasis of the church switched away from monasteries and towards the parishes – because they could be more directly controlled by the central hierarchy.

Of course, all this administration had to be paid for. So the church promoted its own tax. No one could deny that the practice of tithing – the Old Testament practice of the priests taking a tenth of everyone's produce – was scriptural. So the church picked this up and happily gold-plated it. Literally. Curiously, it was less keen to endorse other practices from the same part of the Bible, such as circumcision. But pastors, preachers and televangelists have been bigging up tithing ever since.

The other strange thing was that the tax was imposed much more readily on ordinary working folk than on the old aristocratic families. But then, the ordinary working folk didn't have soldiers.

Highly regarded Hildegard

Mysticism was common currency in this period. In all places, but especially in the convents and the monasteries, there were men and women seeking to be lifted out of the earthly realm. Which, given that the earthly realm was smelly, cold and generally covered in mud, was hardly surprising.

Hildegard of Bingen (1098–1179) was both a mystic and a highly respected intellectual who became the correspondent of a pope, an emperor and Bernard of Clairvaux. She produced a vast range of works including hymns, plays, theology and several hundred letters.

Her first vision came when she was just three years old: 'I saw such a light that my soul trembled,' she said, 'but because I was an infant, I could say nothing of these things.' She would experience a 'fiery light of exceeding brilliance' so that suddenly she 'knew the meaning of the exposition of the Scriptures'.

But this example shows up why mysticism was also suspect. It was a shortcut to God, bypassing the clergy and the sacraments. It's a sign of Hildegard's gifts that she was allowed to remain an abbess and even preach to male clerics. And she had harsh words for monks 'enveloped in the blackness of acrid smoke because of their habitually foul behaviour'. She warned that the church would have to renew itself or be stripped of its wealth and power.

Eventually, of course, she had to be silenced. A year before her death, her convent was put on special measures: the local bishop withheld mass from her and her sisters. For the establishment, leniency has to have its limits, even for a prophetess like Hildegard.

THINGS YOU LEARN FROM CHRISTIAN HISTORY

NO. 7

Heresy is any theological speculation which is not the official theological speculation

Variant: A heretic is someone who is wrong at the time.

Virtually every major Christian thinker has been declared a heretic by somebody, at some point. And some of Jesus' teaching looks a bit unorthodox, if you ask me . . .

7 Beguines, Bibles and Black Death

Christ's substitute

Following Barbarossa's unfortunate drowning and subsequent pickling, his son Henry took over the Holy Roman Empire™. But Henry died while both of his sons were still infants. The result was a struggle for supremacy between two contenders for the throne. Not the infants – they were more interested in who was going to get the biggest rusk – but Otto of Brunswick and Philip of Swabia. Both asked the pope – Innocent III (Pope from 1198 to 1216) – to adjudicate. Innocent replied that it was not the pope's role to choose the emperor. This seemed quite surprisingly hands-off, but then Innocent cleared his throat and clarified: it was not his role to choose the emperor, but it *was* the pope's role to correct the choice, if he felt that the German princes had elected the wrong one.

Innocent came from an aristocratic background, and it showed. Popes had, for a long time, styled themselves 'Vicars of Peter', from the Latin word *vicarius*, meaning 'substitute'. But at his consecration Innocent announced that he was 'the vicar of Jesus Christ, the successor of St Peter, the Christ [i.e. anointed] of the Lord, the God of Pharaoh . . . midpoint between God and man . . . who can judge all things and is judged by no one . . . set between God and man, lower than God but higher than man'. He then shouted 'Who's the daddy?' and tore the Vatican telephone directory in half.

Never mind, Peter. Now hear this: the pope is Christ's substitute.

Argue with that if you dare.

The last Crusade

Sadly, Innocent's credentials as Christ's substitute don't stand up to a huge amount of scrutiny. Not unless you see Christ as someone who really enjoyed starting wars. Because in 1204 Innocent decided that what Europe really needed was another crusade. Yes, other crusades had failed – but they weren't launched by the Vicar of Christ.

It did not go well. (There's a surprise.) The Crusaders decided to attack Egypt first, on the grounds it was the most vulnerable of the Muslim states; but that meant ordering a lot of ships from Venice. Which would have been OK, but when the army assembled in Venice they were dismayed to find out that only 1,500 Crusaders had bothered to turn up. Which meant that they had ordered *way* more ships than they needed. The Venetians insisted, though, that someone had to pay for all those extra ships. So they proposed a deal: the Crusaders could pay for the surplus ships by attacking Hungary first. There was the tiny issue of Hungary being a Christian country, but business is business and someone had to pay for all those boats. When the pope heard of the plan, he was appalled. And he excommunicated the Crusaders.

But then the now unauthorised Crusaders had a visit from Alexius, would-be heir to the imperial throne at Constantinople. He had been usurped by another candidate and he promised that if the Crusaders stopped by Constantinople first and put him on the throne, he would pay for the expedition to Egypt.

So that's what they did. They went to Constantinople and reinstalled Alexius in 1203. But Alexius's promises proved as empty as his treasury: there was no money to pay his 'New Emperor' installation fee. So he melted down church silver and gold and inflicted punitive taxes on the populace. Then some drunken French Crusaders came across a Mosque in the city which had been built for the use of visiting Muslims. Naturally, being (a) Crusaders and (b) drunk, they set fire to it. And in the process, burned a quarter of the city as well. The people had enough: they kicked the awful Alexius out.

The Crusaders went berserk. In one of the most shameful acts in the history of these shameful wars, they attacked Constantinople in a three-day bender of violence and rape. Nuns were raped in their convents. Justinian's magnificent cathedral of Hagia Sophia was ransacked. And – oh, the thigh-slapping hilarity – they sat a prostitute on the throne of the patriarch to dance and sing crude songs.

The Fourth Crusade was about greed and nothing else. It dropped entirely the pretence that the other crusades had clung to: of being somehow holy wars. This was an attack, not against the Muslim infidel, but against eastern Christians. In the Crusaders' eyes these people spoke Greek and had funny names, so that made it all right. A Frankish Crusader became emperor of the east, and the Venetians – who had already stolen St Mark himself from Alexandria – filled St Mark's Basilica with the booty stolen from the greatest Christian city in history.

You might think that this jaw-droppingly awful episode is where the concept of the crusade hit rock bottom. But, oh no. There were still some big holes to be dug.

Heresy. Heresy! HERESY!

Innocent III had originally condemned the attack on Constantinople. But then he realized that, with a western Crusader on the throne of the eastern emperor, he had technically reunited the church. Result! Admittedly, the eastern church saw things rather differently, but their city was in ruins so *ner*.*

And if a crusade could solve that ancient problem, then maybe it could solve the other major issue facing Christendom: heresy. So, in 1209, Innocent launched a sequel. But this time the crusade was not against Christians in Greece, but in France, right at the heart of Europe. The Crusaders were to eliminate heresy in Languedoc, and as a reward they would get to keep the lands of any 'heretics' they were willing to root out and destroy.

The heretics in question have become known as the Cathari, although this is not what they called themselves. Like the word 'Christian' itself, the name was actually applied to the movement by their enemies.† It comes from the Greek word for 'pure', and may refer

---

* There's a marble relief plaque of Innocent III in the US House of Representatives, where he is one of twenty-three historical figures honoured 'for their work in establishing the principles that underlie American law'. Er, what? No, really, *what*?

† Not many people called them Cathari at the time anyway – the term really

to their ascetic lifestyle, but what actually seems to have happened is that heresy hunters found a sect called the Cathari in an eighth-century book on heresies, and simply slapped that label on the radicals in the south of France. 'Aha! You thought the Cathari had died out four hundred years ago. But here they are, alive and well. Be afraid. Be very afraid.'

In fact, very little is actually known about the beliefs of the Cathari. For centuries, based on the accusations of their inquisitors, it was assumed that they were dualists – a rebirth of Manichaeism. But that assumption has now been seriously questioned and it appears increasingly likely that they were simply radical, apostolic Christians.

They encouraged their followers to avoid contact with corrupt priests. They seem to have had versions of the Bible in the vernacular – the book of Acts, at least. They demanded celibacy (including divorce for the married). They were vegans, not out of any concern for animal cruelty but because all animal products were 'the result of fleshly congress'. (However, fish were OK, since everyone knew that they were spontaneously created by water.) They fasted three days a week. They banned all killing, possessions and oath-taking. They allowed women priests, because they believed that bodily differences were irrelevant.

Very few could live up to these demands. So the Cathars, like the clerics in the early church, developed the idea of the 'perfect' – those initiates who lived the full-on ascetic lifestyle – and the 'believers', lay people who supported them.

Whatever the reality, the pope launched a war on heresy. He launched what became known as the Albigensian Crusade (the city of Albi was one of the centres of the cult). But how do you wage war on heresy? Well, you need experts. You need heresy hunters. Theological intelligence operatives.

You need Dominic.

---

became popular in the nineteenth century.

DOMINIC

Dominic. Probably reading someone's secret file

Name: Domingo Félix de Guzmán.
Aka: Dominic.
Nationality: Spanish.
Dates: 1170–1221.
Appearance: Medium height, apparently with strawberry blond hair and beard, and long hands. I don't know why, but I always imagine him with very sharp cheekbones. He was that sort of guy.

Before he was famous: Monk.

Famous for: Founding the Dominicans (aka the Blackfriars). Hunting heretics. Inadvertently inspiring the Inquisition.

Why does he matter? The order he founded, the Dominicans, became the primary teaching order of the church. (They also became its secret police and intelligence officers.)

Could you have a drink with him down the pub? Possibly. But you would have to be very, very careful what you said.

Helping with inquiries

Dominic was a Spanish priest from an Augustinian monastery who was recruited by the church to beef up the campaign against the heretics in the south of France. Dominic realised that if the campaign against heresy was going to succeed, it could not be seen to be waged by rich, comfortable, powerful people: these were exactly the kinds of people the 'heretics' were rebelling against. You don't win a campaign on corruption by sending a load of corrupt priests to order everyone about.

He decided to beat the heretics at their own game. If they lived among the poor, he would live among the poor. And not just he alone. He formed a whole band of preachers who lived a simple life, travelling from town to town and teaching people the truth. They had to know their stuff, so Dominic made sure that they were carefully educated and that they were good at teaching others.

His efforts in the south of France didn't quite go to plan – not least because there were too many people involved in the conflict who preferred old-fashioned brutality to his new-fangled intellectualism. But his basic idea – of a teaching order of monks – caught on rapidly. And they became known as the Dominicans.

Dominic's passion, the mission that drove him, was evangelistic. He was trying to win the Cathars back to what he saw as orthodoxy. But the effect was that the Dominicans became the secret police of the church. From heresy hunting in the south of France they moved into the universities, where they started combating radical ideas put about by academics. The Dominicans gained a reputation for having enormous brains; but their intelligence was used as a weapon: they were intellectual warriors fighting against heresy.

In 1231 Pope Gregory IX took heresy hunting to a new level, with the establishment of the Inquisition. (Nobody, of course, was expecting it.) And he put the Dominicans in charge. The idea was to have an organisation dedicated to rooting out heresy, trying the culprits and having them executed. Obviously, the church couldn't do the actual execution stuff – that would have been wrong. So they just did the investigating and then handed the condemned over to the state to do the actual dispatching.

The Inquisition relied on third-party accusations against heretics. The accused were then tried in secret – without any legal representation, of course. If they confessed, they could often be let off with a penance. Well, and losing all their property. But if they protested their innocence, they were tortured until they confessed. (Torture was officially sanctioned by Rome in 1252.) If they still managed to hold out, they were burnt. Heads I win; tails you are burnt to a crisp.

FRANCIS

Francis. Apparently he was quite a jolly in real life

Name: Giovanni Bernardone.
Aka: Francis ('Frenchy') of Assisi.
Nationality: Italian.
Dates: 1181/1182–1226.
Appearance: Shortish. Round face. Dark hair and black beard. Apparently his 'ears were small and upright'. Thin lips, good teeth. And he had thin legs and small feet.
Before he was famous: Young, wealthy playboy.
Famous for: Founding the Franciscans, the women's Order of St Clare, and the Third Order of St Francis for laymen and women. Writing poetry. Exhibiting stigmata.
Why does he matter? He lived a life of commitment to the poor. The Franciscans – or Friars Minor – became one of the main preaching orders of the church. Francis was a living reminder that Christ lived a life of poverty.
Could you have a drink with him down the pub? I think so. Might have to be organic. Even vegan. He was into that sort of thing.

San Francisco

Much of the heresy that the Inquisition had to be set up to root out arose from one simple fact: that laymen were often more devout than the clergy.

Giovanni Bernardone was the son of a wealthy cloth merchant in Assisi, a flourishing town in central Italy. His father liked to call him Francesco – which was more fashionably French. In fact, it *means* 'French'. Anyway, young 'Frenchy' joined the family firm and enjoyed the benefits of wealth: fine clothes, fast horses and a taste for marzipan. But Francesco grew dissatisfied. He wanted to drop out, but in thirteenth-century Italy there was nowhere for him to drop out to. Punk hadn't been invented. You could go to art college, in the form of an apprenticeship, but, unlike modern art schools, you actually had to be able to paint.

One day – the story goes – he saw a leper in the road. He got off his high horse and embraced the man. Then he had a vision in the church of San Damiano in Italy, where a talking crucifix told him to 'Go, repair my falling house.' So he spent a lot of money rebuilding the local church, which had fallen into ruins. The only problem was that he had 'borrowed' the money from his father. That's borrow as in 'take without asking'.

Then, two years later, he had a Waldensian-style conversion. He heard the story in the Bible of Jesus sending out his disciples and decided that he would do the same. From then on he was committed to a life of radical poverty and service. He called himself Brother Francis. Or, as we know him, Francis of Assisi. From the start, he was a get-your-hands-dirty sort of guy. Get your hands infected, probably, since he and his followers worked alongside the peasants and the lepers and the outcasts.

Pope Innocent was deeply suspicious of this movement. There was only a fag-paper-thin difference between the Franciscans and the Waldensians, and the latter were definitely heretics – it said so in his law books. But the movement was incredibly popular. And, anyway, Innocent had a dream in which he saw Francis holding up a decaying and crumbling church. So he gave the order official recognition, and they became known as the Lesser Brothers or Friars Minor. It was a humble term for a humble community.

Francis' story has certainly been mythologised. But there is a core of genuine, radical goodness. He gathered together a load of followers who were prepared to give up their possessions and become nobodies, in order to serve the great somebody.

Francis was essentially an anarchist. He levelled out the medieval hierarchy that had man at the top of creation. In his famous poem 'The Canticle of the Sun' Francis talks about 'Brother Sun' and 'sister Moon' moving through a world of wind, water, creatures, fire, plants and earth. Humanity didn't appear until a later version. He genuinely hated power. He didn't want to be a leader, yet many people were drawn to his example; and without ever wanting to, he became the leader of a group known as the Franciscans. As soon as he could, though, he handed the leadership over to someone else.

It left him free to pray. He was the first known person to get stigmata – bleeding from the five points where Jesus was pierced on the cross.

Francis spent the last years of his life trying to keep the movement he had reluctantly founded true to his ideals. Just before he died he expressed concerns that his commitment to poverty would not be carried on with such zeal by his followers, and he worried about the fact that they were spending money building enormous convents. He died in 1226 and, within a decade, his followers had built a vast, magnificent church over his tomb – indeed, the pope came and laid the foundation stone.

It was exactly the kind of monument he would have hated.

And the movement fragmented. It split into the Conventuals and the Spirituals. The Conventuals were those who wanted to make the order more like the Dominicans. The Spirituals were those who wanted to stick to Francis' ideals of poverty, simplicity and getting away from everyone. Some of the Spirituals took things to extremes and started preaching the destruction of all authority. And authority was not having any of that. Eventually, surprise, surprise, the Spirituals were condemned as heretical by Pope John XXII. In 1323 he had four of them burned at the stake for the appalling heresy of preaching that Christ had lived in absolute poverty. I mean. As if.

The bulk of the Franciscans, though, carried on in a more moderate vein. Like the Dominicans they became involved in the universities. Like the Dominicans they built monastic communities where the people were. They wanted to interact with ordinary people. Their churches were designed so that people could come in and hear the sermons; their refectories were open to people from the streets to come in and talk to them. Unlike a lot of the monastic communities they wanted people to come in to browse, as it were.

And typically, the two houses – Franciscan and Dominicans – became bitter rivals. They were so alike it was inevitable that they should end up hating one another.

Innocent blood

Back a bit. In 1215 Innocent III called a council at which the Cathars and Waldensians were condemned. This same council officially approved the term 'transubstantiation' to explain what happened during the mass, insisted that all Christians should take Confession and Communion at least once a year at Easter, and prohibited the illegitimate sons of the clergy from inheriting their fathers' churches. Jews were banned from appearing anywhere in public during Holy Week and from having any position that gave them official power over Christians. They also had to wear a yellow star, but that was only, you know, so that Christians didn't marry them by accident. It was more of a food label kind of thing.* Just for good luck it also called for a fifth crusade against Egypt. Some people never learn.†

Innocent died during the council. He had sponsored wars, he had claimed extravagant titles, he had brought heresy hunting right into the heart of the establishment. For a man called Innocent he had a lot of blood on his hands.

Despite the official condemnation, it took decades before the final Cathars were wiped out. Dominic's approach did not succeed: the soldiers in the south of France were not theologically sophisticated – they couldn't tell the difference between who was orthodox and who wasn't, so they tended to kill everyone just to make sure.

The bloody climax came with the capture of the Cathar fortress of Montségur in 1244. The church authorities, borrowing a phrase from Revelation, termed the place a 'synagogue of Satan'. Montségur was captured and over 200 of the Cathars were burned alive. One might speculate as to where the real satanic powers were residing.

Forty years later England, the country where the mass-persecution of heretics had begun, pioneered a new form of expulsion. In 1289 the parliament of Edward I refused to give any more money to the king unless he expelled all the Jews from the realm. So he did, making England the first of the western nations to expel all the Jews from its soil.

---

* To be fair, similar requirements were made of Christians and Jews in Muslim countries. Furthermore, for reasons not entirely clear, all clergy were banned from wearing green.

† The Fifth Crusade did take place, but it achieved very little. After wandering aimlessly around Galilee (where they found one of the genuine water pots used at the wedding of Cana) they went to Cairo, where Francis joined them and tried to convert the Sultan of Egypt.

I know what you did last Summa

When Rome collapsed in the fifth century, many things were lost, including toga-wearing, Roman central-heating technology, some bloke's house keys, a fair bit of loose change, oh, and Aristotle. Not literally. Obviously. The original Aristotle died in 322 BC, but a lot of his *writing* went AWOL. It was not lost completely, though, because a lot of his fans were pagan philosophers, who left to live outside the Christian empire. So when trade started picking up with Islamic lands, it brought not only sugar and silk and spices, but also copies of Aristotle. The result was that in the first half of the twelfth century, 800 years after his death, Aristotle had some new books out, works on science, logic and metaphysics that had been preserved by Muslim scholars, then rediscovered and newly translated.*

The other great philosopher of the ancient world, Plato, believed that there was a higher reality: he pictured this world as a reflection of the eternal, a shadow dancing on the wall of a cave. Discovering the true reality, therefore, is largely a matter of divine revelation, of seeing through the wall to the eternal realities. Aristotle, on the other hand, thought that reality was, well, *real*. The wall of the cave was solid and reality could be encountered only by examination, taste, touch, feel, etc.

Aristotle believed in a prime cause, some kind of god who got the universe started, but you could not have a personal relationship with this force. And, while the universe was, he felt, eternal, souls were mortal. The church, stunned by these radical new 1,400-year-old ideas, immediately banned his books. As did Paris University. But one man realised that you could not solve such ideas by banning them. You had to examine them. Study them. Get, in fact, all Aristotelian on them.

His name was Thomas Aquinas (*c*.1225–74) and he was a Dominican. He chose a life of austere poverty – much to the irritation of his family, who wanted him to be a rich, powerful abbot. They even tried to kidnap him and convert him to 'proper' monasticism by locking him in a room with a prostitute. Thomas whiled away this imprisonment by writing an essay on logic. Eventually his family – and, presumably, the prostitute – gave up.

* Metaphysics is the science of being and knowing. But I'm sure you are and knew that. Aristotle also wrote on theatre. As an eighteen-year-old theatre student I was astonished at his notion that stories had a beginning, a middle and an end. Ground-breaking stuff.

His Dominican masters rather underestimated Thomas: they nick-named him the 'Dumb Ox'. But he went on to study and teach in Italy, Paris and Cologne. And he became the greatest western theologian since Augustine. Thomas *loved* Aristotle, and he loved Christian theology. And his aim was to bring the two together. Faith is always paramount, but reason helps you see faith more clearly. It was possible to be an Aristotelian Christian.

Aquinas suggested that there were two aspects to reality: 'nature' and 'grace'. 'Natural' knowledge was the kind of stuff we humans can work out for ourselves – not only through our five senses, but also through our scientific, rational minds. 'Grace' knowledge was supernatural knowledge – that is, stuff we know only because God has revealed it to the proper authorities. So this included doctrine and dogma, ideas like the incarnation, the Trinity, transubstantiation, and so on.

He summed all this up in his *Summa*: to be precise, his *Summa Theologiae*, which means the 'Sum of All Theology'. Sadly, 'total Theology' was a bit of a misnomer, since it was incomplete. He never finished it. But the bits he did finish became, officially, *the* book of Roman Catholic doctrine.

Perhaps one of his most influential doctrines has been the theory of the just war. 'War,' Thomas asked, 'what is it good for? Absolutely nothing – well, hold on, let me just clarify that.' Actually, Aquinas argued that there were three conditions under which Christians could wage war: (1) sovereign authority – that is, it's ordered by the state (or the pope); (2) a just cause; and (3) an intention to bring about good, rather than evil.

He went on to qualify these ideas, pointing out that the aim of war is, ultimately, peace, that Christians should have a love towards their enemies and that violence should be as limited as possible, and tempered with mercy and forgiveness.

These three principles still serve as the basis for the church's acceptance of war. But Thomas was a monk, not a politician, and ever since his criteria – which were supposed to regulate and restrict violence – have frequently been used as a checklist to justify some very unjust wars. Ordered by the government? Tick. A just cause? Tick. Will it end up in truth, democracy and better shopping? Tick. Right, let's get bombing.

In the end, though, Thomas hit the wall of the cave. All those hundreds of thousands of words, all that stuff about reason and logic in the end proved inadequate. On St Nicholas' Day 1273 Aquinas went to attend mass. In the chapel he had a vision, a mystical experience, a . . . well, the truth is no one really knows what happened. All he said was, 'I can write no more. After what I have seen, everything I ever wrote seems like straw.'

He never wrote another word of the book. He died on the way to the Council of Lyons in 1274, in a donkey-related accident.*

Aquinas' thought became known as Thomism. Not long after his death he was accused of heresy by his very own bishop. The universities of Oxford and Paris banned his teaching. But eventually people came round, and fifty years after his death he was declared a saint. Swings and roundabouts, this theology stuff.

Oh, and he also accidentally invented the limerick.†

AQUINAS

Name: Thomas of Aquino.
Aka: Thomas Aquinas, the 'Dumb Ox', 'Angelic Doctor', 'Doctor Universalis'.
Nationality: Italian, Neapolitan to be precise.
*Dates: c.*1225–74.
Appearance: Heavily built (hence the Dumb Ox jibe). Apparently his complexion was 'like the colour of new wheat'. (Isn't that green?) He had a big head, hardly surprising given the size of his brain.
Before he was famous: Came from an aristocratic family. Dominican monk.
Famous for: Theology. Lots and lots of theology.
Why does he matter? He's the most influential medieval theologian. Famous for trying to reconcile natural reason and speculative theology. His writings are still core teaching for Catholic clergy.
Could you have a drink with him down the pub? Sure – if you could only drag him out of the library for long enough.

---

* He struck his head on the branch of a fallen tree on the Appian way. The donkey, following precedent, refused to talk without a lawyer present.
† A poem in his Breviary runs, 'Sit vitiorum meorum evacuation / concupiscentae et libidinis exterminatio, / caritatis et patientiae, / humilitas et obedientiae, / omniumque virtutum augmentatio.' Hilarious, I'm sure you agree.

Yes we Khan

While it was boom time for Christianity in the west, in the east, things were in turmoil. Russia was overrun by the Mongols in 1237, although, in a dress rehearsal for the Communist years, the church found a way to survive under its pagan overlords. The Mongols also invaded Poland, Austria and Hungary. The pope sent a Franciscan monk to convert the Great Khan, the Mongol leader. When he arrived at the Mongol court, the Khan staged a debate between representatives of various religions, including the Catholics, Nestorians, Muslims and Zoroastrians.* In the end he decided he was quite happy with animism, thanks. Nevertheless, Christianity did make some small inroads. By the end of the thirteenth century there was a church in China and a Franciscan missionary as the Archbishop of Beijing.

Constantinople was now in terminal decline. The Crusaders held it until 1261, but then the Byzantines retook the city. By now, though, the city had been ruined by years of looting and misrule. Desperate, the eastern emperor wrote to the pope in 1274, offering to submit to Rome, if the pope would use his influence to send troops to fight off the growing Turkish threat.

Eastern representatives came to a church council in Lyons, ready to sign up to anything. Papal supremacy? No problem. Western version of the creed – including the *filioque* line? OK. (The pope made them sing it there and then three times just to make sure.) They would do all the cooking and the cleaning and babysitting – they would sign up to the lot. Reunify the church. Just send the troops. And so the deal was done. But when the representatives returned to Constantinople and news spread of what had been agreed, there was outrage. The residents of Constantinople had not forgotten the Fourth Crusade. Rome was not a friend but a bitter enemy – so they rejected the creed entirely. When the pope heard about this, he condemned them in turn.

Christendom was as divided as it had ever been.

---

* Two Jehovah's Witnesses arrived on a door-knocking mission slightly too late.

Sur le Pope d'Avignon

The papal election of 1294 was a long time coming. There had been a vacancy in the papal throne for two years, because the cardinals could not agree on a suitable candidate. Eventually they were sent a threatening letter by a famous eighty-five-year-old Franciscan hermit called Peter Morone, who said that there would be divine vengeance if they did not choose somebody. So they did. They chose him. He was, well a bit of a Morone, actually. His Latin was so bad that he couldn't understand a word the cardinals said to him. Despite choosing Celestine as his papal name, the poor man was so unhappy with his elevated position that he had a small wooden shed built in one of the palatial rooms of his residence and lived in there: it was the only place he felt at home. In the end he gave up and was the first pope in history to resign voluntarily.*

Not that he was allowed to return to his old life. You can't have ex-popes knocking about. No, his successor, Boniface VIII, thought it best to keep Peter somewhere safe, like, oh I don't know, a jail. He spent the rest of his life locked away – and died under suspicious circumstances. The official cause of death was given as infection caused by an abscess, but forensic tests on his skull done in 1988 showed that it had a hole in it made by a nail driven through by an unknown assassin.†

Boniface VIII was a greedy, corrupt individual. The poet Dante was so impressed by Boniface that he assigned him a place buried head first in the eighth circle of hell, among the simonists. And Boniface wasn't even dead when Dante was writing. In 1302 he wrote a document called *Unam Sanctam*, which claimed that 'by necessity for salvation' all human beings – including the most powerful, of course – are 'entirely subject to the Roman pontiff'. (In other words, if you don't obey the pope, you cannot be saved.)

Unfortunately, the King of France disagreed. When King Philip of France put a bishop on trial for treason, Boniface threatened him with excommunication. Philip was so scared he arrested the pope and

---

* He was – until 2013 – the last pope to do so. Significantly, perhaps, Benedict XVI was a fan of Celestine. He visited Celestine's remains after the 2009 L'Aquila earthquake, and left his woolly scarf as a gift. And on the eight hundredth anniversary of Celestine's birth Benedict XVI proclaimed the year to be 'the Celestine year'. Maybe he was hinting at something?

† Reports that Boniface VIII was seen buying a hammer at B&Q earlier in the day are mere rumour.

passed the papacy to a Frenchman – unsurprisingly – called Clement V, who, in 1309, decided that the papacy would be much better off in France. So he moved to Avignon in the south of France, which while not technically at that time in the French kingdom, still had a lot of Frenchiness to it –you could get baguettes, the shops closed for three hours in the middle of the day, and King Philip could still exercise a lot of control.

The move to Avignon merely confirmed what many people thought of the church. This was nothing to do with making history, but everything to do with worldliness, politics, power, luxury and greed.

Fig. XXIII. *In hell, Dante is introduced to a selection of popes guilty of simony*

Contagion

But it was not just the behaviour of the clergy that caused people to ask questions of God. In 1348 the latest eastern import arrived in western Europe: the Black Death.

No one quite knows how it began. It was spotted in Constantinople and Trebizond, trading centres in the east. Then it arrived in Genoa, Italy. And then . . . then, it was *everywhere*. Within forty years a third of Europeans were dead, most of them in the first few years after it struck. It took the high born and the low. It killed the Archbishop of Canterbury in England and King Alfonso in Spain. The statistics are mind-blowing. England lost half its population to the Black Death. Some 1,000 entire villages were wiped out. It killed more people in Europe proportionately than the 1914–18 war: some estimates put the death toll at one in three of the population.

And one of the victims was faith in the church. People looked to the church to protect them, but the clergy seemed as helpless as anyone else. So people turned, like desperate cancer victims, to unsanctioned remedies. Street preachers preached hellfire and damnation. Evangelists walked the streets dressed as skeletons. Groups like the Flagellants, who spent their time beating themselves for their sins, sprang up. The dreadful punishments they inflicted on themselves probably did more to spread the disease than to cure it.

And then people started to think that maybe it wasn't *their* sins that had caused this, but the sins of other people. Jews. Lepers. All this must be happening because we allow *them* to stay here. Anti-Semitism had risen steadily during the twelfth century, but now it burst out like a virulent disease. Like, in fact, a plague. Jews were accused of deliberately poisoning wells. In April 1348 in Toulon, France, forty Jews were murdered. The next year there were massacres across Europe. The worst outrage, perhaps, was in Strasbourg, where on St Valentine's Day, 900 Jews were burned alive. (This was seen as a preventative measure; the plague had not even reached the city, but you can never be too careful.)

To his credit, Pope Clement VI issued a papal bull declaring that those who thought the Jews were to blame had been 'seduced by that liar, the Devil'. But his efforts were completely undone by Charles IV, the new Holy Roman Emperor, who declared that any property of Jews killed in riots was forfeit to the authorities. So killing Jews became both financially advantageous *and* a matter of spiritual health and safety.

Begin the Beguines

When it came to radical, real Christianity, the action was happening elsewhere. In Belgium they were beginning the Beguines.

The Beguines were a female community who renounced property and embraced chastity. But they didn't enter a nunnery. They stayed with their parents or in small communities in ordinary houses. They were a loosely organised network of lay sisters, with no common rule, and no mother superior; independent, autonomous communities, living lives of service and austerity but right in the middle of the towns.*

They were similar to the Franciscan 'spirituals' in some ways. Some Beguines experienced a heightened, intense, almost physical, sensation of union with Christ. They described it as a kind of annihilation, where the soul was taken over, overwhelmed, by the spirit. Their most influential teacher was Marguerite Porete, author of a hugely popular book called *The Mirror of Simple Souls*, a dialogue between Soul, Love and Reason where she describes people who are so abandoned to God's love that they are completely overwhelmed by the will of God. In such a condition, she wrote, they live entirely within God's will and no longer have a 'why' of their own.

The church reacted sniffily. This 'higher plane' stuff smelled of Gnosticism. And things weren't helped when Marguerite described those who had achieved this state as 'the Greater Church', while the organised, official church was the Lesser Church. This was not the kind of language to endear them to the church authorities. What is more, they had the temerity to wear religious habits although they belonged to none of the official orders. They were outside the system: there were even accusations that they did not obey their parish priests.

But they weren't just other-worldly mystics. They had jobs: weaving, spinning, nursing. Many Beguine houses made good money, but they channelled it towards the poor. Mind you, that didn't matter when it came to passing judgement on them. No, they were unlicensed, uncontrolled, loose women.

---

* The male counterparts were called Beghards.

So, inevitably, the Beguines were condemned as heretics, at the Council of Vienne in 1312. Two years before that, Marguerite was arrested and her books confiscated and burned. She refused to defend herself to the Lesser Church. 'This Soul responds to no one if she does not wish to,' she said. On 1 June 1310 she was burned at the stake.

Marguerite's real crime, one suspects, was to operate outside the system. And to do so without testicles. The fact is that for years Marguerite's work continued to circulate, but in a version attributed to an anonymous male author. No one kicked up a fuss because they thought it was written by a man. There is even a 1927 edition rendered in modern English attributed to an 'anonymous Carthusian monk'. And the edition bore the imprimatur of the Cardinal Archbishop of Westminster. It appears, then, that Marguerite's opinions were heretical only when uttered by a woman.*

Let's go back to that name, Beguine. It's not certain where the name comes from, but it appears to be a mocking term, derived from a revivalist preacher called Lambert le Bégue – Lambert 'the Stammerer'. These women, then, were 'stammerers' who couldn't even speak properly. The same habit of seeking to use ridicule to combat heretics can be seen in another significant dissenting group of the fourteenth century: the followers of John Wycliffe, aka the Lollards.

Modern devotion

The Beguines were far from the only grassroots holiness movement. Geert Groote (1340–84) was a Dutchman who claimed to have 'fornicated on every hilltop and under every spreading tree' in northern Europe. Understandably exhausted, he experienced a spectacular conversion, renouncing his past way of life. He spent three years in a monastery, but never became a monk. Instead, he embraced a life of simplicity outside the monastery walls, and invited poor women to live in his family house as a penance.

Given Geert's history, you might have expected the women to be a bit wary of such hospitality. At the very least, I imagine they stayed away from shady trees. But Geert does seem to have been a reformed

---

* It was not until 1946 that it was established that this text was *The Mirror of Simple Souls* and Marguerite was given her rightful recognition as its author.

character and he and his new sisters formed a kind of religious community, holding all things in common and dedicating themselves to prayer, study and charitable acts. In particular, they focused on nurturing a rich, inner devotional life, nourished by reading and imaginative meditation. This became called the *devotio moderna*, or 'the new devotion'. (And their meetings were called 'congregations'.)

Geert became a famous preacher and his movement flourished. He also inspired a monastery at Windesheim that in due course included nearly one hundred houses. After his death the movement became known as the Brethren of the Common Life, and it flourished throughout the fourteenth and fifteenth centuries. They were not monks: they included married couples and families. Their 'houses' were controlled by the local town corporations, not by abbots or bishops.

The idea was that everyone could follow Jesus, an idea summed up by one of their most famous members, Thomas à Kempis, in his book *The Imitation of Christ*. Books and reading were, indeed, key to their approach. Each community had a library and published devout books. And, because reading was so important, they taught other people how to do it: they ran schools, teaching Latin, grammar and rhetoric.

In 1497 a young German schoolboy spent a year at one of their schools in Magdeburg. His name was Martin Luther. We'll *definitely* be meeting him soon.

Prêt-à-porter

When not condemning heretics, the Council of Vienne also directed that Chairs of Greek, Hebrew, Aramaic and Arabic should be set up at the major universities: Paris, Bologna, Salamanca and Oxford. Oxford immediately rushed into action and, a mere 200 years later, appointed someone to do the job. (There is a record of a converted Jew called John of Bristol teaching Hebrew and Greek there in 1320, but apparently he only lasted a year. Well, he came from a red-brick university, what do you expect?)

At the School of Theology in Paris students obviously had to study the Bible. But *which* Bible? How could they make sure everyone was studying the same text? Parisian printers sniffed a business opportunity . . .

The result was the release of so-called Paris Bibles: small, portable

Bibles that included study aids, and that, for the first time, used a standard, uniform way of dividing the Bible into chapters. Chapter division had been used since the days of the great Alexandrian codices – but there was no uniform system. So a university teacher called Stephen Langton devised a number system so that all the students could easily find the same place in the Bible. And it is his chapter divisions we follow today.*

These Bibles also appealed to wandering preachers, ranters or shouty types. The preaching orders – monks like the Dominicans and Franciscans – wanted Bibles to take with them on their quest to save souls, and most Bibles up to then were so big you'd need a wheelbarrow. So the Paris printers and booksellers developed smaller, more portable, Bibles, written on a special type of vellum, scraped as thin as tissue. They made the Bible available to people in a way that had never been known before.

(Meanwhile, the organ continued to go from strength to strength. Churches had official organists – you hear of people called 'John the Organer', which surely ought to be a criminal offence. In Halberstadt, Germany, a huge organ was installed in 1361 that had so much wind pressure from the bellows that the organist had to use the full power of his arm to hold down a key. So he could play only two notes at once.)

The Wyclifites

Making the Bible available was something very dear to John Wyclif (*c.*1325–84), Doctor of Divinity at Oxford University. A distinguished academic, Wyclif followed in the footsteps of the Franciscans by claiming that Christ lived a life of poverty, and that the church he intended to establish was a spiritual body with no earthly possessions. Needless to say, this did not go down well with a number of church authorities, who had quite a lot of possessions and felt perfectly OK about that.

Wyclif's criticisms were not new, but he took them further than others had dared. At the root of his ideas was the Bible, which Wyclif placed above the church and its traditions, above the teaching of the

---

* The earliest known copy of the Bible with this numbering system actually dates from 1231 and was written not in Paris, but in Canterbury.

church fathers and the rulings of the pope. In the Bible Wyclif saw no basis for the idea of transubstantiation. Aquinas had argued that there were two aspects to bread: first, its 'substance', by which he meant its universal, fundamental nature, the sort of *breadiness* of bread. Then there was what he called 'accidents', which means the qualities of an individual piece, for example shape, size, density, amount of poppy seeds, and so on. He claimed that during the mass, the substance of the bread was altered, but the accidents remained the same. It looked like bread, tasted like bread, and so on, but was no longer bread.* Its 'breadiness' had been changed to 'Jesusness'.

Wyclif thought that was rubbish. The mass had become a distortion of the original biblical idea of the Eucharist. Communion was not some kind of conjuring trick played with universals and accidents.

Wyclif also argued that the use of force and the rule of law to support church doctrine was anti-Christian. The pope, in his eyes, was just the Bishop of Rome, no more, no less. Only Christ was the head of the church. What is more, he said that the authority of the pope – or any church leader for that matter – came not from political or military power, but from moral authority. This radical idea meant that the decrees of an immoral pope had no power whatsoever.

Ordinarily, Wyclif would have been dealt with fairly swiftly. But political divisions in the country meant that he was allowed to continue his attacks: the nobility of the country weren't going to clamp down on ideas that, in weakening the church, might bring more power their way.

Eventually, though, he was condemned – at a synod in 1382. The university sacked him, but even then all that happened was that he retired to the small town of Lutterworth in Leicestershire, from where he continued to issue his denunciations of the church, right up until his death two years later.

Wyclif believed that everyone who could read should read the Bible. But it was in Latin. So some of his followers made the first translation of the Bible into English. Although he has been traditionally associated with the translation, which even became called the Wyclif Bible, it was probably the work of two men: Nicholas of Hereford, who did a rather wooden version of the Old Testament, and John Purvey, who revised

---

* Non-alcoholic lager works in much the same way. It looks right, even smells right, and then you taste it...

the Old Testament and completed the work. The translation was condemned as heretical. 'Condemn the word of God in any language as heresy and you call God a heretic,' replied Wyclif.

WYCLIF

Wyclif. An artist's impression. Personally I think he got the nose wrong. At least, I hope he got the nose wrong

Name: John Wyclif.
Aka: John Wycliffe, John Wycliff, John Wiclef, John Wicliffe, John Wickliffe.
Nationality: English.
Dates: c.1330–84.
Appearance: Bald, bandy-legged, monobrowed, hook nosed. But apart from that, curiously attractive.
Before he was famous: Academic at Oxford.
Famous for: Championing the primacy of Scripture. Challenging the status of the pope and traditional teachings about such things as transubstantiation.
Why does he matter? He marks the start of the anticlerical movement in England that was to lead, eventually, to the Protestant Reformation. He was an early opponent of the secular power of the papacy. He also inspired the first English translation of the Bible.
Could you have a drink with him down the pub? Definitely. Pint of ale in the Lutterworth inn.

Banning the Bible

The English authorities were OK with power moving from the pope to the nobility, but they didn't want it moving anywhere else. When the peasants got all revolting in 1381, Wyclif's ideas were blamed. 'You see?' said the powers that be, 'this is what happens when people start reading the Bible for themselves. Anarchy. Rebellion. General revoltingness.' So, in 1407, Thomas Arundel, Archbishop of Canterbury, banned the making and reading of Wyclifite Bibles without the approval of the church – and since there was no way the church was ever going to give approval, this was a big fat *no* to the translation of the Scriptures into English.

The 1407 ban was a stop-and-search law for Scriptures. It allowed the English authorities to search and confiscate any heretical books. No other part of Europe went to such lengths to stop people getting hold of the Bible in their own language. Vernacular translations were not exactly encouraged elsewhere, but they were never made illegal. Yet in England translating the Bible was to remain illegal for another 150 years.

They also tried to clamp down on Wyclif's followers. They called them Lollards, a word that was supposed to imitate the muttering, mumbling sound of a group of lay people stumbling their way through the Bible. Lollards were believed to be threats to the social order – and these fears were confirmed in 1414 when the prominent Lollard Sir John Oldcastle marched on London with a badly thought-out plan to establish some kind of commonwealth. He and his army were easily defeated and Oldcastle was publicly executed. The sentence was heresy and insurrection: in the psyche of the English nobility the one necessarily led to the other.

But Lollardry proved amazingly resilient. Driven underground, it survived and thrived among traders and merchants and the professional classes. Small groups of Lollards continued to meet in secret. They appointed their own leaders, allowed lay people to preach and to officiate at the Eucharist, and they read from their Bibles. And nor were these the outcasts and the poor: these were people from prosperous farming areas such as East Anglia, the Chilterns and the Cotswolds. These were the kinds of people that the authorities really feared: people with cash.

The spread of these groups is reflected in the number of Lollard Bibles that still survive. Over 250 manuscripts of Lollard Bibles survive to this day – mostly copies of all or part of the New Testament. More Wyclifite Bibles survive than any other form of medieval literature. Considering these are only what was left after the purge, there must have been thousands of these things produced.

Because one pope is never enough

In 1377, after some seventy years in France, the latest pope – Gregory XI – returned to Rome for a bit. The state of the city so appalled him that he died a year later. By now the cardinals were largely French, so they wanted to go home at this point, but the Romans having now got them back weren't going to let them go. They forced the cardinals to stay and choose a new pope. An *Italian* pope. So the cardinals quickly elected Pope Urban VI, and the moment the Romans' backs were turned, the cardinals legged it back to Avignon, where they deposed Urban and appointed a French replacement – Clement VII.

This was not, as we've seen, the first time there were two rival popes. But it was the first time that they each had their own cities and courts. And each pope had support from various European rulers. So this time there were two 'real' popes. Two proper primates. This situation continued for thirty years, with Avignon and Rome each electing their own popes.

To try to solve the problem a council was convened at Pisa in 1409. Neither of the current popes attended, which was not a good omen. The council decided to simplify things by dismissing both of the present popes and electing a new one. Genius. Well, it would have been, were it not that both the Avignon pope and the Roman pope refused to step down. And the new pope wasn't going to step down either. So now there were *three* popes.

Scandal in Bohemia

Meanwhile, outside the confines of the papal palaces, the world was changing.

Wyclif's ideas had already escaped the university. They'd flown over the seas, in fact, carried like a virus. In 1382 Anne, Princess of Bohemia, married King Richard II of England, and there was a sudden influx of Bohemian students coming to Oxford. (Bit like the sixties.) There they came into contact with Wyclif's ideas, which they took back to Prague, along with other souvenirs such as their 'My Son Went to Oxford and All I Got Was This Lousy Tabard' clothing and their 'My other heretic's a Lollard' bumper stickers. The ideas were taken up by the Dean of the Philosophical Faculty in Prague's newly established university. His name was Jan Hus and he was a fiery Czech preacher. (Not literally. Obviously. Although, actually, given his fate . . .) Bohemia was a part of the Holy Roman Empire, but it had a strong sense of its own identity. Hus did something incredibly radical: he offered communicants both the bread and the wine, something that had not been done for centuries. He was relying solely on the Bible for his inspiration. Czechs loved these ideas. When one of the three rival popes tried to excommunicate Hus, there was a riot.

In 1411 one of the two original popes declared a crusade against the other one and tried to recruit backers for this by offering free forgiveness of sins for anyone who put money in the pot. When the decree arrived in Prague, Hus condemned both the pope and the decree and had it burnt in the street.

Under Hus arrest

Meanwhile, attempts were being made to sort out the embarrassing multiple-pope situation.

A council was called at Constance in 1414. It took five years, but it eventually sorted out the mess. The idea was that all three current popes would make way for one new one. The most recent pope was persuaded to move downstairs, as it were, and become the cardinal Bishop of Tusculum. The fact that he had been found guilty of heresy, simony, piracy, murder and other unmentionable stuff didn't seem to count against him.

The Roman pope agreed to step down, providing that he could be a kind of deputy pope in the future. Everyone agreed – he was already ninety, so it wasn't going to be a permanent position. (And it wasn't. He died in 1417.)

Only the Avignon pope wouldn't play ball. He refused to resign and declared that he was the real pope, so there, and he was taking his bat and ball and leaving. He retreated to a remote castle in Spain, where he spent six years complaining, before dying in 1423.

The council appointed a new pope. But, fed up with dealing with the mess created by such overweening authority in the hands of power-hungry individuals, the council went all Eastern Orthodox: it declared that in the future, church councils, not the pope, were to be the final authority on ecclesiastical matters. To facilitate this, regular councils were to be called every few years. The pope was not the final master.

And the council promptly showed that it could be just as spiteful and duplicitous as any pope. Wyclif was declared a heretic and condemned to be burnt at the stake. The trouble was he was already dead, so the council ordered that he should be dug up and burnt. And then thrown into a river.

This was OK. But everyone agreed it would be so much better if they had someone actually alive to condemn. So they offered Jan Hus safe passage to come to discuss the unrest in Bohemia. He was given a promise of safe conduct by the Holy Roman Emperor, Sigismund, but the council ignored that, and had Hus arrested and thrown into a dungeon. (Sigismund was furious, but the council told him that promises didn't count if they were given to a heretic.) Hus was put on trial, denied a defence counsel, kept chained up at night and half-starved. In 1415 he was burned at the stake.

His death turned him into a martyr in Bohemia. A mob led by a radical preacher called Jan Zelivsky went to the city hall and threw thirteen Catholics from an upper window to their deaths. (Throwing people out of windows – defenestration, to use the technical term – was to become a habit.) They went on to wreck churches and monasteries. It led to decades of civil war in Bohemia.*

The council might have decided it was the supreme authority, but the new pope, Martin V, managed to avoid letting it meet and actually, like, do anything. He was supposed to call one of the shiny new regular councils in 1423, which he did, but an outbreak of plague allowed him to dismiss it before it could do any harm. And when he died in 1431, his successor Eugenius IV tried to play for time. But this time the council sought the German emperor's support to make sure that not only would a council meet, but that it would actually have the power to do something.

It did meet and it did do something: it reunified the eastern and western church.

---

* The Bohemian army managed to hold off much stronger forces from else-where in the empire through inventing, essentially, the tank: fortified wagons, covered with sheets of iron with slits through which those inside could fire out. These were pulled by horses.

Reunification

By 1423 the Byzantine cause was almost hopeless. The Turks were overwhelmingly powerful and the once-magnificent empire of Byzantium now consisted of Constantinople, a bit of land in southern Greece and some allotments near Thessalonica.

The pope recognised that the situation was critical. He invited the Byzantines to a council. And so, on 8 February 1438, Emperor John VIII of Byzantium and Joseph II, patriarch of the Byzantine church, met with the pope in Ferrara, accompanied by 20 bishops and some 700 priests, monks and lay officials. It was the biggest show of ecumenical unity for a thousand years.*

It was a historic occasion. It was also fabulously expensive. The pope had a hole knocked in the wall of the palace to allow him to ride his horse right up to the throne – because he thought that being seen with his feet on the ground might diminish his prestige. The sheer expense of the occasion soon started to drain the papal coffers and the whole affair had to be moved to Florence as a cost-cutting exercise.

After much negotiation a decree of reunion was agreed. The east was in no position to negotiate, but the council did make some concessions, most notably around our old chum the *filioque* clause: the east accepted it, and in return the west did not require the east to use it.

So east and west were remarried and bells rang out across the city.

But when the Greek negotiators returned to Constantinople, they were met with the same antipathy as before. Even those who had attended the council agreed that they had 'sold' their faith. And all the most reliable Byzantine opinion polls clearly showed that by now most Byzantines would rather be conquered by the Turks than by the pope.†

Faced with such anger and – as they saw it, ingratitude – many prominent Byzantine clerics and scholars packed their bags, headed to

---

* The meeting is recorded in what is the nearest the Renaissance came to an official summit photograph: the painter Benozzo Gozzoli recorded the delegates as characters in 'the Procession of the Magi' on the walls of the Medici Chapel in Florence.

† In any case, the west proved itself unable to deliver on its side of the bargain. When, in 1443, it finally did get round to sending an army to save Constantinople, they got only as far as Bulgaria, where they were slaughtered by the Muslims.

the harbour and got on to a boat back to Italy. Their number included Bessarion, Metropolitan of Nicaea, who had led the pro-union clergy at the council; in 1450 even the Patriarch of Constantinople himself, Gregory Melissenos, fled to Rome.

Along with these high-profile emigrés, thousands of Byzantine scholars, intellectuals, tradesmen and craftsmen found jobs in the west as teachers and tutors. They brought with them hardly anything in the way of money or possessions, but they had skills that to the westerners seemed magical: in particular, they could read and write classical Greek. The Byzantines had developed a system of further education where anyone over the age of fourteen would study the works of the ancient Greek poets, historians, dramatists and philosophers. Any educated Greek in the imperial service, therefore, would have undergone this education.

They settled in many Italian cities, sometimes in significant numbers. By the late 1470s the Greek population of Venice, for example, stood at around four thousand. They were even given a wing of the church of San Biagio in which to worship in their own language.

The end of the east

On 28 May 1453 there was an ecumenical service in Hagia Sophia in Constantinople. For the first time in . . . well, *ever*, Orthodox and Catholic Christians in the city – including the emperor – met together, prayed and shared the mass. And after that they all went out to die.

The Turks had besieged the city for many months. There had been a heroic resistance effort, led by the emperor, but now, on the evening of 29 May 1453, Ottoman forces under Sultan Mehmet I finally conquered Constantinople. Constantine XI, last emperor of Byzantium, was lost among the fighters in the streets. His body was never found. The eastern empire – the great empire of Byzantium – was finished.

There was a day of terror and looting, with bodies piled in the streets, men and women killed, assaulted or taken into slavery. At sundown the twenty-one-year-old Mehmet entered the church of Hagia Sophia and watched while an imam stood in the pulpit and proclaimed, 'There is no god but God and Muhammad is his messenger.' A thousand years after the church had been built by Justinian it had become a mosque.

Fig. XXIV. *Constantinople falls to the Turks*

The news was received with horror in the west. Pope Nicholas V declared another crusade, diverting funds from various art projects, creating new taxation – even selling off books and art to fund it. But no one else shared his enthusiasm. The French and the English were embroiled in the Hundred Years War, which, by now, rather surprisingly, had reached year 116. And anyway, the last time a crusading army had faced the Turks they had been well and truly beaten.

282

It was not, of course, the end of Christianity in the city of Constantine. The church survived. Mehmet appointed a monk, Gennadius, to be Patriarch. But the church was never as influential again, and in later years the post changed hands largely on the basis of who paid the most money. Christians were heavily taxed, forced to wear special clothing and forbidden to evangelise others. They were not allowed to marry Muslims.

And the effect was that Christians in the west simply forgot. They forgot that there had once been a mighty empire in the east, a *Roman Empire* that had stood for a thousand years after the one in the west had declined and fallen. They forgot that Christianity had flourished in the cities of Syria and North Africa and Persia and Palestine long before it had even started in Britain and France and Spain. They forgot that Christianity had been born in Jerusalem, taken its first tottering steps on the streets of Antioch and Alexandria, grown to maturity in Constantinople and Nicea and Chalcedon.

Christianity became what many people around the world still assume it to be: a religion of the west.

THINGS YOU LEARN FROM CHRISTIAN HISTORY

NO. 8

If you encourage people to think for themselves, they will

The Reformation made following God a matter of individual conscience, based on the interpretation of Scripture. Its leaders then got really hot under the collar when people started making their own decisions based on their own readings of Scripture.
Tough.

8 Print, Protestants and Peasants

Johnny Gooseflesh

In 1454, the year after the fall of Constantinople, the world changed. Again.

It was all down to a man called Johannes Gensfleisch. Which literally means 'Johnny Gooseflesh'. Understandably, he decided that he would rather be known as Johannes Gutenberg. And he invented a device called a printing press, where each letter was set in type, character by character. He launched his new invention with an edition of the Bible.

Gutenberg's invention changed the world. It brought him fame, but not riches. Gutenberg was a great inventor, but a rubbish entrepreneur. The first edition of his Bible took him two years, comprised 150 copies and nearly bankrupted him. It was left to others to make a commercial success of printing books, and printing spread rapidly in Italy, France and Germany, aided by another major new technology: paper.* As books became cheaper and smaller, knowledge and ideas could spread further and faster than ever before.

Bibles began to flood from the presses. In the decades following Gutenberg over 70,000 Bibles were printed in Central Europe, not to mention 100,000 New Testaments. They were printed in Latin, of course, but also in High German, Low German, Dutch, Catalan, Middle German, Portuguese, Polish, Lower Left-hand-side German, Czech, French, Italian, Russian and Ethiopian.

---

* I say 'new', although the earliest paper ever discovered was unearthed by archaeologists in a Tibetan desert town and dates to the late third century AD. However, it took a thousand years before the first paper-mill in Europe was founded in Germany in the thirteenth century.

But not English, obviously. We wouldn't want to give people *ideas* now, would we?

Fig. XXV. *In Germany, pioneering printers have a vision*

It wasn't just Bibles, either. As we've seen, the collapse of Constantinople brought many refugee Greeks to Italy and they found work in the printing industry, first as scribes, and then as translators preparing Greek texts for publication. But expertise wasn't the only thing these refugees brought with them: they brought new texts as well – the writings of the classical authors, poetry, drama, scientific treatises, theological works.

In the west, for the first time in a thousand years, people began to study Greek. They also studied Hebrew, although there were a couple of problems with that: (a) it went backwards, and (b) there was always a risk that you might catch Jewishness. Everyone knew reading Hebrew was risky: a monk in Freiburg said, 'those who speak this tongue are made Jews'.

Of course, not all Greeks travelled west. Some priests remained in Constantinople, and the Turkish Empire. But it was Russia and the Slavic nations that were to become the new home of Orthodox worship. And they even adapted the old Roman title for their leader: he became the Caesar. Or Czar, as they termed it. And, just for good measure, they called Russia the Third Rome.

After a thousand years based in Constantinople, Rome had moved to Moscow.

Vive la republic

Politically, Europe was changing. Spain became the new superpower in western Europe. It was determined to be both powerful and pure. So it expelled all the Muslims and Jews within its borders – at least, all who would not convert to Christianity. (England and France had already expelled all Jews 200 years previously.) This zeal for purity so impressed the pope, he gave the king and queen, Ferdinand and Isabella, approval to purge their land of all heretics for good measure. They set about reforming the monasteries, rooting out corruption, educating the clergy. And their tool for doing this was the Inquisition.

In Spain the Inquisition acted with a chilling, ruthless efficiency. Managed by Tomás de Torquemada, it extracted confessions, rounded up suspects and burnt at the stake not only heretics, but Christians of Jewish or Moorish descent who were suspected of backsliding. Around 2,000 people died in this reign of terror.

Meanwhile, the papacy had finally realised that they were never going to be *real* kings – so they settled for living like kings instead. The popes of this time are notorious for having tons of money and virtually no morals. They built splendid new churches and sponsored magnificent works of art, but, in order to fund these, taxation went as high as their church towers, and clerical posts were sold to the highest bidder.

Perhaps the state of the papacy at this time is best illustrated by one of its most notorious members – Alexander VI, formerly known as Rodrigo Borgia. He bribed his way into the post in 1492. Though aged sixty-one at the time, he had a nineteen-year-old mistress whose brother,

Fig. XXVI. *The Inquisition gets to work*

Alessandro Farnese, the pope made a cardinal. Indeed, all his relatives got plum jobs.*

He was a patron of the arts, commissioning works from people like Michelangelo. He also commissioned murders from various assassins. And he staged sex shows in the Vatican.† For the last few years of his life he never appeared in public without a mask, because his face was so badly disfigured by syphilis.‡ Alexander VI, then, was that rare thing in

---

* The word 'nepotism' comes from the habits of popes and bishops who would give places to their 'nephews'. Sometimes these were genuine nephews; sometimes it was a euphemism for their illegitimate sons. Anyway, the Italian word for nephew is *nepote*, hence 'nepotism'. Pope Alexander had first been made a cardinal because he was the nephew of Pope Callixtus III, head of the Borgia family. The practice was ended by Pope Innocent XII in 1692.

† Both of these were probably staged by his cruel and rapacious nephew, Duke Cesare (who was also a cardinal). According to a report from the Venetian ambassador, 'Every night, four or five men are discovered assassinated, bishops, prelates and others, so that all Rome trembles for fear of being murdered by the duke.'

‡ The disease was new – it had arrived with the French soldiers when they invaded Italy in 1494. The Italians called it The French Pox – a name which,

history, a pope with an STD. Should have used a condom. (It didn't kill him, though. He died aged seventy-two, when – allegedly – an attempt to poison one of his cardinals backfired.) In the long catalogue of evil, rapacious, morally bankrupt popes, Alexander VI stands out. Which is saying something.

In Florence there was a Dominican friar called Girolamo Savonarola, a fiery preacher who cut out the middle man and claimed direct communion with God. He hated the wealthy aristocracy who ruled the Italian states at the time, especially the Medici in Florence, the Duke of Milan and, most of all, Pope Alexander VI:

> Popes and prelates speak against worldly pride and ambition and are plunged in it up to their ears. They preach chastity and keep mistresses . . . They think only of the world and worldly things; for souls they care nothing . . . They have made of the Church a house of ill fame . . . a prostitute who sits upon the throne of Solomon and signals to the passers-by . . . O prostituted Church, you have unveiled your abuse before the eyes of the whole world, and your poisoned breath rises to the heavens.

He prophesied a flood of biblical proportions and the arrival of a new mighty warrior, like Cyrus in the Bible, and coming from the north. So when the French army arrived in Florence, it seemed like his prophecy had come true. The French ousted the ruling house of Medici (who left to concentrate on their greetings-card business) and left the city in the control of Savonarola.

Savonarola's Florence was a 'Christian and religious republic' – indeed, the first truly modern republic, as in 'ruled by the whole people'. The new constitution granted every citizen in good standing the right to a vote in a new parliament: the Great Council. It is a debt that is rarely acknowledged by modern republics, but the basic idea of modern democracy was invented by a rogue Catholic monk. However, there were limits to this new-found freedom. The city also enforced a strong moral code, banning same-sex relationships, adultery, public drunkenness, and young men – a sort of Savonarola Youth – roamed the streets telling people off if they were immodestly dressed. There were also regular 'bonfires of the vanities' during which citizens would come to chuck their mirrors, make-up, fancy

---

much to the irritation of the French, was quickly adopted throughout Europe.

clothing and paintings on the fires, along with worldly books, musical instruments and even games such as chess. (Tragically, the paintings burned included several by Michelangelo and Botticelli.) It was Puritan England, only warmer and with more olive oil.

The pope ordered the arrest and execution of Savonarola. Savonarola was excommunicated and, when the brave new world he'd promised failed to arrive, the Florentine people lost faith in their fiery priest and handed him over, along with two associates. They were tortured, and on 23 May 1497 the three were led out into the Piazza della Signoria in Rome, stripped of their Friar's robes and hanged. For good measure a fire was lit under them, so that Savonarola would burn just like all those vanities the pope loved so much.

But Savonarola cast a long shadow. (Not literally, though. He was described as only being 'of middle height'.) His body was burned, but the words he wrote in prison spread around Europe. And he became a kind of symbol of all that the authorities – ecclesiastical and secular – were up against. Nearly a hundred years after his death the Grand Duke of Florence was still forbidding monks, friars and nuns in the city even to mention his name.

So, to sum up this bit, the reign of Pope Alexander VI saw the invention of several features of modern life, notably republicanism and syphilis. Oh, and colonialism. Because in 1493 the pope gave official approval to the dividing up of Africa and America.

Brave new world

The naval empires of Spain and Portugal had been busily exploring. Columbus had made the grave error of discovering America in 1492. The Portuguese, under the aptly named Prince Henry the Navigator, had been happily navigating up and down the west coast of Africa. Vasco da Gama and Bartolomeu Dias had rounded the Cape of Good Hope and opened up a sea route to India.

In order to make sure that everyone played nicely, Pope Alexander issued the decree of *Inter cetera divina*, which drew a line down the Atlantic. Spain had the trading rights to everything west of the line, Portugal to the east.* When this finally came to the attention of

---

* The line was later moved somewhat to the west in 1494, so that the Portuguese

other nations, they took no notice of it whatsoever. 'I should like to see the clause of Adam's will that excludes me from a share of the globe,' said the French king rather grumpily. But it set a precedent that many many people around the world were going to regret. It allied the church with colonialism. Because this wasn't just about trade: it was about converting people, whether they wanted to be converted or not.

Spanish colonisers conquered South America, taking Catholic religion with them in the form of Franciscan and Dominican missionaries. By 1530 Cortes had trashed the Aztecs in Mexico, and Pizarro had crushed the Incas in Peru. And full-speed conversion was underway. In Mexico one pair of Franciscans worked a baptism production line, baptising 200,000 people. (Their output peaked at 14,000 in one day.)

It was easy to see why the natives so readily embraced this new life. Mainly because if they didn't, they would have the old life forcibly removed. They were given an ultimatum: become a Christian and be baptised, or lose all your lands and your possessions and become slaves. Although, to tell the truth, even if you did accept this great free offer, you were pretty much a slave anyway. Those who ticked the box marked 'Yes, I'd love to take up my free trial of Christianity and the benefits of European governance' found themselves herded into labour camps, where the joys of learning how to be good Christians were accompanied by disease, foul living conditions, back-breakingly hard work in the mines and a life expectancy of about two years. Still, at least they were saved. So *that* was all right.

The net result of all this was wholesale decimation of the population. Those who weren't killed by the executions and the forced labour were carried off by diseases to which they had no immunity. By 1550 it is estimated that the population of South America had dropped by as much as 95 per cent.

The astonishing thing is that many of those involved in these atrocities genuinely believed they were doing God's work by rescuing the natives from vice and superstition.* Columbus believed that God had made him the messenger of the new heaven and new earth . . . and he

_____

could claim Brazil.

* Well, some of them believed that, anyway. When Pizarro was reminded about his duty to provide religious instruction for his slaves, he replied, 'I have not come for any such reason; I have come to take away their gold.' At least he was honest.

showed me the spot where to find it.' Those he found living there were less excited. The celebrated explorer was an incredibly cruel and heartless dictator. His slaves had to deliver him a quota of gold, for which they received a copper token. Any slaves who failed to earn their token had their hands cut off and were left to bleed to death. Enjoy Columbus Day, everybody.*

There were many truly Christian missionaries, though, who were appalled at the mistreatment and suffering. When the Dominican Antonio de Montesinos spoke to a load of Spanish dignitaries in Hispaniola in 1511 he let them have it with both barrels:

> You are all in mortal sin, and live and die in it, because of the cruelty and tyranny you practise among these innocent peoples. Tell me, by what right or justice do you hold these Indians in such a cruel and horrible servitude? On what authority have you waged such detestable wars against these peoples, who dwelt quietly and peacefully on their own land? . . . Are these not men? Do they not have rational souls? Are you not bound to love them as you love yourselves? Don't you understand this? Don't you feel this? Why are you sleeping in such a profound and lethargic slumber?

Montesinos denied confession to his listeners, one of whom was a labour-camp manager called Bartholomew de las Casas (1484–1566). Later Bartholomew became a Dominican priest and, after witnessing appalling atrocities during the conquest of Cuba, he released his own slaves and spent the rest of his life campaigning for the rights of the natives. When he was Bishop of Chiapas in 1544–47, he refused mass to some slaveowners – which almost got him lynched. He was a gifted writer and passionate activist, who acted as a kind of frontline journalist, sending back to Europe reports of the atrocities and massacres. Later, Protestants started to use these reports as anti-Catholic propaganda, so his books were banned and burnt. But he did manage to persuade the king to pass laws in 1542 restricting the labour camps.

* Mind you, we should not romanticise some of the cultures that were overrun. These cultures had engaged in a *lot* of human sacrifice. Shortly before the Europeans arrived an estimated eighty thousand victims were sacrificed to the gods. As always, it was the poor people at the bottom of the Aztec pyramid who got killed.

He was, perhaps, the first human rights campaigner in colonial history. And his example inspired many later Catholic priests. Back in Spain he was called 'Protector of the Indians'. He also managed to influence Pope Paul III, who in 1537 made statements in support of the rights of the natives, declaring that 'the Indians, like all other peoples, may not be deprived in any way of their freedom or property (even though they do not belong to the religion of Jesus Christ), and can and must enjoy them in freedom and legitimately'. Given that by that time millions of them had died and the continent had been divided between the powers, it was perhaps a little late. But good on him, anyway.

Meanwhile, the Portuguese had made inroads into Africa. Or in rivers, actually. They had sailed up the Congo and encountered King Nzinga a Nkuwu of Kongo, whom they baptised and renamed John I. His son, Alfonso, created the Roman Catholic church of Kongo (or possibly the Roman Katholic Church of Congo). The country provided slaves for the plantations of the new world, to replace all those South Americans who had ungratefully died of disease, labour camps, acts of Spaniards, and so on.

Other Portuguese explorers sailed around Africa and on to India, where they were a bit surprised to find that Christianity had got there first. In India they discovered the remains of the Nestorian Christians who claimed that Thomas had brought the gospel to their land – an unverifiable legend, but one that made the Portuguese look like newbies anyway.

It didn't stop the Portuguese trying to convert them to Catholicism, though. Elsewhere, Christianity proved itself attractive to those at the bottom of the scale. Hindu pearl fishers were low-caste members of society, who were subject to attacks by the Muslims. They became Christians and put themselves under the protection of the Portuguese. The whole population of between 10,000 and 20,000 living on the east coast of India were baptised in 1536. Must have been a big font.

ERASMUS

Erasmus. Apparently wearing a turnip on his head

Name: Herasmus Gerritzoon (i.e. Erasmus, son of Gerard).
Aka: Erasmus Desiderius.
Nationality: Dutch.
Dates: c.1466–1536.
Appearance: Urbane. High cheek-bones. The pictures are accurate.
Before he was famous: Scholar. Writer. Illegitimate son of a priest.
Famous for: His edition and translation of the Greek New Testament.
Why does he matter? His version of the Greek New Testament formed the basis for translations by people like Luther and Tyndale. His questioning, critical approach heralded modern biblical criticism.
Could you have a drink with him down the pub? A glass of sherry, certainly.

Come to your senses

Around 1400 only a very small percentage of people could read. But by 1650 literacy rates had soared – as many as eight out of ten males could read in some cities. Which is a higher literacy rate than among tabloid journalists and footballers even today. Even out among the yokels, rural literacy might reach 30 per cent.

The church recognised that this spelt danger. In Venice, in the late sixteenth century, a silk worker was denounced to the Inquisition because, it was said, 'he reads all the time'. Women were thought to be especially vulnerable to new ideas. So, to protect them, it was recommended that they should not learn to read at all. This is one reason why pictures of the Virgin Mary reading – which were relatively common in the Middle Ages – largely disappear after 1520. Reading was not a respectable habit – not even for the mother of Jesus.

The fact is that nothing liberates people more than reading. When people can read stuff for themselves, they can draw their own conclusions. They no longer have to believe everything that they are told. Christians began to explore the Bible for themselves, and as they did so they found some puzzling omissions. There was no pope (or patriarch for that matter), no purgatory, no penance. Someone had taken the Ps out of the Bible! This, combined with the radical thoughts shared by the wandering preachers on the one hand, and the teachers in the university on the other, meant that the pillars of the church were wobbling a bit, and one of the chief pillar-wobblers was a man called Erasmus.

He was born Herasmus Gerritzoon, and he was actually the illegitimate son of a humble priest. He became a monk, and soon distinguished himself as a writer, scholar and satirist. And, as the craze for Greek took hold, he rebranded himself 'Erasmus Desiderius'. Desiderius is in fact the Greek version of Erasmus. Erasmus: so good he named himself twice.

He was the first superstar of the age of print. He wrote the first printed bestseller – an annotated collection of proverbs. And, although an orthodox Catholic, he satirised the excesses of the church: his tract *Julius Barred* depicted the then late, unlamented Pope Julius arriving at the gates of heaven only for Peter to tell him that he wasn't on the guest list.

In February 1516 Erasmus published the *Novum Instrumentum Omne* – a Greek New Testament with accompanying Latin translation. This was the first modern critical edition of the New Testament, drawn from a variety of Greek manuscripts. The book unleashed a storm of controversy.

He retranslated some of the key terms of the New Testament. The Greek word *ekklēsia* became *congregation*, 'congregation'. Not 'church'. In John 1 Erasmus translated the opening phrase, 'In the beginning was the sermon' – *sermo*, meaning the 'spoken word'. And every good churchman knew that it was through inflammatory sermons that heresies were promulgated. And then there was the little booby trap of Matthew 3.2. For a thousand years the Vulgate text had John the Baptist calling out *poenitentiam agile*, 'make penance'. From this the Catholic Church had built an enormous system of penances, indulgences and other ways of making up for bad behaviour. But Erasmus translated it as *resipiscite*, 'repent', 'come to your senses'.

But it got worse. Erasmus based his translation on the earliest Greek manuscripts he could find. And when he examined those manuscripts, he realised that some passages that had always been in the Vulgate were not actually in the earliest Greek text. Bits like the longer ending of Mark's Gospel, and the story of Jesus and the woman caught in adultery. Suddenly some familiar, well-loved texts were no longer 'the Word of God'.

People didn't like this. They didn't want the text questioned and forensically examined in this way. But Erasmus was at the forefront of a number of writers and scholars known as 'humanists'. They were people who had rediscovered the 'humane literature' of ancient, classical times. They were people who questioned. It was the humanist scholar Lorenzo Valla who exposed the blatant forgery of the Donation of Constantine. They gleefully attacked the superstition of medieval Christianity: with its emphasis on – as they saw it – patently fake relics, the sale of indulgences, ignorant priests mumbling their way through mass in a language they could barely understand.

But for all their cynicism, they were not reformers in the sense of those who came after them. Humanists like Erasmus wanted reform, perhaps, but in a peaceful, humane, reasonable, civilised way.* Erasmus wanted ordinary people to read the Bible. He wanted it read by 'the farmer, the tailor, the mason, the prostitute, the pimp, the traveller and the Turk'. 'Do you think that the Scriptures are only fit for the perfumed?' He made the mistake of so many civilised liberals: he thought everyone was as civilised as he was.

By the time he died in 1536 his approach had been adopted, adapted and abused by more passionate, more furious and far less reasonable people.

Like Luther.

---

* There were limits to his 'humanity'. He was, like so many of his contemporaries, deeply anti-Semitic. 'If to hate Jews is to be a good Christian,' he wrote, 'we are all abundantly Christian.' And he wrote admiringly of the French for having banished all the Jews after 1348.

LUTHER

Luther. There's that turnip again

Name: Martin Luther.
Aka: Er . . . Martin Luther.
Nationality: German. Very German.
Dates: 1483–1546.
Appearance: Generally, he did not look well.
Before he was famous: Monk. Doctor of Theology.
Famous for: Writing. Bible translating. Probably not actually nailing things to doors.
Why does he matter? One of the most influential figures in history. Began the Protestant Reformation in 1517. Challenged some of the basic tenets of Roman Catholicism. His emphasis on personal conviction had a profound effect on western Europe.
Could you have a drink with him down the pub? Absolutely. Ein maß, Herr Landlord!

Luther is relieved

One of the most influential figures in church history, Luther's life is an everyday story of heroism, intellectual courage, religious conviction, bigotry, intestinal problems and a gift for self-promotion that borders on genius.

The son of a miner, Luther had a harsh, brutal upbringing. Then one day in 1505 he found himself caught in a thunderstorm and made a vow that if he survived he would become a monk.

He survived. And became a monk.

He was ordained a priest in 1507, and went to Wittenberg to become a lecturer at the new University.* In 1511 he became Doctor of Theology

---

* If he'd gone to Battenberg he would have become a cake-maker and the whole course of history might have been changed.

and Professor of Scripture. In 1515 he was made a vicar of his order – a post that put him in charge of eleven Augustinian monasteries. As monastic careers go, it was all going tremendously well.

Except that it *wasn't*. Luther had problems. He simply could not be sure of his own salvation. He would go to confession and confess for hours on end, trying to rid his soul of every tiny stain, only to leave the confessional and remember something he should have mentioned.

That wasn't his only problem. Another place he would go to for hours on end was the toilet. Luther was a man in thrall to his colon. He struggled all his life with severe constipation – probably brought on by all that Bratwurst and Sauerkraut. That was not his only physical ailment: he claimed that the devil would roar and whistle in his ears, that his head would start spinning and his heart race so fast that he would actually fall out of his chair. Some doctors think that maybe he had Meniere's disease – a condition that attacks the middle ear – and causes severe problems with equilibrium. This would also explain why, in 1541, he became deaf, after experiencing bad earaches and a discharge from his ears. He also appears to have had extremely high blood pressure that eventually led to heart disease.

It's a good thing, therefore, that he had an extremely calm personality and that he took care to keep calm and not get involved in any major arguments.

What? Oh.

Anyway, back to the toilet. It was there, *in cloaca*, as he put it (or on *das klo*, as the Germans call it), that he had his ground-breaking insight.*

It is known as the *Turmerlebnis* or Tower experience. Usually dated between 1512 and 1515, Luther was sitting, er . . . *contemplating* . . . when he had a revelation. He became convinced of two things: first that believers could be saved only by faith, and second, that there would come a day when the world would be ready for quilted toilet paper.†

For a long time Luther had been oppressed by a sense of guilt, sinfulness and failure. No amount of penitence and confession, of attending mass and doing good deeds could assuage this. He was rotten inside

---

* In fact, the toilet has recently been discovered by archaeologists, leading to the rather wonderful BBC headline 'Luther's lavatory thrills experts'.

† The Chinese had already done this, actually. By 1391 the Bureau of Imperial Supplies in Peking was producing 720,000 sheets of toilet paper every year. But they also produced some luxury sheets, 'thick, but soft and perfumed', for the royal family.

– and he wasn't talking about his toilet issues, either. Luther knew that when it came to judgement, God would have to damn him: because that was the way the whole system worked.

Then he started to read Erasmus' Greek New Testament, and he found himself deeply disturbed. He began to think about the words of Paul's letter to the Romans 'All have sinned and fall short of the glory of God, and are now made righteous by his grace as a gift.' What if God could actually *make* people righteous? Augustine had claimed this to be the case, but Augustine believed that God made people righteous by enabling them to keep his laws. To Luther this was impossible. No one could keep all those laws. Works couldn't possibly get you to heaven. Only Christ was that perfect.

But what if when Christ died, his righteousness was transferred to us? Credited to our account? That's where Paul's idea of justification by faith came in. In the words of Romans 5.1, 'By faith we have been made acceptable to God.' This belief changed everything. Confession, absolution, penitence, prayers to the saints – none of this made any difference. Faith in Jesus: that was the only thing that mattered.

'I felt myself reborn,' Luther wrote later. 'I had looked through the gates of paradise.'

Now that is what I call relieving yourself. But in subsequent days, and on subsequent visits to the tower, presumably, Luther thought more on this, and pushed it to its logical conclusion.

It was to bring him into direct conflict with the authorities – and the pope himself.

Indulge me for a minute

In 1517 Pope Leo X* embarked on a massive scheme to beautify the Basilica of St Peter's in Rome. Born Giovanni de Medici, from the wealthy and powerful Medici family, Leo had become an abbot at the age of just eight and a cardinal aged just thirteen. Let's just say money may have changed hands. Anyway, his career was headed in only one direction. Becoming Pope was just the icing on the cake, and, on his election, he said to his brother Giuliano, 'Since God has given us the papacy, let us enjoy it.'

Enjoy it he did. He gave lavish banquets, spent a fortune on his art

* No relation to Malcolm X.

Fig. XXVII. *Tetzel's sale of indulgences was proving very popular*

projects, and paraded around Rome at the head of processions featuring as a star act his pet elephant, Hanno. Hanno was a rare white elephant, a gift from King Manuel I of Portugal on his coronation. Sadly, he died two years later after someone tried to treat his constipation with a gold-enriched laxative. (That's Hanno who died, not the King of Portugal. Anyway, it's a good thing Luther couldn't afford the same treatment.)

Leo's lifestyle was not cheap. Gold-enriched elephant laxative doesn't grow on trees, you know. And the lavish renovations Leo had in mind for St Peter's were eye-wateringly expensive. So Leo launched a pan-European fund-raising campaign selling papal indulgences.

In Germany one of the main salesmen was a man called Johannes Tetzel, who made outrageous claims of the power of his indulgences, including the catchy rhyme

As soon as the coin in the coffer rings
The soul from Purgatory springs.

The ruler of the region where Luther lived, Frederick III, banned the sale of these things, but even so people started turning up at confessions with copies of their indulgences, claiming that they no longer had to repent of their sins, since the document promised absolute forgiveness.*

Luther went ballistic. He was outraged that forgiveness – a free gift from God – was being peddled for cash. So he wrote out a response: ninety-five bullet points, known as the Ninety-Five Theses.

Luther and the Wittenberg door

It is one of the most celebrated events in Reformation history. On 31 October 1517 Martin Luther strode to the Castle Church in Wittenberg and nailed his Ninety-Five Theses to the door. It must have brought tears to his eyes.

The act, which has been described by Luther fan-boys as 'the hammer blow of history', has become one of the key symbols of the Reformation. But it may not actually have happened. Luther himself never referred to it and the story doesn't even appear until after his death, and was written by Luther's friend Philipp Melanchthon, who didn't arrive in Wittenberg University as a professor until 1518.

We do know that Luther wrote a letter to his superiors on 31 October 1517 denouncing the sale of indulgences and asking that the money be repaid to those he felt had been conned. And with this letter he included his Ninety-Five Theses, which were intended to be a basis for discussion. So it may be that Luther never intended to debate the theses openly, but merely to discuss them quietly with his superiors. Doesn't *sound* like him, I know . . .

Whatever the case, news of Luther's opposition got out. A local printer got hold of the document, made copies and started distributing them. The theses had hit the fan.

The authorities tried to stifle this, but they were foiled. First, they

---

* Wittenberg was not exactly a superstition-free zone. The Castle Church had over 5,000 holy relics. It was particularly strong in what you might call the ante-natal department, including vials of milk from the Virgin Mary, straw from Jesus' manger and the body of one of the children massacred by King Herod. But it also contained bread from the last supper, a branch of the burning bush from which God spoke to Moses (thankfully no longer alight – heaven knows what would have happened if that touched the hay from the manger).

discovered that it was really difficult to stop printers printing controversial things if the controversial things they were printing sold well. Second, the political situation was not in their favour. Frederick III and his neighbouring ruler, George, Elector of Saxony, saw in Luther a useful weapon against the power of Rome and the Holy Roman Empire™, so they protected Luther from arrest. Third, many German nobles were fed up of sending money to Rome just so that the pope could purge his elephants, and thus they backed Luther's cause. Fourth, the people themselves were fed up with being used as a cash cow for the church. So, for a time, Luther had a lot of popular support. Finally, and perhaps most importantly, Luther was a tough, unyielding opponent. He was a theological street fighter. And he was *always* up for a fight.

At a disputation in 1519 papal envoys accused him of contradicting official papal teaching on indulgences. But Luther refused to recant his ideas. For him it was impossible that the church could overrule the Bible. So he ended up denying the primacy of the pope and the infallibility of the general councils.

Ladies and gentlemen, welcome to the Reformation.

The year of living dangerously

The year 1520 was a bit of a big year for Luther. He was excommunicated by the pope, his writings were publicly burnt and he wrote three pivotal works.

An den Christlichen Adel deutscher Nation (To the Christian Nobility of the German Nation) was addressed to the German princes and called on them to abolish tributes to Rome, the celibacy of the clergy, masses for the dead, pilgrimages, religious orders and other Catholic institutions.

This was a huge hit, which led Luther to release the catchily titled *Von der Babylonischen Gefängenschaft der Kirche* (The Babylonian Captivity of the Church), which compared the 'spiritual' captivity of the laity to the Babylonian exile of the Jews. It called for the laity to actively participate in communion and to receive both bread and wine, denied the doctrine of transubstantiation and held that only Baptism and the Eucharist were sacraments. (Apart from this it was completely uncontroversial.)

The final part of the trilogy was *Von der Freiheit eines*

Christenmenschen (The Freedom of a Christian Person), in which Luther proclaimed that it was faith alone which brought salvation. He did not condemn works, but the belief that good works brought righteousness. He declared that 'A Christian man is the most free lord of all, and subject to none; a Christian man is the most dutiful servant of all, and subject to every one.' Well, maybe not *every* one: he rejected the Pope as 'a man of sin and the son of perdition.'

The church responded by issuing a papal bull, *Exsurge Domine*, which branded Luther as a heretic, demanded that he retract forty-one of his ninety-five theses and threatened him with excommunication. (When he received his personal complimentary copy, Luther burned it.)

Things came to a head at the Diet of Worms, which is not, as the name implies, the latest Hollywood weight-loss programme, but a meeting of German princes and bishops, chaired by the Emperor Charles V at the German town of Worms (pronounced Vohrms).

Luther attended – after receiving a guarantee of safe conduct. Given what had happened to Hus, this was a risk, but the fact was that Luther now had real celebrity status. And several of the rulers of German states rather agreed that maybe it was time for a bit of Teutonic independence.

So he went. At the Diet Luther was accused of arrogance. How come only Martin Luther understood the true meaning of Scripture? What about all those learned men who had gone before? Luther gave that argument a thorough kicking, pointing out that most of the popes and the councils had actually contradicted one another. 'Unless I am convinced by Scripture and plain reason,' he replied, 'my conscience is captive to the word of God. I cannot and will not recant anything, for to go against conscience is neither right nor safe. God help me.'

And then he added the famous words 'Here I stand, I can do no other.' (Or maybe he didn't. History is slightly opaque.) But Luther was setting his individual conscience against the pope, the church fathers, the massed books of theology and the councils of the church. It was one man against the system.

And so it was that, just after 6 p.m. on 17 April 1521, Luther invented the modern world.

Here's the thing. Savonarola had invented the democratic rights of citizens. But Luther was giving voice to the idea of freedom of conscience, of one man's – or woman's – right to decide for themselves. Once you say a man is justified by faith, it follows that he is free.

And that is why, just a short while afterwards, Luther was kidnapped. He left the council, whereupon the Elector of Saxony staged a fake kidnapping and took Luther to safety in the Wartburg (pronounced Vortberg). This was for his own safety, because after the council he had been condemned by Charles V (pronounced Charles W).

There, disguised as a knight called Jünker Georg – Sir George – he spent the next eight months writing. He worked at a furious pace, fuelled by his sense of injustice, by his passionate commitment to the faith-lives of ordinary people and, one imagines, by the sheer intellectual excitement of what he had stumbled upon.

Leo X died in 1521. He had spent so much during his reign that he was reduced to pawning palace furniture, silver plates, jewels, even statues of the apostles. He died of malaria, but if he'd known what Jünker Georg was up to in the Wartburg he'd probably have keeled over from a heart attack anyway.

Because Sir George was translating the Bible.

A mean German

In the Wartburg Luther suffered from insomnia, constipation and depression. Pretty much life as normal, then. But he still managed to translate the New Testament into German and write twelve books. Heaven knows what he'd have achieved if he'd been healthy.

As we've seen, this wasn't the first translation of the Bible into German. But Germany was a land of many different mini-states and dialects. So Luther developed a kind of common German – a 'mean German' he called it, one that was intelligible from Saxony in the east to the Rhineland in the west.

He used Erasmus' Greek New Testament, a Latin version and, just as importantly, regular trips to the market place to hear how people actually spoke. Luther's translation – like Luther himself – used the language of the people. And when it was published in 1522, it sold like the proverbial hot-küchen. Luther's enemies were so alarmed that Duke George the Bearded – a man whom Luther, with typical politeness called 'the Dresden Hog' – made it a criminal offence to buy the book and offered to buy back the copies of anyone who had already purchased it. Only four people took him up on his offer, however. Johannes Cochlaeus, the administrator who was tasked with trying to stop this phenomenon, lamented that 'even tailors and cobblers, even women and other simple folk who had only learned to read a little German in their lives, were reading it with great enthusiasm as though it were the fount of all truth, while others carried it around, pressed to their bosom, and learned it by heart'.

It was an international bestseller. When he retired in 1572, the Wittenberg printer Hans Lufft had printed some 100,000 copies of Luther's translation. But it also formed the basis for translations into many other languages. There were Dutch, Danish, Swedish, Hungarian, Lithuanian, Polish, Romanian, Bohemian, Slovenian, even Icelandic, translations.

Luther really understood the new information technology of print. He realised that you couldn't easily silence a mass-produced book. He made his books powerful, compelling, polemical, urgent. They were incredibly popular. There were door-to-door pedlars who sold nothing but Luther's writings. Not including the Bible translations, over 3,700 separate editions of his books or pamphlets were published in his lifetime.

Kiss me Katie

Meanwhile, things were really kicking off in Wittenberg. Luther's friends and supporters took over the church and shaped it around Luther's ideas: priests recited the mass in plain clothes and in plain language (German). Following Hus, communicants ate the bread and drank the wine. Priests even got married. Fast days and masses for the dead were scrapped.

But with all this heady freedom about, things got out of hand and violent disorder started to break out. So Luther returned to Wittenberg and took command. He actually suspended all these changes, and reintroduced them more gradually. (Some he never brought back.)

Luther got married himself in 1525. His wife was a nun, Katharine von Bora. Luther – obviously learning from the whole kidnapping routine – arranged to have her, and some other nuns, smuggled out of the local convent in the back of a fishmonger's wagon, alongside barrels of herring. They had six children of their own and adopted four orphans. Luther loved his wife, whom he called 'my Lord Katie' and 'my chain'. And he *loved* his wife, if you see what I mean. He talked about marital sex as being about more 'than is necessary for the begetting of children'. This was a genuine break with the Augustinian view of sex as a necessary evil.

Martin and Katie sort of invented the ideal of the Protestant household. A home could be a place of sanctity and prayer, just as much as a monastery. Before the Reformation, men and women sat or stood separately in church, but when pews were introduced, they sat together as families.

He was able to do all this largely because the emperor was busy elsewhere. He spent nine years in Italy fighting the French. Or possibly in France fighting the Italians. Either way, he was fighting a lot of people somewhere. This gave Luther the freedom not only to establish his ideas in Wittenberg but also to write and to travel.

The result was that reform spread throughout Germany and into Switzerland. The Waldensians reappeared and joined in. The Hussites were delighted to come along for the ride. In Denmark the ruling classes embraced Lutheranism as a chance to throw off the control of unpopular foreign clerics; in Sweden they embraced it as an excuse to throw off the control of unpopular foreign Danes. Reform took many forms, but it shared an emphasis on Scripture, on preaching, on belief in justification by faith and, of course, on a complete abandonment of the idea of allegiance to Rome.

Luther is a complex character. Protestants, like the Orthodox and Catholics, have a habit of creating saints, even if they don't call them that. But Luther was far from saintly. He was a dogmatic, argumentative man and his language is truly potty-mouthed. Even when he was preaching he was incredibly crude. Because he felt so keenly that he was under attack, his writing and sermons frequently teeter on the edge of paranoia. Tragically, as he got older, more ill, more disillusioned with the activities of some of his followers, he lashed out in pain.

His disillusion turned into blind hatred, expressed in some truly appalling writing. In his youth he had been personal friends with many Jews and naively believed that the Jews would see the glories of Protestantism and convert, that they had always been put off Christianity not by Christ, but by Catholicism. When the Jews rejected the joys of Lutheranism, he started condemning them in extreme – not to say unhinged – ways. His later tracts, particularly the notorious *On the Jews and Their Lies*, advocated banning all rabbinic teaching, burning Jewish homes and synagogues and expelling from Germany all Jews who would not convert.

ZWINGLI

Zwingli. Looking rather two-dimensional

Name: Huldrych Zwingli.
Aka: Ulrich Zwingli.
Nationality: Swiss.
Dates: 1484–1531.
Appearance: Contemporary portrait shows him as pale and with only one eye. Oh, hang on, it's just a side-on profile.
Before he was famous: Pastor.
Famous for: Being Lutheran. And then falling out with Luther. Emphasised a plain, stripped-down church worship.
Why does he matter? He believed that the Eucharist was purely symbolic. Nothing happened to the bread and wine in a physical sense. (Apart from being swallowed. Which is pretty physical.)
Could you have a drink with him down the pub? Tricky, because he cut back their numbers, and their opening hours, and ordered publicans to report any instances of blasphemy. Probably safer to share a Toblerone.

From bad to Würst

Challenges to the ecclesiastical authorities came in many forms. In Zurich they came in the form of a sausage. On 12 March 1522 a printer ate some sausage and egg on Ash Wednesday. This was Lent, and he had broken the fast. When the city council investigated, he told them that he was hungry. And anyway, Ulrich Zwingli said it was OK.

Zwingli was a preacher in the city. He had been present at what has come to be called Sausagegate* and he sprang to the printer's defence. Zwingli claimed the only 'law' over Christians was the Bible and there was nothing in there about Lent. A debate was called at which Zwingli

* It's only called that by me.

argued that 'God does not desire our decrees or doctrines if they do not originate with him.' The council agreed, Zwingli was free to preach – and Zurich went Protestant.

Zwingli was a disciple of Luther, but, like many of Luther's 'children', he was more radical than his spiritual dad. Under Zwingli's influence Zurich stripped the churches of images. Ministers in plain clothing served Communion from a table in the midst of the congregation. Monasteries were closed and their buildings used for teaching or to house and care for the poor.

(In a move to delight music lovers everywhere, the Minster organ was bricked up. While Martin Luther supported the use of the organ, Calvin and Zwingli outlawed it. So they weren't all bad.)

Zwingli was a hardliner. Luther kept robes and some rituals; Zwingli saw them as the work of the Antichrist. But the issue that really divided them was the Eucharist. Luther believed a kind of watered-down version of transubstantiation. He talked about the 'ubiquity' of Jesus Christ: Christ could be at the right hand of the Father and, somehow, at the same time in bread and wine.

Zwingli was having none of that. The Eucharist was a reminder of the death of Christ. It was a spiritual act, but not a piece of magical trickery. Bread was bread and wine was wine and sausage was sausage and that was that.

In time, though, people in Zurich began to out-Zwingli Zwingli. A scholar called Conrad Grebel looked at the Bible and failed to find any infant baptism there. Instead he found the words 'Believe and be baptised.' If, as Zwingli argued, the sacraments had no mystical powers in and of themselves, but were merely expressions of faith, then baptism had to be the same: it was for believers.

This was too much even for Zwingli. Infant baptism was about inclusion, about making sure that everyone entered the church, part of the fabric that bound society together. Grebel's ideas would essentially turn Christianity into a voluntary organisation. But Grebel followed through with his ideas, and refused to have his children baptised.

In January 1525 the council gave Grebel and his followers an ultimatum: they had eight days to get their children baptised, or else be expelled from the city. So on 21 January Grebel held a baptism. Not of children, but of adults, who repudiated their baptism as infants on the grounds that they could not possibly have been believers as babies. They stated that theirs was the first true baptism in the church for 1000 years. This group of dissenters went on to refuse to work for the state. They were pacifists.

They were expelled from the city. And they became known as rebaptisers or, in mock-Greek, the Anabaptists. And they were bitterly persecuted by the other Protestants. They were harried and chased and exiled. They became a kind of Protestant underground. Most Anabaptists tried to live quiet, inoffensive lives, building small communities and practising a Christian communism. These were people who based their lives on what they read in the Gospels and Acts.

Grebel had been expelled from Zurich, but subsequently the city authorities went much further. In 1527 an Anabaptist called Felix Mantz was drowned in the River Limmat in a cruelly ironic execution. The Protestants had started killing their own heretics.

The Anabaptists were the reds under the bed of the Reformation. And they were treated brutally by both sides. The Anabaptist leader Michael Sattler was charged with denying transubstantiation, infant baptism and last rites, and for despising the Blessed Virgin. He was also accused of saying that it was wrong to fight the Turks. He was horrifically executed and his wife was drowned for good measure.

Then there was Jakob Hutter, leader of an Anabaptist community in the Tyrol. This group practised an early form of communism, banning private property and sharing everything in common – straight out of the pages of Acts. Hutter was caught in 1535, part drowned, then tortured and burnt at the stake. His followers, the Hutterites, moved from place to place across subsequent centuries, eventually moving to America in the nineteenth century (where they continued to be ostracised and abused). Today, happily, they are thriving, mainly in Canada.

Similarly, the Dutch Anabaptist Menno Simons started a community that became the Mennonites. He planted congregations in the Netherlands and Germany and spent twenty-five years underground, secretly spreading the Anabaptist gospel.

League of Protestant Gentlemen

Why, you might be asking, didn't any of the big players in Europe simply gang up on these newly Protestant states and force them back into the Catholic fold?

Good question. Glad you're paying attention. Well, part of the reason was that Europe was seriously disunited. At one point the troops of Charles V even occupied and pillaged Rome, and took the pope prisoner. Not much unity there. And then the Turks invaded Hungary, which took everyone's mind off the trouble in Germany.*

Charles V did make diplomatic attempts to solve the crisis. In 1529 he called a diet of all the German rulers at Speyer, which decreed that Protestant states must return to the Catholic fold. But six princes and fourteen cities refused and delivered an official letter of protest – a document known as the Protestation. And that, children, is why they became known as Protestants.

Charles realised that he really needed to bring unity, and if that meant making compromises with the Protestants, then so be it. So he called another council – this time at Augsburg in 1530. It was attended by Luther's deputy, Philipp Melanchthon, who was far more patient and far less potty-mouthed than his mentor. Melanchthon prepared a kind of Protestant statement of faith for the occasion, which became known as the Augsburg Confession.

This was to become the central doctrinal document of Lutheranism. It went as far as they felt they could go towards Catholicism: choosing to skate over contentious issues such as purgatory, it concentrated on the positive, accentuating things like justification by faith and the importance of preaching.

It worked. Sort of. I mean, it didn't convince the Catholics, obviously, but it brought the Protestants far more support. And these Protestant states gathered together in the unwieldily named Schmalkaldic League, which was the strongest league in Europe right up to the time of the Premiership.

Zwingli didn't join them. He was in a strop, his own statement of faith having been effectively ignored by the Diet. He formed his own league – an alliance of Swiss Reformed cities. Eventually there was a civil war between these cities and the ones that had remained Catholic. Zwingli died in battle, hacked to death by Swiss Catholic soldiers armed, presumably, only with their standard issue pocket knives. His body was burnt and mixed with manure to stop his followers venerating his remains. He ended up, literally, in the brown stuff.

---

* The Turks reached Vienna, but then had to retreat. Before they went, the Viennese had looked at the crescents on their flags and invented a new pastry. Yes, the Viennese Whirl. Or maybe the croissant. One of the two.

Münster Inc.

Sixteen years before Luther probably didn't nail his theses to the door a man called Joss Fritz went to church.

He didn't go to worship, but to protest. He walked in and placed a banner over a picture of the crucified Christ. On the banner was the laced boot of a peasant and the phrase 'Nothing but the Justice of God'. Over the next three decades there were repeated uprisings by the peasants against the landowners, calling for an end to oppression, an end to taxes, tolls and tithes, and free use of common land, rivers and woods and, generally, a society based on the Bible and divine justice.*

From the start these grievances were rooted in the Bible. But as time went on they took on a much more reforming character. It was a Protestant pastor, Christoph Schappeler, who, along with a tanner called Sebastian Lotzer, wrote the peasants' manifesto, the *Twelve Articles of the Peasants*, in March 1525. This called for the reform of rents, taxes and servitude, but also for the reform of the church, including the removal of pictures and images, the preaching of the 'pure' gospel, and the right to elect the parish priest, whom they would then support from tithes collected in a way of their own choosing, with any surplus going to the poor.

Between Fritz's banner and Lotzer's pamphlet, of course, Luther had risen to prominence. The peasants looked to Luther for support but, although he had sympathy with some of their concerns, he hated the idea of rebellion. He argued that the Bible clearly supported slavery – after all, didn't the patriarchs of the Old Testament have slaves? Didn't Paul tell slaves to be obedient?

In his dealings with the peasants Luther was out of his depth. He wanted church reformation, not political revolt. But it felt like a terrible betrayal. And when the violence started to rise, when things started to get bloody, Luther went into a panic and abandoned them to their fate. In a typically polemical tract, *Against the Robbing and Murdering Hordes of Peasants*, he declared that anyone who killed a rebellious peasant was doing God's will.

* The uprising Joss planned for 1502 was betrayed and Joss had to flee for his life. He organised another one in 1513, but that was betrayed and he . . . er . . . had to flee for his life. He organised another one in 1517, but this was betrayed and . . . well, you can guess the rest. Friedrich Engels called Fritz a 'model conspirator', by which he presumably meant 'completely hapless failure'.

Over 100,000 peasants were slaughtered in 1525 alone.

The end to this terrible recurring story of crushed revolts comes a decade later. In the German city of Münster a former Lutheran Pastor called Berni Rothman started to preach that the second coming of Christ was imminent, and that Münster would be the new Jerusalem. The city soon became a nexus for all sorts of disenfranchised, extreme Anabaptist groups. Jan Matthys replaced Rothman as leader and urged a violent revolution. His fellow-leader, the dangerously unbalanced Jan Beuckelszoon (aka Jan of Leyden), took things even further. He banned all books except the Bible. You want *sola scriptura*? You got it. The situation descended into diseased chaos. The forces of the Bishop of Münster and his troops blockaded the city. The food ran out. Anarchy. Jan of Leyden declared himself the new Messiah, the successor to King David, playing out the life of an Old Testament king, practising polygamy and living in luxury while all around him the people starved and their fevered dreams died.

In the end there could only be one outcome. In 1536 the city was captured; the new Jerusalem was brutally and sadistically crushed; the leaders were tortured and executed and their bodies hung in cages from the tower of the city church.

You can still see the cages there today.

THINGS YOU LEARN FROM CHRISTIAN HISTORY

NO.9
Without love, it's all just noise

Or, in the words of 1 Corinthians 13.1-3:

Though I spake with the tongues of men and angels and yet had no love I were even as sounding brass: or as a tinkling cymbal. And though I could prophesy and understood all secrets and all knowledge: yea if I had all faith so that I could move mountains out of their places and yet had no love I were nothing. And though I bestowed all my goods to feed the poor and though I gave my body even that I burned and yet had no love it profiteth me nothing.

© Paul of Tarsus, 54
  In this version, © William Tyndale, 1525

9 Calvinism, Counter-Reformation and Commonwealths

The salt of the earth

The same year that the peasants were publishing their manifesto another new incendiary book was published in Worms. Well, not exactly a new book: it was the New Testament. But it was in English.

It was the work of one of the greatest figures in English history – a man who has changed our culture more profoundly than virtually any mitred archbishop, or miracle-working saint, or any playwright or poet. His name is William Tyndale (c.1494–1536). He was born in Gloucestershire and, after studying at Oxford, conceived the idea of translating the Bible into English. He wanted to give the Bible to everyone, even 'the boy that driveth the plough'.

Naturally, this being England, his enthusiasm was frowned upon (a) because it was illegal, and (b) because the English frown upon enthusiasm of any sort. So Tyndale had to work in secret. But after a few months his plan was discovered and he was forced to flee the country. He went to Wittenberg – Protestant Central – and within a year had completed his fresh, vibrant translation. What made it different was that Tyndale had gone back to the Greek (the Lollard Bibles used the Vulgate). And he was a truly great translator. No, scratch that: a truly great *writer*, full of vigour and energy. We still use many of his original phrases today: 'lead us not into temptation, but deliver us from evil', 'a law unto themselves', 'knock and it shall be opened unto you', 'the apple of his eye', 'a land of milk and honey', 'let there be light', 'the powers that be', 'the salt of the earth', and many more, come straight out of Tyndale's translation.

As we've seen, this activity was illegal in England, so his books were smuggled in and distributed on a kind of Bibles black market, and it became a huge underground success. If you knew where to look – in the Tudor equivalent of car parks, perhaps – there were distributors, winding down the windows and saying, 'I've got some Galatians, if you're interested.' 'Any Romans?' 'Nah, I don't deal with the hard stuff.' One of his main distributors was a man with the fantastically New Testament name of Simon Fish.*

Even in mainland Europe Tyndale was not safe. He was forced to go on the run. His writings had made him enemies. It wasn't just the New Testament: his book *The Practyse of Prelates* opposed Henry VIII's proposed divorce, making an enemy of the king. His most vehement, relentless opponent was Thomas More, who pursued heretics with a murderous zeal: those found aiding distribution of Tyndale's works were burnt at the stake.

Tyndale, in fact, was full of seditious ideas. He believed that it was better to try to convert the Turks than kill them. He disagreed with the death penalty for theft. Or for heresy, in fact. He was seditious because he believed God's law was above that of the king.†

Tyndale's enemies caught up with him. He was betrayed to the authorities in Antwerp, condemned for heresy and in 1536 was burned at the stake. As an act of mercy and in the light of his fame he was allowed to be strangled at the stake before the flames were lit. His last words, according to *Foxe's Book of Martyrs*, were a prayer for Henry VIII, that his eyes would be opened.

And, indeed, they were.

---

* Fish was a writer himself. His pamphlet *Supplication of Beggars* was an attack on the abuse of power by the church. It centres around a notorious case of suspicious death while in the custody of the Bishop of London. A man called Richard Hunne refused to pay a burial fee to his parish priest for the burial of his child. Hunne was arrested on charges of heresy and taken to the Bishop of London's prison. (What? Doesn't *every* bishop have his own prison?) Two days later he was found hanging dead in his cell. The authorities said it was suicide, but the coroner found signs of foul play and the evidence pointed to the chancellor of the Bishop of London, Dr Horsey. The bishop obtained a royal pardon for Horsey and no charges were ever brought.

† By now More was dead as well. Thomas More lied to Parliament, lied to the public and was involved in acts of torture, and sent countless people to their deaths. He's also the patron saint of politicians and statesmen. 'Irony' doesn't quite cover it, somehow.

I'm Henry the Eighth I am

It was not actually the English authorities who killed Tyndale. It was the troops of the Holy Roman Emperor Charles V, who at that time ruled an empire covering Spain, Burgundy, chunks of Italy and Germany and the Low Countries.* Henry VIII, or his officials at any rate, actually tried to get Tyndale released.

Why? Because in 1534 England had gone Protestant. Henry had separated from Rome and established the *Anglicana Ecclesia* – the C of E.

This was the mother of all U-turns, given that, only a few years before, he had been a very keen Catholic. He had even written books on it. And the pope was really a big fan. *Loved* his work. Henry's response to Luther's *Babylonian Captivity* earned him the title 'Defender of the Faith' from the pope. The title is still used of British monarchs today. Few people know that it was the pope who first bestowed it on the monarch while he was actually defender of a slightly different form of the faith.

But then something happened that shattered the faith of the defender of the faith. His wife, Catherine of Aragon, had not given him a son, so Henry sought a new wife and was after an annulment of the marriage from the pope. Normally this would have been no problem. Money might have changed hands, the whole thing could have been agreed easily. But Catherine was the aunt of Charles V who, at that time, had control of the pope. And, as we've seen, much of Europe. There was no way he was going to let Aunty Cathy be disgraced by the English king.

So Henry underwent a double separation: first he divorced Catherine, and then he divorced himself from the pope. Henry became the 'supreme head on earth of the Church of England'. Now, Henry was no reformer. His England was Anglo-Catholic, not Lutheran. But his new wife, Anne Boleyn, was very influenced by Protestant thinking, and the real architect of the changes was a Cambridge don called Thomas Cranmer, who became Archbishop of Canterbury.

The English Reformation – for Henry at least – was less about theology and more about those three old gods, money, sex and power. Sex? Well that was Anne, until the old monster got tired of her, framed her on

---

* I've just found out that Charles's parents were nicknamed Philip the Handsome and Joanna the Mad. That marriage guidance counsellor must have had his work cut out.

witchcraft charges and had her killed. And cutting the ties with Rome gave Henry more political power. And money? Well, that came from the monasteries. In 1536 Parliament passed Acts dissolving the smaller monasteries; in 1539 they went after the big ones as well. Henry's attack-dog was a man called Thomas Cromwell, who took the title Vicar-General. Using a decidedly dodgy dossier of monastic abuses he closed all the nunneries, friaries and monasteries in England and Wales and confiscated their lands and treasures. Whatever the faults of the monastic orders, it was one of the greatest acts of cultural vandalism ever committed.

Note that the people didn't welcome all this with open arms. In Lincolnshire there was a protest march/armed uprising led by a shoemaker who became known as Captain Cobbler. (His real name was Nicholas Melton – clearly he's the world's first superhero.) This was suppressed, but was immediately followed by a more extensive uprising in York, which became known as the Pilgrimage of Grace. Led by a barrister called Robert Aske, the insurgents captured York and returned expelled monks and nuns to their houses. Then around 30,000 gathered at Doncaster. Henry was forced to negotiate: he promised that he would listen to their grievances and issued a general pardon to all involved. As soon as they disbanded, though, Henry rounded up the rebel leaders and killed them. Over 200 people were executed by the king, including members of the nobility, abbots, priests and monks. That, people, is how you defend the faith.

We need to talk about Calvin

On 18 October 1534, a month before Henry VIII invented the Anglican Church, his French counterpart, King Francis I, saw a poster attacking the Catholic mass. That would have been bad enough, but somehow the poster had been affixed to his bedroom door. It was like Luther's theses (or maybe not) all over again.

He immediately investigated, and found that these posters were all over Paris. 'Mon dieu!' he exclaimed. 'Zut Alors! Sacré bleu! Gerard Depardieu!' And other Gallic sayings. There was a clampdown. Some thirty-five suspected Protestants were executed as part of the purge.

Some, though, managed to flee, among them a twenty-five-year-old lawyer called Jean Calvin (1509–64). He went to Basle, which was a Swiss Reformed city. There he wrote his *Institutes of the Christian Religion* – a kind of primer in the basics of Protestantism. Well, I say 'wrote'. He started writing. Over the next twenty years he continually added to it, so much so that, by the time he'd finished, Calvin's *Institutes* was fourteen times the length of the Bible. He was nothing if not thorough.

Calvin was recruited by the French preacher William Farel to stay and help to establish Protestantism in the city of Geneva. He proposed major reforms. Communion was to be monthly, instead of annually as before. A network of spies, sorry, overseers, was to monitor the population. Evil-doers, the immoral, slackers, those who 'do not belong to Jesus,' would be identified and sent to the naughty corner. Or the 'excluded from Communion, and ostracised until they mended their ways' corner at any rate. Everyone had to sign up to a new Reformed creed: if you didn't you would be excommunicated. It was like those old Roman imperial certificates of pagan orthodoxy, only reinvented by Christians.

The council reluctantly accepted his ideas, but the people rebelled. Calvin was accused of being a French spy. There were riots in the streets and shots outside his window. Calvin and Farel excommunicated their critics. But the council disagreed and in 1538 evicted them both from the city.

Three years later he was back. There had been riots and unrest: the city needed a firm hand. And the council, shamefacedly, turned to the strongest hand they knew: the one attached to Calvin. In 1541 he returned, somewhat reluctantly, to Geneva, took over the running of the place, and turned it into the über-Protestant city. The church was reorganised along what Calvin believed to be a New Testament model. Churches were stripped of all their decoration. Psalms were sung, but nothing like Luther's hymns. He also shut down all the pubs, and banned dancing, theatre and fashionable trousers. It became illegal to give your child a name that was not in the Bible. Indiscretions were reported and punished by the Consistory – the main disciplinary body in Geneva. Three young men who had eaten too much pâté were locked up for three days with only bread and water. An atheist called Jacques Gruet was convicted of dancing and claiming that Calvin had 'the airs of bishop'. He was tortured and beheaded.

The thing about Calvin is that he was a lawyer to his core. That is, I think, what makes him fundamentally such an unlikeable and cold human being. He was a legal system on legs. The *Institutes* are a logical systematic theology, with no gaps. And that makes them slightly chilling.

Calvin was utterly convinced of the majesty and authority of God.

Whatever happened in human history, God was in complete control. There was no such thing as 'chance' – didn't Scripture say that every hair on our head was numbered? So Calvin concluded that every single event in human history has to be not only known about, but ordained by God.

OK. But how does that square with people becoming Christian? Calvin believed that God already knew about that. In fact, he ordained it. It is a natural development of Augustine's idea of predestination. God ordains everything that happens. So if people become Christians, it's because God chose them to be saved. They are the elect.

But if God has chosen only some people to be saved, then . . .

Yep. Calvin took the idea to its logical extreme. He believed that God also predestines some people to be damned. If he chooses some to be saved, then he must, logically, select others for the damnation pile. For Calvin this showed the majesty of God. But then Calvin was in the elect. He was saved, no doubt about that, matey. For others, this is the big problem with a rigid form of predestination: if God has chosen who will be saved and who will be damned. And there's not much you can do about it.

Calvin stared into the abyss and didn't blink. He looked into the logic of predestination, dispassionately confronted its darker side and endorsed it. Luther, typically, agreed with 'double predestination' (salvation and damnation from the beginning of time) – but chose not to talk about it. Calvin was too rigid, too honest, too dispassionate to cavil like that.

And that's the difference between them. Luther was a foul-mouthed, anti-Semitic bigot who would dissemble for the cause and who fell out with virtually all of his friends. But there was hot blood running in his veins. Calvin was an android. (Not literally. Obviously. Although it would explain a lot.) You could have a drink with Luther. But you could never enjoy a drink with Calvin. For one thing, he'd shut down all the pubs.

Calvin's Geneva became the Disneyland of European Protestantism. Immigrants and refugees flooded there from throughout Europe. It hummed with Bible printing and biblical scholarship. In 1551 a French scholar-printer called Robert Estienne (or Stephanus) issued an edition of the Greek New Testament in Geneva that was notable for featuring verse references. A couple of others had done this before, but it was Estienne's verse division that stuck and that we follow today. Later English refugees created one of the great monuments of English literature: the Geneva Bible, the world's first study Bible.

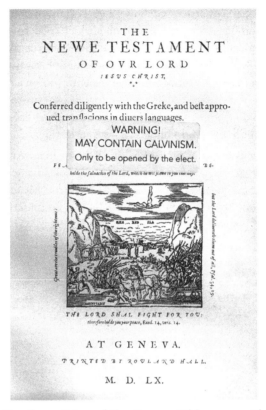

THE
NEWE TESTAMENT
OF OVR LORD
IESVS CHRIST,
.

Conferred diligently with the Greke, and beft appro-
ued tranflacions in diuers languages.

WARNING!
MAY CONTAIN CALVINISM.
Only to be opened by the elect.

THE LORD SHAL FIGHT FOR YOU:
therefore holde you your peace, Exod. 14, vers. 14.

AT GENEVA.
PRINTED BY ROVLAND HALL.

M. D. LX.

Fig. XXVIII. *The first edition of the Geneva Bible came with the usual health warnings*

Calvin never held an official position within the Genevan government – which, frankly, allowed him to keep his hands clean. But Geneva was Calvin's thought made real. And he was directly involved in the killing of a man called Michael Servetus. Servetus' crime was heresy: he had questioned the idea of the Trinity. He was a Unitarian. This meant that he was hated not just by Calvin but by Lutherans, Anglicans, Catholics; you name it. Calvin had had a lengthy and fractious correspondence with Servetus, which, in the end, he gave up in frustration. (He was particularly irritated when Servetus sent him a heavily annotated copy of the *Institutes*, which pointed out errors in the book.) Servetus stated that he would come to Geneva and meet Calvin. Calvin wrote to Farel that if Servetus did come, 'as far as my authority goes, I would not let him leave alive'.

To be fair to Calvin, Servetus had already been condemned to death in several other countries, Catholic and Protestant (although Basle didn't support it). Not only that, but he had tried to persuade the Council of Geneva to expel Calvin and give Servetus all of Calvin's possessions. So Servetus hadn't exactly gone out of his way to be friendly to Calvin. But having a lot of people agree with you on a crime doesn't make it less of a crime. Calvin did try to get Servetus to repent. And when that didn't work, Calvin asked the council to behead Servetus, as it was a more merciful killing. That's comforting.

Servetus was burnt at the stake in Geneva in 1533. Another victim at the altar of theological correctness. Protestants and Catholics burnt and branded and slaughtered and killed. Meanwhile, those who spoke out against such behaviour had to go underground. And hide.

CALVIN

Calvin, enjoying a joke.

Name: Jehan Cauvin.
Aka: Jean Calvin; John Calvin.
Nationality: French.
Dates: 1509–64.
Appearance: Long nose, long face, long beard. *Really* long beard. Intellectually he had depth; physically he majored on length.
Before he was famous: Lawyer. Possibly an android.
Famous for: Institutes of the Christian Religion; Calvinism; predestination; running Geneva.
Why does he matter? Calvinism, the theological system that grew from his teachings, was widely adopted among Reformed, Congregational and Presbyterian churches. His theory of predestination has proved hugely influential.
Could you have a drink with him down the pub? No. He shut them all down. (Although his contract to run Geneva did entitle him to seven barrels of wine.)

The X Men

For nearly twenty years the Catholic Church had been losing ground – both metaphorically and literally – for large chunks of territory had gone Protestant. It had to counter the Reformation with something. So it did, with the imaginatively named Counter-Reformation.

Many Catholics agreed with the Protestants on one thing: the need for reform. They also followed the Protestants with an emphasis on the word: their view was that better teaching and preaching would counter the spread of Protestantism. What was needed was far deeper, more personal, faith.

Perhaps the most famous example of this is found in the work of Ignatius of Loyola (1491–1556). Badly wounded while serving as a soldier, he took to prayer and developed a kind of course book of Christian meditation called *Spiritual Exercises*, which used the imagination to help people to move closer to God. Despite the close attentions of the Inquisition, who were never sure he was entirely orthodox, in 1534 he and his followers founded the Society of Jesus – aka the Jesuits. The next year the Jesuits gained official recognition from the reform-minded Pope Paul III (helped by the fact that, along with the usual monastic vows, they added a vow of obedience to the pope). The pope encouraged other new orders intended to breathe new life into the Catholic Church: the Theatines and the Ursulines were dedicated to living in parishes and promoting spiritual renewal among ordinary people.*

The Jesuits were dedicated to mission, and while Ignatius stayed in Europe many of his disciples went far afield to spread the word. The most famous of these was Francis Xavier, who arrived in India in 1542 and embodied the kind of servant values that the church needed. Having heard that the previously converted pearl fishers had lapsed a bit, he spent eighteen months living among them trying to win them back. He is said to have founded 45 Christian settlements. To make things easier to learn, he turned the creed into poetry.

It was Xavier who famously said, 'Give me the children until they are seven, and anyone who likes can have them afterwards.' He baptised ten thousand people in one month at one point. But he also claimed

---

* Unlike the Ovaltines, who were largely dedicated to serving hot milk-based drinks.

to have seen miraculous healings as a result of his Gospel readings.*

Seven years later he went on to Japan, on the advice of a Japanese outlaw whom he had met in India, who told him that people in Japan were very keen to learn about 'both God and the world'. They weren't that keen, actually. They were polite, sure. But keen? No.

Xavier worked hard to convert them, but with limited success. His monastic poverty – so impressive in other places – only offended the Japanese. Again some commoners and low-status people accepted Catholicism, but only about 200 in two years. Xavier died while on a journey to China. His efforts eventually bore fruit, however, and after his death some of the local warlords of Japan started to embrace Catholicism. By 1587 there were perhaps 300,000 Catholics in areas around Nagasaki.

IGNATIUS

Ignatius, in his battle gear

Name: Ignacio de Loyola.
Aka: Ignatius of Loyola.
Nationality: Spanish.
Dates: 1491–1556.
Appearance: Balding. Bearded. Walks with a pronounced limp.
Before he was famous: Soldier.
Famous for: Prayer. Meditation. The *Spiritual Exercises.* Founded the Jesuits.

Why does he matter? Founded the Society of Jesus (Jesuits) and was its first Superior General. The approach to meditative prayer in his *Spiritual Exercises* became known as Ignatian prayer.

Could you have a drink with him down the pub? Well, you could *imagine* having a drink with him down the pub. Now what is God saying to you through that?

---

* Heaven knows how he also found the time to found a team of mutant superheroes.

Musical differences

Paul III also commissioned an internal enquiry into the state of the church. When it reported in 1537, its harsh conclusions were leaked and gleefully printed by Protestant presses. It was one of the first leaked enquiries in history.

But the Protestants were leaking as well. (Not literally. Obviously. Well, in some ways, I suppose, but let's not go there.) In 1540 Philip of Hesse, the leading Protestant aristocrat, decided to make an honest woman of his mistress, Margaret, and married her. Unfortunately, he forgot the little matter of his being already married, and so was technically a bigamist. This would have been terrible PR for the Protestant cause had it been revealed (not to mention the fact that bigamy carried the death penalty in the empire), so he more or less forced Luther, Melanchthon and Bucer – the Protestant leader in Strasbourg – to approve the marriage and prepare a document providing theological support for bigamy. To help them come to the right decision he added that if they didn't approve of this marriage, he could always go back to the Catholics.

But it was impossible to keep hidden. Luther proposed that they should issue 'a good, strong lie'. Melanchthon, who was less morally flexible, fell ill under the stress. The scandal meant the end of Philip's leadership of the cause. (Luther's willingness to be economical with the truth has also rather been swept under the carpet.)

Talking of marriage, Bucer and Melanchthon were among those who were still hoping for a reconciliation between Protestant and Catholic. They attended talks in Regensburg in 1541, which were attended by delegations of both Protestants and Catholics. They managed to pass a number of agreements, but the problem was that every time they moved forward either Luther, or the pope, or both, would repudiate what had just been agreed.

Frankly, it was too late. The marriage was over. There were irreconcilable differences. The moderates were beaten, the hardliners had won and all that was left was to argue over who got custody of the heretics. Indeed, Cardinal Contarini, who had led the papal delegation to Regensburg, returned to Rome, was accused of heresy and died under house arrest. In his place a hardline traditionalist, Cardinal Carafa, took charge. He was head of the Roman Inquisition and utterly dedicated to rooting out Italian Protestants and crushing them. Carafa took his job so seriously he had a new house built for himself, with its very own dungeons. Talk about taking your work home with you.

In 1545 Pope Paul decided the time had come to return to traditional means. He called that most traditional of things, a church council. It met in Trent. Not the river in Nottingham, but Trento in Italy. And it was a biggie. In all, the council meetings lasted for a whopping eighteen years, split into three chunks.

Fig. XXIX. *The Council of Trent gets down to business*

It was not what you might call a broadly based council: out of about 600 Catholic bishops in Europe, only 28 actually attended. This was an elite group of power brokers. Trent concluded that the Bible could not be the only source of truth: the church is also the vehicle of divinely ordained doctrine and traditions. And while clearly the church could not veto bits of Scripture, it could declare that no one should use their own judgement 'to distort the Scriptures in accordance with his own conceptions' which meant in any sense other than 'that which the holy Mother church holds.'

Among its other conclusions were a reaffirmation of the seven sacraments, and a condemnation of the idea of justification by faith alone. Justification was offered by God on the basis of human co-operation: it was not the simple 'one-way' gift which Luther had preached. Original sin was reaffirmed – a pop at many Anabaptists who had denied it and gone all Pelagian.

The Council of Trent was the first time that Catholicism was called 'Roman'. It was also the first council to ban a musical interval: the augmented fourth, aka the diminished fifth. It was thought to be the 'devil's interval'.

Bloody Mary

By 1555, then, significant lumps of Europe were Protestant: the majority of Germany, the Swiss cities, Scandinavia. And England . . . oh, no, hang on. No, England had reverted. They had woken up and smelt the burning.

Despite the six marriages, Henry VIII died leaving only one son and two daughters. Edward became king, aged nine, and was taken in hand by Protestants. A Protestant liturgy – modelled on Luther's services – had been produced by Archbishop Cranmer. English Bibles had been printed. A new Prayer Book had been produced, which omitted many traditional rites and rituals.

But Edward died young. And in 1553 he was succeeded by his elder sister, Mary. She is known as Bloody Mary and is the only queen to have a cocktail named after her. Unless there's a Queen Harvey Wallbanger out there somewhere.

Mary was Catholic with a capital CATH. Her mother was Catherine of Aragon, the divorced and embittered first wife of Henry VIII. Her life had been ruined by the Reformation and now it was payback time. Mary was determined to rid England of Protestantism by whatever means necessary. And she wasn't entirely alone in her wish; the pace of change in the reign of Edward VI had unsettled many people. There was even an uprising in the south-west of England, where the leaders called not only for the restoration of the Latin mass, but also for a ban on the English Bible.

Within a month of ascending the throne she banned the public reading of the Bible. The English Bible was not to be used in church services, and Bibles placed in church were taken out and burned.

Then she started burning people. In her reign 300 Protestants were burnt, including 5 bishops, one of whom was Cranmer, the Archbishop of Canterbury. (Archbishop Cranmer initially recanted to save his life. But Mary decided to burn him anyway, so he withdrew his initial

recantation and plunged the hand that had written it into the fire first.)
The bulk of those martyred under Mary, however, were not famous or
wealthy or influential: they were ordinary tradesmen and labourers and
women. It was not only cruel and barbaric; it was incredibly dumb:
Mary's policy created a wealth of Protestant martyrs whose courage
did more to establish Protestantism than the Prayer Book ever did.

Nevertheless, it was the kind of policy that thrilled the new pope,
none other than Pope Paul IV – the artist formerly known as Cardinal
Carafa, he of the feature article in *Home and Torture Chamber* maga-
zine. Paul IV banned travelling entertainers and dancing, and had fig
leaves painted on the nude figures of the Sistine Chapel. He was a kind
of reverse Calvin. A Nivlac. What Paul IV really excelled at was hatred.
And he was an equal-opportunities hater. It wasn't just the Protestants:
he hated Jews, humanists, Spaniards . . . In 1557 he also started one
of the Catholic Church's most notorious practices – the Index of
Forbidden Books. It listed some 550 authors whose works were not to
be read, including theologians like Luther and Calvin, works of botany
and geography, and the complete run of *Venetian Playboy.**

But his hatred went on to find more disturbingly physical form. He
rounded up the Jews in Rome and forced them into ghettos. They had
to wear yellow hats. His paranoia convinced him that the Jews were
secretly in league with the Protestants.

Paul IV died in 1559 and the people of Rome immediately acted like
people coming out of the control of a dictatorship. Which, in a way,
they were. The offices of the Inquisition were destroyed and the prisoners
released. All the files were burnt and the pope's statue was dismembered.

Moderate Queen Bess

The year before Pope Paul IV died, the other big fan of tough-love
Catholicism, Queen Mary, died as well. And she left no heir. The crown
went to Elizabeth, the daughter of Henry VIII and Anne Boleyn. And
Anne had been a strong, Bible-believing Protestant – the very reason,
in fact, that the Church of England was invented.

---

* Its last major update was in 1948, but it was officially abolished in 1966 by
Pope Paul VI who, like everyone in the sixties, was probably keen to read
some Jean-Paul Sartre.

So England sort of snapped back in the other direction. But it didn't go as far this time. Elizabeth managed to ensure that England stayed Protestant, but without entirely ridding the country of all traces of traditional Catholicism. There were still robes and vestments, saints' days, stained glass and ornaments. And although many Protestants hoped she would move further in the direction of Geneva, as it were, she never did. She and her advisers had invented an expression of Christianity in which virtually everyone was perpetually mildly disappointed; or, to use its technical name, Anglicanism.

Many refugees who returned from Geneva hated Elizabeth's 'middle way'. They became known as Puritans. Deeply opposed to the Anglican establishment, they saw the church as still infected with the 'dregs of popery'. Their movement had significant support, and, learning from Luther, it harnessed the power of the new media: the printing press. The bestselling book was John Foxe's *Book of Martyrs*, which listed in gruesome detail the martyrdoms of Protestants, not just during Mary's reign, but during Henry's as well.

But like a really annoying driver on the motorway, Elizabeth refused to budge from the middle lane. Under Elizabeth, Anglicanism was fanatical about only one thing: moderation. And, grudgingly, the various factions accepted it. After all, the only alternatives were Mary Queen of Scots, who had the backing of the French as the rightful queen, and Philip of Spain. And no one wanted either of those.

Our friends in the north

Mary's hold on the throne of Scotland, however, was decidedly dodgy. She was a Catholic, but her own land was rigorously, thoroughly Protestant.

Scotland's religious landscape was dominated by the preacher John Knox. He was a man who had suffered for his Protestant beliefs – he had spent a year and a half as a galley slave for his role in a Protestant uprising, after which he had been a refugee in both England (under King Edward) and then Geneva. This was not a man whose life had been a bundle of laughs. Except at the burning of Michael Servetus. He was present at that, and found it quite amusing, apparently.

The rest of the time, though? Well, let's just say he was winner of the 'Man Least Likely to be Nicknamed Chuckles' award thirteen years running. And Scottish Puritanism reflected that grim tone. These were people who thought that Calvin was a bit too happy-go-lucky. In May 1559 Knox led an armed uprising and gained power, even though Mary remained on the throne. All Catholic expressions of Christianity were outlawed. It was McCalvinism.* Knox applied what became known as a Presbyterian system of church government (from that old Greek word *presbyteros*). There was a nationwide network of presbyters, who gathered together in national synods to make decisions. One presbyter, one vote.

Mary, however, refused to toe the line. She deliberately carried on with her Catholic observance. (Not to mention her scandalous sex life.) It was a classic power struggle between the queen and the Parliament. And the queen lost. In 1567 she was forced to abdicate in favour of her one-year-old son, James. She fled south to England, seeking the protection of her stepsister.

James remained in Scotland, to be brought up by Scottish Calvinists in what was possibly the least fun childhood ever. And he never forgot it.

The reign in Spain

Protestantism was often tied to nationalism. The Netherlands, for example, were actually ruled by Catholic Spain, so Lutherans, Calvinists and Anabaptists were able to ride a wave of anti-Spanish feeling. (An uprising led by William of Orange in 1566 was brutally crushed, which only added to the support for Protestantism.)

France, meanwhile, was in chaos. The king had died in a bad jousting accident. And then his successor (who doubled as the husband of Mary Queen of Scots) died after eighteen months. The next king in the queue was only nine, so control of France passed to the Italian queen mother – Catherine de Medici. Protestant aristocrats saw their chance for a coup.

Reform had spread in France, albeit underground. But now these some 1,000 congregations saw their chance. They took over Catholic churches and put armed guards on the doors to stop them being repossessed. Queen Catherine tried to broker a peace and, in 1562, she issued

---

* Knox wrote a book called *The First Blast of the Trumpet Against the Monstrous Regiment of Women*, which probably tells you all you need to know. Unless he was just playing hard to get.

a decree which demanded that the Protestants should vacate the churches they had seized, but that they would be permitted to worship freely outside French cities. It didn't work. Riots broke out and anti-Protestant violence spread. The country descended into civil war.

A peace deal was worked out which allowed Protestants their own places of worship. To seal the deal a leading Protestant nobleman married the young king's sister in Paris in 1572. The Calvinist Admiral de Coligny, arrived in Paris for the wedding, along with thousands of other Protestants. Then someone shot the admiral. He survived, which you might think was a happy ending. But Catherine was so scared of Protestant reprisals that she ordered a pre-emptive strike. Thousands of Protestants were killed in Paris and throughout France in what became known as the St Bartholomew's Day massacre. It was not the first wedding to end in violence, but it was the bloodiest. It triggered violence throughout the country, the peace was shattered and war, once again, descended on France.

The unrest spread to the Netherlands, where a war of independence broke out against Spain. It was a long, drawn-out affair, and ended with the north gaining independence and becoming a republic, while the south stayed Catholic and under the control of Spain. Eventually these regions became Holland (the north) and Belgium (the south). But Protestantism in the north was wildly diverse, with no one type of Protestantism dominating, so the area became a kind of haven for Protestant dissidents.

Meanwhile, Mary, erstwhile Queen of Scots, had a cunning plan: she would become Queen of England. And so, aided by a group of English Catholics, she plotted a coup. But the plot was discovered and Mary was executed. Before she died, however, she named a successor to the English throne, which she viewed as hers. It was not her son, James, but Philip of Spain. This was all the excuse Philip needed. He launched a mighty Spanish Armada against the English . . .

. . . which was utterly destroyed by a marvellous combination of the English navy, and unfavourable storms and winds.

The Armada was intended to return England to Catholicism – among the 19,000 soldiers on the ships there were 180 monks – and in its defeat, therefore, the English saw the final, incontrovertible proof that God was indeed a Protestant.

Elizabeth was now secure on the throne, so she was free to crack down on those troublesome moaning Puritans. Many of them went

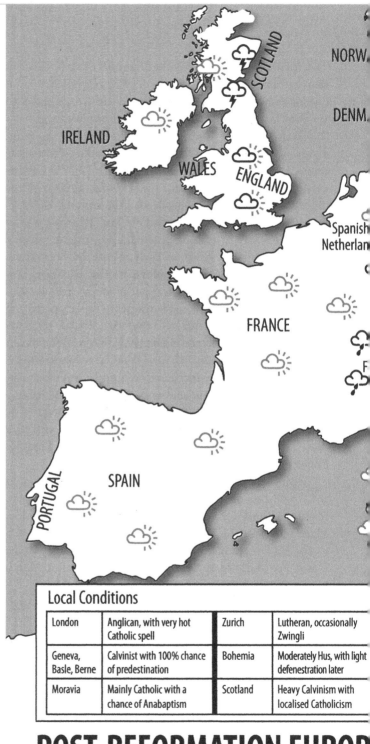

SCOTLAND

NORW.

DENM.

IRELAND

WALES

ENGLAND

Spanish
Netherlan

FRANCE

F

PORTUGAL

SPAIN

Local Conditions

London	Anglican, with very hot Catholic spell	Zurich	Lutheran, occasionally Zwingli
Geneva, Basle, Berne	Calvinist with 100% chance of predestination	Bohemia	Moderately Hus, with light defenestration later
Moravia	Mainly Catholic with a chance of Anabaptism	Scotland	Heavy Calvinism with localised Catholicism

POST-REFORMATION EUROP

From around 1560 onwards

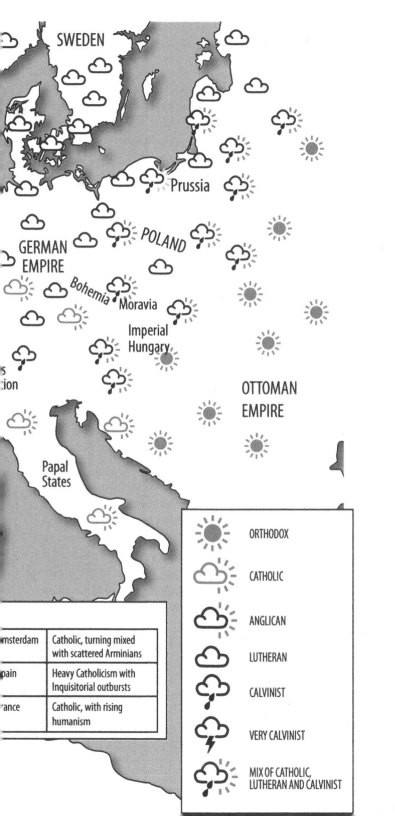

SWEDEN

Prussia

POLAND

GERMAN
EMPIRE

Bohemia

Moravia

Imperial
Hungary

OTTOMAN
EMPIRE

Papal
States

msterdam	Catholic, turning mixed with scattered Arminians
pain	Heavy Catholicism with Inquisitorial outbursts
rance	Catholic, with rising humanism

ORTHODOX

CATHOLIC

ANGLICAN

LUTHERAN

CALVINIST

VERY CALVINIST

MIX OF CATHOLIC,
LUTHERAN AND CALVINIST

underground. And many of these more radical Puritans discovered the joy of running their own – albeit hidden – independent congregations. This way the state had no control over the local congregation: each local meeting was self-governing, free to worship in what it considered an authentic way, and empowered to elect its own ministers.

They were known as the Separatists. Sometimes this separation cost them a lot. In 1595 the Separatist leaders Barrow, Greenwood and Penny were convicted of sedition and separated from their heads. Their congregations fled to Holland.

Meanwhile, the wars of religion in France finally came to an end. Henry IV had come to the throne in 1589, when the previous Catholic monarch had been assassinated, confusingly by a monk. Henry was a Protestant, but chose to convert to Catholicism to secure the throne. The Protestants were outraged, but in 1598 Henry oversaw the introduction of the Edict of Nantes, which gave Protestants freedom and legal status.

God's silly vassal

In 1603 Elizabeth I of England died. She had never married and, in consequence, the throne passed to James VI of Scotland, the son of Mary Queen of Scots. This united the Scottish and English in perfect harmony – and they have been bickering ever since.

James's life had not been without its challenges. Throughout his upbringing he had struggled against the oppressive influence of the Scottish Calvinists, who were so strict they made the English Protestants look like woolly liberals. Their attitude of superiority can be summed up in the comment made by Andrew Melville, Rector of St Andrews University, when he told the king, 'Sirrah, ye are God's silly vassal; there are two kings and two kingdoms in Scotland: there is king James, the head of the commonwealth; and there is Christ Jesus, the king of the Church, whose subject James the Sixth is, and of whose kingdom he is not a king, not a lord, not a head, but a member.'

When you're the king and someone calls you 'God's silly vassal', well, let's just say, you take note of that kind of thing. Certainly in later life James became a passionate believer in the absolute divine right of kings. He wrote two books, *The Trew Law of Free Monarchies* and *Basilikon Doron* (Royal Gift), which outlined his ideas that kings, far from being 'silly vassals', were higher beings than other men.

James was a Protestant, which made him acceptable to the English, but he was about as far removed from Calvin's kind of Protestant as it is possible to imagine. He was scandalously bisexual and profligate with money.* Elizabeth's death gave him the opportunity to (a) escape the influence of these people, and (b) to escape Scotland.

In the south, though, English Calvinists were really excited. They thought that someone raised by John Knox and his chums was bound to be on their side. This was the chance the Puritans had been waiting for to make the changes to the church that Elizabeth had refused them.

They didn't even wait for him to arrive in London. While he was still making his way south from Scotland, he was met by a deputation of Puritans asking for church services to be modified. James agreed to moderate a conference to be convened at Hampton Court in 1604, but when it came round he utterly refused to make any changes. At the conference the Puritan divine John Reynolds called for a new translation of the Bible – what he probably wanted was the official adoption of the Geneva Bible. James torpedoed that one as well: 'I could never yet see a Bible well translated in English,' he replied, before adding, 'but I think that of all, that of Geneva is the worst.' James did suggest a uniform translation done by 'the best learned of both Universities'. But he insisted that the new translation should be entirely without marginal notes, 'for in the Geneva translation', he said, 'some notes are partial, untrue, seditious and savouring of traitorous conceits'. He had in mind the note at Exodus 1.17, which suggested that the Hebrew midwives were right to disobey the Pharaoh's command. 'Their disobedience herein was lawful,' ran the note, 'but their dissembling evil.' To James, disobedience to a royal command – any royal command – was seditious.

So the Puritans quickly decided that they hated James.† They

---

* In Scotland he was suspected of being lured into 'carnal lust' by the Earl of Lennox – the first of a succession of male favourites. His extravagance was notorious. In 1614 relations with Parliament collapsed because Parliament was no longer willing to fund the extravagance of the court, with its sexual scandal, intrigue and licentiousness.

† As did the Catholics. They hated him so much that they wanted to fire him

wanted the Scottish Presbyterian system introduced. But James replied, 'No bishop, no king.' He insisted that all clergy should declare their approval of bishops and the entire contents of the Prayer Book. Ninety refused and were evicted from their posts.

Meanwhile, the work on the new Bible was completed in 1611. The result was the King James Bible, one of the monuments of English culture. But it was never intended – as the Geneva was – as a Bible to be read. It was intended, rather, to reinforce the system.

AUTHORISED VERSION

The first edition of King James's new Puritan-footnote-free Bible

Name: The Authorised King James Version.
Aka: The Authorised Version, King James Version, KJV, AV.
Nationality: English.
Dates: 1611 to present.
Appearance: Varies. But the first one was black, leather-bound and the size of a small table.
Before it was famous: It was other versions: Tyndale's, Coverdale's, the Geneva Bible.
Famous for: Sounding brilliant. Being the sole allowable version in American fundamentalist churches.
Why does it matter? It's a cultural cornerstone. It has shaped our language. (But it's not the most accurate translation in the world.)
Could you have a drink with it down the pub? It's a Bible. It doesn't drink.

– literally. In 1605 an Italian called Guido Fawkes was found under the Houses of Parliament with barrels of gunpowder. He was executed and the plot broken up. And it is commemorated every year as one more example of the perfidy of those pesky papists.

Lift and separate

The Separatists were also leaving. Many of them followed their earlier brethren to Amsterdam. The trouble with Separatists is that, once they've separated once, they tend to get into the habit. In Amsterdam they acted like good brassieres: they kept dividing and separating.

One of the most radical of the radical Separatists was John Smith, which sounds like an alias, but was actually his real name. He fell out with his fellow-Separatists over a number of things. Taking Bible purity rather seriously, he insisted that the Bible should be read only in Greek and Hebrew in church. Given the Protestants had spent a lot of effort trying to translate it out of Latin this seemed a bit of a backward step. Initially, Smith had carried on with infant baptism, but in 1609 he rejected it and adopted the Anabaptist stance: that only believers should be baptised. At the same time he rejected Calvinist predestination, deciding that only those who choose to believe will be baptised, and then become members of the church.

And so it was that he invented the Baptists.

Smith was such a fan of baptism that he even baptised himself, unable to think of anyone more qualified to do it. But then he regretted this action, so he had someone else baptise him again – the third time in his life. This so annoyed his fellow-leader Thomas Helwys that the Baptists split over it. Still, they had been 100 per cent united for a year, so they'd had a good run. (Since their ethos was very close to the Mennonites, Smith ended up joining the Mennonite Church.)

Helwys, however, returned to England, taking with him ten Baptists. He decided that he couldn't stay safe in exile when others were living in ignorance back home. He died in prison in about 1615.

Later on, different Baptist groups appeared who, unlike Smith and Helwys, did adopt Calvinism. These became known as the Particular Baptists, to differentiate them from those wishy-washy general, or non-Calvinist Baptists.

Some of the Separatists decided what was really needed was to separate themselves even further. They set sail for the New World. The most famous of these groups sailed on the *Mayflower* to America in 1620. After a journey of some three months, they landed in New England, which was a bit of a surprise, since they were aiming for Virginia, some 500 miles south.

Fig. XXX. *The pilgrims arrive in America*

Holy propaganda

America wasn't the only place benefiting from a fresh batch of Christians. In Asia too the message of Christianity was spreading. In Vietnam the Jesuits made thousands of Catholic converts. In China a Jesuit named Matthew Ricci arrived in Macau in 1582. There he spent twenty years becoming a Mandarin scholar, before he ever breathed a word about Jesus. This was a man who knew what it was to earn respect. And he knew what it was to value a culture. The version of Catholicism developed in China was rather 'liberal'. Converts were allowed to maintain traditional veneration of their ancestors and of Confucius. The danger was that Jesus became more like a Confucian wise man than the Son of God. Even so, by the time Ricci died, three thousand people had become Catholics.

Meanwhile, in India, a Jesuit called Robert de Nobili (1577–1656) took the unprecedented step of actually dressing like normal people. Although the normal people in this case were those living in Southern India. Nobili lived with the people, embraced the culture and ate the food (he turned vegetarian). He pioneered a kind of Hindu-Christian fusion: those he converted kept a lot of their Hindu practices, except those involving the worship of idols. When the authorities in Rome heard about his approach, they accused him of watering down the gospel. He argued that it was not his business to turn Indians into little Europeans: he wanted them to become Christians in their own culture. His approach seems very modern. But he went, in some ways, too far. In deference to the Indian caste system he fed communion to the untouchables – the Dalits – on the end of a stick. Creating the communion kebab was inventive, but it's not, perhaps, quite what Jesus would have done.

Nevertheless, the Catholic Church was embracing mission in a big way. In 1622 the pope established what was the first ever mission agency – the Sacred Congregation for the Propagation of the Faith. And from the Latin version of its name we get the English term 'propaganda'.

Through the round window

The Separatists weren't the only ones having rows in Holland. A Calvinist pastor and academic called Jacob Arminius was given the task of defending predestination against the attacks of a Catholic humanist with the utterly brilliant name of Dirk Coornhert.* Trouble was, he actually found Coornhert's arguments quite compelling. (And he wasn't the only one: he was the third Calvinist pastor who had been given the task, and all three ended up agreeing with Dirk. That, my friends, is the power of the Coornhert. Or the Dirkmeister, as I shall now call him.†) Coornhert believed that it was possible for a man to live like Christ. Very difficult, admittedly, but possible.

Arminius developed a new theory. Although, for fear of reprisals, he kept it under his hat for a long time. (Not literally. Obviously. Although he probably did have a big hat, because a lot of them did in those days.) His theory was this: everyone who became a Christian was automatically saved; but God, being God, could see who would or would not become a Christian with his help. So he 'chose' them and gave them the ability to recognise the truth. For Arminius, 'God has decided to save believers through grace, that is, through gentle and sweet persuasion, agreeing or congruent with their free choice.'

---

* Arminius is actually Jacob's Latin pen name. His real name was Jakob Hermanszoon.
† Or I would call him, if I were actually going to mention him again in this book. Which I'm not.

When he eventually released his ideas, they caused a storm of controversy. And in the end the Calvinists held their very own council – a national synod at Dort in 1618. They condemned what they called Arminianism, and forbade its preaching. The Synod's ninety-three canons defined Proper Grown-up Calvinism and formed the basis of the Dutch Reformed Church. Indeed, they defined Calvinism more rigidly than Calvin ever had, and he was so inflexible you could have used him as a tent pole. It was like the Orthodox councils of old. *Plus ça change*, as Jean Calvin might have said.

Calvinism was still officially illegal in the German Empire, although several states were Calvinist. There was a three-way struggle in central Europe between Lutheranism, Calvinism and Catholicism. Then, in 1617, Archduke Ferdinand, the King of Bohemia and next in the queue to be Holy Roman Emperor, decided to clamp down on the freedom that Bohemian Protestants enjoyed in the land of Hus. He sent imperial representatives to issue his commands, and the Protestants in Prague chucked them out. Literally. Through a window. The event – known as the 'defenestration of Prague' – launched a revolt, then a coup, then an alliance between Bavaria and Spain, then a counter-attack, then the Thirty Years War. It all goes to show you should be really careful what you chuck out of a window.

The Thirty Years' War was a horrible, energy sapping, attritional, deeply unholy holy war, which drew in Sweden, France, Spain and Germany. Gradually, the original religious causes of the war were subsumed in a protracted, attritional fight for territory, during which Germany was pretty much brought to its knees. Shades of wars to come.

More than ten million people are estimated to have died through the war. By the time the war finished in 1648 no one had really won anything very much. But one thing seemed to have crystallised in the European mind: religion was not really worth fighting over. The French *eminence grise*,* Cardinal Richelieu, said 'the interests of the state and the interests of religion are completely different things'. For the best part of 120 years Europe had been wracked by the wars of religion. They were worn out by it. From now on Europe was set to become gradually, but increasingly, secular.

---

* French for 'greasy eminence'.

Viva la commonwealth

The same could not be said of Britain. There, politics and religion were so completely intermixed as to be virtually indistinguishable. And, in the same year that the Thirty Years' War concluded, the Puritans were finally to get their longed-for wish of power as King Charles I surrendered to Parliamentary forces and Oliver Cromwell turned the whole country Puritan and London into Geneva-on-Thames.

It began as a religious conflict. James I's son Charles was brought up with the same high regard for the monarchy that his father had had. And when he ascended to the throne in 1625 he started to restore a more traditional ritual to British churches. It was what people were to call Anglo-Catholic. It had vestments and incense and ceremonies. Yes, it kept the liturgy and creed intact, but it added a whole lot of what its enemies called 'popery'. His archbishop, William Laud, maintained that England had never actually stopped being Catholic, nor had it really split from Rome. It was not that England was Protestant: it was more that it was very Reformed Catholic. And so the Puritans began to find themselves pushed out. Their preachers were banned. Calvinism was evicted and Arminian teaching adopted.

To a lot of people, though, it was the thin end of the wedge. Charles had married a Catholic queen – Henrietta Maria of France. She had been allowed to keep her own court and her own form of worship in Somerset House – a little piece of Catholic France right in the middle of Protestant London. And they assumed that she was luring the king in the same direction.

It had the effect of energising even the most moderate of the Protestants. They voiced their objections through Parliament, so Charles decided to dissolve Parliament and rule by himself.

Problem. He had no money. Without Parliament he couldn't raise taxes. That was, after all, why kings had parliaments. It wasn't that they wanted to listen to them; it was so that they could get tax laws passed.* Charles tried to raise money himself, using long-forgotten laws and levies, but that just plunged him to new depths of unpopularity. Charles is venerated in some circles today, but honestly, he was one of the most inept kings England has ever had. And his ineptitude reached new heights – or depths – when he took on the Scottish.

---

* Still the same today. Only replace 'king' with 'Prime Minister'.

343

James I had eventually taken his revenge on all those annoying Puritans in Scotland by reintroducing bishops, bribing the nobility with grants of land to ensure their support. Charles decided to reclaim this land for the church, which made him popular with Scottish bishops and, er . . . nobody else. Charles then forced a new prayer book on Scotland. On Sunday 23 July 1637, the Dean of Edinburgh read it in public for the first time and was promptly hit on the head by a stool. The woman who threw it shouted, 'Daur ye say Mass in my lug?'

The Scottish general assembly then convened and not only threw out the prayer book, but all the bishops as well. Charles refused to acknowledge the authority of the assembly – and the Scots invaded England.

But Charles had no money to pay an army to defend England, because he had abolished Parliament. So he was forced into a humiliating climbdown. He recalled Parliament. And they had the king over a barrel. They abolished all the Catholic innovations Charles had introduced. And the relationship inevitably descended further into conflict. Parliament pressed for deeper and more radical reform. Charles dug his heels in. In 1642 the two sides went to war.

The war showed everyone what kind of world the Parliamentary forces intended to enforce: they scrapped the Prayer Book and abolished all bishops. In return for support from the Scottish, they promised to implement the full presbyterian system. Archbishop Laud was tried and executed on charges of treason – charges that were palpably not true.

But, just as in other Protestant takeovers, there was an apparently irresistible move towards radicalism. Cromwell rose to prominence through his policy of rewarding actual ability in his soldiers and commanders. His New Model Army brought military success after early Parliamentary setbacks. And so, in 1648, Charles surrendered. His queen escaped to France, along with their sons.

And now the Parliamentarians had a bit of a problem. What do you do with an ex-king? Most of them weren't in favour of executing him, but the radical fringes demanded the king's execution and drove out every MP who disagreed.

Meanwhile, in defeat Charles seemed to find a new strength. He refused to admit the authority of the court arraigned to try him. And when, in the end, the radical elements of the Parliamentarians took over, and the king was sentenced to death, he went with equanimity and courage. He was pretty useless as a king, but in the end he proved himself a courageous man.

In many ways the culmination of Reformation ideas took place on 30 January 1649, when the English Puritan Parliament beheaded the king. The effect of this was profound. To many of the people the king was not just another leader, but a divinely appointed individual.

To them, the Puritans, in killing the king, had beheaded God.

Fig. XXXI. *In revolutionary London, King Charles has a bad day*

THINGS YOU LEARN FROM CHRISTIAN HISTORY

NO.10
Not everyone welcomes revival

Virtually every revival movement
has been criticised for being
simplistic, or populist, or just plain
vulgar. Leaders want more people
in church, sure – but always
provided they are the right kind of
people.

10 Revolution, Reason and Radicals

Galileo, Galileo, Galileo figaro

In 1543 the Polish astronomer Copernicus wrote a book suggesting that the earth was not actually the centre of the universe, and that it really went round the sun instead of the other way round. Since it was obvious to everyone that the earth stayed still and the sun moved, no one took him very seriously at the time.

Then, in 1608, some Dutch spectacle makers arranged two lenses in a tube and invented the telescope. The next day a work-experience boy in the lab painted the eyepiece with ink and invented the practical joke. And the next year the Professor of Mathematics at Pisa University made his own – much more powerful – version. (Only without the ink.) His name was Galileo Galilei, and using this powerful tool, he saw things that no man had witnessed before: it enabled him to see craters on the moon, the moons around Jupiter, ten times as many stars as anyone had seen before and, just as importantly, right through the windows of the nunnery across the road.

He used these and subsequent observations (not the nunnery – that was a joke) to prove that Copernicus was right: the sun was the fixed centre of the universe, not the earth. Earth was one of several planets that orbited the sun.

His theories caused outrage – although not with the pope of the time, Urban VIII, who accepted them. Others were not so relaxed. After all, didn't the Bible say that God 'has established the world; it shall never be moved'?* Galileo was not an atheist. He was a devout Catholic.†

---

* Psalm 93.1, in case you're wondering.
† In his early life he dabbled with the idea of becoming a priest. Later, though,

But Galileo's observations of nature conflicted with the literal statements of the Bible. So which was right?

The Inquisition let it be known that they were keeping a close eye on Signor Galileo. For a while he and his supporters were allowed to continue with their researches, as long as it was made clear in their writings that it was all a kind of 'what if', a series of hypothetical observations, rather than definite statements. It's hard to play 'let's pretend' for long in such circumstances, though, and in 1630 Galileo dropped the pretence. His book *Dialogue about the Two Major World Systems* made it clear that he believed his observations, not the declarations of dogma. Pope Urban was under pressure to crack down from reactionary forces within the ranks. And so Galileo was asked to come for an 'interview'. (In fact, the Inquisition had already passed the book as OK, but then they had second thoughts when it was pointed out to them that it definitely wasn't OK and that if that kind of thing went on they'd have to start 'interviewing' themselves.)

Galileo broke down under torture and threats . . . oh no, hang on, he didn't. From the start of the interview he maintained that he had never believed in the Copernican universe, or rather that he had once agreed with it, but then sided with the church in condemnation of the ideas. It's fair to say that both sides were playing the game. Galileo remained under house arrest for the rest of his life, and his books were officially condemned – but he was hardly the martyr that he is sometimes made out to be.*

Which is not to say, of course, that the Inquisition and the church hierarchy knew what they were doing. But then, it's hard to see the stars when your head is so firmly stuck in the sand.

Descartes before the horse

In France René Descartes (1596–1650) read Galileo's work and was thrown into turmoil by the conflict between what Galileo was saying and what the Catholic doctrine had proclaimed. So he decided to rethink things from scratch.

He started from the first principles: his own thoughts. 'I think,' he wrote

---

he had three children out of wedlock. He put the two girls into a convent to become nuns because he believed them unmarriageable.

* His books remained condemned for two hundred years. The *Dialogue* was officially banned for Catholics until 1835.

famously, 'therefore I am.' And then he added, 'I drink, therefore I need a coffee.' But while the kettle was boiling he made a big jump: the idea of God is too perfect to have occurred to a simple man: so it must have been *put* in someone's mind by God. So that proved God. Two sugars, please.

It's not really entirely convincing. But it reflects a new approach – an experimental approach, if you like, to theology. Descartes was beginning from a sceptical position.*

It's not enough just to state things: you have to work them out for yourself. Both Descartes and Galileo were Christians, but they reserved the right to think for themselves.

Digging and levelling

On 1 April 1649, four months after the king was executed, some twenty poor men took possession of a plot of common land in Saint George's Hill, Surrey, and started to dig. They were henceforth known as the Diggers, and the Surrey community was the first of over thirty communities that held property in common and sought to reclaim the land they believed had been taken from them. Their leader, Gerrard Winstanley, called for land captured during the Civil War to be redistributed. That, he claimed, would 'turn swords into ploughshares and settle such a peace in the earth, as nations shall learn war no more'.

It was a time of radical movements. Understandably, because radical Puritans were in control of the entire country. After abolishing the monarchy, Parliament abolished the House of Lords and then went all John Knox on everyone. Swearing was declared illegal, dancing was banned, along with maypoles, the theatre and sport on Sunday. Churches were stripped of their ornaments. Statues were broken, stained glass smashed. The inns and alehouses were largely

---

* And from a prone position. Much of his best thinking was done in bed, where he would stay, writing, until noon. Later he had to abandon the whole bed-based routine: when he was appointed tutor to the twenty-two-year-old Queen Christina of Sweden, he would get up at five every morning, according to the queen's demand. Not surprisingly, the strain was too great and he died a year later aged just fifty-three. Although it could have been that he caught pneumonia from the French ambassador. However, I blame the early mornings. And since I'm going to be the same age soon, for my own safety I'm going to take up the bed-based routine, starting immediately.

closed. And then they cancelled Christmas. And Easter.

If this sounds repressive, there were some good things. First, the Puritans destroyed most organs. (Often these were taken to private homes, or torture chambers.) Organ-builders almost disappeared. Second, there was genuine freedom of conscience, and religious tolera-tion. You were free to go to church or not as you chose. You were free to start your own church or denomination.* The result was a wild flowering of new sects and radical beliefs.

The Muggletonians, for example, strongly believed that anyone who knowingly rejected their teachings was going to hell. So, to avoid inflicting this fate on others, they decided not to tell anyone what they actually believed. They were the first Christian sect to ban evangelism. Amazingly, they survived until the 1970s. They didn't even worship together, choosing just to meet up for discussions. Then there were the Adamites, who certainly met for worship, but were accused of doing so in the nude. The Grindletonians from Yorkshire believed that true Christians could achieve perfection on earth, although how that was possible in Yorkshire they didn't say. And then there were the Ranters, who were a kind of catch-all bogeyman heretical sect, who believed in Pantheism and discarded all worldly moral rules.

This lot were at the stranger, seriously unworldly end. But there were several movements, like the Diggers, that had a much stronger emphasis on politics and social change.

Perhaps the most famous of these political activists were the Levellers, led by John Lilburne. He was a devout Christian who had been in trouble with the authorities since before the war. He relentlessly campaigned for his 'freeborn rights' – which earned him the nickname of 'Freeborn John'. The Levellers, like the Diggers, pointed to the example of the Garden of Eden, where 'all men were Levellers'. They preached equality for women, called for all working men to have the vote, for one-year Parliaments, the abolition of the House of Lords, religious toleration. They also called for MPs to have no outside interests. Still some way to go on that one . . .

For both the Diggers and the Levellers things ended in violence. The Digger communities were broken up by landowner-orchestrated campaigns of violence, harassment and arson. The Levellers were marching on London when they were captured and confined in the

---

* This did not apply to non-Christians, or even non-Protestants, of course. Catholics, Jews and Muslims need not apply.

church at Burford.* Three days later, on 17 May, three of their leaders were taken out and shot while the remainder watched from the rooftop.

A year later there was another significant development for western Christendom: the first coffeehouse opened in Oxford in 1650 (followed by one in London in 1652).† Coffee had developed in the tenth century in Ethiopia, eventually arriving in Europe via Mecca, Turkey and then Spain. I'm not sure when it was first served after church services, but whenever it was it definitely (a) tasted rubbish, and (b) was served in those cheap green cups with the three rings going round them. It has since become as much a part of Christian life as reading the Bible, saying your prayers and sleeping through the sermon.

In Bunhill Fields

In London, just north of Liverpool Street Station, you enter Nonconformist territory. Well, maybe not these days, given the number of pin-stripe-suited individuals you encounter, but in the seventeenth and eighteenth centuries this was where you came if you were into dissent. On one side of the road was Wesley's House and Chapel; on the opposite side was a gated entrance to Bunhill Fields. The name comes from Bone Hill – this was originally a burial ground for plague victims, but then it was taken over by a Mr Tindall, who turned it into a burial ground for anyone who could afford the fees. And this is where the Nonconformists came to be buried, for the simple reason that their refusal to join the 'established' church denied them burial in the consecrated ground of churchyards. So they found a resting place here.

And there are some major players buried there. The poet, artist and borderline loonie William Blake lies close to the novelist Daniel Defoe. Opposite them is the tomb of John Bunyan. Beyond him, John Wesley's eccentric mum, Susannah. Isaac Watts the hymn writer, Thomas Bayes the mathematician. Others, less well known: Thomas Buxton, abolitionist, prison reformer, tireless campaigner against the death penalty. (He never saw it abolished in his lifetime, but he did manage to reduce

* On the lead font, you can still see the engraved graffito of one of their number: 'Anthony Sedley. 1649. Prisner.'
† A Parisian coffeehouse had opened in 1643, but, knowing French coffee, it was probably rubbish.

the number of crimes punishable by death from more than 200 to 8.) Thomas Newcomen, who invented the first steam-powered water pump and was also a teaching elder in his local Baptist church.

These are the 'dissenters'. The outsiders. Refuseniks. Weirdos. People who, even in death, refused to lie down quietly and compromise.

The radical movements of the 1640s led to some of the most influential movements in Christian history. Their members include great artists, poets, writers, campaigners, businessmen, scientists . . . They paid a high price for their beliefs. Bunyan spent a third of his adult life in jail. Many paid the ultimate price. If you pass through Bunhill Fields, you come to the Quaker garden, the burial place of the Quakers. And there on the wall is a plaque:

'Near this spot George Fox was interred in 1690, previously Edward Burrough and some Ninety other Martyr Friends Who died in London Prisons.'

GEORGE FOX

George Fox. Preparing to quake

Name: George Fox.
Aka: None.
Nationality: English.
Dates: 1624–91.
Appearance: He was 'graceful in countenance, manly in personage, grave in gesture, courteous in conversation'. Had quite a big nose, though.
Before he was famous: Shoemaker.
Famous for: Quaking. Experiencing the inner light. Pacifism.
Why does he matter? He founded the Society of Friends. His conviction that everyone has the inner light meant that Quakers fought for equality, against slavery, and for a wide range of radical social action.
Could you have a drink with him down the pub? A small one. Probably outside. He disapproved of excessive drinking.

Crazy like a Fox

The Quakers were the longest-lasting and most influential of the radical sects. They were founded by a cobbler called George Fox (1624–91) who, after seeing God in a dream, became a wandering preacher in 1643. Fox knew Christ 'experientially': he had had a direct experience of Christ without the need for the institutions of the church. And he came to believe that all people had this ability, that everyone had an inner light from God, which was all the religion necessary.

'Quakers' was a belittling nickname. They were properly known as the Society of Friends, but their enemies claimed that they shook when under the inspiration of the inner light. Fox was following what he read in the Gospels – the *euangellia*, 'evangels', in the Greek. These people who emphasised a personal experience were to become known as 'evangelicals'. He sought to direct people to 'their Inward Teacher, Christ Jesus, who would turn them from darkness to the light'.

This extremely radical idea has some enormous ramifications. Most Christians – whether Protestant, Catholic or None of the Above – believed that God's presence was mediated through institutions like theology, the sacraments, church. But if everyone had the inner light, then the church became unnecessary. So Quakers abandoned all the rituals of the church, which they dismissed as mere externals.

And if what qualifies you for ministry is the Holy Spirit, then anyone has the right to minister: men, women, children, even. The inner light makes everyone equal. So they refused to doff their hats to their elders and betters; they insisted on interrupting sermons and correcting the minister; and they allowed women to preach.* Probably Fox's first follower was a woman, Elizabeth Hooton (1600–72), who, although well into middle age, left her family and followed George into a career as a wandering teacher. In 1662 she left England and journeyed across the Atlantic to the New World. Where she was arrested, beaten and left to die in the wilderness. But she was made of tough stuff. She survived, returned to England and then went back to the New World twice more,

---

* Of course, it went to some people's heads. In a kind of Münster-lite moment, one Quaker leader's inner light informed him that he was, in fact, Jesus. So he rode into Bristol on a donkey.

where she was beaten up again. Finally, she joined a group of Quaker missionaries and went to Jamaica, where she died, aged seventy-two.*

And here's the thing: although Fox used and valued the Bible, Quakers' inner guide was just as, if not more, important. One effect of this was that the Quakers became anti-slavery campaigners long before other Christians. To other Christians the Bible seemed to accept slavery; the Quakers didn't care about that: their inner light *told* them it was wrong.

Fig. XXXII. *George Fox seeks new converts*

---

* Hence the famous joke – Elizabeth Hooton's gone to the West Indies. Jamaica? No, she was following the inner light. (I'll get my cloak.)

Champagne Charlie

In the end the people quickly tired of puritanical rules. Cromwell's commonwealth soon descended into a totalitarian police state. England was both frightening and deadly dull at the same time. With the death of Cromwell things unravelled quickly and in 1660 Charles II reclaimed the throne of England. It says something about the Puritans that the people of England preferred a man of such vacuous superficiality.*

After 1660, and the end of Cromwell's Commonwealth, most people had a shopping list of desires. They wanted the alehouses and theatres reopened. They didn't want any more fanaticism and 'enthusiasm'. And they wanted a quiet life. (The latter was made harder by the fact that church authorities invited two Germans over to teach them how to build organs again.)

Charles II insisted – initially, at least – on toleration for religion. This was less out of a general sense of justice and more because he was actually a closet Catholic. He restored the bishops. And the Act of Uniformity was passed, which required all Anglican services to use the Book of Common Prayer. But he resisted, at first, calls for revenge on the radicals who had led England for a decade.

Then, on 6 January 1661, fifty men from a movement known as the Fifth Monarchists marched on London. They believed that in 1666, Jesus Christ – the eponymous fifth monarch – would return.† In order to get things ready they decided to march on London, reclaim it for King Jesus, and help the apocalypse along a bit. Their coup was crushed and the leaders executed for high treason.

This uprising panicked the authorities and led Charles to start suppressing the Nonconformists. He introduced a new prayer book in 1662, which was anti-Puritan in tone. Puritans were forbidden to work for the state or the church. Puritans became outsiders again. Baptists and Quakers were outlawed. Angry mobs were allowed to attack their meetings without any comeback. Many Quakers were

---

* Cromwell was dug up, hanged and beheaded. His head stood on a pole for twenty-five years as a warning to anyone who might think of killing another king. In 1685 a storm blew the pole down. After this the head moved around between private collectors. It was probably not buried until 1960, three hundred years after the restoration.

† The first four were King Arthur, King Prawn, Old King Cole, and King Sizeduvet. Or possibly the four rulers listed in Daniel 2.

locked up in prisons, where they died from the insanitary conditions.

The Fifth Monarchist may have been wrong about the return of Jesus, but the times did have an apocalyptic feel. In 1666 London was decimated by the Great Fire. The year before, the city had been hit by the Great Plague. In echoes of plagues long past in Alexandria, most Anglican vicars took off for the country; many Puritans stayed with their flock. Later, Parliament, believing them to be intrinsically infected, banned them from coming within five miles of any city. So they left.

Many went overseas, to America, a place where Separatists could be separate and Puritans could be pure. In New England Puritans founded a land where people were free to believe whatever they wanted, as long as it was congregationalism. When a Baptist called Roger Williams moved to Rhode Island and established a settlement based on ideas of religious liberty, the Puritan authorities expelled him. It was a very mixed picture out there, in contrast perhaps to received wisdom regarding free conscience. In what was called New Netherlands the aim was to establish a monopoly of religion for the Dutch Reformed state-supported church; in the four southern colonies a kind of diluted Anglicanism became the established church. The Quaker William Penn established Pennsylvania. Maryland, appropriately given its name, was originally planned as a Catholic colony.

Fig. XXXIII. *In the colonies, negotiations with the natives are going well*

Glorious Revolution

When Charles died, he was succeeded by his brother James II.* Where Charles had kept his Catholicism under wraps, James came out of the closet. He was a Catholic, and he was proud of it.

This put Parliament into an uncomfortable position. Some supported James on the basis that he was the legitimate heir, a son of Charles I, and he should therefore be king, never mind his religion. These became known as the Jacobites or 'tories'. In the opposing camps were the 'Whigs', who wanted to stop James becoming king. At first the Tories won: James ascended the throne in 1685. But he was disastrously lacking in tact and diplomacy. He gave all the top jobs in the country to Catholics. Jesuit missionaries started to enter the country. Religious toleration was proclaimed. Then in 1688 he had seven bishops who had criticised him arrested and tried. Suddenly everyone had had enough. James was forced to flee the country, deposed by his own daughter and son-in-law, the joint monarchs William and Mary.

Parliament had reasserted itself. What is more, it had changed king without bloodshed. And this was called the Glorious Revolution. Dissenters – who had supported the move – were rewarded with legal status. Catholics were not.

Apple pi

One of those who escaped the 1665 plague in London was Isaac Newton. He retreated to the country, where he sat under a tree and an apple fell on his head. He simultaneously invented gravity, apple crumble and concussion. In 1687 he published *Principia Mathematica*, which contains his theory of gravitation, and his famous three laws of motion.† What was radical about Newton's ideas was the underlying thesis that the laws of physics – rather than, or as well as, the laws of God – governed the universe. Newton went on to develop theories about optics, mathematical calculus, the binomial theorem and an approximation of pi.

* Although Charles fathered many children, not a single son was actually legitimate.
† The most famous one is 'for every action there is an equal and opposite reaction'. These rules do not apply on social media, where for every action there is an unequal and opposite overreaction.

Newton – like Galileo – was a devout Christian, albeit a slightly unorthodox one.* 'Gravity explains the motions of the planets,' he said, 'but it cannot explain who set the planets in motion. God governs all things and knows all that is or can be done.'

But Newton had set things in motion, to coin a phrase. Geologists began to argue that the world was far older than the account in Genesis allowed for. The English philosopher John Locke was a champion of 'reason' and argued for 'reasonable Christianity'. No mystical mumbo-jumbo, no blind faith in church authorities: everything had to be tested. Locke believed in God and he defended religious freedom too; except – obviously – for Catholics and atheists, both of whom he considered utterly unreasonable.

Dei-o

Ideas of reason and scientific enquiry were chipping away at doctrinal certainty. But even those who jettisoned traditional Christianity were not prepared to jettison religion. The result was deism, which was sort of a general worship of common sense.

Deism held that reason was true religion. Or the heart of true religion, anyway. All the other ones had branched off into various kinds of superstition. Miracles and all those things were rather vulgar bits of folklore. Virtually all the church's historic doctrines were inventions. Religious ceremonies were just silly. There was God, and there was basic morality, and we should acknowledge God's existence and worship him and . . . well, that was it really.

Deism was a bit of an upper-class hobby, but it was taken up by a Frenchman, François Arouet. We know Arouet better by his pen name: Voltaire. His book *Letters on the English* was published in 1734 and praised English tolerance: 'An Englishman, as one to whom liberty is natural, may go to heaven his own way,' he wrote. The book was immediately banned in France – largely on the ground of praising the English. But Voltaire became a famous and prolific author, publishing everything from plays to history.

* He denied the doctrine of the Trinity, but believed devoutly in the second coming and made dense mathematical calculations based on the dimensions of Solomon's temple.

He was a champion of all the values that became associated with the Enlightenment: reason, free speech, scepticism, wearing wigs, taking snuff, and so on. He mocked Catholicism for all kinds of things: its love of the Scriptures, and its hatred of the Jews who wrote them; for promoting a God who craves worship and punishes doubt; for preaching the love of your neighbour while 'hating your neighbour for his opinions'.

For Voltaire, traditional non-rational Christianity was crowd control, a method of commanding the masses and ensuring their obedience. 'If God did not exist,' he wrote, 'it would be necessary to invent him.'

Deists believed in God – just not the kind of God that orthodox Christians did.

Mission impossible

In 1712 Abraham Jordan proudly showed off a new invention, which he called a 'swelling organ'. Naturally people flocked to the church of St Magnus-the-Martyr to see it, only to be disappointed to find out it was really just a musical instrument with a volume control.

Talking of swelling, in China things had gone so well for the Jesuit missionaries that there was now an official Chinese bishop and liturgy and hundreds of thousands of baptised Catholics.

But back home, suspicion still lingered over Ricci's rather liberal accommodation of traditional Chinese ways within Chinese Catholicism. Eventually, the pope stepped in and forbade any use of Confucian terms, and the veneration of ancestors. The result was a disaster: the emperor expelled any cleric or missionary who followed the orders of the pope – whom he saw as an enemy emperor. The Catholic Church in China withered and died.

Meanwhile, in Japan, the rulers were getting ever more paranoid about foreign influences. In 1622 fifty-one Christians were killed in an attack on a church. In the persecution that followed, missionaries were burnt at the stake and native converts executed in the most horrible ways. Some were crucified or boiled alive. But the Japanese, like the Romans, found that these martyrdoms actually impressed people with the courage of the Christians, so they took to torturing Christians into submission. By the end of the century Christianity had virtually disappeared, or been driven underground, and Japan had retreated into isolation.

Up until now Protestant interest in overseas mission had been, well, non-existent, really. It also heralded a sea change in Protestant attitudes towards overseas mission. Luther had more or less ignored overseas mission, choosing to believe that the missionary command had been carried out in apostolic times. But increasingly, as Protestantism became a settled faith, missionaries went out to all parts of the world.

In 1698 the Anglicans formed their own 'propagandists' in the form of the SPCK, the Society for Promoting Christian Knowledge. Three years later a different group formed the Society for the Propagation of the Gospel in Foreign Parts (1701). Initially the aim of the SPG was to support the colonists in America, but then they expanded their vision to include the 'evangelisation of slaves and Native Americans'. Missionaries started to go from Europe to America. And among them were two brothers: John and Charles Wesley.

Heartburn

The travelling Wesleys had a terrible time in America on their first mission trip. The Wesleys' foray into mission ended in scandal. John tried to seduce a young woman – her family tried to have him arrested. He had to flee.

But the journey itself proved to be crucial. Because, on the trip, John Wesley (1703–91) came into contact with Moravians. These – as the name implies – came from Moravia and were loyal followers of Jan Hus. They had been driven out of their homeland, and in 1722 a group sought asylum on the lands of one Count Nikolaus von Zinzendorf. He became their leader – and let's face it, if *your* name was Nikolaus von Zinzendorf, *you'd* be leader. They formed a community, a bit like a Protestant monastery only with women, and without the head shaving and the celibacy. They also sent missionaries to North and South America, to Greenland and the West Indies and to heathen lands like . . . er . . . England. And Germany. Deeply pious, in America these old-school radical Christians scandalised everyone, preaching to every-body, regardless of racial distinctions.

They believed in 'heart' rather than 'head' religion. Abstract theology was rejected in favour of emotion and feeling. God, they preached, cared for each individual as a person: all individuals, therefore, had to make a commitment, had to ask Christ to enter their hearts.

The Moravians first came to John Wesley's attention when he noticed that they weren't screaming. The boat had got caught in a storm and all the English started panicking. But the Moravians stayed calm and carried on with their service. These people had a kind of certainty that Wesley lacked. While he was in America, he met with the leader of the Moravians, Spangenberg, who asked him a very powerful and personal question: Did Wesley really know Jesus Christ? And was he really saved?

Once back in London Wesley spent more time with the Moravians. He began to see that he had an intellectual, rational belief in God, but nothing in the gut, no heartfelt faith. Then, on 24 May 1738, he went 'very unwillingly' to a Moravian meeting when, listening to the preacher, 'About a quarter before nine, while he was describing the change which God works in the heart through faith in Christ, I felt my heart strangely warmed.' It was not that his hot water bottle had burst. It was that he suddenly felt that 'I did trust in Christ, Christ alone, for salvation; and an assurance was given me that He had taken away my sins, even mine, and saved me from the law of sin and death.'

JOHN WESLEY

John Wesley, thinking about his method

Name: John Wesley.
Aka: n/a.
Nationality: English.
Dates: 1703–91.
Appearance: Shortish. Strong. Probably bandy-legged, due to the fact he rode a reputed 250,000 miles during his preaching career.

Before he was famous: Student. Failed missionary.
Famous for: Founding Methodism. Being warm-hearted.
Why does he matter? Methodism was all about a personal experience of Jesus. Wesley was a superb preacher, but he was also a great organiser: thousands of people joined his small groups. And he appointed itinerant, unordained preachers.
Could you have a drink with him down the pub? Yes. But he'd probably start preaching to the bar staff.

Oh, Mr Whitefield!

He was not alone. In the 1730s and 1740s there was heartwarming going on on both sides of the Atlantic. In Britain it was the Evangelical Revival; it was the Great Awakening in British America.* Different names, but the same experience: revival, people experiencing Christ in an entirely new way.

Fig. XXXIV. *George Whitefield turns his disability into an advantage*

And one of the great preachers of this mass heartburn was a friend of Wesley's called George Whitefield (1714–70). Whitefield had been banned from preaching in the state churches, because of his radical

* I like that phrase 'British America'. Happy days.

idea that a lot of people in Anglican churches might not *actually* be Christians. He responded to this prohibition by preaching outdoors. In fields, market squares, anywhere where he could gather a crowd.

And he was a fabulous preacher. It was not that he was in any way glamorous – on the contrary, he was severely cross-eyed – but he could command the attention of the crowd in a way few others could. David Garrick, the greatest actor of his age, once said that he would give 100 guineas 'if I could say, "Oh!" like Mr Whitefield'. His first sermon was said to have driven thirteen people mad.*

We're all doomed

Whitefield was a transatlantic preacher. He made thirteen preaching trips to North America. There he built on the work of preachers like Jonathan Edwards (1703–58). A boy genius, who entered Yale College aged just twelve, Edwards decided to become a minister when he experienced a 'divine and supernatural light'.

Edwards believed that God's love shone like a 'divine light' over the universe. Believers – anybody at any time – could sense this light through the Holy Spirit, and 'apprehend the things of God'. He couldn't stand the passive, superficial religious observance he saw around him, and insisted on real commitment. His sermons are passionate, outspoken, built on the concept of justification by faith – and full of the language of hellfire and damnation. It was time for sinners to get real and get saved. It was Edwards's sermons that really started the Great Awakening in British America.

Later on he fell out with the members of his church over a theological argument. He was forced out of the church and became pastor of a frontier mission church in Stockbridge, Massachusetts, and a missionary to the local Indian tribe.† He became president of the College of New Jersey (now somewhat better known as Princetown). When a smallpox epidemic hit town, he decided to get inoculated to show people that it was safe and effective. He caught smallpox from the inoculation and died on 22 March 1758. Oops.

---

* I've preached sermons like that. Although I tend to drive people hopping mad.

† The Housatonic Indians. As opposed to the Isotonic Indians, who were fond of Lucozade.

The great unwashed

Back in Britain Wesley followed Whitefield into the fields and other outdoor spaces, and all heaven was breaking loose. Tears were commonplace. Not to mention convulsions, collapses, shaking, fits, uncontrollable laughter, miraculous healings, exorcisms and divine visions. The state church was prepared to admit that Jesus and the disciples did such things – but that was back in pagan times when people didn't know any better. Surely Britain – Christian Britain – didn't need such signs and wonders? It was all very vulgar.

As were the people to whom Whitefield and Wesley preached. Vulgar people. Common. People who lived in poverty and neglect. People who had never before been told that God actually cared about them.

They were thirsty for faith. The size of the crowds was astonishing. On one night 3,000 people gathered to hear Wesley preach in a field. The crowd was down a bit, but, be fair, it was a Monday night. He got more later in the week. In Blackheath he preached to nearly 14,000 people. He rode 3,000 miles a year on his preaching journeys and often preached more than 1,000 times a year. He devised a method of voice projection that was close to singing, which allowed his voice to be heard outdoors.

Wesley, though, had something a lot of the other preacher-evangelists didn't have: the ability to organise. He understood that you needed to nurture new converts and support them. So he organised a system of weekly study groups who would listen to teaching, pray, sing and be accountable to one another. He wasn't trying to set up a new denomination: he was trying to breathe new life into the Anglicans; but, inevitably, there was to be a parting of the ways. He used lay leaders (this was a matter of practicality as much as anything else: he originally wanted ordained clergy to lead the groups, but hardly any of them wanted anything to do with Wesley). And he even allowed – wait for it – *women* to lead.

It is hard nowadays – when Methodism has become so respectable – to get our heads around the outrage and the disdain of those days. The revivalists were beaten up by mobs. They were showered with stones, rotting fruit, fire-bombs even. They were rounded up by clergy and local officials.

But the ordinary people loved it. Around 30,000 people signed up to Wesley's groups. He had a network of more than 100 preachers. Wesley pushed himself continually to the limits. And by now he'd more or less given up on the Anglican Church. He started ordaining his own leaders (much to the shock of his brother, who became a famous hymn writer) and he rewrote the Book of Common Prayer.* Despite the fact that his books brought him an annual income of up to £1,400, he insisted on living on £30 – the average wage of an ordinary worker. He gave the rest away. No wonder the fat cats in the Anglican Church hated him so much.†

In the industrial towns of Britain these 'dissenters' saw huge growth. Twenty years after John Wesley's death 5 per cent of Britain's population belonged to his Methodist societies. (The name was a mocking nickname, originally applied to all evangelicals but coming to be used of only Wesley's followers.) They were by far the largest of the dissenting denominations and their following was especially strong in the industrial towns of the north.

And there were other mini-Wesleys at work. In 1800 a man called Hugh Bourne preached to thousands of workers in Harriseahead, Cheshire, a neighbourhood he described as the most 'ungodly and profane' in England. He earned a reputation as a zealous preacher, albeit very shy – he was so embarrassed by the whole thing that he spent the whole sermon with his hands over his eyes. He rejected the, by now, traditional Methodist service as being boring and out of date and developed a camp-style service with open-air preaching, public confession of sin, group prayer, and hymn singing, and by 1804 revival had spread to the neighbouring towns. The Methodist leadership, far from welcoming this, felt his methods to be inappropriate. In 1807 the Methodist Conference said that 'It is our judgement, that even supposing such meetings to be allowable in America, they are highly improper in England, and likely to be productive of considerable mischief; and we disclaim all connection with them.' They expelled him and refused even to let those converted by Bourne enter their churches. So Bourne created the Primitive Methodists. And the whirring sounds of the industrial north were augmented by the sound of Wesley spinning in his grave.

* He also came into conflict with other revival leaders over the issue of predestination. Whitefield accepted it, but Wesley said that 'It represents the most holy God as worse than the devil.'
† Not all Anglicans hated him. Evangelicalism hit the Anglican Church as well. Leaders like John Newton, the former slave trader and hymn writer, preached the evangelical need to be born again.

Sunday schools

Bourne's movement recognised that there was more to evangelicalism than just a spiritual experience. Like many other dissenting movements he spoke out against the drunkenness and alcoholism that served to make the conditions of working people slightly more bearable. He encouraged lay preachers – indeed, many early trade union leaders learned their skills as Primitive Methodist preachers.

And he promoted education for the working class. In this he was following in the footsteps of Robert Raikes (1736–1811). Raikes was a publisher, the proprietor of the *Gloucester Journal* and a committed Christian who came to see that many people were trapped because they had no access to education. Raikes started a school for boys in the slums, and, since most of those boys worked during the week, he ran it on a Sunday. It was the world's first Sunday school. The first school opened in 1780, in the home of a Mrs Meredith. Raikes paid for the schooling himself, and used his newspaper to publicise and promote his work. Within two years several schools for boys and girls had opened around Gloucester.

Some were outraged. The schools were mocked as 'Raikes' Ragged School'. But by 1831 Sunday schools in Great Britain had a weekly attendance of 1,250,000 children – an astonishing 25 per cent of the child population. They are the forerunners of the state school system, a system that was not put in place until the Elementary Education Act of 1870.

I never knew it would happen, with the MP from Clapham

In 1785 an MP called William Wilberforce (1759–1833) got 'saved'. Two years later he came into contact with a group of anti-slavery activists who persuaded Wilberforce to take up the cause.

Europe had built its colonial power through the use of slaves. Over 100,000 slaves were trafficked across the Atlantic each year to work in the plantations in America and the West Indies. Conditions on the slave ships were horrific and a high percentage of the captives never survived the journey.

In some ways, though, the abolitionists were drawing on a radically different reading of the Bible. Read the Bible literally and uncritically and it is hard to find a condemnation of slavery.* On the contrary, both the Hebrew Tanakh (the Hebrew Bible) and the Christian New Testament take the condition of slavery for granted.

Wilberforce and his circle – known as 'the Clapham Sect' after the south London village where they lived – were therefore arguing for a different way of reading the Bible. This was reading from the standpoint of natural justice: it was just plain *wrong* for people to be slaves. So we must re-examine the Bible to find evidence to substantiate our arguments.

Wilberforce devoted the rest of his life to the abolition of slavery. Trading in slaves was finally abolished throughout the empire in 1807, but it was still legal to own them. And those born to slaves were still slaves. It was not until 1833 that slavery was finally abolished throughout the British Empire. Wilberforce never got to see it: he died a month before the vote was passed. But by then he knew that it was going to happen, and he died knowing that his life's work would come to fruition.

Encyclopedic knowledge

On All Saints' Day in 1755 an earthquake hit Lisbon, Portugal. It was Sunday, so the churches were packed. The earthquake shattered buildings; a tsunami hit the harbour, fires broke out throughout the city. Some 30,000 people lost their lives.

It was an event that shattered many Europeans' image of God as a benevolent creator. The writer and thinker Voltaire wrote a poem – 'Poem on the Lisbon Disaster' – in which he railed against the idea that the world was under the detailed control of God. In France Denis Diderot published the *Encyclopedia*, which included many dangerous new ideas. It openly attacked Christianity. It was banned, and copies were burned, but it was widely read all the same.

Others attacked the credibility of the Scriptures. At Hamburg University a Deist scholar called Hermann Reimarus (1694–1768) wrote a critique of the Bible (he kept it unpublished until after he was dead and safely out

* The only overt statement against the trade in human misery comes from that subversive commie tract, Revelation, which talks of Babylon's evil trade in 'slaves and human souls' (Rev. 18.13).

of the way. (Perhaps he hid it under Arminius' hat.) He was interested in establishing its history: How did this document come to be written? What were the sources? What picture did it really show? He decided that the Gospels really depicted Jesus as a preacher and political activist whose career ended in failure and whose followers created the myth that he had returned from the dead largely to avoid having to go back to fishing for a living. Reimarus's ideas were influential and were really the beginnings of modern revisionist historians of the historical Jesus school.

This type of approach – sceptical, questioning, focusing on reason – has become known as the Enlightenment. It was not a movement without faith. Many of its proponents were deists, but more, they also had a deep faith in human progress, a faith that, in the long run, was to prove rather unreasonable in itself.

Witch! Witch! WITCH!

One of the few things on which Catholics and Protestants could agree were witches.

Witches were bad. They were in league with the devil. They wore big pointy hats and coveted ruby slippers. Concerns about witches went back to the early fourteenth century, when Pope John XXII commissioned a team of theological experts to look into the phenomenon. In 1327 he issued a bull, *Super illius specula*,* which confirmed that yes, witches were real, that magical practices were heretical and, look out! She's got a broom! But after that nothing much happened for a long time.

Then in 1487 the whole thing was given new impetus by the publication of a witch-hunter's textbook, called *Malleus Maleficarum* ('Hammer of Witches'). And from then on Europe – and subsequently America – was convulsed by bouts of witch-hunts. It has been estimated that between forty and fifty thousand people were killed for being witches between 1400 and 1800.

Different places peaked at different times. Witch-hunting was particularly virulent in Germany until, in 1691, a Dutch Reformed pastor called Balthasar Bekker wrote *The World Bewitched*, a book that tore the

---

* The follow-up was called Expialidocious.

process to shreds and shamed many Protestant leaders into stopping the trials. One of the most intense persecutions was in Scotland, in the mid-seventeenth century, where the Church of Scotland invented the torture of sleep deprivation in order to extract confessions. Their invention is still used by many a secret policeman around the world today. Indeed, the last witch to be executed in Britain was in Scotland, where, in 1727, a poor, mad woman was accused of turning her daughter into a pony. She was burned alive.

In America the worst excesses were at Salem, Massachusetts, in 1692. There the Quaker leaders gave in to a kind of mass paranoia, interrogating some 150 suspects and executing 19 of them. One of the judges at the Salem witch trials, Samuel Sewall, later issued a public apology for his actions and asked for forgiveness. He later wrote a pamphlet supporting the anti-slavery movement which is, perhaps, some form of amends.

Fig. XXXV. *The Salem witch trials get out of hand*

Being Jesuitical

Has anyone heard from the pope recently? No? Me neither. And there's a reason for that. The position haemorrhaged power over the centuries. The old arguments about who should appoint bishops were long lost: the Catholic powers had all made bishops answerable to their heads of state rather than to Rome.

And the Jesuits – set up, you'll recall, to reform the Catholic Church and propagate Catholicism – had gone the way of all the other movements before them, amassing their own power and wealth. They were widely detested, even outlawed. Throughout the 1760s the Jesuits were banned in Portugal, France and the Spanish Empire.

Pressure was put on the pope to abolish the order. He offered to reform it, but France in particular was having none of it and in the end the Society of Jesus was dissolved in 1773. Or almost. It actually survived in countries where you'd least expect it – countries outside the control of Rome, like Protestant Prussia and Orthodox Russia. Their policies of toleration meant that the Jesuits could continue underground, as it were. Covertly.

Expect great things

By the late eighteenth century, the British Empire was the global superpower. The sheer expanse of their holdings offered opportunities to missionaries to travel to far-flung climes and convert the heathen.

William Carey (1761–1834) has been called the Father of Modern Mission, a title which only works if you ignore about 200 years of Catholic missions. But he was certainly a remarkable man, and the first major missionary from the ranks of the Dissenters. He was a cobbler in Northamptonshire who taught himself Greek and Hebrew and went to India, founding the Baptist Missionary Society along the way. Carey's great motto was 'Expect great things from God; attempt great things for God.'

He was also a great Bible translator. Carey printed the first Bible in Bengali. Unlike Catholic missionaries, the Protestant approach could not rely on the images and objects that priests used to tell the story. Nor could they point to a wide roster of different saints. They had the Bible. And that needed translation.

Translation was tricky. There were the difficulties of squeezing the Bible into languages that sometimes contained only a few hundred words. Translation meant finding out all they could about the culture – there is a story of one native whose name for the missionary was 'the white man with the book who torments us with questions'. In countries that have never seen a sheep, what word do you use for the Lamb of God? (The translator working among the Inuit went for 'seal-pup'.)

Many times it went wrong, as in the story of the missionary who purportedly translated 'Heavenly' as 'sky Blue', encouraging the prayer, 'Our sky-blue father . . .'

When Luther translated the Bible into German, only 15 translations of the Bible had been made. By 1600 that figure had risen to 40; by 1700 it had risen to 52. By the start of the nineteenth century the Bible had been translated into about 70 languages, mostly those of middle Europe and the Mediterranean region. In the next century the pace of translation was to accelerate markedly. In 1804 the British and Foreign Bible Society, dedicated to translating and printing the Scriptures and distributing them around the world, was founded, and over the next two centuries they were to make the Bible available in over 800 languages. No organisation in history has done more to make the Bible available throughout the world.

Independence Day

Three years after the demise of the Jesuits, America chucked a lot of tea about and declared war against the Brits, which they won due to (a) not fighting fairly, and (b) having the support of the French, who were just bitter about losing Canada. Of course you can't have a Church of England in America. Well, you could, but it wouldn't have been tremendously popular. So the Anglicans had a marketing meeting and rebranded themselves as Episcopalians, that is, The Church of Bishops.

The Episcopalians were just one of several denominations that had established themselves in America: there were thriving communities of Baptists, Quakers, Congregationalists. So when the constitution was finally agreed in 1787, Congress agreed that there should be no official state religion and that no one should be kept out of office for religious reasons. For the first time since Constantine there was an official separation between church and state.

And that is why every president since then has had to be a Christian. Er . . . hang on. I'll get back to you on that one.

Anyway, one of the effects of independence was that the Americans could start printing their own Bibles. Before then, as a British colony, it was illegal to publish any Bible in English. All Bibles had to be imported from England. The first book printed in English in the newly formed United States was the New Testament, printed in Philadelphia in 1777 by Robert Aitken. And, significantly, it was the King James Version. (They didn't call it the Authorised Version: no King had any right to authorise anything in America any longer. Or even 'authorize' as they would spell it.) As the first printed book in America, it gained a certain mythic status: it was one of the country's founding documents, a book that bound the fledgling nation together.

And, with typical American entrepreneurial flair, Bibles were printed in enormous numbers and sold cheap. The result was that in the United States – more even than in Britain – the KJV became sacred. Today the Bible Belt of the United States has a deep dedication to the King James Version. The King James Bible was produced under the supervision of a spendthrift, heavy-drinking, bisexual king, who agreed to it only because he wanted to quash some republican marginal notes. And it has become the beloved holy book of the American right-wing, teetotal, ultra-Republican Bible Belt.

Officially, though, the USA was a multifaith country. In 1791 the Bill of Rights secured freedom of religion. And United States law does not designate Christianity as its official faith. Today four other world continents house more Christians than North America, yet, more than any other nation, the USA is seen as a 'Christian' nation. Officially it has always shied away from that. If anything, it is Deist. The coins bear the motto 'In God we Trust'; the Pledge of Allegiance talks of one nation under God. Jesus is never mentioned.

A similar ambivalence can be seen in the religion of the founding fathers. The famous cannabis farmer George Washington* was happy to talk about providence but avoided getting any more specific. Benjamin Franklin was a typical product of the Enlightenment. As an old man he said he would find out the truth about Jesus when he died. Thomas Jefferson spent his spare time cutting out all the

---

* In his diary for 12–13 May 1765 he records that he 'sowed hemp at Muddy Hole by swamp'.

miracles from the Gospels and compiling a scrapbook of Jesus' moral teachings.

Revolting French

Britain had had the Glorious Revolution. America had had its revolution against the English. France was feeling left out.

There was widespread famine. The land was ruled by an arrogant, unfeeling aristocracy. You could be sentenced to death for making your own salt. The church owned – scandalously – up to one fifth of France. Small wonder there were mobs on the street. Its parliament hadn't met for, oh, about 200 years. In the end Louis XVI ran out of cash and the inevitable happened: the commoners took over. They declared the Rights of Man, they abolished tithes – the tax paid to the church – and they confiscated all church property. The monasteries were closed and it was declared that from then on the clergy would be elected by the people.

Parliament started abolishing things, including slavery, the church, King Louis XVI (he was beheaded) and God. Christianity was replaced by a new shiny Cult of Reason. Churches were ransacked and turned into Temples of Reason. Crosses were removed from graveyards, whose gates now bore the cheery inscription: 'Death is an eternal sleep'. The altar of the cathedral of Notre Dame was replaced with an altar to Liberty. Saints' days were scrapped and replaced with fruit, vegetable and flower days. (It shows that whatever else about church you annul, the flower arrangers will always survive.) The old sabbatarian seven day system was decimalised: weeks now consisted of ten days.

It was the first full-scale state-wide attack on the church in Europe since the days of the Roman Empire. But the madness was everywhere. There was a reign of terror, when thousands of suspected counter-revolutionaries were summarily executed. As stability and security collapsed inside the regime, they tried to focus on enemies outside, declaring war and invading Belgium and Holland.

This war saw the rise of a small man from Corsica. The up-and-coming general Napoleon Bonaparte led the army to victories in Italy, even capturing Rome and the pope himself. In 1799 he returned to Paris and staged a coup, disbanding parliament and declaring himself emperor.

Napoleon worshipped, but only when he looked in a mirror. He was the hero of his own story and the only object worthy of his own veneration. But he banned the Cult of Reason and cut a deal with Pope Pius VII. If the church approved of Napoleon's regime, he would restore the property and prestige that had been lost during the French Revolution. Pius agreed and, in 1804, travelled to Paris, where he was supposed to crown Napoleon Emperor. It was the Holy Roman Empire™ all over again (although that was finally closed down the same year, when the last emperor was persuaded to relinquish the title and became just the Emperor of Austria). In the event, the pope was humiliated. At the last moment Napoleon took the crown from the pope's hands and crowned himself. There was, after all, only one man in the world good enough to crown Napoleon, and that was Napoleon.

Napoleon was finally defeated in 1815 by the general they named the boots after. Wellington. Or possibly Doc Marten. One of the two.

So the Catholic church was back. And they got back the Papal States (which Napoleon had confiscated). The Jesuits returned as well. And, indeed, the middle ages generally, because the next Pope along put all the Jews back in the ghettos. It was just like the good old days.

THINGS YOU LEARN FROM CHRISTIAN HISTORY

NO.11

Just because you shout louder, doesn't mean you're right

Fundamentalism was a response to criticism. As was papal infallibility. But just saying something firmly and in a loud, determined voice doesn't change reality.

11 Mormons, Missionaries and Monkeys

Waiting for rapture

America provided a place where Separatists could be free to dream their dreams and create their ideal societies. When a teacher and spiritual leader called Johann Georg Rapp (1757–1847) was expelled from the German Duchy of Württemberg in 1805, he and 800 followers made their way to America – or, as Rapp called it, the 'land of Israel'. There, known as the Harmonites, they set up three model communities, named Harmony, New Harmony and Economy. These were attempts to build the New Jerusalem in Pennsylvania and Indiana.

Similar communities were established by the Shakers, a community that lived a simple lifestyle of shared possessions, celibacy, worship and fabulously beautiful furniture. They were led by a woman, the charismatic 'Mother' Ann Lee. They emigrated to America in the late eighteenth century and built up more than twenty settlements, attracting over 20,000 converts during the next century. Their name was yet another nickname: from 'shaking Quakers', a dismissive description of their ecstatic worship.

The communities were celibate for the same reason that the apostle Paul advocated celibacy: the end was nigh. The Harmonites even made specific predictions. Rapp believed that Napoleon was the Antichrist and that Jesus Christ would return on 15 September 1829. When Jesus rescheduled and failed even to leave a message, a third of their members left.

There was discord among the Harmonites but elsewhere, in a remote farming community in Vermont, William Miller (1782–1849) pored over his King James Bible and discovered the truth: the second coming would happen on 22 October 1843. When the date came and nothing happened, he recalculated and announced that it was due in 1844. He and his followers gathered in the desert and . . . nothing happened. The non-event was given the rather depressing title of 'the Great Disappointment'.

Miller returned to Vermont to work out what had gone wrong. He took with him a better abacus and a group of true believers in the advent of Christ, including a visionary teenage prophetess called Ellen G. Harmon. Her two thousand visions and keen fondness for vegetables and roughage formed the basis of a new movement, the Seventh-Day Adventists. They celebrated the Sabbath on Saturday, as the Jews did. And one of their benefactors was a man called Dr Kellogg, who put Ellen's ideas on roughage into practical and profitable form.

They proved to be a fractal denomination of endlessly splintering subsets. One Millerite group was the Jehovah's Witnesses: pacifists who predicted that the war of Armageddon would start in 1914. What happened in 1914 certainly had some Revelation-like qualities, but it was not the end of the world. Then they moved the date to 1925, then 1975, then . . . well, you get the idea.

Second comings are like buses. There will always be another one due in a minute.

The Plymouth Brethren began in Dublin sometime around 1828. They had a touch of the Quakers about them, rejecting all church traditions and employing no leaders. Everyone was allowed to preach and administer the sacraments. (Apart from women, obviously.) One of the leaders of the Brethren was John Nelson Darby (1800–1882), a former Anglican who developed a growing interest – you might say an obsession – with Revelation and the idea of the end times. He invented two theories. The first was based on Matthew 24.36–44, where Jesus describes his return and how one man would be whisked away, while another would be left behind. Unable to read the passage in any way other than literally, Darby came up with the idea of the Rapture, where on Christ's return believers would be suddenly lifted up. Christ would then rule the earth for 1,000 years from his base in Israel.

This is, of course, our old chum: the millennium. Having failed to turn up for its own party in 1000, and then in 1030, and then in 1666, apocalypse-obsessives began ever more tortuous and detailed analyses of Revelation to work out what was going on. Or wasn't going on. Naturally, they splintered into many different groups, but there were two main strands of interpretation. Darby's came to be called 'premillennial' from the idea that Christ's return would *precede* the millennium.

The opposing view, based on earlier interpretations, but which was held by Jonathan Edwards among others, was that the second coming of Jesus Christ would arrive after the thousand-year golden age, rule of the saints. This is known as 'post-millennial'.

Another core idea of these groups was dispensationalism: the idea that God had divided human history into dispensations – historical eras – of different kinds of divine activity. So there was the period of law in the Old Testament, followed by the era of grace. In the period of dispensation marked 'end times' there would be great tribulations, cataclysmic battles between good and evil, and at the end Christ would come riding in like the cavalry, to defeat Satan and establish the New Jerusalem.

Darby's ideas are still very much in evidence. Just try typing the word 'rapture' into Google.* The habit of predicting the end of the world is as popular – and as wrong – as ever. And the one thing all these groups have in common is that they have all been proved wrong.

The Book of Mormon

Perhaps the strangest mutation of apocalyptic thought is British and American Israelitism, which identified Britain and the USA as the lost tribes of Israel. The British Israelites believed that the British monarch was descended from King David and the coronation stone in Westminster Abbey is actually the same stone on which Jacob laid his head when he saw his famous ladder.†

It's batty. But it wasn't a new idea. There was something about America that reminded people of the Promised Land. The early Puritans believed they were building a holy kingdom: 'We shall be as a City upon a Hill, the eyes of all people are upon us,' wrote the Puritan John Winthrop.

* Actually, don't.
† Their founder, Edward Hine, predicted that Britain would never fight a war with Germany. And also that the two nations would always preserve a strict Sabbath. So far not only have we fought Germany twice, but every Sunday we shop at Aldi and Lidl.

The imagery of the Promised Land filled their rhetoric. The Separatists identified with the ancient Hebrews. The New World was the New Canaan. George Washington was the 'American Joshua'. When it came to designing the nation's new Great Seal, Benjamin Franklin wanted a picture of Moses dividing the Red Sea, while Thomas Jefferson proposed the Pillars of Fire and Smoke. If they were the new Israel, then the Native Americans were the Canaanites: God had given the land to his people – now the chosen had to drive the enemy out.

Among those who took this idea to extremes was a man called Joseph Smith, who had a visit from a Native American. A Jewish Native American. A *dead* Jewish Native American. The spirit, whose name was Moroni, returned from the dead to tell Smith that the Native Americans were really the lost tribes of Israel, who had come to America in 600 BC. Smith translated history using a pair of magic spectacles and the result was the Book of Mormon (the name of Moroni's father). Smith and his followers moved west, where he announced that polygamy was allowed and declared himself a candidate in the 1844 presidential election. When a local newspaper published an exposé of Smith, he organised a bunch of disciples to shut it down by force. This angered the governor, who sent in the troops and arrested Smith and his brother. On the night of 27 June 1844 an armed mob stormed the jail and shot them dead. Whether it was because of the newspaper, or because Smith had nicked all the women, isn't clear.

These were just a few of the many new denominations, sects and brands of Christianity available in the Land of the Free®.* The increasing emphasis on personal conversion, being born again, brought opposition in the mainstream churches. But the American dream, people's gung-ho 'you can do it' philosophy, meant that instead of submitting to authority, people just headed off to start their own church. There was something for everybody.

---

* Small print: full membership of Land of the Free® does not include slaves. Or Native Americans. Terms and conditions may apply.

Let my people go

Not everyone welcomed American independence. When the British withdrew from Georgia, a man called George Lisle (1750–1820) decided to go with them. It wasn't that he wasn't keen on liberty. On the contrary, going with the Brits was the only way he could be sure of staying free. Because George was an ex-slave. And he figured that if he stayed in the American south he would be taken back into slavery.

George had been freed by his Baptist master, Henry Sharp, who had recognised George's gift of preaching. After his release, he and his family spent time in Savannah, Georgia, where he helped lead a Baptist congregation. In 1780 he went to Jamaica with his wife and four children. He was the first black missionary. His preaching gathered many followers and he was able to found a church of some 350 people – including some white attendees. He was helped financially by British supporters. But the British authorities in Jamaica were not quite so keen: they kept a close eye on him and censored his sermons and even his prayers.

The liberation of America was not extended to its slaves, who were almost universally regarded as a subhuman species. Indeed, there were questions asked as to whether they were even worthy of baptism. Admittedly, there was that bit in Paul about there being no difference between slave and free, but you could get round that by reading it really quickly and hoping no one would notice.

One would expect that people kept in such a situation would reject everything about their oppressors. But one of the amazing things about Christian history is that the slaves adopted the faith of the white men. They co-opted it; subverted it. They looked into the Bible and saw the real story: a story of Exodus, of powerful overlords brought down and a nation released from slavery. They turned these stories of release into songs – 'spirituals' – that used biblical code language to share their hopes that, one day, they would be released.

Fig. XXXVI. *Slaves in the plantations realise something is wrong*

In 1800 the slaves revolted in Virginia, led by a blacksmith called Gabriel (1776–1800). He and twenty-five followers were hanged. In reaction Virginia and other state legislatures passed repressive new laws, which prohibited the education of slaves and curtailed their rights of assembly and free speech. You can see why they were worried: around 40 per cent of the population of Virginia were slaves at the time. Gabriel had ordered his followers not to kill any Methodists or Quakers, both of which groups were vocal in their opposition to slavery.

Thirty years later a slave called Nat Turner led a slave revolt that killed 60 whites. He was captured and hanged, along with at least another 100 blacks during the uprising, with many more killed or beaten during the mob reprisals that followed. What was interesting about Nat was that he was a devout Christian. He was often seen reading his Bible, and he experienced visions that he believed were messages from God. He also led Baptist services among his fellow-slaves.

Services were generally seen as ways of controlling the slaves, endorsing the status quo and preaching the virtues of obedience – but this approach was dangerously double-edged. And many Christians were involved in helping slaves to escape. One of the best-known escape routes was via the so-called Underground Railroad, a resistance movement and network of safe houses by which slaves from the south could find their way to northern free states or to Canada.

By 1860, according to the US census, there were nearly four million slaves in service. In the end it took the bloodshed and horror of the American Civil War to bring an end to slavery in the USA. Suddenly, over a third of the population of the southern states of the Union, previously enslaved, were set free. Their reward was lives of poverty, unemployment and ongoing racial segregation.

Oxford movements

Christianity was booming in America. Back in Blighty, though, some people thought that the church was in a bad way. In 1833 John Keble, an Oxford academic, preached a sermon accusing Britain of becoming an ex-Christian nation. He was worried that the church had gone too far in the direction of Wesley and all those Nonconformist bods. What he wanted was more bishops, a stronger, more authoritarian church hierarchy, and the return of the doctrine of transubstantiation. Catholicism, in other words. He and his friend Newman wrote a series of tracts, culminating in 1841 with the imaginatively named Tract 90, a piece of revisionist theology which argued that the Thirty-Nine Articles of the Church of England were, in fact, perfectly in agreement with the Roman Catholic council of Trent. It was all a dream . . .

It was known as the Oxford Movement.* Inevitably, a lot of other Anglicans disagreed; so in 1845 Newman, along with a few hundred of his followers, packed his chasuble, left the Church of England and joined the Catholics. But others who thought similarly stayed within Anglicanism, where they established the Anglo-Catholic party. Which was quite like the Protestant party, except you got to wear nicer frocks.

Tractarians were big in leafy Oxford, but not so much in grimy Oldham. In northern Britain the Industrial Revolution was now in full swing. Britain was the world leader in manufacturing. Not to mention its status as world leader in industrialised misery, slum landlords and rickets.

---

* The other name was Tractarianism, from all those tracts they kept pushing out.

Fig. XXXVII. *In Lambeth Palace, the Archbishop of Canterbury shows a basic misunderstanding of Anglicanism*

Critical Germans and depressed Danes

In 1835 a German theologian called D. F. Strauss published *The Life of Jesus*. The book argued that the Gospel stories were not lies in the sense that Reimarus had stated, but were 'myths' – that is, fictions that in a symbolic way speak of the true meaning of Jesus. They were not historical facts, but reworkings of Old Testament stories to show how he fulfilled the Jewish hopes.

Strauss had studied at Tübingen University, where his professor, F. C. Baur, was also looking hyper-critically at the Gospel accounts. He came from a different direction. Noting the argument in the early church between Paul and Peter, he deduced that these must be representative of two opposing factions within the early church: the Jewish and Gentile groupings. And more: since only four of Paul's letters mention the argument, he concluded that the rest were forgeries. It's not a theory that is taken seriously today and it falls down on a number of points (such as there not being a shred of proof for any of it) but what it did was kick off a way of looking at the New Testament that is still prevalent today.

Other scholars brought a much more 'hands-on' approach to their research. Constantin von Tischendorf (1815–74) was the Indiana Jones of Bible manuscript studies. Having published a new edition of the Greek New Testament when he was just twenty-seven, he then deciphered the previously impenetrable manuscript Codex Ephraemi using nothing but his naked eyes. He was acclaimed as the world's greatest palaeographer.

Then, in 1844, he went on a hunt for rare manuscripts to the remote monastery of St Catherine on Mount Sinai. Inside he found a time capsule: a living relic of Byzantine monastic practices from the time of Justinian. There were twenty-two chapels; there were Byzantine mosaics; there was a mausoleum guarded by the Stephanos, the monastery caretaker. (Rather inconveniently, he had died some 1,100 years before, but they left his skeleton in place. After all, he had never *actually* resigned.)

And he found what turned out to be the world's oldest complete manuscript of the Bible. It took many years, several visits and heavyweight backing from the Czar, to persuade the monks to part with it. And to this day there are still arguments over whether Tischendorf borrowed or purchased it. But Codex Sinaiticus – written between 325 and 360 – has proved to be one of the most valuable manuscripts for establishing the original text of the Greek New Testament.*

The American explorer Edward Robinson travelled throughout Palestine, mapping hundreds of ancient biblical sites, as well as discovering the remains of Hezekiah's tunnel in Jerusalem. In 1868 a German missionary discovered the Moabite Stone – a monument carved with the oldest Hebrew script known, commemorating the defeat of Israel by Mesha, king of Moab. In Mesopotamia thousands of cuneiform tablets were discovered in the abandoned libraries of long-forgotten emperors. And two British archaeologists, Grenfell and Hunt, found a treasure trove of papyrus fragments – wills, receipts, letters, accounts – the kind of writing that opened up the world of ordinary Greek-speaking people from the time of the New Testament.

Meanwhile in Denmark, Søren Kierkegaard (1813–1855) was very gløømy. Lots of people were, are and always have been gløømy in Denmark; it's that kind of place, but Søren took gløøminess to a whole new level. He was particularly upset about the way that a liberal, complacent Christianity had taken all the really serious stuff out: sin and salvation and the fear of God.

---

* The Bolsheviks sold it in 1917 and today it is in the British Museum. Well, most of it. Some bits are still in Sinai and elsewhere. But you can view the complete version online.

He was sick of this abstract thinking, and sick of everyone demanding evidence. Humans had to be weaned from their insistence on 'visible evidence'. Instead, it was all about the faith of the individual. 'Science and scholarship want to teach that becoming objective is the way. Christianity teaches that the way is to become subjective, to become a subject.'

All this stuff about what is objectively true, or what is rational, is mere footling. In his journal he wrote that 'the thing is to understand myself, to see what God really wishes me to do: the thing is to find a truth which is true for me, to find the idea for which I can live and die'.

Had he been French, and born a hundred years later, he would have sat in cafés smoking Gauloises and wearing black polo neck jumpers and shrugging a lot. But as it was, he was Danish, so he was just assumed to be a bit bonkers. And he died without anyone realising that he'd invented existentialism.

Exterminate all the brutes

Britain had lost America, but elsewhere it was business as usual. And 'business' was the word. The empire was driven by commercial interests and huge companies – like the East India Company in Asia or the Van Diemen's Land Company in Tasmania. Some missionary work brought the missionaries into conflict with these interests. The famous explorer David Livingstone (1813–73) was sponsored by the London Missionary Society. He was a tireless advocate for the rights of the African natives – a message that did not go down well with the commercial and state interests that were seeking to exploit these huge new territories.

The Far East was opening up as well. Another London Missionary Society worker was Robert Morrison (1782–1834), a Scottish Presbyterian who was sent to China by the London Missionary Society in 1807. Like Carey he was not welcomed by the British East India Company, nor, indeed, by imperial China. It was hard work: it took him seven years before he reported a single baptism.

Fifty years later Japan was prised open. The country had been closed to foreigners for 200 years. In 1857 America used its powers of persuasion (an enormous gunboat parked in the harbour) to persuade the

Fig. XXXVIII. *Stanley finally meets Livingstone*

country to open up to foreign trade. And when French missionaries managed to enter the country they discovered that there was still a church there. The Catholics who had gone underground two centuries before had survived in hidden churches dating back to the time of Francis Xavier. The French missionaries immediately pointed out to these plucky survivors everything that they were doing wrong, thus splitting the church straight away. Not only that but the Japanese suddenly became aware of the Christians' presence, and exiled some 40,000 of them, thus making this the least successful missionary visit ever.

Africa had been parcelled up between the European nations, and the missionaries usually arrived on the same ships as the colonial administrators and the merchants. Some of them became little more than chaplains to the imperialist forces, the nineteenth-century Protestant equivalents of the Catholic priests in Spanish and Portuguese South America.

It was not that they weren't sincere. They believed utterly that they were saving souls. Nor is it that they did not bring benefits to the regions they served. There are plenty of examples then, as now, of hospitals and schools being built. But the issue often was that for them the ascendancy of spiritual concerns obscured their vision on worldly issues, that spreading the good news in the colonies required turning a blind eye to the activities of the colonial powers.

Every colonial power has its skeletons in the cupboard. When Britain colonised Australia, the Van Diemen's Land Company took over the running of Tasmania. Many of the natives were slaughtered. By 1820 the local press of the settlers was demanding that the natives should be relocated, and if they refused they should be 'hunted down like wild beasts and destroyed'. In 1829 the government let loose British prisoners to hunt down natives and bring them into an 'assembly' camp. It is estimated that for every native who made it to the camp, nine were killed out in the bush. By 1830 there were only three hundred Tasmanians left.

Perhaps the most notorious cases of cruelty come from the rule of King Leopold II (1835–1909) of Belgium. The Congo was Leopold's personal possession, and his agents exploited the rubber tree plantations with a brutal aggression. If African workers on the plantation didn't work hard enough, they could have their right hand and forearm cut off. Belgians in the Congo killed millions of Africans. Back in Europe people heard rumours of this cruelty, of course, and tried to raise the issues, but Africa was a long way away, and anyway these people were inferior races.

Science had proved it.

Planet of the apes

In December 1831 a young amateur naturalist went on a journey. Before the voyage he was supposed to have been embarking on a career in the church. Instead, he embarked on a boat called the *Beagle* and went to the Galapagos Islands. And when he returned, with notebooks stuffed with drawings and a head stuffed with ideas, he had invented evolution.

Charles Darwin (1809–1882) returned from the Galapagos Islands in 1836. But it wasn't until 1859 that he published his landmark book *On the Origin of Species*. In between the two events there had been other notable scientific discoveries that had rocked the Christian world. The discovery of fossils, for example, put a serious crimp in the whole 'the universe was created in six days' theory.

But it was *On the Origin of Species* that really put the cat among the finches. Darwin showed how finches on different islands were almost but not quite the same as each other – and that they had adapted to their various environments. From that, he developed the idea of survival of the fittest. Animals were not, in his theory, created as one-offs by God: they adapted, mutated and changed through natural selection. He followed this up with *The Descent of Man*, in which he put forward the idea of evolution. Humanity had evolved from the apes.

It was, on the face of it, a massive challenge to the traditional doctrines of the church. If there were no Adam and Eve, then what did that make of Genesis? And what happens to doctrines such as the creation of the universe and the fall of humans?

Many Christians simply embraced the theory. They saw God at work through evolution. Genesis was a story that told a deep truth, but it was not a scientific thesis. Others, however, reacted more angrily. There was a famous debate between Bishop Samuel Wilberforce and the Darwinist Thomas Huxley (1825–95). (Darwin didn't want to take part.) Huxley wrote that 'the historical trustworthiness of the Jewish scriptures' meant that the foundations of Christianity were built upon 'legendary quicksands'. The debate itself was not quite the knock-down victory it is often portrayed to be; Darwin himself thought Wilberforce's scientific counter-arguments 'uncommonly clever'. But it did give the impression of a church that hadn't quite grasped the issues and was on the defensive.

In 1869 Huxley – who possessed some of the finest sideburns ever seen – coined a word to describe his own faith, or lack of it: agnosticism. It was not an outright disbelief, just an intellectual shrug, a not-knowing.

The church went on the defensive; it began to retrench, to batten down the hatches. It not only affirmed the Bible as inerrant; it set its dogma in stone as well. It was at the First Vatican Council of 1870, for example, that the doctrine of papal infallibility was formally defined.

And Darwinism had its dark side, in the sense that it became possible to talk, quite openly, about lesser species. Darwin himself had seen that in action: on his return journey he had stopped in Tasmania and seen what his countrymen had done to the natives. By the time *On the Origin of Species* was published there were only nine Tasmanian women left, all of them too old to bear children. Survival of the fittest led to extinction: and if some tribes, some peoples, were being wiped out . . . well, what can we say? It's a jungle out there.

Fig. XXXIX. *Darwin was always at work*

Workers of the world unite

The Industrial Revolution made many people wealthy and brought to the known world the benefits of railways, cotton mills and tuberculosis.

Some people got very wealthy indeed. Others, largely those who did the actual work, lived in dire poverty and terrible working conditions. Christians tried to address this. The great Quaker families – Cadburys, Rowntrees, Terrys and Frys – all worked within the confectionery industry. They built model factories for their workers, provided them with excellent housing and introduced schools and even leisure facilities and, probably, ruined their teeth for ever.

But they were the exceptions. And as a result there was a steadily growing undercurrent of unrest among the working class.

In 1844 a German called Friedrich Engels described their plight in *The Condition of the Working Class in England*. He wrote of slum conditions, lack of sanitation, families of eight or ten sharing a single room. Three years later he and his friend, the German economist and philosopher Karl Marx, took over a socialist organisation called the League of the Just.* They rebranded it as the League of Communists and the following year collaborated on the *Communist Manifesto*, which called on workers to revolt and seize the means of production. Marx dismissed religion as a drug – an opium of the people, keeping them placid and easily controlled.

The Communism that eventually emerged from Marx's writing was hostile to Christianity. But there were many socialists who combined both radical political beliefs and their faith. The result was Christian socialism: many of the leaders of the labour movement in Britain came from the Nonconformist chapels and the dissenting churches.

The plight of the urban working class was of particular concern to a Methodist minister called William Booth (1829–1912). He formed the Salvation Army – a kind of uniformed Christianity. It was teetotal: Booth saw alcohol as one of the great problems of the urban life. The Army reached out to people who were left behind by the mainstream denominations. It became a movement known for its commitment to social welfare. The movement embraced innovation. 'Does it signify by what novel and extraordinary methods we get hold of drunkards, wife-beaters, cut-throats, burglars and murderers so that we do get them?' they asked. So they formed bands, wrote new lyrics to popular songs, toured the pubs. The Salvation Army are now such a part of our social fabric that it is hard to realise just how radical – and how persecuted – they were when they started. In 1844 alone, 600 Army preachers were jailed, and many more ordinary members assaulted.

Booth was not an easy man to work with. He was dictatorial and had a medieval popelike love of appointing his family to official positions. The philanthropist, politician and evangelist Lord Shaftesbury even went so far as to describe Booth as the 'Anti-Christ'. But much of the antagonism was based on a misunderstanding of what the Sally

---

* Later becoming the famous superhero group the Justice League, whose members include Superman, Batman, Wonder Woman and Dialectical Materialism Boy.

Army was all about, and when he died – 'promoted to glory' as the Army called it – forty thousand people attended his funeral service, including Queen Mary, who crept in and sat, almost unrecognised, at the back.

Nearly infallible

The year 1848 was a good year for revolutions: they popped up in France, Germany, Czechoslovakia, Ireland and Italy, forcing Pope Pius IX (1792–1878) to flee Rome disguised as a woman.

Maybe dressing up as a woman gave Pius ideas. In 1854 he issued a papal bull declaring the doctrine of the Immaculate Conception, the idea that the Virgin Mary was 'from the first moment of her conception . . . preserved free from every stain of original sin'. The doctrine hadn't been mentioned before the 12th century and heavyweight critics like Bernard of Clairvaux and Aquinas had dismissed it. But the Pope was the one wearing the trousers. Or the trouser suit, anyway.

For centuries Italy had been a patchwork of separate states; now they had come together to fight for independence from their Austrian masters and for unification into Italy. This was opposed by the pope on the grounds that he didn't want to lose any of his lands. And when I say 'opposed', I mean opposed. He recruited an army, which was enlarged by the addition of Catholics from across Europe. And in 1860 they marched into battle. And lost. Italy united, and it took its revenge. The pope lost all the Papal States and was left with just Rome. This was bad news for the pope, but good news for all the Jews, who no longer had to live in the papally endorsed ghettos.

Pius IX holed up in Rome and four years later published his *Syllabus of Errors*, a bullet-point list of everything that he considered anti-Christian. It included republicanism, democracy, the separation of church and state, and liberalism. He outlawed any Catholic movements for political reform and even ordered Italian Catholics not to vote.

In 1869, after he'd spent a decade as a 'prisoner' in Rome, he called a council. The First Vatican Council was the first ecumenical council for 300 years. The council declared that when speaking about faith and morals 'in the exercise of his office as pastor and teacher of all Christians', the pope was 'infallible'. A sizeable minority of those attending opposed the idea on the basis of . . . well, the entire history of the papacy, to be honest, but in the end the doctrine was voted through.

Diplomatically, all but two of those opposing decided not to attend the final vote, on the grounds of having some 'really quite important other things to do'. Some of them even formed a splinter church: the Old Catholics.*

Pius worked on the principle that if you said something with enough certainty and confidence, then reality would be frightened into submission. But reality had other ideas. The pope had been maintained in Rome through the support of the French army. But in 1870 Prussia went to war with France, so the French troops went back to join in the fight. Suddenly, Rome was at the mercy of the newly united Italians. They seized the moment, captured Rome and offered the citizens the chance to vote on whether they wanted to be ruled by the pope or become part of Italy. The Roman citizens, remembering their centuries-long association with the papacy, showed the full extent of their gratitude and appreciation by voting in favour of joining Italy by a margin of 100 to 1.

Über-Darwin

Meanwhile, the Prussians easily beat the French and Bismarck unified Germany. One of those who fought in the Franco-Prussian War was a young philosopher called Friedrich Nietzsche (1844–1900). He went on to become a professor of classical philology aged just twenty-four.† He became the prophet of ultra-Darwinism. Survival of the fittest was his religion. Judaism, he believed, had once been a proper man's faith: one of vigour and conquest with lots of blood everywhere. But Israel was defeated and, instead of accepting their weakness as a sign that they had been out-evolved, their religion changed, to bang on about love and how God was on the side of the poor and the needy and, well, Nietzsche just wanted to shout a great big *Nein*! to that.

And Christianity? That was even worse. It hadn't even bothered to have a brutal conquering phase. Nietzsche despised it and called it 'one

---

* As opposed to the Really Old Catholics, which would be the Greek Orthodox Church.
† Philology is stamp collecting. Probably.

of the most corrupt conceptions of the divine ever attained on earth'.
Here are a few of his cheerier jottings:

What is good? – Whatever augments the feeling of power, the
will to power, power itself, in man.

What is evil? – Whatever springs from weakness.

What is happiness? – The feeling that power increases – that
resistance is overcome . . .

The weak and the botched shall perish: first principle of our charity.
And one should help them to it.

What is more harmful than any vice? – Practical sympathy for the
botched and the weak – Christianity . . .

Nietzsche believed that the essence of life was the will to power. Or
Ze Vill to Power, in the original German. Nature rewards the strong,
not the weak and the botched. He rejected completely Judaeo-Christian
ideas of compassion: his philosophy was red in tooth and claw. And
in the end it devoured him. He spent the last eleven years of his life
insane. But, strangely, it never seemed to occur to him that nature had
simply deselected him.

It is not hard to see in Nietzsche the seeds of the horrors which were
to consume Europe in the twentieth century. Genocide, eugenics, Nazism
– it's all in his dark vision. Once you have decided that some species
are doomed to extinction, it is not hard to make the same conclusions
about races, or individuals. Darwin never dreamed of such a thing, but
others took his ideas to their logical conclusion. Darwinism gave a
scientific authority to ideas of racial superiority. And as European
colonialism spread across the globe it promoted the idea of the fitness
to rule – and to survive – of the white races. It led to genocide.

On 19 January 1864 the Anthropological Society in London arranged
a debate on 'the extinction of the lower races'. During the debate A. R.
Wallace – who co-discovered the theory of evolution with Darwin –
talked about racial extermination as simply another name for natural
selection. This understanding became a core part of colonial theory.

And not just out in the colonies. There was mass murder closer to home too. For eight centuries Armenian Christians had lived under Turkish rule. There were two million of them living in the country. When rebellion broke out in some Armenian towns, they were massacred. Between one hundred and three hundred thousand Armenians lost their lives and many others were forcibly converted to Islam.

Meanwhile, Russia's ancient, creaking feudal system was close to collapse and in 1881 the Czar – the Caesar – was assassinated by anarchists. The rumour spread that the assassins were Jewish (they weren't) and between 1881 and 1884 a wave of persecution was launched against the Jews in Russia. An estimated 20 per cent of all Jews lived in the country, and in 1881 over 200 pogroms were launched against Jewish communities, often supported by the Orthodox Church and carried out with the active participation of the police. Many went to America. A million went to Europe, where they all lived happily ever after . . . er . . . wait, I'll get back to you on that one.

In 1898 Lord Salisbury, the English prime minister, gave a lecture in the Royal Albert Hall. 'One can roughly divide the nations of the world', he said, 'into the living and the dying.'

Armenians. Jews. Were they living or dying?

THINGS YOU LEARN FROM CHRISTIAN HISTORY

NO.12
Nothing is ever really new

Christianity is on a voyage of perpetual rediscovery.

12 Fundamentalism, Fascism and Females

The third blessing

On 31 December 1900 Charles Parham, an itinerant evangelist who had started his own Bible College in Topeka, Kansas, was teaching his students about the book of Acts. They had not got far – just to the bit about being filled with the Holy Spirit at Pentecost. Parham suggested that one of the signs of being filled with the Holy Spirit was the ability to speak in a different language – and he encouraged his students to seek this gift. The next day, a woman called Agnes Ozman started 'speaking in tongues'.

It was 1 January 1901. The first day of the new century.

Others soon joined in. But they weren't speaking any known language. So what was this? Parham concluded that this was the language of heaven – the tongues talked of by Paul in his letter to Corinth. An ecstatic experience that theologians call *glossolalia*. Parham, borrowing a phrase from Acts, called this experience 'baptism in the Holy Spirit'. And, because this was another Pentecost, the movement that it spawned became known as Pentecostalism.

It proved to be the fastest growing type of Christianity ever.* In 1906 in Los Angeles one of Parham's students, an African-American Pentecostal pastor called William Seymour, started prayer meetings for revival at his mixed-race chapel in Azusa Street. Thousands experienced what was now termed 'the third blessing'.† In a forerunner of many of these Pentecostal outbreaks many people visited the church, experienced the blessing and took it back with them to their home church.

---

* Apart from the original one.
† Blessing no. 1 was salvation; blessing no. 2 was sanctification. Not sure what blessing no. 4 is. Possibly it's liturgical dance.

To traditionalists these scenes were alarming. To them the tongues seemed more like possession by the devil, not by the Holy Spirit. Pentecostals responded that if you could not recognise this for what it was, that only showed how spiritually dead you really were.*

The blessing even travelled abroad. Europeans came to America, caught the fire and took it back with them. Especially Scandinavians. Well, they needed something cheerful after Kierkegaard. Pentecostal missionaries were sent out in their hundreds.†

Of course, some took it to extremes. In 1910 in Tennessee a Pentecostal minister, George Hensley, was preaching on the text 'they shall take up snakes' at the end of Mark's Gospel. A literalist, he immediately grabbed hold of a rattlesnake and commanded his flock to prove their holiness by doing the same. Hensley kept on snake handling for forty-five years. In the end he died when a piano fell on him. No, just kidding. He was bitten by a snake, of course.

Nearly infallible (2)

They were reviving in Wales as well. In 1904 the country was engulfed in a national revival. Daily prayer meetings were filled to the brim. Rugby matches were cancelled so that worshippers could attend meetings. This was a period of large-scale evangelism not seen since the days of Wesley and Whitefield.

In fact, it has been estimated that the high point of British church-going was in 1904, when out of a population of thirty million, some four million people went to church every week. From there, though, it was a story of steady decline. The church – not just in Britain, but in Europe generally, was battered on one side by science, and on the other by liberalism and a lack of confidence in the Bible.

The church responded in different ways. Liberals put the emphasis on social action. In fact, even the new pope went all liberal. Well, relatively. In 1891 Pope Leo XIII issued an encyclical, *Rerum Novarum* ('New Stuff'), which supported the rights of workers, rejected both

---

* Things were not helped by the fact that Seymour was (a) black, (b) ran a mixed-race church that emphasised unity in Christ, and (c) supported women in church leadership. Heretic!

† The death toll among Pentecostal missionaries was high, because they trusted so much in the power of healing they didn't bother to get inoculated.

communism and unrestricted capitalism, approved trade unions and called for social justice. In an unprecedented move, *glasnost* came to the Vatican. He opened the Vatican archives, re-founded the Vatican Observatory and was the first Pope to be filmed. He even made friendly overtures to Protestants and the Orthodox.*

Evangelicals, on the other hand, responded to this new changing world by heading bravely into the past. They retreated into fundamentalism, rigid dogmatism and endless statements of faith. Conservative Catholics had the infallible pope; conservative Protestants had the infallible Bible. Evangelicals had, for 150 years, been concerned with social transformation, but now they focused more and more on believing the right things and being born again.

Between 1910 and 1915 a group of rich Americans self-published a twelve-volume collection of essays called *The Fundamentals,* prompted by their dismay at wishy-washy, liberal church pastors. It was a modern church council: but where Catholics and the Orthodox had bishops, Americans had businessmen. Three million copies were printed. Copies were sent to every minister, missionary, Sunday School superintendent and theology student in the USA. Frankly, if you looked holy and wore sandals you got a copy.

Subtitled, 'A Testimony to the Truth', its contents covered everything from 'Is there a God?' (answer: yes) to 'the Decadence of Darwinism'. The conclusions were pretty much what you'd expect: Jesus is God, the virgin birth is true, Jesus died and rose again, and he will return for his 1,000-year reign. Oh, and Popes are Not A Good Thing. Finally, the Bible was declared to be literally, absolutely true and without error.

The believers who grabbed hold of what these volumes espoused were known as Fundamentalists.

Commies. Commies! COMMIES!

Volume 4 of *The Fundamentals* contains an entertaining essay on 'the Church and Socialism', which begins, 'the sudden rise of Socialism

---

* There were limits, though. When a Catholic theologian called Alfred Loisy wrote a book which accepted some of the German Protestant scepticism about the Bible, Leo excommunicated him. Mind you, Loisy also penned the memorable statement: 'Jesus came preaching the kingdom and what arrived was the church.'

is the most surprising and significant movement of the age. A few years ago the term suggested a dream of fanatics; today it embodies the creed and the hope of intelligent millions.'

Two years after this was written, in 1917, there was revolution in Russia. The Czar was deposed in 1917 and the Bolsheviks took over. Communist Russia was an atheist state. Initially, the movement's leader, Lenin, decreed religious toleration, but then, as his brave new world began to fill up with starving old peasants, he didn't want them rallying around the Russian Orthodox Church. So he dismantled it. Church schools were shut, monasteries became army barracks. Atheism was now the faith of Russia. Well, that and terror: in the first five years of the Bolshevik regime, 28 bishops and 1,200 priests were executed.

Fig. XL. *The official photo for the Communist Party was no time for joking*

It was the start of a long period of persecution for the Russian Orthodox Church. During a famine in 1922 the Communists confiscated church treasures for famine relief. Those who refused to hand over church valuables were arrested and executed. Churches were closed and tens of thousands of clergy were shot dead. Various patriarchs were thrown into jail, and replaced by a group of Communist sympathisers called the Renovationists or 'Living Church'.

Women. Women! WOMEN!

Fig. XLI. *A suffragette campaigns for justice*

Socialism wasn't the only disturbance in the social fabric. On 4 June 1913 a Christian called Emily Davison went to the races. As the runners in the Epsom Derby rounded the corner, she rushed out among them, hands raised above her head. She was trampled to death by a horse owned by George Frederick Ernest Albert of Saxe-Coburg and Gotha. Or George V as he was more widely known. She died four days later. Emily probably did not intend to commit suicide. It was more a naive publicity stunt gone wrong. But at her death she was seen as a martyr. Emily was a suffragette. Founded in 1903, the suffragettes campaigned for women's rights. Emily was a committed Christian and a member of the Anglican Church League for Women's Suffrage. In an unpublished essay called 'the Real Christianity' she argued that the teaching of the church was a horrible distortion of Scripture; that when real Christianity happened, men and women would be equal. She likened the persecution of the Suffragettes to that faced by the early church.

The war to end all wars

In 1910 there was a World Missionary Conference, which gathered hundreds of missionaries together and declared the aim of planting in 'every non-Christian nation an undivided church of Christ'.

It was a good dream. And it looked for a moment as though peace and unity might really be possible on a global scale. And then, four years later in Sarajevo, all hell broke loose.

People still argue about what actually caused the First World War. Probably the answer lies in that acute historical analysis of Blackadder: 'The real reason for the whole thing was that it was too much effort not to have a war.' The assassination of the Archduke Ferdinand in Sarajevo set in motion a chain of events that led to millions of deaths.

The horror was worldwide. In Turkey the Christian Armenian community was forcibly deported. The Turks, fearing that the Armenians would fight on behalf of their enemies, drove some two million people out of their homes and into a forced march across the wilderness. About half were killed during the journey.*

There were revolutions. Easter 1916 saw a wartime uprising in Ireland. It was brutally suppressed by the British troops, with the result that, in the election of 1918, Sinn Fein won a record number of seats and immediately declared Irish independence. There was more fighting, and in the end Ireland was divided into the Catholic south and the (mainly) Protestant north. The Irish had a brief civil war over whether to accept the offer, and the pro-division party won. And they all lived happily ever after . . .

The First World War shattered the sense of Victorian optimism. The liberal theory of history – that the world was getting better morally,

---

* The figures are hard to gauge since, even today, Turkey denies the nature and scale of the incident and refuses to term it 'genocide'.

spiritually and economically – was gunned down on the fields of Flanders. But it also added to the disenchantment with traditional religion. Each side in the war had been certain that God was on their side.

Fancy nipping down the church for a quick Eucharist?

For some fifty years the evangelicals had been preaching the virtues of teetotalism, and, indeed, many American states had prohibited alcohol for some time. But in 1919 the Eighteenth Amendment to the US Constitution made it officially illegal to sell or drink alcohol anywhere in the nation. The ban came as a result of a concerted campaign that brought together Catholics, Protestants, Fundamentalists, and probably Zoroastrians for all I know. Even the Southern Baptists got involved, and they were still grumpy about the North's role in the Civil War.

It was a tremendous success. Oh, sorry, no, that was the drink talking. It was a complete failure. Far from making the nation purer, it provoked widespread illegality. Smuggling skyrocketed, there was a massive black market in alcohol and many 'speakeasy' joints sprang up, serving illicit liquor. During prohibition attending mass suddenly became incredibly popular – at least to judge from the production of communion wine, which was exempt from the ban: production rose by 800,000 gallons a year. The ban lasted till 1933, when President Roosevelt declared, 'I think this would be a good time for a beer.'

Evolution was also prohibited. Or at least the teaching of it: in 1925 a politician called W. J. Bryan had persuaded fifteen states to draft legislation banning the teaching of Darwin's theories. So in a stunt organised by some Methodists, a science teacher in Tennessee deliberately taught his class about evolution in order to provoke a court case (and also to boost the local economy with a bit of sensationalist PR). His name was John Scopes, and his trial became a cause célèbre. Everyone went ape over the 'Monkey Trial'. So many people turned up to watch that they had to hold the hearings outside on the lawn. Fans of each side could buy memorabilia: Bibles for one side, little toy monkeys for the other.

It was not exactly unbiased. The judge opened each day's proceedings in prayer and, curiously for a dispute about scientific theory, banned the defence from using any actual science. So the defence simply called W. J. Bryan to the stand, asked him to defend Genesis and tore him to shreds. Scopes was actually convicted, but his conviction was overturned on a technicality in the Tennessee Supreme Court. The law was never actually challenged, W. J. Bryan died of embarrassment and everyone agreed Never to Talk of This Again.

In a way both sides lost. Or, at least, neither side won. Like the Bibles and the monkeys, you pays your money and takes your choice.

Seven hundred and fifty million, Vatican included

After the war women were allowed the vote, and they started their long, hard struggle towards full emancipation. Ahh. Bless.

Having got the vote, there was pressure on the church to allow women ministers. Since the days of the early church – since Montanus and his enthusiastic women, in fact – the role of women had been widely discussed. Mainly by men. By the first half of the twentieth century, many denominations – such as Baptists, Congregationalists and Pentecostals – had allowed them for some time. Not the Church of England, though. For them dresses were still for men.

But the church knew that it had to change. Many denominations started merger talks: Canadian Methodists, Presbyterians and Congregationalists joined up to form the United Church; in India, the Methodists rejoined the Anglicans. The Old Catholics – yes there were still a few around – started sharing communions with the C of E.

Then the pope – Pius XI – offered reunion with both Protestants and Orthodox. With just one tiny condition: that they all became Catholics. When this move wasn't immediately and joyously embraced, he banned Catholics from religious conferences with other Christians. Still, he had his mind on other matters. In 1929 he cut a deal with the Italian authorities. In return for renouncing any claim on the Papal States and the city of Rome, he was given sole rule of the Vatican State – a parcel of land 0.5 km long and containing 700 people. He also got 750 million lire thrown in.

Fig. XLII. *In the Vatican, crowds waiting for mass spot a problem.*

The Italian leader with whom he made this deal was a man called Mussolini.

Dark forces were gathering. In 1924 Lenin died and Stalin started to take over Russia. In 1925 Hitler published *Mein Kampf.*

(Possibly worst of all, in 1926 the *Orgelbewegung*, that is, The Organ Revival Movement, was founded, dedicated to reviving the art of the oldest organs. A terrorist organisation if ever there was one.)

'Positive Christianity'

The clouds were gathering. In 1932 a pipe organ in Atlantic City was revealed with 33,000 pipes, 4 manuals, and a full list of stops, whatever that means. Its claim to be the loudest musical instrument ever constructed, however, can be challenged (a) on the use of the word 'musical', and (b) on the fact that scientists later created Dame Shirley Bassey.

Meanwhile, Germany was in turmoil. When the victors sent in the final invoice for the First World War it came to £11 billion. Today that's the lunch allowance for the European Parliament, but in 1918 it was a massive amount. The result was an economic meltdown. The exchange

409

rate started multiplying faster than a rabbit on Viagra. The country went through eighteen governments in just fifteen years.

In such a situation a firm hand was needed. Unfortunately, the firm hand Germany got was attached to the upraised arm of Adolf Hitler.

The historian Eric Hobsbawm described the twentieth century as 'an era of religious wars, though the most militant and bloodthirsty religions were secular ideologies of nineteenth-century vintage'. Hitler's religion was that of the prophet Nietzsche: the religion of racial purity, Ze Vill to Power, the declaration of perpetual war and the crushing of lesser breeds.

Hitler came to power in 1933. He quickly instituted measures against the Jews, banning them from holding state office or teaching in schools. In this he was backed by large sections of the church, particularly a group of Fascists who called themselves 'German Christians'. They wanted to purge the church of Jewish practices, like saying 'Amen' and 'Hallelujah'. They sacked anyone married to a Jew (thus technically outlawing Peter and James, among others).

The German Christians adopted a kind of Nazi theology which claimed that Jesus was a true Aryan whose ideas had been corrupted by that fiendish Jew 'Rabbi' Paul of Tarsus. This was called 'Positive Christianity'. Standing against this were Christians like the Lutheran pastor Martin Niemöller, and the theologian Karl Barth, who formed an organisation called the Confessing Church.

Barth (1886–1968) was the moving force behind the Barmen declaration, which attacked the German Christians and rejected any subordination of the church to the state. The church is 'solely Christ's property'. The declaration ended with a promise: 'therefore, Fear not, little flock, for it is your Father's good pleasure to give you the kingdom'. Barth personally mailed a copy to Hitler.

He was sacked from his professorship at the University of Bonn in 1935 for refusing to swear an oath of allegiance. The same year, Hitler passed the Nuremberg laws, prohibiting Jews from marrying an Aryan or being a German citizen. He was supported by the Archbishop of Freiburg, who said that 'No one should be prohibited from safeguarding the purity of their race.'

Hitler was not a Christian in any shape or form. He used the church cleverly, and manipulated the stupidity and greed and complacency of its leaders. But he despised the 'Jewish religion' and derided the notion of turning the other cheek as a 'Jewish doctrine'.

Red dawn rising

As in Nazi Germany, so in Stalinist Russia. In the 1930s Stalin launched an all-out assault on the Orthodox Church. Over 57,000 churches had been active in 1914; by 1941 there were around 4,250 left. Only 30 of the estimated 1,500 convents and monasteries remained open. The church was driven underground. Many Orthodox priests died in Stalin's labour camps. Stalin launched a re-education campaign, with museums and university departments dedicated to the teaching of atheism.

In Italy Mussolini was in power. And in Spain there was civil war, which was won by the fascists. During this war Communist soldiers killed 8,000 Catholic clergy.

No, this is the war to end all wars

By now most people knew that war was returning to Europe, but few people wanted to admit it.

Hitler had made an agreement with the Vatican, but carried on dismembering the church. In the end Pope Pius XI issued an encyclical, *Mit brennender Sorge*, which condemned Nazi ideology. The only papal encyclical ever to be written in German, copies had to be smuggled into the country so that it could be read in the churches.

In the early hours of 10 November 1938 the Nazis unleashed a wave of destruction against Jewish shops, homes, schools and synagogues. The attacks left the streets covered with so much broken glass it became known as Kristallnacht. It was also Martin Luther's three hundred and fifty-fifth birthday. From then on Jews were banned from driving, owning businesses, going to school or even visiting the cinema. They had to wear a yellow star to identify them. Later, the Nazis revived another longstanding Christian tradition by cramming Jews into ghettos.

Hardly any German church leaders spoke out against Hitler, except when he tried to impose euthanasia on Germans. Other church leaders remained quiet as well. Pius XI died in 1939 and his successor, Pius XII, said nothing. One of the first things Pius XII did was suppress a draft encyclical prepared by his predecessor that would have condemned all racism. Even after the war, when many church leaders admitted their guilty silence or how little they had spoken out, Pope Pius said nothing.

411

One of those who did stand against Hitler was Dietrich Bonhoeffer (1906–45), perhaps the only Lutheran pacifist spy. Bonhoeffer, best known for his 1937 book *The Cost of Discipleship*, believed that churches had diluted the demands of discipleship to the point where it was simply too easy, too respectable. What was needed, he believed, was a return to 'costly grace', a willingness to follow Jesus Christ, even if 'it costs a man his life'. Bonhoeffer had the chance to escape Germany and teach in New York. But he chose to return to Germany and work on behalf of (a) the Confessing Church, and (b) the resistance. He was recruited by the Abwehr – German Military Intelligence – but this was a cover for anti-Hitler activities and his courier work for the German resistance movement. He was arrested by the Gestapo in 1943, who suspected him (rightly) of knowing about plots to assassinate Hitler. Two years later he was hanged.

Two horrors marked the ending of the war.

In August 1945 the USA dropped two atom bombs on Japan. Oppenheimer, one of the scientists whose work made the destruction possible, looked on at a test bombing and quoted a line from the Hindu Bhagavad Gita: 'I am become Death, the shatterer of worlds.' What more was there to say? Humanity had achieved godlike powers of destruction.

Seven months earlier, in January, Soviet troops liberated the Auschwitz extermination camp in Poland. It was later discovered that 1.3 million people died there, 90 per cent of them Jewish. As the Allies liberated Europe they discovered more camps – Concentration Camps, Forced Labour Camps and the Death Camps. Millions of people had been killed in these places: Christians, Socialists, Communists, Homosexuals, Gypsies, Prisoners of War – but mainly Jews.

During the Second World War six million Jews were systematically killed. For Judaism it was incomprehensible. How could God abandon them this way? Where was he? For Christians it raised horrible spectres of the past. Individual Christians had acted heroically, but the church as a whole had done little to stop it. Nourished by Nietzsche's über-Darwinism, Nazism took anti-Semitism to a new level. But there was plenty of precedent on a much smaller scale in previous Christian attitudes towards the Jews. It was time for Christianity to renounce anti-Semitism permanently.

Behind the Iron Curtain

After the war the Iron Curtain descended across Europe. (Not literally. Obviously. It was mainly barbed wire and wood.) Christians behind the Iron Curtain were harassed, persecuted, jailed and generally silenced.

The western powers, meanwhile, came up with the idea of giving the Jews a place to live: Palestine. The United Nations tried to secure a partition of the country between the Arab inhabitants and the Jewish immigrants who flocked there after the war, but the plan failed and in 1948 the state of Israel was established. And so they all lived happily ever after.

Well, no, of course not. Trouble ever since, really. In trying to solve western guilt, it created a whole new set of problems, because Muslims saw it as an attack on Islam. They attacked the new country, and were repulsed.

And the situation led to confusion in the minds of many Christians as well. 'Christian America', in particular, developed strong ties with Israel. Some forms of conservative Protestantism – historically some of the bitterest enemies of the Jews – became highly supportive of Israel. It's a very odd thing, though, because the support of Zionist Christians is based on a theology that Jews would utterly repudiate: the idea that when all Jews return to Israel, the second coming of Christ will be triggered. It's a literal reading of – what else? – Revelation.

Revelation also contains that stuff about the Antichrist. And after the war two organisations which have frequently themselves been identified as the Antichrist – at least by sundry and various nutters – were born. The first is the World Council of Churches, which met for the first time in 1948, in Amsterdam. Now this really was an ecumenical council – 147 denominations were represented from around the world. They agreed a basic creed – which boiled down to accepting 'our Lord Jesus Christ as God and Saviour'. In keeping with the councils of old, various churches refused to attend. Some evangelical churches viewed the World Council of Churches as irredeemably liberal. Pope Pius XII stood aloof. He acknowledged its presence but refused to join it. It was like Nicea all over again.

The second organisation was the European Union, which grew out of European trade organisations set up in the 1950s. There are many stories on the internet about the satanic, beastly qualities of the EU, not least that the seat number 666 in the European Parliament is kept vacant, ready for the Antichrist to slip into when he appears. Sadly, it's not true.*

After Stalin died in 1953 Khrushchev took over in the USSR. Relations with the west thawed slightly, but persecution of Christians continued. Christians were imprisoned on any manner of trumped-up charges. Half of the churches were closed again and children were banned from attending the churches that were left. In some cases children were even removed from Christian families for 're-education'.

But there was still a spiritual hunger. In Russia in the 1970s a Bible could command two weeks' wages on the black market. A number of organisations began to smuggle Bibles across the border. Perhaps the most famous of these Bible smugglers is 'Brother Andrew' of Open Doors, who began taking Bibles across the border in 1957. In 1968 he took a van-load of Bibles into Czechoslovakia, at exactly the time when the country was invaded by Soviet tanks. Later, he received a letter from a mother in the Soviet Union which thanked him for 'giving our son a Bible when he was occupying Czechoslovakia'.

Communism spread into the Far East, in Vietnam and Korea. Even where the church was allowed, it was heavily monitored and regulated. In 1949 China became a Communist state under the leadership of Mao Tse-Tung. Immediately all foreign missionaries were expelled. The Chinese church remained optimistic, and hoped to form a new kind of non-western Christianity. But the state had no intention of letting that happen. They arrested hundreds of Chinese priests, closed all the Christian schools and hospitals and what churches remained were subject to strict controls. The real church went underground, into secret house churches. Fifteen years or so later, in 1966, Mao launched the Cultural Revolution, a three-year assault on intellectuals, and, of course, Christians. The handful of official churches were closed. Christians were rounded up and taken away to labour camps. Secret Christians were handed over and killed.

The one exception to all this was South Korea, where Christianity was growing. And after the Second World War Japan became an industrial powerhouse. Churches were free to rebuild, but they remained a small minority.

---

* An insider revealed that at one stage the seat was occupied by an Italian MEP. 'He has a reputation for being a sleazeball, but it's probably a bit of a stretch to call him the Antichrist,' he said.

Black and white

The same year that the World Council of Churches were world-council-of-churching for the first time, the National Party came to power in South Africa.

It introduced apartheid, a system that segregated whites from blacks and 'coloureds' – to this day the only political system based on the instructions on a washing machine. It was Nazism in the sun. The master race were the whites – and they held the power. Interracial marriages were banned (and interracial sex for that matter). The best places, services and jobs were reserved for the whites. And once again it received support from a church: the Dutch Reformed state church endorsed the system and gave it a spurious theological backing. God, they argued, was a God of separation. Look at, er . . . Genesis, where he did all that separating the land from the sky stuff. That shows that he really likes keeping things apart. Then there was the Tower of Babel. And . . . well, there was probably some other stuff as well.

Other churches – in South Africa and around the world – condemned it.

African Christianity, by the way, was growing massively. African nuns made up a third of all nuns in the world. Even in South Africa itself one in three black South Africans was a Christian.

As the years went by South Africa became a more and more oppressive regime. It removed the vote from all non-whites. When unarmed non-violent protestors organised a demonstration in a place called Sharpville, they were massacred. The end came in 1994. After years of negotiations between President de Klerk of South Africa and Nelson Mandela, South Africa had its first multiracial elections. Apartheid was over. There was – and is – a long way to go, but the system had been killed off.

Christians were deeply involved in its demise. Archbishop Desmond Tutu of Capetown, chaired hearings of the Truth and Reconciliation Commission – a process which was more about repentance than revenge. (Among those repenting was the Dutch Reformed Church which finally acknowledged its guilt in supporting apartheid). The anthem of this new South Africa was a hymn written in 1897 by a Methodist schoolteacher with the wonderful name of Enoch Sontonga. Nkosi Sikelel' iAfrika: 'Lord, bless Africa . . . May her glory be lifted high, Hear our petitions, God bless us, Your children!'

Vatican II, Conservatives 0

Britain after the war was a drab, grey land. Rationing was still in place. The workforce had been depleted by the war and so a call went out to the colonies, as it were. Two hundred and fifty thousand immigrants arrived from Jamaica from 1951 onwards, as well as many from other parts of the world, such as India and Africa. Most were Christian. Many went to church, found it either (a) lifeless, (b) boring, (c) racist or (d) all three. So they set up their own churches, the majority of which were Pentecostal.

In 1954 the WCC met again, this time in Illinois. This time they were discussing evangelism, which, they concluded, was A Good Thing. This time the Pentecostal churches attended. Their leader, David du Plessis, prophesied that the Holy Spirit was ready to revisit the 'old' churches, which must have come as a bit of a shock to all those who felt that the Holy Spirit had never actually left them. The WCC affirmed that Pentecostals were actually Christians after all. The pope still didn't turn up.

Four years later Pope Pius XII died. He had been Pope since 1939 and it had been a turbulent time. He was succeeded by an Italian peasant, who became Pope John XXIII. It seemed to be a stop-gap appointment; after all, the new boy was seventy-seven years old. He would presumably just keep things ticking over.

So everyone was rather surprised when he called a second Vatican council and started to rewrite the Catholic faith.

The Second Vatican Council convened in 1962.

At the time it was rather overshadowed by other events, notably the publication of Amazing Fantasy no. 15 (the first appearance of Spiderman), the release of the Beatles' 'Love Me Do', and the Cuban missile crisis.* But once the Russians had backed down and everyone had stopped reading their comics and taken off their Beatles wigs, Vatican II addressed itself to the issue. And the issue was, what should the church be? Pope John addressed the 2,500 participants, and talked of 'a new world order of human relationships'. It was all very new (although the address was in Latin, so not *that* new). The pope died in 1963, by which time the council hadn't really decided anything. But his successor, Pope Paul VI, continued the council and the reformers started to make headway.

---

* One of the pope's first acts was to excommunicate Fidel Castro.

It was the biggest change in Catholicism for hundreds of years. A thousand years, in one instance, because one of the things they did was edit and translate the mass from Latin into ordinary languages. Now children everywhere could be bored in their own language! Priests were instructed to face the congregation. And lay people were allowed both the bread *and* the wine. Catholics were encouraged to read the Bible in translation (they were even allowed Protestant versions). The Index of Forbidden Books was scrapped. Pope Pius IX's *Syllabus of Errors* was rejected as being a bit of an error.

Protestants and Orthodox were referred to in surprisingly warm terms – as 'separated brothers' – and mutterings were made about rectifying the damaging split. Muslims and Jews were also brothers. Everyone was a brother. (This was the sixties after all.) It was, like, really cool man. And, crucially, the Jews were finally, officially, absolved of guilt for the crucifixion. (Although it has to be said that some 250 delegates voted against this amendment.)

Then, like all sixties stars, Pope Paul went on tour. He became the first pope ever to go to Jerusalem, where he even shared communion with the patriarch of Constantinople.

There were still some major sticking points. Vatican II did not rule on marriage between non-Catholics and Catholics. Nor did it say anything about contraception. Paul VI cautiously allowed the first, but issued an outright ban on the second (despite the recommendations of a commission he had set up). Contraception was out. The only form allowed was what became known as the rhythm method. Paul, though, was taken aback by how badly this ruling was received, especially in the west. But then, most white Europeans have never had much rhythm.

On the buses

In 1955 a white man boarded a bus in Montgomery, Alabama. He walked to where a black woman was sitting and demanded her seat. According to the law, the woman – Rosa Parks – was obliged to give up her seat and move to the back of the bus. Rosa refused. She had had enough. And she was arrested.

But Rosa was a Christian and her case ignited a fire in a local Baptist pastor, Dr Martin Luther King (1929–1968). He organised a boycott of the bus company. King had been influenced by Gandhi's non-violent campaign for Indian independence – a campaign which itself had been inspired by Jesus' words in the Sermon on the Mount. And so he began a campaign to bring an end to racial segregation and race laws.

The campaign rapidly gained momentum. In 1963 peaceful protesters, including children, were attacked in Birmingham, Alabama, by armed police officers. There was national outrage. A quarter of a million people marched on Washington, where King gave one of the great speeches of history – a speech drenched in biblical imagery and delivered in the style of a black Pentecostal preacher at full power. The prophet and the people had spoken, and the next year segregation was outlawed in the USA.

Still the police in the south had not given up their use of violence. King led more protests, and there were more assaults. He faced pressure to abandon non-violence, but he refused to back down on his adherence to the principles of the Sermon on the Mount. Non-violence was not weakness: it was a subversive strength. And in the end African-Americans gained the right to use their votes.

In April 1968 Dr King gave one of his most famous speeches to a group of striking sanitation workers in Memphis. Drawing on consciously Old Testament iconography, he spoke like Moses on the mountain top: 'I may not get there with you, but I want you to know tonight, that we, as a people, will get to the promised land.'

The following day he was shot dead.

Hands down, who wants coffee

The 1960s saw new technology, better music, shorter skirts and a much more libertarian view of life. Britain was suddenly in Technicolor. Divorce was readily available. There were different attitudes to homosexuality and abortion. People were more mobile than ever before, leading to societies that were much more mixed and multicultural. Everything was fab and groovy and the church seemed part of a distant, old-fashioned world.

Elsewhere, though, Christianity was growing fast. The 1960s saw the peak years of American churchgoing as well, when 70 per cent of American citizens attended church.

The Pentecostal movement was breaking boundaries. Mainstream churches were being influenced by their style of worship, and also by their expressions of the 'gifts' of the Holy Spirit. Baptists, Methodists and Episcopalians started speaking in tongues, praying for healing. It was the start of a broader charismatic movement within the church. And, in order not to break with long-standing tradition, many of these ministers were expelled from their churches – or at least asked to tone it down a bit.

Soon, though, every major denomination in North America and Europe had its charismatic stream. And the effect was often to bring different denominations together. Charismatic churches from different denominations often found they had more in common with each other than with more traditional churches from their own denomination.

Yet the old divides were still painfully evident in some places. In Northern Ireland atrocities were done under the banner of identification as 'Catholics' or 'Protestants'. None of the people committing these deeds had, in truth, anything to do with Jesus Christ, but those were the labels under which they decided to fight.

Liberators

European Christianity was in decline, but in the lands to which the Europeans had exported Christianity the inhabitants started to make it their own.

In South America they developed liberation theology, which is what happens when you leave poor, oppressed, marginalised people alone with the Bible. The love child of Christianity and Marxism, at its heart was a gospel of freedom and social justice. 'The revolution is not only permitted but is obligatory for Christians' said the Colombian priest Camillo Torres. And, 'If Jesus were alive today, He would be a guerrillero.' Torres was killed in battle in 1966.

The liberationists were sort of like Marxist Wesleyans in that they developed small groups, what they called 'base communities' of believers who studied the Bible and then took action against the forces of oppression: landlords, factory owners, the ruling classes. It was a Peruvian priest, Gustavo Gutiérrez, who gave theological shape to the movement, in his 1971 book *A Theology of Liberation*.

They were distrusted by the hierarchy in Rome. Their opponents claimed that liberation theology was simply secular Marxism with a thin veneer of the Bible. But in Latin America they had some significant representatives among the church leadership. Dom Hélder Câmara (1909–99) was an archbishop who chose to live and dress like one of the poor. Archbishop Oscar Romero of San Salvador preached constantly and heroically against the murder and torture of dissidents. In 1980 he was shot and killed, probably by government death squads. During the rule of various military juntas and dictators, many priests, monks and nuns were also killed. Overall, though, the Vatican made moves to silence these theologians and dismantle the base communities.

This emphasis on social change was worrying – especially to the more conservative and evangelical wings of the church. Evangelicals held their own version of Vatican II in Lausanne, Switzerland, in 1974. Along with a renewed emphasis on the need for evangelism and the authority of Scripture, there was a return to some of their roots in a recognition of the need for social justice. Evangelicalism too was rediscovering its social conscience.

And in the end

Not all of evangelicalism, mind you. The rise of TV meant the rise of televangelists, particularly in the USA, where tub-thumping, money spinning entertainer-evangelists filled the airwaves. The use of mass media was nothing new: early pioneers like the tent-crusading Aimee Semple MacPherson and the Catholic priest Father Charles Coughlin had used radio to great effect. But TV gave them previously unimaginable scale and reach. The first major TV evangelist, Rex Humbard, built a $4 million Cathedral of Tomorrow church in Ohio, specially designed to accommodate the equipment and crew for his weekly TV show – along with a ~~studio audience~~ congregation, of 5,400 people.

They were overtly political. The right-wing demagogue Jerry Falwell claimed that 'Jesus was not a pacifist.' He must have missed that bit in Matthew. Another bit that most of them missed was all that stuff about not having any money, because a lot of these shows peddled a 'health and wealth' prosperity gospel. It was unliberation theology. If you honoured God, he would honour you. And honouring God in this context meant making a donation to whichever shyster happened to be filling the screens at the time. With so much money washing around, scandal was sure to follow. Jim Bakker was revealed to have spent time with a prostitute and was later incarcerated for fraud. Another evangelist, Jimmy Swaggart, was twice caught using the services of prostitutes. The first time he made a much-televised repentance. The second time he told his accusers, 'The Lord told me it's flat none of your business'. The Renaissance popes were alive and well and living in La-La Land.

Another frequent feature of the televangelists' shlock was the idea that we were in the end times, that Christ would return soon.

In 1967 Israel completely defeated Egyptian, Syrian and Jordanian attackers in just six days – the famous Six Day War. It enabled Israeli forces to take control of the West Bank and the entire city of Jerusalem. For the first time since AD 70 the Jewish people were in charge of the city of Jerusalem. But it pushed their Muslim opponents to more extremes. Increasingly, Muslims were drawn to radical teachers who saw that a return to a kind of fundamentalist Islam was the only way to defeat the evil west.

But the strength of Israel, and their effective recapture of Jerusalem, lent fresh impetus to the prophets of the end times. Hal Lindsey published *The Late Great Planet Earth*, which interpreted Revelation and other biblical texts to prophesy that Christ would return 'within forty years or so of 1948'. We're still waiting, sadly.* But the belief that the end is nigh was very strong – and remains so. One man declared that 'Everything is in place for the battle of Armageddon and the second coming of Christ.' That wouldn't have been so worrying had it not come from the mouth of Ronald Reagan, then President of the USA.

Glasnost

Pope John Paul II was the first pope from Poland and the first non-Italian pope since the Reformation. In Poland things were changing. The Solidarity Union was leading protests against the ruling junta. John Paul II made several visits to his homeland, but despite his apparent support, Prime Minister General Jazuzelski crushed the protests and took its leaders into prison.

But these were the first cracks in the façade, the first tiny dents in

---

* And Lindsey is still prophesying. His latest prediction was that Barack Obama is preparing the way for the Antichrist.

the Iron Curtain. The fact was that the Soviet system was bankrupt. Years of corruption and mismanagement had left the USSR close to collapse. When Mikhail Gorbachev became the Soviet leader in 1985, he promised more freedom. The Russian Orthodox Church came in from the cold. The Berlin Wall was torn down. Gorbachev visited the pope. Solidarity came back in Poland. In Romania protests that began in churches led to the fall of the dictator Ceaușescu. The church was back and bigger than ever.

Then, after the horrors of the Cultural Revolution, China started to open up to the west. Cautiously it started to allow Christianity to emerge from hiding, and doing so revealed an astonishing fact. Before Communism about 1 per cent of the population had been Christian. After years of repression that number had risen towards 5 per cent. The church had grown while it was supposed to be in shutdown.

In 1992 revolution came to the Church of England's General Synod when it voted to allow women priests. It had taken its time: the Episcopal Church of Canada had started to ordain women priests in 1975, and the US Episcopalians in 1977.

This is an apology on behalf of Christendom

In March 1998 Pope John Paul II issued a statement called 'We Remember'. It was a historic apology for Christian abuse and treatment of Jews. He didn't go as far as accepting any responsibility on behalf of the church, but it was a welcome correction – and when he went to Jerusalem and prayed at the Wailing Wall it was clear that times had changed.

Two years later he went further. According to one newspaper report, the pope 'electrified ranks of cardinals and bishops'. Which is, I suppose, one way of keeping them awake during the speech. He went on to commit the church to not repeating its mistakes. 'Never again,' he said. He sought forgiveness for sins committed against Jews, heretics, women, Gypsies and native peoples.

He listed seven categories of sin for which the church needed to repent: 'general sins; sins in the service of truth; sins against Christian unity; against the Jews; against respect for love, peace and cultures; against the dignity of women and minorities; and against human rights'. Which more or less covers everything in this book, really. At the same event

Cardinal Joseph Ratzinger, who went on to become Pope Benedict XVI, confessed to the sins of the Inquisition.

Seeking forgiveness became a bit of a theme of John Paul II's papacy. As well as apologising for treatment of the Jews, he also apologised for the Crusades, the massacre of French Protestants, the trial of Galileo, the cancellation of the 10:15 from Paddington, the Maradona handball in the world cup and Simon Cowell.

Some argued that he should have kept quiet. Some even suggested that the gesture would be interpreted as a sign of weakness by secular opponents and Muslims.

But it was a time of healing old wounds. In spring 1998 the British government signed the Good Friday Agreement with Sinn Fein, promising power sharing in Northern Ireland. Protestant–Catholic divides ran deep, but again, it was a start.

Meanwhile, things weren't looking too hot for British churches. Despite various charismatic movements, like the Toronto Blessing, despite the fact that the nineties had been declared 'the Decade of Evangelism', by the millennium church attendance had dropped by 25 per cent.

The Twin Towers

On February 23, 1998 the leader of a small Muslim underground organisation declared war on America. In a *fatwa* issued from somewhere in Afghanistan, he declared it 'an individual duty for every Muslim' to drive the 'crusader armies' out of the Islamic lands and to 'liberate the al-Aqsa Mosque' in Jerusalem.

His name was Osama bin-Laden. Six months after this announcement his organisation – Al Quaeda – bombed US embassies in Kenya and Tanzania. The bombs killed 223 people, only 12 of whom were Americans.

Three years later, two planes appeared over the skies of New York.

Conclusion

Over two billion

Two thousand years after the birth of Jesus Christ, 2.3 billion people around the globe claim to be his followers.

2.3 billion.

OK, so if this history proves anything, it proves that not all of those two billion will be that observant of their faith. Not all of them will be what you might call orthodox. Many of them might have a shaky grasp on some of the basics of Christianity (but then, again, so did many Christian leaders). Many might, indeed, seem to be acting in flat opposition to the values Jesus espoused.

But 2.3 billion.* That's a third of the world's population, which makes Christianity by far the biggest faith in the world.

Reports of Christianity's death are greatly exaggerated.

A global faith

In the 1930s Hilaire Belloc wrote rather smugly that 'Europe is the faith' and 'the faith is Europe'. Even allowing for the fact that he completely ignored Christianity's origin and history in the east, you could see his point: in 1900 over 80 per cent of Christians lived in Europe and North America, and the overwhelming majority of Christians were non-Latino whites.

But history has a habit of suddenly switching directions. In his book

---

* According to figures released by the Centre for the Study of Global Christianity. Oh yes, actual, real, reliable research. Better late than never.

The Napoleon of Notting Hill Belloc's friend, the far more talented G. K. Chesterton, describes one of humanity's favourite games, a pastime he calls 'Cheat the prophet':

> The players listen very carefully and respectfully to all that clever men have to say about what is to happen in the next generation. The players then wait until all the clever men are dead, and bury them nicely. They then go and do something else. That is all. For a race of simple tastes, however, it is great fun.

Nothing exemplifies this more than Christianity. Just when you think it is going in one direction, the players reverse direction and do something else. And today Belloc's confident assertion looks, to use a technical historical term, utter pants.

Although Europe is still home to some 588 million Christians, Latin America is coming up fast, with 544 million. Africa has 493 million, Asia 352 million and North America about 286 million believers. Today, then, Europe and North America combined have less than 40 per cent of the world's Christians. The centre of Christianity has shifted. Again.

All change

We should not be surprised. If there is one thing that the history shows us it is that Christianity, for all its emphasis on tradition and foundations, has an incredible ability to adapt to its surroundings and reinvent itself. Ironically, Darwin would be impressed.

How has it done this? How has it survived?

It has survived because it has always been carried on by ordinary people. Any history of Christianity is naturally dominated by the big beasts: by the Pauls and the Augustines and the Gregorys and the Luthers. And of course those guys matter. But the people who have really and always carried the story forward are those on the ground, the footsloggers. Real Christianity has always, in fact, been the stubborn faith of exploited and oppressed people. Through times of power and times of weakness, under good leaders and bad leaders and downright despicably evil leaders, there have always been the real Christians, struggling on, trying to follow Jesus and do the kinds of things they believed he wanted them to.

Today, though, many of those people have one thing that their fore-bears never had.

They have a voice.

One voice

So what are they saying?

Well, a huge number of them are demanding the right to worship in freedom. Of those 2.3 billion Christians, perhaps as many as 100–200 million of them live under conditions of oppression or persecution. The situation is particularly bad in countries that either have an extremist Muslim government or where extremist Islamic fanatics wield strong influence. With a long history of antagonism and incomprehension between the two faiths, dialogue is difficult, but absolutely vital. In the meantime we should be aware of those who are denied their religious liberty.

Many of them are demanding the right to participate. It has probably not escaped your notice that there are these people, to be found all around the world, called women, for example. And in the last 100 years, in the west at least, their position has utterly changed. You can argue all you like about what Paul actually meant in 1 Timothy – or even whether he wrote it at all – but the fact is that for the bulk of 2,000 years women have provided the backbone of the church. We should not be surprised if, at last, they are beginning to show some spine.

Quite a lot are demanding decentralisation. Not perhaps in so many words, you don't see a great many 'Decentralisation Now!' marches being organised, not least because there's nobody in a central enough position to organise them. But the idea of the old style monarchical bishop has gone. Whatever statements are issued by the Archbishop of Canterbury, the pope, or anyone else, people are making up their own minds anyway. It is undoubtedly the case that Catholics in the west are using contraception, despite the official policy. Everybody has just agreed not to talk about it.

There is a call for accountability and transparency. The scandals in the church over finance and corruption and, most of all, over child abuse have been made so much more appalling by attempts to cover them up. The church as an institution has tried to tough out scandals, circle the wagons and wait for the enemies to exhaust themselves. But that doesn't work any more.

A lot are demanding choice. In western Europe the ecumenical movement has basically just stopped, because people are quite happy with variety. They don't mind. People no longer care about structural reunion anymore, for the simple reason they don't much care for structures. And the one-size-fits-all view of Christianity just doesn't work any more. The current arguments about homosexuality, for example, show the huge gulf between different churches – or even between different groups within the same church. The fact is that there is no way to come up with one statement that is going to make everyone happy.

Most of all, though, I think people are demanding the same things as the Patarines in Milan, or Paul writing to the Corinthians, or the desert fathers, or the Wyclifites: they want authenticity. They want leaders who will walk the talk.

Holding out for some heroes

As I write this, a new pope has just been enthroned. While I was writing history, he was making it. He is the first pope from Latin America. He took the name Francis – which no pope has taken before. He was the first Jesuit to assume the throne. He refused to wear the fancy ermine or the red shoes that were traditional, and kept on the sturdy black boots someone had given him. Before leaving for his official enthronement he stopped off to pay his hotel bill. He talked about the Jews and the Orthodox as brothers. Four days ago, as I write this, he went on a Maundy Thursday visit to a youth detention centre and washed people's feet, including, shock horror, the feet of Muslims and women.

It's early days, of course. And by the time this book comes out it might all have gone pear-shaped. He might prove to have a dodgy past. He might fall foul of the powerful Vatican bureaucracy. He might champion an entirely new and even more powerful form of church organ. And even if he doesn't, with the Catholic Church riven by scandals about banking, about corruption, and especially about sexual abuse, there is an awful lot to clear up. He won't, and can't, please everyone, and is unlikely to make any major changes in Catholic theology. But it's a good start. And the media reaction shows just what can happen when someone comes along and starts acting all Christianly.

People want and need examples, people to look up to. One of the real tragedies of the Christian church has been that just placing someone in an official position automatically granted them respect and honour. Nobody thinks that way, not nowadays. And maybe, judging from that story we started with, of old Barsanuphius in his cave, maybe not many ever really did.

The fact is this: the world needs more than people with a topcoat of Christianity. It needs people – popes, priests, archbishops, patriarchs, vicars, monks, nuns, you and me – whose Christianity runs deep.

Renewal

Of course there are big challenges. In America and Britain, especially, there has been a rise in a militant atheism, but for all their blustering rhetoric perhaps the more potent threat to the faith is a comfortable indifference. The west is, despite the best efforts of certain rogue bankers, a wealthy and hedonistic place. Where Christianity is thriving it is doing so among the poor, the hungry and the marginalised. Perhaps these are the people who will teach the complacent west how to read the Bible afresh.

And there is a sense of unease. The events of the last few years have shown that there is a healthy distrust of the 'powers' of the world. Perhaps western Christianity, for so long one of those powers, needs to rediscover its roots among the outcasts of the world.

I am certain that Christianity will continue to renew itself. As we saw at the beginning of this journey, it began in a graveyard outside Jerusalem. The movement began at the very point when everyone thought it dead and buried. And that's what Christianity always does: reinvent itself. Rise again.

It's the resurrection, stupid.

Timeline

*c.*300 BC	Ctesibius of Alexandria invents the organ.
AD 33	Jesus rises from the dead. Pentecost. Followers start the church.
*c.*34	Conversion of Paul.
*c.*40	Antioch church founded. First use of term 'Christian'.
44	Death of Herod Agrippa I.
47–57	Paul makes series of trips around Asia and Greece establishing churches, spreading the gospel and getting into fights.
49	Christian Jews, including Priscilla and Aquila, expelled from Rome.
54	Priscilla and Aquila return to Rome.
60	Paul lives under house arrest in Rome.
*c.*60s	Gospels are compiled.
62	James killed.
64	Great fire of Rome.
64–68	Persecution of Christians by Nero. Peter and Paul executed during this period.
66–70	Jewish revolt. Christians leave Jerusalem. Somebody hides the Dead Sea Scrolls.
67	Nero introduces the organ to Rome.
68	Nero commits suicide.
*c.*69	Ignatius becomes Bishop of Antioch.
70	Destruction of the Temple.
*c.*92	John the Elder, *Revelation*.
95	Persecution of Christians by Domitian.
*c.*100	Simeon, nephew of Jesus, is executed. Clement of Rome writes to Corinth.

*c.*107	Ignatius writes seven letters while being taken to Rome. First recorded use of the term 'catholic'.
*c.*110	Pliny the Younger writes to Trajan about Christians.
*c.*130	Justin Martyr becomes a Christian at Ephesus.
132–35	Second Jewish revolt. Roman away win. Jerusalem renamed Aelia Capitolina.
*c.*140	Marcion moves to Rome.
144	Marcion is kicked out of the church.
*c.*155	Justin moves to Rome.
156	Polycarp martyred in Smyrna.
*c.*165	Justin beheaded.
*c.*170	Tatian compiles the *Diatesseron*. Rise of Montanism in Phrygia.
177	Martyrdom of Christians in Lyons. Irenaeus becomes bishop. Abgar VIII becomes king of Edessa.
180	Christians martyred in Carthage, North Africa. Irenaeus, *Against Heresies*.
*c.*189	Victor becomes first 'monarchical' Bishop of Rome. Invents excommunication.
*c.*190	Clement of Alexandria becomes head of catechetical school.
192	Commodus strangled in his bath.
*c.*197	Tertullian becomes a Christian.
*c.*200	Christianity established in Edessa. Christians in the state build the first public church building in the world. Minutius Felix, *The Octavius*.
202	Persecution forces Clement to flee Alexandria. Origen takes over his job.
203	Perpetua and companions martyred in Carthage.
*c.*207	Tertullian becomes a Montanist.
211	Death of Septimus Severus brings chaos to the empire.
213	Tertullian, *Against Praxeas*. First explicit use of the term 'trinity'.
226	Ardeshir I becomes ruler of Parthia. Zoroastrian revival.
230	Origen settles in Caesarea after a row with his bishop. Begins the *Hexapla*.
*c.*248	Origen, *Against Celsus*.
*c.*250	Cyprian becomes bishop of Carthage. Novatian sets

		himself up as alternative leader. Novatianist schism will last for next two centuries.
250		Emperor Decius orders universal sacrifice to Roman gods. Origen arrested and tortured.
251		Cyprian, *On the Unity of the Church.*
254		Origen dies.
256–57		Cyprian falls out with Bishop Stephen of Rome.
258		Cyprian martyred in Carthage.
***c.*270**		Anthony becomes a monk. Goes into the desert.
***c.*280**		Christianity taken to Armenia by Gregory the Illuminator.
***c.*300**		Christianity becomes official religion of Armenia.
303		Persecution of Diocletian.
306		Constantius I dies at Eburacum (York). Succeeded by his son Constantine.
311		A group of African bishops refuse to acknowledge Caecilian as Bishop of Carthage. They choose Donatus instead. Beginning of Donatist schism.
312		Constantine marches under the sign of the Chi-Rho and defeats Maxentius at Milvian Bridge. Constantine becomes emperor of the west.
313		Edict of Milan promises tolerance to Christians.
314		Council of Arles. Donatists behaving badly.
316		Constantine orders confiscation of Donatist churches.
319		Arian controversy begins.
320		Pachomius founds first monastic community in Egyptian desert.
324		Constantine defeats Licinius, the emperor of the east. Becomes sole emperor. Eusebius, *Church History.*
325		Council of Nicea. Produces a creed with the word *homoousios* – i.e. 'one substance'. A lot of people go, 'Huh?'
326		Helena discovers the true cross. Follows this success by founding churches in Jerusalem and Bethlehem.
330		Constantine dedicates city of Constantinople.
335		Synod in Tyre supports Arian and exiles Athanasius to Trier. The first of many exiles.
336		Arius dies in Constantinople.
337		Death of Constantine.

*c.*350	Production of great codices Sinaiticus, Vaticanus, Alexandrinus.
351	Constantius II defeats Magnentius, becomes sole emperor.
354	First mention of Christ's birthday as being 25 December.
357	Constantius issues the Declaration of Sirmium. Supports Arianism, outlaws use of *homoousios*, *homoiousios* and other such words. A lot of people go, 'Wha?'
361	Constantius dies. Julian the Apostate comes to power.
363	Julian dies in battle. Jovian succeeds him.
366	Damasus elected Bishop of Rome.
372	Martin becomes Bishop of Tours. Founds abbey at Marmoutier. People either love Marmoutier or hate it.
373	Ambrose becomes Bishop of Milan.
378	Valens dies in battle with the Visigoths.
379	Theodosius I becomes emperor in the east. Death of Basil of Caesarea.
380	Priscillian's teaching condemned. He is exiled.
381	First Council of Constantinople. Resolves the Arian controversy. Produced the expanded version of the so-called Nicean creed. A lot of people go, 'Eh?'
383	Jerome publishes his first revision of the Gospels.
384	Jerome forced to leave Rome. Moves to Bethlehem.
*c.*384	Augustine converts to Christianity.
386	Priscillian is tried by Maximus and is executed. First Christian to be executed by Christians.
390	Jovinian teaching in Rome.
391	Augustine becomes Bishop of Hippo.
398	John of Antioch becomes Bishop of Constantinople.
*c.*400	Pelagius teaching in Rome.
401	Visigoths invade Italy.
404	John Chrysostom exiled.
406	Jerome finishes his Latin translation of the Bible. Barbarians cross the Rhine into Gaul.
407	Death of John Chrysostom.
410	Visigoths sack Rome. Pelagius and Celestius go to

	Africa. Roman legions depart from Britain and leave the key under the mat for Jutes, Angles, etc.
*c.*415	John Cassian founds two monasteries (one for men, one for women) near Marseilles.
418	Pope Zosimus excommunicates Pelagius.
428	Nestorius made Bishop of Constantinople.
430	Death of Augustine.
431	First Council of Ephesus. Nestorius condemned and deposed. A lot of people go, 'Hmm.'
440	Leo I becomes Pope.
448	First Council of Constantinople condemns Eutyches for teaching monophysitism. A lot of people go, 'Hmm.'
449	Second Council of Ephesus reverses the decision of the first.
*c.*450–60	Patrick evangelising in Ireland.
451	Council of Chalcedon. Produces the definitive statement of orthodoxy. A lot of people go, 'Whatever.'
452	Attila the Hun retreats from Rome.
455	Rome captured by the Vandals. They vandalise. A lot.
476	Romulus Augustus, last emperor of the west, is deposed.
488	Ostrogoths arrive in Italy.
493	Ostrogoths capture Ravenna and make it their capital.
*c.*496	Baptism of Clovis, king of the Franks.
527	Justinian I becomes Emperor in Constantinople.
529	Benedict founds monastery at Monte Cassino. Or possibly a casino at Monte Monastery.
533	Justinian launches campaign to retake Africa and Italy.
535	Belisarius invades Italy.
536	Byzantine army retakes Rome.
540	Ravenna becomes Byzantine capital in Italy.
552	Byzantines drive the Goths out of Italy.
553	Second Council of Constantinople. Condemns Nestorius (and Origen for good measure). A lot of people take no notice.
562	Consecration of Hagia Sophia in Constantinople.
590	Gregory becomes Pope.

597	Gregory sends Augustine to England. Conversion of the Angles.
598	Gregory makes peace treaty with the Lombards.
602	Augustine meets with Celtic bishops. It does not go well.
622	Muhammad forced out of Mecca to Medina.
635	Nestorian missionary Alopen arrives in China.
638	Jerusalem captured by Muslim forces.
664	Synod of Whitby. Approves Roman practices against the Celtic version.
672	Muslim army attacks Constantinople. Repulsed.
698	Arabs conquer Carthage.
711	Arabs cross to Spain.
726	Leo III destroys images in Constantinople.
732	Arab army defeated by Charles Martel at the Battle of Tours. Or Poitiers. No one's quite sure, but the Franks won.
751	Lombards conquer Ravenna.
754	Pope Stephen II crowns Pepin the Short. Pepin grants the papacy the Papal States.
771	Charles (aka Charlemagne) becomes king of the Franks.
780	Empress Irene restores icons to the churches.
787	Second Council of Nicea confirms use of icons.
793	Vikings attack Lindisfarne.
800	Charlemagne crowned Holy Roman Emperor by Pope Leo III.
809	Council in Aachen endorses use of *filioque* clause.
813	A hermit 'discovers' the tomb of 'St James'. Spanish tourist board hold a massive party.
814	Charlemagne dies.
828	Venetian traders nick, sorry, rescue the bones of St Mark.
846	Arab forces sail up the Tiber and plunder St Peter's (then outside the city walls of Rome).
849	Pope Leo IV leads forces against the Arabs. Arab navy destroyed.
851	Danes ransack Canterbury Cathedral.
862	Methodius and Cyril go to Moravia.

866	Danes capture York.
870	Edmund of East Anglia killed by the Danes.
871	Alfred becomes king of Wessex.
878	Dane army routed at Battle of Edington. Danes become Christian. Guthrum takes name of Ethelstan. (Presumably because Ethelstan didn't want it.)
896	Trial of the late Pope Formosus: the 'Cadaver Synod'.
910	Establishment of Monastery of Cluny.
911	Norsemen given lands in northern France, thus becoming the Normans.
962	Otto I crowned Emperor by the pope. Restoration of the Holy Roman Empire.
963	Establishment of monasteries on Athos.
988	Baptism of Vladimir I, king of Rus.
996	Otto III crowned as Holy Roman Emperor.
999	Election of Pope Sylvester II.
1000	Millennium. World is supposed to end. Nothing happens. First of many such disappointments.
1009	Symeon the New Theologian exiled from Constantinople.
1010	Caliph al-Hakim bi-Amr Allah destroys the Church of the Holy Sepulchre in Jerusalem.
1022	Synod at Pavia prohibits marriage for all clergy.
1049	Bruno, Bishop of Toul, becomes Pope Leo IX. Starts reforming the church.
1054	Schism between Roman and Eastern church.
1059	Lateran synod reforms the way the pope is elected. From now on popes will be chosen by the College of Cardinals. A pig flies by.
***c.*1070**	Patarines start campaigning in Milan.
1071	Byzantine army defeated at the Battle of Manzikert. Turks take control of Asia Minor.
1073	Hildebrand becomes Pope Gregory VII.
1074	Gregory declares compulsory clerical celibacy and excommunicates married priests.
1075	Gregory publishes the *Dictatus Papae*.
1076	Gregory excommunicates Emperor Henry IV.
1077	Henry goes to Canossa to seek absolution.
1084	Henry IV enters Rome, chooses new pope and then

	scarpers before the Normans arrive. The Normans arrive and destroy the city of Rome. Gregory exiled. First Carthusian monastery established in France.
1085	Muslims driven out from Toledo. Spanish tourist board hold another party.
1091	First Cistercian monastery.
1095	Council of Clermont. Pope Urban II proclaims the First Crusade.
1096	First Crusade leaves for Jerusalem.
1097–98	Crusaders capture Antioch.
1098	Baldwin founds Christian County of Edessa.
1099	Crusaders take Jerusalem.
1115	Bernard founds Abbey of Clairvaux.
1131	Peter of Bruis killed by a mob in St Gilles.
1140	Abelard and Arnold of Brescia condemned at Rome as heretics.
1144	Arabs capture County of Edessa.
1145	Pope Eugenius declares the Second Crusade.
1153	Death of Bernard.
1155	Arnold of Brescia hanged in Rome.
1165	Henry II of England kills German heretics near Oxford. First mass persecution of heretics in Europe.
c.1170	Peter Valdes starts teaching in Lyons.
1187	Saladin defeats the Crusader army and recaptures Jerusalem.
1189	Barbarossa and his all-star Crusaders set out on the Third Crusade.
1190	Barbarossa drowns in Cilicia.
1191	Crusaders capture Acre.
1192	Crusaders sign a peace treaty with Saladin and go home.
1201	Innocent III declares himself 'the vicar of Jesus Christ'. Launches the Fourth Crusade.
1204	Crusaders sack Hungary and then Constantinople.
c.1208	Francis founds the Order of the Friars Minor, aka the Franciscans.
1209	Innocent declares Albigensian Crusade against heretics in France.
1215	Fourth Lateran Council condemns the Cathars and

Waldensians. Officially approves the term 'transubstantiation' to explain what happened during the mass. Innocent III dies during the council.

1216 Pope Honorius III gives official approval to Dominican order.

1223 Pope Honorius III gives official approval to Franciscan order.

1226 Death of Francis of Assisi.

1231 Pope Gregory IX establishes the Inquisition.

1237 Mongols invade Russia.

1241 Mongols invade Hungary, Poland and the Balkans and then go home.

1244 Cathars butchered at Montségur.

1261 Crusader rulers thrown out of Constantinople.

1272 Thomas Aquinas, *Summa Theologiae*.

1273 Aquinas has a vision. Gives up writing.

1274 Death of Aquinas. Council of Lyons agrees reunification of Roman and Eastern church. Later rejected by citizens of Constantinople.

1289 Edward I expels the Jews from England.

1309 Pope Clement V decides to move to Avignon.

1310 Beguine leader Marguerite Porete burned at the stake.

1312 Beguines condemned as heretics at the Council of Vienne. (Rescinded in 1321.)

1318 Pope John XXII condemns the Spiritual Franciscans.

1348 Black Death arrives in Europe. Massacre of Jews across Europe.

1378 Two rival popes elected. Beginning of papal schism.

1381 Peasants' revolt in England.

1382 John Wyclif condemned. Retires to Lutterworth.

1384 Death of Wyclif.

1401 Persecution of Lollards in England.

1407 Authorities ban the making and reading of Wyclifite Bibles in England.

1409 Council of Pisa tries to solve problem of two popes, but actually elects another one. Now there are three.

1414 Council of Constance resolves the multiple-pope problem.

1415	Execution of Hus.
1438	Council of Ferrara agrees reunification of Roman and Eastern church. Again. Rejected by citizens of Constantinople. Again.
1453	Constantinople captured by the Turks. End of Byzantine Empire.
1454	Gutenberg invents printing press. Beginning of mass printing of books.
1479	Beginning of Spanish Inquisition. Spanish tourist board not sure how to play this one.
1490	Savonarola starts preaching in Florence.
1492	Rodrigo Borgia becomes Pope Alexander VI. Columbus reaches America. Colonisation of the 'New World' begins.
1494	Pope Alexander VI splits America between Spain and Portugal. Spanish tourist board get into fight with Portuguese tourist board over who gets to go on the trip.
1494	Savonarola establishes 'Christian and religious republic' in Florence.
1497	Savonarola executed in Rome.
c.1512–15	Luther has his tower experience.
1516	Erasmus compiles *Greek New Testament*.
1517	Pope Leo X launches campaign of selling indulgences. Luther publishes his Ninety-Five Theses.
1519	Zwingli attacks traditional church in Zurich.
1520	Luther, *To the Christian Nobility of the German Nation*, *The Babylonian Captivity of the Church*, *The Freedom of a Christian Man*. He is branded a heretic.
1521	Diet of Worms. Luther attends, then taken to Wartburg. Loyola injured, and has deep experience of God.
1522	Luther translates *German New Testament*.
1525	Luther marries Katharina von Bora. Anabaptists expelled from Zurich. Peasant wars in Germany. Over 100,000 peasants killed. William Tyndale translates *New Testament*.
1527	Anabaptist Felix Mantz executed in Zurich. Imperial troops attack Rome.
1529	Diet of Speyer calls Reformist states to return to the

Catholic fold. A lot of people go, 'We protest' – hence birth of Protestantism. Lutherans and Zwinglians fail to agree at Marburg. They also fail to agree to disagree, come to that.

1530	Council of Augsburg. Melanchthon prepares the Augsburg confession.
1531	Zwingli killed in battle.
1532	Thomas Cranmer becomes Archbishop of Canterbury.
1533–35	Rebellion in Münster.
1534	England splits with Rome. Calvin leaves Paris for Basle. Ignatius of Loyola founds the Society of Jesus, aka Jesuits.
1536	Jakob Hutter killed in the Tyrol. Menno Simons becomes Anabaptist. Tyndale executed. Calvin, *Institutes* (shorter version). Calvin moves to Geneva. Parliament dissolves the smaller monasteries.
1538	Calvin evicted from Geneva.
1541	Calvin returns to Geneva.
1542	Francis Xavier arrives in India.
1543	Copernicus suggests the earth goes around the sun. Nobody pays him any attention.
1545	Council of Trent. It lasts until 1563. There are intervals though, for coffee, etc.
1549	Xavier goes to Japan.
1551	Robert Estienne compiles *Greek New Testament* (first with modern verse references).
1553	Servetus executed in Geneva. Death of Edward VI in England. Succeeded by Mary. England returns to Catholicism.
1555	Cardinal Carafa becomes Pope Paul IV.
1557	Pope Paul IV institutes the Index of Forbidden Books.
1558	Mary dies. Elizabeth I becomes queen. England returns to Protestantism.
1559	John Knox seizes power in Scotland.
1560	Presbyterian system set up in Scotland. *Geneva Bible*.
1562	Civil war in France between Protestants and Catholics.
1566	Netherlands revolt against Spanish rule.
1567	Mary Queen of Scots forced to abdicate. James VI becomes king of Scotland.

1572	At least 3,000 Protestants killed in Paris in St Bartholomew's Day massacre.
1582	Matthew Ricci arrives in Macau.
1593	French wars of religion come to an end.
1598	Edict of Nantes gives Protestants freedom and legal status.
1603	Elizabeth I of England dies. James VI of Scotland becomes James I of England.
1604	Hampton Court conference. Robert Nobili goes to India.
1607	Virginia is first permanent English colony in North America.
1609	John Smith forms first Baptist church in Amsterdam. Death of Arminius.
1611	*Authorised Version of the Bible.*
1617	Defenestration of Prague. Beginning of the Thirty Years' War.
1618	Council at Dort condemns Arminianism. Issues ninety-three canons defining 'Calvinism'.
1620	Pilgrim Fathers sail on the *Mayflower* to America.
1622	Pope Gregory XV establishes the Sacred Congregation for the Propagation of the Faith. Persecution of Christians in Japan.
1625	Death of James I. Charles I becomes king.
1630	Galileo, *Dialogue About the Two Major World Systems.*
1637	Charles tries to impose new prayer book on Scotland. They don't like it. Scots invade England.
1642	Civil war breaks out in England.
1643	George Fox founds the Society of Friends, aka Quakers.
1648	Charles surrenders.
1649	Execution of Charles I. Diggers take possession of land in Surrey. They start to dig. Levellers march on London. They are rounded up by Cromwell and their leaders are shot.
1660	Restoration of the English monarchy. Charles II becomes king.
1661	Fifth Monarchists march on London.

1662	Charles brings in new prayer book.
1666	Great Fire of London.
1685	Charles II dies. James II becomes king.
1687	Newton, *Principia Mathematica*.
1688	James II forced to leave England. Replaced by William and Mary.
1692	Witch trials in Salem, Massachusetts.
1698	Formation of Society for Promoting Christian Knowledge.
1701	Formation of Society for the Propagation of the Gospel in Foreign Parts.
1709	Formation of Scottish Society for the Propagation of Christian Knowlege.
1710	Formation of Society for the Propagation of Tomato Plants.
1722	Count Nikolaus von Zinzendorf forms the Moravian Brethren.
1735–37	The Wesley brothers working in Georgia.
1736	George Whitefield begins open air preaching.
1738	Wesley goes to Moravian meeting and feels his heart strangely warmed.
1739	Whitefield starts preaching in America. John Wesley starts open air preaching in England.
1773	Pope Clement XIV dissolves the Jesuits. (But they hang on.)
1776	Americans are revolting.
1780	Robert Raikes opens first of his 'Ragged Schools'.
1787	William Wilberforce takes up anti-slavery cause.
1789	French are even more revolting.
1795	Foundation of London Missionary Society.
1804	Foundation of the British and Foreign Bible Society.
1807	Trading in slaves abolished throughout the empire. Robert Morrison goes to China.
***c.*1828**	Plymouth Brethren founded in Dublin.
1829	Tasmanian genocide.
1831	Darwin travels on the *Beagle*.
1833	Slavery finally abolished throughout the British Empire.
1836	Darwin returns from the Galapagos Islands. An idea is forming . . .

1841	Keble and Newman publish Tract 90. Start of the Oxford Movement. Søren Kierkegaard breaks off his engagement and starts brooding . . .
1844	Death of Joseph Smith. Tischendorf finds Codex Sinaiticus.
1845	Newman joins Catholic Church.
1848	Loads of people are revolting, including in France, Germany, Czechoslovakia, Ireland and Italy. Pope Pius IX flees Rome. Marx and Engels, *The Communist Manifesto*.
1854	Pope Pius IX issues Papal bull declaring immaculate conception of Mary. Commodore Perry persuades the Japanese to open up a bit.
1859	Darwin, *On the Origin of Species*.
1860	Papal forces defeated by Italian independents.
1864	Pius IX, *Syllabus of Errors*.
1865	End of the American Civil War brings an end to slavery in the USA. William Booth founds the Christian Revival Association, becomes the Salvation Army in 1878.
1869	Huxley coins the term 'agnosticism'.
1870	First Vatican Council formally defines the doctrine of papal infallibility.
1871	Darwin, *The Descent of Man*.
1881	Pogroms against Jews in Russia.
1883–85	Nietzsche, *Thus Spoke Zarathustra*.
1901	Students of Charles Parham in Topeka start speaking in tongues.
1904	Welsh revival.
1906	Pentecostal revival in Los Angeles, based at Azusa Street.
1910	First World Missionary Conference.
1910–15	Publication of *The Fundamentals*.
1914–18	First World War.
1916	Uprising in Ireland.
1917	Russian Czar deposed. Russians are revolting.
1918	Sinn Fein declare Irish independence. Armenian genocide.
1919	Karl Barth, *Commentary on Romans*. Prohibition begins in the American states.

1924	Lenin dies, Stalin takes over Russia.
1925	'Monkey trial' in Alabama. Hitler, *Mein Kampf*.
1929	Pope Pius XI makes deal with Mussolini. Vatican state established.
1930s	Stalin persecutes Orthodox Church in Russia.
1933	Hitler gains power in Germany.
1936–39	Spanish civil war.
1937	Bonhoeffer, *The Cost of Discipleship*.
1938	Nazis attack Jewish property in Kristallnacht.
1945	USA drops two atom bombs on Japan.
1948	First World Council of Churches. National Party gains power in South Africa. Beginning of apartheid. State of Israel established.
1953	Stalin dies. Khrushchev takes over. Persecution of Russian Christians continues.
1954	Second meeting of the World Council of Churches.
1949	China becomes a communist state under the leadership of Mao Tse-Tung.
1955	Rosa Parks refuses to give up her bus seat to a white man in Alabama. Beginning of American civil rights movement.
1962	Second Vatican Council brings big changes to Catholic Christianity. A lot of people go 'Wow. Groovy.'
1963	Civil rights march on Washington, led by Martin Luther King.
1966	Cultural Revolution in China.
1967	Israel wins Six Day War.
1968	Brother Andrew begins smuggling Bibles into communist lands. Assassination of Martin Luther King in Memphis, Tennessee.
1971	Gustavo Gutiérrez, *A Theology of Liberation*.
1978	John Paul I becomes Pope. Dies a month later and is succeeded by John Paul II.
1980	Assassination of Oscar Romero.
1985	Mikhail Gorbachev becomes Soviet leader. Beginning of glasnost.
1992	Church of England votes to allow women priests.
1994	End of apartheid.
1998	Pope John Paul II issues 'We Remember'. British

government signs the Good Friday Agreement with Sinn Fein, promising power sharing in Northern Ireland. Osama bin Laden declares a jihad against America.

2001 Destruction of the Twin Towers on 9/11.

2013 Election of Pope Francis I. First pope from South America. First Jesuit pope. First pope called Francis. A lot of people go, 'Oh please be a good one.'

Index